GUANTÁNAMO

GUANTÁNAMO

★ ★ ★ ★ ★

AN AMERICAN HISTORY

★

JONATHAN M. HANSEN

★ ★ ★ ★ ★

HILL AND WANG

A DIVISION OF FARRAR, STRAUS AND GIROUX   NEW YORK

Hill and Wang
A division of Farrar, Straus and Giroux
18 West 18th Street, New York 10011

Distributed in Canada by D&M Publishers, Inc.
Printed in the United States of America
First edition, 2011

Library of Congress Cataloging-in-Publication Data
Hansen, Jonathan M.
    Guantánamo : an American history / Jonathan M. Hansen. — 1st ed.
        p.   cm.
    Includes bibliographical references and index.
    ISBN 978-0-8090-5341-4 (cloth : alk. paper)
    1. Guantánamo Bay Naval Base (Cuba)—History. 2. Guantánamo Bay (Cuba)—
History. 3. Americans—Cuba—Guantánamo Bay—History. 4. United States—Foreign
relations—Cuba. 5. Cuba—Foreign relations—United States.   I. Title.

VA68.G8H36 2011
359.7097291'67—dc22

                                                                2011008442

Designed by Abby Kagan

www.fsgbooks.com

1   3   5   7   9   10   8   6   4   2

FOR MY PARENTS

CONTENTS

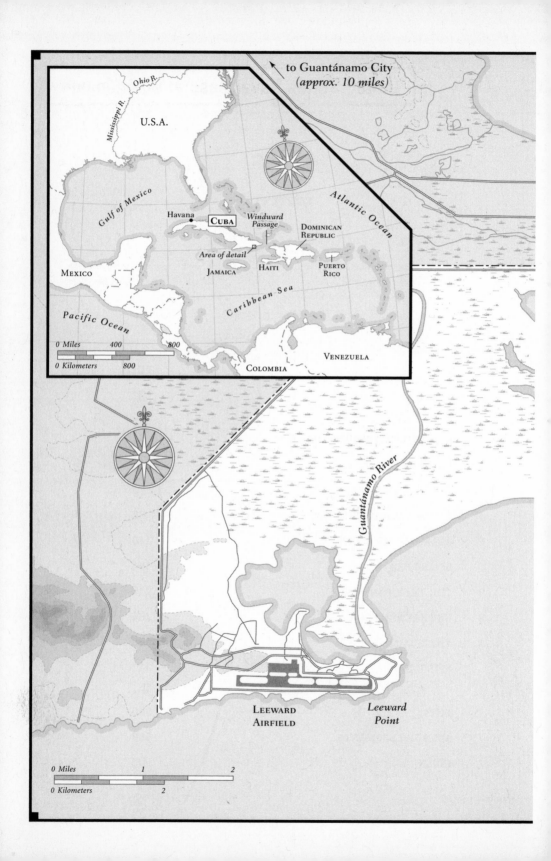

to Guantánamo City
(*approx. 10 miles*)

U.S.A.

Ohio R.

Mississippi R.

Gulf of Mexico

Havana

CUBA

Windward
Passage

DOMINICAN
REPUBLIC

Atlantic
Ocean

Area of detail

JAMAICA

HAITI

PUERTO
RICO

MEXICO

Pacific Ocean

Caribbean Sea

0 Miles   400   800

0 Kilometers   800

COLOMBIA

VENEZUELA

Guantánamo River

LEEWARD
AIRFIELD

*Leeward
Point*

0 Miles   1   2

0 Kilometers   2

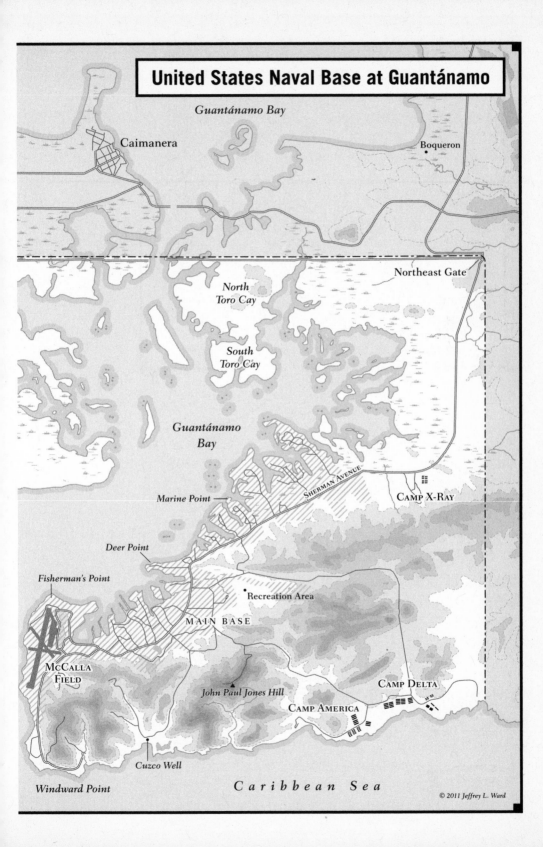

United States Naval Base at Guantánamo

Guantánamo Bay

Caimanera

Boqueron

Northeast Gate

North Toro Cay

South Toro Cay

Guantánamo Bay

SHERMAN AVENUE

Marine Point

CAMP X-RAY

Deer Point

Fisherman's Point

Recreation Area

MAIN BASE

McCalla Field

John Paul Jones Hill

CAMP AMERICA

CAMP DELTA

Cuzco Well

Windward Point

C a r i b b e a n   S e a

© 2011 Jeffrey L. Ward

PREFACE

A trip to the U.S. naval base at Guantánamo Bay, Cuba, introduces you to far more than a notorious prison. It takes you back in time to before the United States was even a country, connecting recent developments in the war on terror to epochal events in the nation's history—and, indeed, in the history of the Atlantic world. At Guantánamo, the past comes at you in all colors and from every angle with no chronological formalities and no mercy for the faint of heart.

My odyssey began before I had even left the United States. I first flew to Guantánamo in October 2005 aboard a rickety charter out of Fort Lauderdale, Florida, with room for about sixteen passengers. Most of the passengers on my plane were Filipino laborers. Men ranging in age from thirty to forty, they were headed to the bay to help build and maintain the prison in exchange for $2.60 an hour. The Philippines is a long way to go for cheap labor, and I wondered what made Filipinos suitable for such work in the eyes of the U.S. Department of Defense. I wondered, too, if the Filipinos knew how the United States came to occupy Guantánamo Bay. For Cuba and the Philippines share a common history. Along with Puerto Rico and Guam, they were liberated from Spain by the United States in 1898, only to discover that freedom has its conditions. Cuba would get independence so long as it acknowledged the U.S. right to intervene at will in Cuban affairs and acceded to the leasing of the naval base. The Philippines would undergo a pe-

riod of U.S. tutelage until it proved itself ready for self-government. In
the Philippines these conditions sparked revolution; in Cuba they
spawned resentment that festers to this day. At Guantánamo, I quickly
discovered, past and present confront you in unexpected ways.[1]

Ask a navy official at Guantánamo Bay to explain how the United
States came to occupy this remote corner of Cuba, and he or she will
respond with the gripping story of gallant U.S. marines seizing the bay
from Spanish regulars in the first pitched battle of the so-called
Spanish-American War. But this doesn't really answer the question.
How the United States captured the bay and how it has managed to
hold on to it are two very different things. On several visits to the naval
base, I heard this story repeated over and over again with a zeal bordering on zealotry. It is a story Guantánamo officials have been telling
themselves with little variation for more than a century, which is enough
to make a historian suspicious. Every generation rewrites its own history, the saying goes—except, apparently, at Guantánamo Bay.

The story of the taking of Guantánamo is only the first chapter in a
larger myth, remarkable for its constancy and consistency, about
America's century-long occupation of the bay. In abridged form, the
myth runs something like this: Columbus first discovered Guantánamo
Bay on his second voyage to the new world in April 1494. Centuries
later, a newly liberated and infinitely grateful Cuba consented to the
U.S. occupation of Guantánamo at the end of the Spanish-American
War. In the ensuing years, U.S. forces based at Guantánamo repaid
Cuba's faith, acting the part of the good neighbor, stimulating Cuba's
economy, and gently but firmly intervening in Cuba's volatile eastern
provinces to safeguard personal liberty and protect private property.
Sadly, Castro's rise put an end to this idyllic situation. The cold war
threw up an impenetrable barrier between natural allies and high-
lighted Guantánamo's strategic importance as the guarantor of liberty
in the region. If some personnel at the base found the closing-off of
Cuba stultifying, many more came to regard Guantánamo as a haven
of safety and security from a U.S. society beset by political violence,
cultural radicalism, and moral decay. Such a haven it remains to this
day. It's not the prison camp so much in the news this past decade that

defines contemporary Guantánamo, but the hospitable and whole-some community in which everybody knows your name.

Like all creation myths, this one serves the interest of those who espouse it, celebrating certain groups and individuals and inviting cer-tain questions while ignoring or obscuring others. It would have been news, for example, to Cuba's Taino "Indians" to hear that Columbus discovered Guantánamo Bay, just as it must have been humiliating to Cuban insurgents to read American journalists disparaging their con-tribution to the defeat of Spain. Moreover, it is inaccurate to suggest that Cuba welcomed the U.S. occupation of Guantánamo Bay. The Guantánamo myth is full of such self-serving valorizations that have never been exposed to historical scrutiny. History is often inconve-nient to the powerful. Several times on my first visit to Guantánamo I reached for news clippings about racial discrimination or labor exploi-tation or gender bias on the base, only to be asked by my host, who had failed to beat me to them, "Why are you interested in that?"

Guantánamo's climate is comparable to San Diego's. Two short rainy seasons in May and October deliver just over twenty inches of rain per year on average, not enough to alter impressions of a landscape dry, rug-ged, and unforgiving—if starkly beautiful. On a typical October day, it showers for a few hours in the late afternoon. The autumn of my first visit to the bay, the rains came early and hardly let up. Taking advan-tage of a break in the weather, I ventured out on the water with the base naturalist. If inconvenient, the rain was transformative. The bay called to mind California's Marin County in the spring. Hillsides glis-tened in knee-high grass. Palm trees produced new fronds. Cactus and manzanillo bloomed. Mangroves bobbed with pelicans, bitterns, ibis, herons, and hawks. In a region of the world whose resources have been ravaged by poverty, the base presented a striking anomaly. The U.S. Navy describes the base as a wildlife sanctuary, among other things, and I saw nothing to refute that characterization at first glance.

Columbus "discovered" Guantánamo Bay in May 1494, at the end of one such rainy season. I asked my host to take us out into the open sea, the better to see the bay as the admiral himself might first have glimpsed it. Puerto Grande, Columbus reportedly christened the bay, and indeed its grandness was the first thing that came to mind. Twelve miles long, six miles wide, and ranging from thirty to sixty feet deep, Guantánamo is dotted with cays and inlets that make it seem both limitless and inviting. Like San Francisco Bay, it is ringed by hills, in this case the granite escarpment of Cuba's Sierra Maestra, the highest, most picturesque mountains in the land. Columbus was disappointed to find the bay uninhabited. It appears underinhabited to this day. The navy has developed few of the forty-five square miles that comprise the base, and most of the development is tucked behind Windward Point, the peninsula at the southeast entrance of the bay, out of sight to incoming traffic.

European explorers of the new world had very specific ideas about what constituted legitimate land use. Columbus assumed Guantánamo to be uninhabited because it remained undivided, unalloted, unfenced. And yet evidence suggests that the Taino people who welcomed Columbus to southeast Cuba had been making efficient use of the Guantánamo basin as a game preserve. I was intrigued to hear that the navy, not known for its environmental and cultural stewardship, carries on Taino traditions to this day—in its own way. It is true that Guantánamo remains largely undeveloped, but it is not the pristine place it appears to be. "We can't go there," my host remarked, pointing to a flooded plain on Leeward Point, at the southwest corner of the bay. "That area's closed on account of unexploded ordnance," the result of U.S. target practice. What's that? I asked. "A bombing range." Over there? "More unexploded ordnance." There? "An old minefield. Strictly off-limits." And so this wildlife sanctuary is safe from human incursion. But how do the animals fare? Any casualties from unexploded ordnance or unrecovered land mines? I wondered. "Nothing," my host replied, "besides the occasional deer."

One afternoon, I toured the fence line that separates the base from Cuba. My tour began at the Northeast Gate, site of countless altercations between U.S. soldiers and their Cuban counterparts over the decades, as well as more constructive meetings between U.S. and Cuban military officials in recent years. The official contact point between the base and Cuba, the Northeast Gate is where a dwindling

number of Cuban "commuters," as Cuban laborers are called, enter
the base each day for work. I was struck by the utter desolation of the
place. No hostility. No people to sustain a grudge—in fact, no people
at all. An old barracks that held up to 150 U.S. marines at the time of
the Cuban Missile Crisis is the solitary reminder of the gate's symbolic
importance. Also empty is the U.S. marine observation point, or MOP,
that soars over the gate. In fact, very few of the MOPs along the base's
seventeen-mile perimeter are still manned, and these less to keep an
eye on a hostile enemy than to track the movement of asylum seekers
desperate enough to attempt to pick their way though a Cuban minefield onto the U.S. base.

   In the several years before 9/11, the base functioned at "minimum
pillar," navy parlance for maintaining just enough U.S. presence at the
bay to prevent Castro from claiming that the base had been abandoned.
From an outsider's perspective, minimum pillar persists. The perimeter
road on the U.S. side of the fence has all but eroded, quite a contrast
to the pristine Castro Bay Area Road on the other side. The base's general state of disrepair became starker still in contrast to the new prison
camp, where on my three visits to the bay everything appeared amply
funded. We cruised by the so-called playground where "good prisoners"
are allowed to take fresh air. "Fifteen million dollars," muttered my
host. "That's the site of the new twenty-five-million-dollar permanent
prison . . . There, the twenty-million-dollar mental health clinic." Navy
people console themselves that without the base you couldn't have the
prison, but from a visitor's perspective it seems that the prison has all
but become the base.

"An Eisenhower-era community perched alongside an Eisenhower-
era country." These are the words of the public works officer who took
me on a drive around the base's residential neighborhoods. With
stucco homes, pristine lawns, scattered toys, SUVs, and the odd boat
trailer, the U.S. enclave at Guantánamo redefines the term "gated
community"—with Subway, McDonald's, Starbucks, and the Navy
Exchange just down the street. I found it odd that a place notorious for
abusing prisoners could feel so familiar, so safe. But *safety* is the buzz-
word in these suburbs, where "there is no traffic, no drugs, no crime,

and where you can go out alone at night without having to lock your doors."

The prison camp lies along the Cuban coastline, separated from the hub of naval activity by a range of hills. Navy folks like to think of their side of the hills as the "real Guantánamo" (sometimes the "good Guantánamo"), leaving the visitor to conclude what he or she may about the prison. But the prison wouldn't be here without the navy. And the navy wouldn't be here without the U.S. government's decision to retain the bay at the end of the war with Spain. Finally, none of this would be here today without the tacit consent of the American people, whose standard of living the U.S. government and military is sworn to protect. Up close, a chasm seems to separate Americans who, apparently for the first time in the nation's history, tried to write torture into U.S. law from those who reject torture unconditionally. But through the lens of history, the differences blur and Americans become one people, just as Guantánamo becomes one bay.

This book is a story of nation making and empire building. It is a U.S. story, to be sure, but it is also a chronicle of Cuba, and of Cuba's attempt to realize its independence with an imperial juggernaut on its back. Besides Americans and Cubans, the cast includes Ciboney and Taino Indians, Spaniards and Englishmen, Italians and Portuguese, Chinese and subcontinental Indians, Jamaicans and Haitians, as well as countless peoples known to the modern world as the "stateless," from pirates and refugees to enemy combatants. This story features world-historical figures—Columbus, Castro, and Kennedy, to name a few—and many the world has long forgotten: the sailors, saloonkeepers, and prostitutes; planters and farmers; stevedores, janitors, and maids who built, occupied, lubricated, and maintained the base for more than a century. This is a story of the transformation of a bay into a naval base, and of that base into a prison. But it is also the history of an immense drainage basin and body of water and of the myriad flora and fauna it continues to support. This is on balance a twentieth-century tale, but one that begins in the geological upheaval of the Mesozoic era, some 180 million years ago, and gathers pace in the social dislocation of the sixth century CE and thereafter, which peopled the islands of the Greater Antilles with, first, "Indians," and then Europeans, Africans, and Asians.

This is, in short, a history of a once treasured, recently ignored, now notorious place, a natural and juridical wonder that sits athwart the social and political fault lines of the modern world. Guantánamo has much to teach us about the character and contours of that world, *our* world, foremost perhaps that liberty and empire make awkward bedfellows at best.

GUANTÁNAMO

1

★

REDISCOVERING GUANTÁNAMO

On the afternoon of April 29, 1494, Guantánamo Bay bustled with activity. Hunters from a village up the Guantánamo Valley gathered food for a celebratory feast.[1] Using traps, nets, hooks, and harpoons, and perhaps working from canoes, the hunters were having a good time of it. Within a few hours, they had hauled in roughly one hundred pounds of fish, which they set about preserving for the journey home. Meanwhile, a second group of hunters pursued alligators that made their homes along the banks of the rivers that fed Guantánamo Bay. They, too, were enjoying a good day, and before long the bay was perfumed by wood smoke from fires sizzling with fresh fish and alligator meat hung from wooden spits.[2]

An ordinary day at Guantánamo became memorable sometime in the midafternoon, when three large vessels topped by billowing white sails appeared off the entrance to the bay. News of the foreign fleet's return to the Americas had preceded it to Cuba, borne by fleeing villagers from nearby Hispaniola.[3] With scarcely time to conceal themselves, the hunters withdrew into the hills and bushes bordering the bay, leaving their game roasting over the fires. Aware of the strangers' advantage in weaponry, the hunters could only watch as the strangers disembarked and devoured the fish, all the while eschewing the alligator, the more precious delicacy in local circles.[4]

With their stomachs full, the strangers set out to explore the sur-

roundings, as if to identify if not thank the people who had so amply
provided for them. Still, the hunters shrank back, until finally appoint-
ing an envoy to find out what the strangers wanted. Moving forward,
the envoy was met not by one of the newcomers but by a fellow
Arawak speaker whom the strangers had snatched off one of the Bahama islands.[5] Convinced at last that the strangers had stopped at the
bay for only a quick visit, the hunters abandoned their hiding places
and approached their guests with caution and generosity. Never mind
the hundred pounds of fish, the interpreter was assured; the hunters
could recover that in a matter of hours. There followed an exchange of
gifts and pleasantries, after which the strangers reboarded their vessels and went to bed, the better to rise early, set sail, and finally put to
rest the impious notion that Cuba was an island and not the continent
of Asia.[6]

The people who discovered Columbus helping himself to their dinner
that day had preceded him by nearly a millennium. The Taíno, as Columbus's unwitting hosts are known today, were themselves recent arrivals in eastern Cuba.[7] They had been beaten to the bay by still earlier
discoverers, who began to harvest Guantánamo's resources as early
as 1000 BCE.[8] Guantánamo's first discoverers hailed from the west,
hopping over islands, now submerged, that once connected Central
America to Cuba via Jamaica some seven thousand years ago.[9] These
so-called Casimiroid people found in Guantánamo a cornucopia of
flora and fauna with no one to compete for it. The Casimiroids exploited Guantánamo Bay more as a hunting ground than as a home.
For them, the bay comprised part of a larger ecosystem that met the
requirements of Stone Age living. From the mudflats and mangrove-
lined terraces of the outer harbor, the Casimiroids took shellfish, fish,
and game, and materials for the simple tools that facilitated their hunting and scavenging. Along the streambeds and river valleys that fed the
inner harbor, they drew water and collected wild fruit and vegetation.
Theirs was a difficult, prosaic life. Their impact on the Guantánamo
Basin was negligible. The vast bay easily absorbed their sparse population, and for their first two thousand years in Cuba, they had few if any
rivals.[10]

As the Casimiroids were wending their way toward Guantánamo, another people—horticultural, sedentary, ceramic—began to stir deep in the Orinoco River basin of South America. These were the ancestors of Columbus's Taíno hosts. What set them in motion is anybody's guess, but sometime after 2000 BCE they took to the sea, riding a branch of the South Equatorial Current along the northeast coast of South America, over the equator, to the base of the Antilles archipelago. Over the next two thousand years, they migrated up the archipelago from island to island, all the while appropriating cultural elements of the Stone Age peoples they displaced. By the late first century BCE, they had arrived at Hispaniola, where Taíno civilization reached its zenith several centuries before Columbus. The Taíno first crossed the Windward Passage from Hispaniola to eastern Cuba around 700 CE. There their westward progress stalled, their assimilative powers outmatched by the guns, germs, and steel of the conquistadors.

In the American imagination, Columbus's so-called discovery of America in 1492 represents a watershed second only to the birth of Christ. In the eyes of Columbus and his royal sponsors, the mission to the Orient was merely a logical extension of the *reconquista*, the centuries-old (and vastly expensive) effort to drive the Moors (and Jews) from Spain. Only in hindsight can the expulsion of the Moors in 1492 be taken for granted. At the time Columbus was charting his journey west, the success of that battle could hardly be assumed, and Spain's newly consolidated kingdom of Aragon and Castile wanted nothing so much as funds sufficient to finish the job. Promise of access to lucrative Oriental markets induced Castile's queen Isabella to sponsor an audacious navigator from Genoa.[11]

On the Iberian Peninsula, the rise of Aragon and Castile was achieved by the creation of what were in effect colonies established in the wake of the retreating Moors. King Ferdinand and Queen Isabella granted rights to their most trusted and valued lieutenants to rule over these new colonies in their names. But there were only so many such grants to be won at home, and after 1492 the *Orbe Novo* beckoned to a cohort of second-tier conquistadors flush from the heat of battle, no less ambitious for fame and fortune, and no less committed to the project of making the world safe for Christianity than the royal favorites themselves. Columbus was more sailor than warrior, but warriors

accompanied him on his several voyages to the Americas, where violence became the Spaniards' stock-in-trade.[12]

Columbus's brief sojourn at Guantánamo signaled the beginning of
a cataclysmic social and economic revolution that permanently transformed not only Cuba and Hispaniola but North and South America,
Europe, and Africa besides. The islands and continents that Columbus and his successors "discovered" at the end of the fifteenth century
were worthless without a labor force. Spain was merely the first in a
series of aspiring European and North American empires that defended the enslavement and annihilation of millions of indigenous
inhabitants and imported Africans on the basis of putative cultural
and racial differences. The contradiction between the universalism
latent in Western theology and philosophy and the West's historic
treatment of Indians, slaves, and countless "others" inspired a long argument about just who was fit to be counted as a "human being," an argument that continues to this day (women? indigenous Americans?
African slaves? stateless enemy combatants?). But all of this was unimaginable upon that first encounter at Guantánamo Bay.[13]

No doubt Columbus's impatience at Guantánamo Bay suited the
Taíno hunters just fine. With the admiral on his way to China, they
were free to complete the task that had brought them to the bay. Compared with their cousins on Hispaniola, they had gotten off easily that
day. At Isabella, Columbus's headquarters across the Windward Passage, the psychological and physical demands of conquest had begun
to take a toll on the Europeans, with one of the first formal incidents
of Spanish-on-Taíno violence recorded earlier that same month.[14] A
local Indian had allegedly stolen a Spaniard's clothes; as punishment,
one of Columbus's lieutenants cut off the ear of a Taíno vassal, taking
into custody the responsible cacique and several members of his family. Columbus wanted to teach the Indians a lesson by cutting off all
his prisoners' arms, but a Taíno ally dissuaded him. Nevertheless, a
precedent had been set, and over the course of the next twenty years,
the Spanish so brutalized Hispaniola that within a single generation
there remained scarcely any Taíno left.

Cuba, meanwhile, enjoyed what can only be called a grace period, its inhabitants going about their lives as if they could avoid their neighbors' fate simply by ignoring it.[15] When Spain finally turned its attention to Cuba in 1511, it did so with brutal efficiency. To pacify Cuba, the Crown selected Diego Velázquez de Cuéllar, author of spectacular atrocities in the Spanish conquest of Hispaniola, including the burning alive of eighty-four Taíno caciques assembled at the village of Xaragua in autumn 1503.[16] Velázquez arrived in Cuba with a vengeance, indeed, in hot pursuit of a cacique named Hatuey, who had fled across the Windward Passage rather than submit to Spanish authority—a capital offense.[17]

By 1511 the Crown had introduced in Hispaniola a scheme of land and labor distribution called encomienda, a feudal system for the New World. By the terms of encomienda, Spanish colonists received land along with right to the labor of the Indians who dwelt upon it. Technically, the Indians owned the lots on which they lived, and if less than independent, they were not formally slaves. Until they ran away, that is, thus depriving the Spanish encomendero the means of making a living (and the Crown itself its reason for being in the New World). A Taíno in flight from encomienda was for all intents and purposes a runaway slave, and no amount of hand-wringing by Bartolomé de las Casas and a whole order of Dominican monks could alter his or her fate.[18]

Hatuey landed in Cuba at Punta de Maisí, just across the Windward Passage from today's northwest Haiti. Punta de Maisí lacks a harbor, so Velázquez headed for Guantánamo Bay, hoping to corner Hatuey in the eastern end of the island and thereby stop the rebellion from spreading. For three months, Velázquez combed the mountains east of Guantánamo in search of a leader who knew his pursuer too well, and who aimed to avoid a face-to-face showdown at all cost. Cuban history is full of guerillas; Hatuey simply wanted to be left alone. But with eastern Cuba rallying around the Taíno chief, Velázquez treated the region to a barn burning, razing villages, terrorizing women and children, and torturing local residents for information.[19]

Before burning Hatuey at the stake, Velázquez offered him the opportunity of redemption. When a Catholic father asked Hatuey if he wanted to be baptized into the Christian faith, Hatuey wondered why he should want to become a Christian when Christians were the source of his undoing. Because Christians go to heaven and remain in the company of God, came the reply. Are you going to heaven? Hatuey asked. Of course, replied the father, like all who are holy. Then no thanks, said Hatuey, who had had quite enough of Christian company already. A match was struck, and the Taíno resistance went up in smoke.[20]

Guantánamo's centrality in these early cultural encounters will be surprising only to readers who have forgotten their natural history. The genesis of this "Great Port" (Puerto Grande), as Columbus named it, dates back to the geological upheaval that splintered the supercontinent Pangaea some 180 million years ago, when, driven by upwelling magma along a rift that would become the mid-Atlantic ridge, "North America" pulled away from "Africa" and "South America." At first the rupture left only a teardrop, an intimation of the Gulf of Mexico. But the drop became an ocean whose relentless expansion sundered Pangaea into bits.

Tectonic activity of this magnitude produces considerable flotsam. Off the western coast of the Americas sat chunks of the continental margin, as if patiently awaiting conveyance. Conveyance arrived, for some at least, in the form of the Caribbean plate. Originating in the Pacific Ocean, the plate moved north and east like a saucer. Along its starboard rim, like running lights, perched a volcanic island arc. This arc would become the islands of the Lesser Antilles. Nearby, on the leading edge of the saucer, rode pieces of future Cuba, Hispaniola, and Puerto Rico, not yet in recognizable form. Hispaniola and Puerto Rico clung to Cuba's southern coast as the saucer shot the gap between the Americas, scraping off Jamaica from the Yucatán along the way. For several thousand miles, the saucer sped unimpeded toward the northeast. It slammed to a halt at the Bahama Banks, southern boundary of North America, where a combination of oceanic and upper mantle crust, continental margin, and island arc stacked up to produce the foundation of today's Cuba, one of the most complex geological conglomerations on earth.[21]

Toward the end of this monumental migration, Cuba sat along the southern rim of the North American plate, originally little more than a chain of islands. Meanwhile, southeast Cuba, future home to Guantánamo, constituted a world of its own. In the immediate aftermath of the collision, it straddled the boundary of the North American and Caribbean plates, Hispaniola and Puerto Rico still firmly attached. But the forces propelling the saucer were unassuaged. With its passage northward blocked by the Bahamas, the saucer veered sharply east in a wrenching motion that nearly carried southeast Cuba out to sea. Southeast Cuba held as Hispaniola and Puerto Rico tore away, exposing a gap along the Cuban coastline that would become the setting of Guantánamo Bay.

Guantánamo Bay is located at W 75°9' longitude and N 19°54' latitude, about three quarters of the way along Cuba's southeast coast, running west to east. Southeast Cuba is extraordinarily rugged. Comprising roughly one fifth of Cuba's territory, it boasts more mountains than the rest of Cuba combined. The Guantánamo Basin is the notable exception in the region. Its 250-odd square miles lie at or close to sea level. Backed by the sea and surrounded by mountains, the basin resembles a vast amphitheater, with the bay itself at center stage.

Guantánamo Bay is very young geologically. It assumed its present shape as recently as 6000 BCE. The principal agent in Guantánamo's creation was water. Since first arriving at the Bahama Banks forty million years ago, Cuba has been repeatedly inundated by and drained of seawater, a result of fluctuating global temperatures and the rise and fall of the Cuban landmass. Flooding seas littered coastal Cuba with marine terraces, inland lakes, and seabeds. Ebbing seas produced erosion, the source of river valleys, basins, and bays. Guantánamo is the sum of these geological processes, of the wearing away of old terraces and seabeds by erosion and the subsequent drowning of the hollows and cavities the erosion left behind.

Officially Guantánamo Bay extends ten miles long by six miles wide and measures between thirty and sixty feet deep. But practically speaking, it consists of two discrete bodies of water, an inner and outer harbor, connected by a narrow strait. The inner harbor is large and shallow. It has a smooth, billowing shoreline and resembles a good-size lake. The outer harbor is ragged and irregular. Smooth to the west, it is rough to the east, and its north is strewn with cays. The contrast between the two harbors derives from their different physical composition. The inner harbor rests atop an old tidal flat that yielded easily and evenly to erosion. The outer harbor is lined by fossilized coral terraces, harder and more defiant of erosion. Where there is fossilized coral at Guantánamo, there will be found the cays, coves, and promontories that comprise the outer harbor (home of the U.S. base); where coral is absent, the shoreline will be smooth and uniform, as along the lower western shore of the outer harbor and throughout the whole of the inner bay.[22]

Individually distinctive, the two harbors combine to create a coastal environment of wondrous diversity. From the sea, Guantánamo stands out among the world's great bays for its accessibility. Some bays are so camouflaged by the surrounding countryside that it is possible to sail right past them without noticing. The harbor entrance at Santiago de Cuba, for instance, is so tortuous and cluttered that it has confounded sailors for centuries. By contrast, Guantánamo's entrance is deep, uncluttered, and virtually impossible to miss. Now nearly two miles wide, it sits within a wide gap in the mountain rampart of southeast Cuba detectable far out to sea.

The narrower a harbor entrance, the more vulnerable approaching vessels to the whims of those who call the harbor home. The mouths of many Cuban harbors are not only narrow but sheer, affording hosts the advantage of significantly higher ground. Again, Santiago de Cuba comes to mind, where Morro Castle commands the harbor from high atop an imposing bluff; again, Guantánamo presents a striking contrast. Windward Point, the southeast corner of the bay, rises four hundred feet above sea level, but not until a half mile from the coast. Meanwhile, Leeward Point remains flat for several miles, barely reaching thirty feet above sea level. Guantánamo's broad mouth would make it a challenge to defend in the years before modern weaponry. Conversely, ships that dared not test the welcome at Havana or Santiago would find Guantánamo Bay an open and inviting place.

On approach, Guantánamo Bay appears not only welcoming but vast. Beyond the entrance to the bay, the Guantánamo Basin seems to stretch out indefinitely, making the bay feel much larger than its sixty square miles. Once inside the bay, visitors confront a wealth of possible destinations, further adding to the sense of scale. Immediately inside Leeward Point, moving clockwise around the bay, is a channel two hundred feet wide and a mile long that is both the estuary of the Guantánamo River and the passage to secluded Mahomilla Bay. The Guantánamo River is brackish well before it meets the bay, but it is navigable far upstream, thus connecting the outer harbor to the Cuban hinterland and providing its only access to freshwater.

Just past the estuary lies Hicacal Beach, three miles of coarse sand carved from the delta of the Guantánamo River. Most of Guantánamo Bay is sheltered from the prevailing southeast wind by the hills of Windward Point. Hicacal Beach is decidedly not. It meets the prevailing southeast wind, brisk by early afternoon most days, squarely on the nose, taming its often boisterous waves and deflecting them harmlessly up the channel. The most exposed territory in Guantánamo Bay, Hicacal is also the most dynamic. Reshaped by tides and passing storms, its fertile and abundant seabeds suggest the benefits of its buffeting by wind and sea.

From its foot inside Leeward Point, Hicacal Beach arches sharply north and east, directing incoming traffic toward the opposite shore. The eastern shore of the outer harbor is a peninsula roughly six miles long and tapering from five to three miles wide as it frames the southeast corner of the bay. Down the spine of the peninsula is a range of hills, nearly five hundred feet tall, that dominate the outer harbor and the nearby Cuban coastline. At the base of the hills, along the outer shore of the peninsula, lies a broad, flat terrace, current site of the U.S. prison camp. Along the inner shore of the peninsula, old coral terraces protrude like fingers into the bay. Roughly thirty feet high, these terraces range from several hundred yards to half a mile long, creating a succession of natural coves and jetties. The terraces proliferate across the top of the outer harbor, too, where some take the form of islands. Here the terraces tend to be long and the coves deep; a few reach inland for nearly a mile. The net effect of this diverse seascape is a prized refuge and an explorer's paradise: behind every promontory a little cove, within every cove a beguiling shoreline.

Past the old coral terraces at the top of the outer harbor lies the opening to the inner harbor, a broad, uncluttered expanse notable less for its topographical interest than for its geographical orientation. If the outer harbor belongs inexorably to the sea, the inner harbor is indisputably Cuba's own. It sits at the foot of the Guantánamo Basin, an ancient drainage system laced with rivers and streams and tied to the rest of Cuba by a ribbon of fertile plain. In contrast to the inhospitable terrain that surrounds the outer harbor, the land framing the inner harbor is irrigated, arable, and hence suited to human habitation. Rich salt deposits line the shoreline; the harbor itself fairly boils with fish. But it is as a link to the outside world that the inner harbor is most significant. Communication is cumbersome in this rugged corner of southeast Cuba, making access to the sea a condition of its economic and cultural vitality.

In sum, the two harbors are complementary, their differences felicitous, at least so long as traffic between them remained open and unfettered. Together, they sustain distinct yet interdependent worlds. Divided, their value depreciates, as, landlocked the one and exposed the other, each becomes merely the sum of its individual parts. Since 1898, when the United States first occupied the outer harbor in the Cuban Spanish-American War, the U.S. naval base has effectively cut the bay in two.[23]

Magnificent in its own right, Guantánamo Bay occupies a strategic geographical position in Cuba, the Caribbean Basin, and the Western Hemisphere. Paradoxically, Guantánamo's significance within Cuba derives from its isolation from the center of Cuban social and political life. Six hundred miles distant from the capital, Havana, and surrounded by mountains, Guantánamo has functioned historically as Cuba's safety valve—a land of exile and refuge accommodating marginalized people from within Cuba and across the Caribbean basin.

Guantánamo's role in Cuba is a function of the island's natural history. Tectonic boundaries tend to be mountainous. Plate collisions cause tectonic folding, and volcanoes are common along plate seams. Scientists call the process of mountain formation orogeny, and southeast Cuba is a case in point. The region consists essentially of two large mountain chains, the fabled Sierra Maestra and the no less formidable Nipe-Sagua-Baracoa Massif. The Sierra Maestra rises just west of Guantánamo Bay and runs 180 miles down the coastline to Cabo Cruz, southeast Cuba's westernmost tip. Pico Turquino (6,476 feet), Cuba's tallest peak, commands the middle of the range.

Slightly lower than its rivals in Jamaica and Hispaniola, Pico Turquino is comparable in height to New Hampshire's Mount Washington (6,288 feet) and North Carolina's Mount Mitchell (6,684 feet), the highest elevations in the eastern United States. For much of its span the Sierra Maestra climbs straight out of the sea, which lends it extraordinary grandeur. Its status is enhanced by the celebrated people who have sought the sanctuary of its caves and copses over the centuries, starting, it is said, with Hatuey, and continuing through the runaway slaves, insurgents, revolutionaries, and counterrevolutionaries of more recent days.

To the east of Guantánamo Bay rise the foothills of the Nipe-Sagua-Baracoa Massif. The great massif sprawls in a sideways V shape one hundred or so miles from Guantánamo Bay to Punta de Maisí, then back to the high plains over Bahía de Nipe. Less magnificent than the Sierra Maestra, its effect on Guantánamo is more constant. Green, luxuriant, expansive, the Nipe-Sagua-Baracoa Massif is a jealous sentinel, at once protecting the bay from wind and weather while simultaneously cheating it of meaningful rainfall. Few roads connect the great massif to the rest of Cuba. Relatively few people live there. Among these few are said to be the final remnants of Cuba's Taíno people.[24]

Remote from the heart of Cuba, Guantánamo enjoys a front-row seat along the Windward Passage, one of the hemisphere's busiest sea-lanes and an integral link in the circum-Caribbean communication system. The passage takes its name from the breeze that blows in off the Atlantic between Cuba and Haiti, hurtling crews and cargo into the heart of the Caribbean basin. From its perch along the passage, Guantánamo affords access not only to the Antilles archipelago and the Gulf of Mexico, but also to coastal Central and South America and the Pacific Ocean, via the Isthmus of Panama.

Fifty-five miles wide, the Windward Passage is exceptionally deep. The passage marks the eastern end of the Cayman Trench, a 1,000-mile-long gash in the Caribbean floor formed by the easterly lurch of the Caribbean plate, which separated Cuba from Hispaniola 40 million years ago. At its deepest, the Cayman Trench plummets over

25,000 feet. The Windward Passage plunges only about one-fifth that deep, but it does so vertiginously, dropping from 60 feet at the mouth of Guantánamo Bay to 1,500 feet a mile out, to 5,760 feet within 25 miles. Ships and cargo lost in the passage are lost forever. More than merely menacing, however, the passage is a boon to Caribbean ecology, allowing nutrients from deep ocean waters to ventilate and replenish the Cayman and Yucatán basins. The passage also proved a benefit to the U.S. Navy and its submarine training program, which has enjoyed the rare luxury of deepwater access just minutes out of port.[25]

The Windward Passage is Guantánamo's ticket to ride. No sooner had the North and South American plates separated from Europe and Africa than temperature and wind and their constant companion current conspired to reunite the hemispheres in an oceanic conveyance system that laid the foundations for the modern Atlantic world. To a considerable degree, that world revolves around Cuba and Guantánamo Bay.

The system draws its energy from the sun. Due to the tilt of the earth's axis, the sun strikes the earth more directly at the equator than at the tropics and poles. When hot air rises over the equator it leaves behind a vacuum of low pressure that draws in cooler, more pressurized air from the tropics in the form of wind. This is the source of the trade winds, the steady easterly breeze that blows between latitude 30° and the equator in both the Northern and Southern Hemispheres. The trade winds blow east to west, thanks to the eastward rotation of the earth, which bends prevailing winds to the right north of the equator and to the left south of it, a result of the so-called Coriolis effect.[26]

But the trade winds are only part of what makes the Atlantic world go round. There is no limit to the amount of sunshine that warms the equator, but there *is* a limit to how high hot air can rise through the earth's atmosphere: approximately ten miles. At that point the rising air hits an atmospheric ceiling called the tropopause and is propelled toward the poles by still more air behind it, where it begins to cool. This equatorial air can go only so far toward the poles due to resistance from air already there. The air pressure thus increases just as its temperature drops, returning the air to the surface of the earth. This happens, north and south, at approximately latitude 30°, creating bands of high pressure known as tropical highs. Much of this highly pressurized air gets sucked back into the vacuum of low pressure over the equator, but not all of it. Another band of low pressure at 60° draws some of the cold, dense, highly pressurized air still closer to the poles, again in the form of wind. This wind, too, is bent to the right north of the equator, and to the left south of it, generating west-to-east winds this time, the so-called westerlies, a source of weather systems on the North American continent.

Just as heat generates wind, so wind generates current. North of the equator, the two bands of prevailing wind produce the North Equatorial and North Atlantic currents. The North Equatorial Current flows east to west between the equator and the tropics; the North Atlantic Current flows west to east between the tropics and 60°. Like the winds that spawn them, these currents also bend in the direction of the earth's rotation, creating the North Atlantic Gyre, a vast clockwise rotating current system that facilitates navigation in the North Atlantic.[27]

It is no coincidence that Christopher Columbus first made landfall off eastern Cuba and the entrance to the Windward Passage, somewhere in the vicinity of Grand Turk Island.[28] Before wind yielded to steam in the second half of the nineteenth century, ships bound to the Americas from Europe and the Mediterranean rode the Canary Current, eastern boundary of the North Atlantic Gyre, down the coast of Africa, past the Canary Islands, in search of the trade winds. The trade winds blow in a belt roughly two thousand miles wide between the tropics and the equator. Vessels originating from the north join the belt at first opportunity—just past the calm of the Horse Latitudes— in the neighborhood of 25°.[29] Allowing for five or ten degrees leeway, the sideways skid of a vessel before the wind, and the absence of contravening action, ships will arrive in the Western Hemisphere off the Turks and Caicos Islands, beyond which lie the Windward Passage and, ultimately, Guantánamo Bay.

After capturing Hatuey, it took Velázquez and his lieutenants a matter of weeks to subjugate Cuba. Over the course of the next five years, Velázquez parceled out the country on terms of encomienda, resettling natives, introducing livestock, and establishing seven major towns. In the zero-sum game that was Spanish mining, the discovery of gold in the hills of central Cuba drained Hispaniola, Jamaica, and Puerto Rico of settlers. When these local settlers were joined by an influx of colonists from Spain, Cuba experienced a population boom. The colonization of Cuba coincided with the launching of Spain's continental empire in the New World, for which Cuba proved an ideal staging ground. There followed a decade or more of steady development, as if Cuba might avoid the boom-and-bust cycle plaguing the rest of the Antilles archipelago.[30]

By 1525, Cuba had become a casualty of the continental exploration it helped launch. The discovery of vast silver deposits in Mexico and later Peru did to Cuba as Cuba had done to its neighbors, depleting it of human and material resources. When no amount of threats by Spain's Council of the Indies could compel Spanish colonists to remain in Cuba, the Crown ultimately gave up. By mid-century, Cuba had been virtually abandoned, its capital, Santiago, reduced to thirty households, its Spanish population down to seven hundred solitary souls.[31]

And yet a phoenix stirred among the ashes. The very mines of Mexico and Peru that had been the cause of nascent Cuba's undoing became the source of its regeneration. Cuba became essential to the task of transporting the bullion back to Spain. The quantity of silver found in Mexico and Peru exceeded anyone's imagination. More than creating a few fortunes, it promised to reshape the political map. France and England had long looked skeptically on Spain's claim to exclusive sovereignty in the New World. Now they began to prey on Spanish galleons and settlements, at the same time that they began to contemplate settlements of their own. At the very least, they would severely tax Spain's harvest of treasure.[32]

Cuba commands the three essential passageways of the communication system that unites the Atlantic world: the Windward Passage, the Yucatán Channel, and the Florida Straits. It was simply a matter of time before Cuba became the focus of imperial competition in the New World. To patrol all three Cuban passages simultaneously was beyond anyone's ability; Spain devoted its resources to the Florida Straits, egress of the Gulf of Mexico and Caribbean Sea, and site of a spacious harbor at Havana. Spain made Havana, moved to its current location in 1519, the base of the flota, the yearly rendezvous of Spanish treasure galleons for the journey home. Now an indispensable link in the Spanish empire, Havana became the recipient of royal largesse and soon developed into Cuba's most important city.[33]

Havana was not the sole beneficiary of the flota. The scale of the rendezvous promoted new industries and markets and spawned new communities and towns throughout western Cuba. As the sixteenth century progressed, increasing numbers of sailors, soldiers, administrators, craftsmen, and laborers poured into Cuba, along with the personnel of associated hospitality industries.[34] Fortifications needed erecting, munitions provided, security maintained. The yearly visit of the fleet swelled the streets of Havana with thousands of Spaniards, who provided the local population with all means of opportunity for work. Food, shelter, entertainment for the men, on land and at sea; rigging, furniture, navigational equipment; new ships, tender ships, coast guard ships—there was plenty of work and increasingly people to do it, compounding the need for housing, food, clothing, and other commodities, and thus contributing to Havana's transformation into a major Caribbean market. The bustle of Havana spilled over into the adjacent countryside, where a domestic market emerged tied to international commerce, and through which local farmers and ranchers exchanged produce for manufactures made in or filtered through Havana. In 1553, Spain's Council of the Indies formally recognized Havana's ascendance, declaring it the residence of the governor of Cuba. In 1594, Havana achieved the status of city, along with which came commercial prerogatives and trading rights, and increased scrutiny. Finally, in 1607, Havana's position as Cuba's first city was formally acknowledged when the Crown split the island into two jurisdictions, "Havana" in the west and "Cuba" (Santiago) in the east. Havana became the island's capital and seat of the governor and captain-general.[35]

In Spain's overextended empire, the rise of Havana and the West precipitated the neglect of Santiago and the area around Guantánamo Bay. In 1608, Havana's population exceeded ten thousand, more than half that of the entire island. Official Crown policies contributed to the demographic imbalance. Rather than encouraging the development of a network of commercial centers throughout the island, Crown officials named Havana Cuba's official seaport, restricting Santiago and other seaports to the coasting trade. Economically, culturally, socially, Santiago and eastern Cuba lagged behind Havana and its surroundings. The domestic production and internal markets that developed in the west did not emerge in the east, where a lack of human investment compounded inadequate material commitment. In Santiago, all but the most essential political and military offices remained vacant, leaving eastern resources untapped and communities there isolated and stunted.[36]

Which is not to say that nobody benefited from the official neglect. The downgrading of Santiago and the disregard for the east created opportunities as well as adversity. Unable to count on royal largesse, the east became less dependent on the Crown for its welfare, more imaginative, more ingenious. Perhaps predictably, eastern Cuba attracted a population different from that of tightly controlled Havana. The people in the east met their needs in unconventional ways, tapping less coveted resources and striking irregular alliances. In Cuba, east and west regarded one another with mutual suspicion. As if the independence and recalcitrance of eastern settlers were not bad enough, French corsairs began buzzing southeast Cuba in the early sixteenth century, preying on Spanish shipping, raiding farms, and sacking towns. By the end of the century, British pirates and privateers had joined the fray.[37]

The general lawlessness of eastern Cuba would vex the Crown for three centuries running. Jealously opposed to the contraband activity, the Crown was in no position to do much about it. Fight it here, it rears up there; Crown resources were perennially overstretched. At one point, Crown officials contemplated depriving black marketeers of their market by resettling colonists in a tight nucleus around Santiago, just as they had resettled Indians a century before. But depopulating southeast Cuba would only make the region more vulnerable than ever to foreign incursion. Instead, the Crown took no initiative whatsoever, leaving southeast Cuba largely unsupervised and underdeveloped.[38]

Both in Spain and throughout the New World, the Crown's policy of emphasizing mineral procurement over agricultural and commercial development inspired criticism on political, economic, and moral grounds. Extractive industries such as mining are hard on natural resources as well as people. Mining promotes a uniquely narrow concept of the value of land. So long as minerals are present, the land is valuable; when the minerals are gone, the miners move on. To get to the minerals, owners will stop at nothing, regardless of the human or environmental cost. Moreover, while Havana's development spawned new industries and even an internal market, the balance of Spain's New World trade remained radically skewed in favor of silver. By the turn of the seventeenth century, silver constituted 80 to 90 percent of Spain's New World exports, leaving little room for investment in other minerals, manufacturing, or agriculture.

The Crown's narrow focus on silver left Spain vulnerable to the larger, diversified naval and merchant fleets of rivals England and France.[39] Moreover, Spain's policy of treating local populations as nothing but means to imperial ends was as politically misguided as it was morally indefensible. Once the vast scale of the continental treasure became known, Spain elevated its scrutiny of Cuba and other colonies, centralizing and honing its administration in order to wring from them every last ounce of profit. When the new Bourbon monarchs came to power in the early eighteenth century, they were determined to usher Spain into a modern political economy. But well past mid-century, modern accounting practices vied with Crown-dominated trading monopolies to discourage individual initiative and enterprise. The fate of early Cuban tobacco production is a case in point. Thanks in part to increasing demand in Europe, tobacco production accelerated in Cuba in the first few decades of the eighteenth century, affording local farmers in places such as the Guantánamo Basin an opportunity to dabble in the world market. But soon royal officials curtailed this activity, regulating production, setting prices, and marketing the tobacco abroad. When the Crown was not appropriating outright the farmers' product, it was overtaxing their profits, inspiring a series of armed showdowns between tobacco farmers and Spanish officials.[40]

A Cuban myth suggests that the U.S. occupation of Guantánamo Bay in 1898 robbed Cuba of one of its great harbors and doomed the Guantánamo Basin to economic and cultural stagnation.[41] While there

can be no denying Guantánamo's virtues, the underdevelopment of
the bay and basin preceded the U.S. presence there. For two centuries
before the United States arrived at Guantánamo, Spanish and Cuban
officials implored the Crown to populate and develop the region. For
two centuries the Crown refused, thus setting the stage for the final
collapse of the Spanish empire in the New World.

Two centuries after Velázquez first parceled out Cuba among a
small circle of barons, the Guantánamo Basin remained sparsely settled, its lands formally monopolized by absentee landlords, who regarded their estates more as status symbols than as sources of income.
Over the course of the next century and a half, efforts to populate
and develop the Guantánamo Basin met with little success, in part
because the landlords themselves had a stake in the flourishing contraband trade.[42] By the end of the seventeenth century, only the
Catholic Church had succeeded in making inroads in the east, though
these were meager. They included the establishment of San Anselmo
de los Tiguabos, a small church located twenty-five miles up the
Guantánamo Basin in a hamlet inhabited mostly by Indians. Around
1695 the official neglect of Guantánamo Bay and its surroundings,
together with the much-regretted attention of pirates and smugglers,
induced Severino Manzaneda, governor-general of Cuba, to launch
the first in a series of sustained appeals to Spain's Council of the Indies to develop Guantánamo Bay. Empty, Manzaneda observed, Guantánamo would remain a site of illicit activity; populated and developed,
it might emerge as one of Cuba's great ports. Manzaneda's call went
unheeded.[43]

Which is more or less where things stood on July 18, 1741, when British admiral Edward Vernon led sixty-two ships bearing three thousand
British troops plus one thousand Jamaican slaves through the entrance
of Guantánamo Bay. Among the British troops were several hundred
American colonists, survivors of a much larger colonial contingent
that had joined a British expeditionary force the previous autumn targeting Spain's New World settlements in the War of Jenkins' Ear.[44]

Vernon took an immediate liking to Guantánamo Bay. Indeed, he
had been at the bay not ten days before renaming it, along with two

rivers, and selecting the ideal spot on which to build a new city. (He called the bay Cumberland Harbour, after Prince William, Duke of Cumberland, younger son of George II.) He was not alone in thinking this "the finest harbor in the West Indies," with "room for all the shipping in the Thames." The "Americans," too, he was quick to report, "begin to look on it as the Land of Promise already."[45]

Vernon had charted a circuitous course to the Land of Promise. Santiago de Cuba, not Guantánamo, was the intended target of the flotilla that cleared Port Royal, Jamaica, on the thirtieth of June. Vernon had set his eyes on Cuba only after a humiliating retreat from the Spanish bastion Cartagena the previous month. By taking Santiago, haven of Spanish privateers, he thought to burnish his image while redeeming at least a fraction of the colossal expenditure of blood and treasure his expedition had cost the king. The British force assembled at Port Royal on the eve of Cartagena had been the largest ever to visit the New World. All England expected something to show for it.[46]

Vernon's American charges had come by the Land of Promise no less fortuitously. Just a year earlier most of the 3,300 colonists mustered into the British ranks at Port Royal had been struggling to make ends meet in a sluggish colonial economy. While opportunity abounded for individuals from well-connected families with access to land and capital, the majority of colonists coming of age at mid-century had reason to regard the future warily. At home, a burgeoning population combined with conflict along the colonial frontier to limit access to land; abroad, a Spanish monopoly on trade to the West Indies throttled colonial commerce and industry. The result was a society characterized by frenzied geographical mobility. Whether running from debt, skirting the law, or leaping at chance, this generation was desperately on the move.[47]

No wonder, then, the "vast number of spectators" assembled in Boston on April 19, 1740, to hear Massachusetts governor Jonathan Belcher announce a levy of troops to fight in the newly declared war with Spain. The king had resolved "to distress and annoy" Spain's "most considerable Settlements in the West Indies." Massachusetts would do its part by enlisting all willing and able-bodied men under the most generous terms: arms, clothing, payment, conveyance, and "a Share in any Booty which shall be taken from the enemy."[48] Belcher had read his audience astutely. Massachusetts had to turn away four hundred volunteers. Other colonies met with equal success—such as Maryland, which sweetened the deal with debt, tax, and toll relief.[49]

If war is plunder, as Governor Belcher's proclamation suggests, plunder was both the trigger and the underlying cause of the conflict that introduced Americans to Guantánamo. For decades leading up to April 1740, colonial newspapers bristled with tales of abuse visited on British shipping by privateers policing Spain's West Indian monopoly—a monopoly made all the more vexing by Spain's refusal to take advantage of it.[50] In the twenty-six years leading up to the war, Spain's desultory trading fleet sailed but nine times. In one seven-year period, it never left port at all. Not content to squander an opportunity, British merchants took up a lucrative smuggling operation checked only by Spain's licensed pirates, who found it more convenient to raid British vessels than to engage in legitimate trade themselves.[51] One such raid, at the hands of the notorious Juan de León Fandino and "his crew of Indians, Mulattoes and Negroes," relieved Robert Jenkins, captain of the British merchantman *Rebecca*, of his ear.[52] When, eight years later, Jenkins paraded his pickled ear before an exercised Parliament, Britain declared war on Spain.[53]

Making the rounds of their final good-byes in autumn 1740, the sons of Massachusetts and Maryland and the other colonies might have been excused for exuding a certain level of confidence. The troop levy whose unanticipated success they embodied coincided with news out of Jamaica of Admiral Vernon's capture of Porto Bello the previous November. In the run-up to war, Vernon, then sitting in Parliament, had boasted that he could take the Spanish stronghold with just six ships. In England, news of Vernon's feat sparked jubilation.[54] In the colonies, it inspired visions of a grand payout. Typical is a column from the *Boston Post Boy*, which, after noting how amply Vernon's men had "enriched themselves with the Plunder of one Town," invited readers to imagine "how much more will those who serve in this Expedition enrich themselves by the Plunder of *many*!" And not "of Towns only, but of a wide extended Country, abounding in Gold, Silver, and every other sort of Riches." So confident was Vernon in the odds of the new campaign that before re-embarking for the West Indies, he commissioned medals depicting his Spanish adversary, Admiral Blas de Lezo, kneeling at his feet.[55]

American hopes for the expedition faded upon the colonists' arrival in Jamaica. Within a matter of days some three hundred American troops were stricken with yellow fever, which, along with dysentery, cholera, malaria, and scurvy, would claim more lives than did any Spanish arms. Inexplicable delays plagued the campaign from the start. For over two months the British force languished in Port Royal, thus forfeiting the element of surprise, inviting further disease, and introducing the colonists to that peculiar brand of snobbery known as British disdain. Going out, the Americans regarded Spain as the principal impediment to colonial interests. Heading home, their perspective had changed considerably. Surely, being included on this campaign reinforced some colonists' sense of Britishness.[56] But more seem to have developed lasting resentment toward their British cousins, who treated them like pawns, splintering colonial companies to fill shipboard vacancies, setting Americans to common labor alongside Jamaican slaves, and using Americans and Jamaicans as cannon fodder to clear the way for British regulars.[57] British army officers, particularly, refused to undertake any action that might be perceived as benefiting specifically colonial interests.[58]

In this unhappy climate Vernon stood out not only for regarding British and colonial interests as one and the same but also for his frank solicitude for the Americans. Though not beyond branding some as lazy, he took pains to assure his superiors that "the Americans have had nothing to complain of from the Sea, and have never expressed themselves dissatisfied at being employ'd on board his Majesty's Ships."[59] An experienced politician as well as a seasoned sailor, Vernon was drawn to the more cultivated Americans, and to one in particular, Lawrence Washington, a twenty-three-year-old captain in one of the Virginia companies. British-educated and immensely ambitious, Washington came to Vernon's attention for his leadership in one of the signal achievements of the ill-fated Cartagena campaign, the storming of the Barradera battery, which helped open the harbor to the British fleet. In the end no amount of individual daring could overcome the incapacity of the British army and navy to act in concert. British forces withdrew from Cartagena in mid-April 1741, after six weeks' futile engagement and amid heavy losses due mostly to disease.[60]

Later, at Guantánamo, Vernon would demonstrate intimate acquaintance with the motives and aspirations of the colonists.[61] At Port Royal, he struck up a lasting friendship with the young Washington before embarking for Cuba. To Washington, Vernon's attentiveness almost made up for the discomfort and inconvenience of Port Royal. "We are all tired of the heat and wish for a cold season to refresh our blood," Washington wrote his father, Augustine. "I mentioned the extravagance of this Island before but they have now raised the prices of everything so that I really believe I shall be under a necessity of drawing Bills" (i.e., taking out a loan). Nor was Washington's regiment receiving the treatment he had expected. Still, he assured his father, "I have remained on Admiral Vernon's ship . . . vastly to my satisfaction."[62]

No record survives of Washington and Vernon's conversation in the wardroom aboard the *Boyne*, but it is possible to imagine something of its content. Washington likely confirmed Vernon's impression that all talk in the colonies was of land.[63] Washington himself grew up in a family for whom land was a vehicle of wealth and advancement rather than the means of subsistence. From the year 1657, when Lawrence's great-grandfather John Washington first appeared off the mouth of the Potomac, the Washingtons had proved themselves keen speculators and cunning bachelors, snatching up much of the tidewater's prized real estate along with several of its most eligible brides. Augustine Washington, Lawrence's father, was a surveyor, a vocation that afforded him firsthand knowledge not only of the Virginia countryside but also of the frontier territory west of the Appalachians. British treaties with the Indians and French delayed opening the so-called Ohio Country to colonial settlement until after Augustine had died. But Augustine was among the first colonists to tap iron deposits around Fredericksburg, Virginia, eventually trading his local mining rights for a large stake in a London mining and manufacturing firm.[64]

Lawrence Washington was every bit his father's son. Exposure to the ravages of war could not distract him from the issue of the day. "I hope my Lotts are secured," he wrote Augustine from Port Royal, "which if I return I shall make use of as my dwelling."[65] The "lotts" in question consisted of 2,500 acres along Little Huntington Creek, Virginia, which Augustine had transferred to Lawrence just before he embarked for the West Indies. Called Epsewasson at the time, Lawrence's Virginia estate would be renamed Mount Vernon after his Port Royal interlocutor.

Besides describing his plans for Epsewasson, Lawrence likely confided to Vernon his hopes for the Ohio Country, which, judging from his activity upon returning to Virginia, was always topmost in his mind. Home by January 1743, the year his father died, Lawrence carried on in the family tradition, marrying the wealthy Anne Fairfax, forging powerful social and political alliances, and pursuing his land and iron interests back and forth across the sea.[66] Lawrence's transatlantic peregrinations paid off in 1747, when, along with a group of prominent Virginia and English investors, he founded the Ohio Company of Virginia, eventually winning a grant of two hundred thousand acres near present-day Pittsburgh, Pennsylvania. Given the competition from like-minded colonists (Benjamin Franklin was a partner in the rival Vandalia Company; Thomas Jefferson's father, Peter, in the Loyal Land Company), never mind the standard established by his forebears, the king's endorsement of his land scheme could be counted a crowning success.[67]

But those who thought to tap the resources of the Ohio Country had to figure out a way to bring its fruit to market. It was simply too hard to carry it east over the Appalachian Mountains to the old ports of New York, Philadelphia, and Baltimore. Better to ship it down the Allegheny and Ohio Rivers, ultimately to the Mississippi River and Gulf of Mexico. This only raised bigger questions about access not only to the French port of New Orleans but also to regional and hemispheric shipping lanes, then largely in the control of Spain.

Here is where Vernon must have cut in. By the time Washington came to his attention at Cartagena, Vernon had been commuting between England and the West Indies off and on for forty years. Later, in Cuba, when his hopes for Guantánamo seemed to be disintegrating on the shoals of army indifference, Vernon reminded his superiors back home that his estimation of Guantánamo's virtues was based on unrivaled knowledge of the Indies.[68] Had Washington not already heard it from his father, the surveyor, he would almost certainly have learned from Vernon that plans for developing the American hinterland hinged on command of three key waterways: the Yucatán Channel, the Florida Straits, and the Windward Passage. The Mississippi River drains into the Gulf of Mexico, as everybody knows, but the Gulf of Mexico is part of a regional circulation system that governs access to its various parts. Current in the Gulf of Mexico flows clockwise, entering through the Yucatán Channel, between today's Cancún and northwest Cuba; it exits through the Florida Straits, between north-central Cuba and the Florida Keys. In the age of sail, travel against this current was difficult, often impossible, which meant that ships accessed the Gulf of Mexico through the Caribbean Sea. The Caribbean, in turn, has many entryways but few deep passages, none deeper and more convenient to Europe and North America than the Windward Passage, home to Guantánamo Bay.

At the time Washington was hatching his land scheme, Spain dominated both the Caribbean Sea and the Gulf of Mexico. Spain patrolled the western side of the Windward Passage from the port of Santiago; Spain's ally, France, the eastern side from today's Port-au-Prince. Both the Yucatán Channel and the Florida Straits were convenient to Spanish-held Havana and to Spanish Florida. Cuba, Vernon well knew, was the gravitational center around which this system churned. The country that controlled Cuba would command the trade and traffic not only of the Atlantic seaboard and North American continent, but of the Western Hemisphere itself.

Vernon and Washington prepared to depart for Cuba in late June 1741. After Cartagena, Vernon had thought to remain in Port Royal for six weeks, giving men and ships ample time to recover. But Port Royal proved no healthier than before. In six short months, twelve thousand men had been reduced to three thousand, and Vernon resolved to engage the enemy while there remained troops at his command. Havana and Vera Cruz were among the targets considered by a British council of war meeting in mid-June.[69] Ultimately, it settled on Santiago de Cuba, which, if less significant than the other ports, was crucial both "to the security of British trade," as the council put it, and to "cutting off the baneful correspondence between the Spaniards and [the French at] Hispaniola."[70]

Vernon had had his eye on southeast Cuba for some time. While pooling local resources in advance of Cartagena, one of his lieutenants captured a British privateer, pressing its "marooning" crew into the king's service. Among the harvest taken on that raid was a displaced New Englander named John Drake who had been plying the waters of the western Atlantic for over two decades and whose description of southeast Cuba changed Vernon's understanding of the goal of this campaign.[71]

In a deposition obtained on board the *Boyne* as Vernon sailed for Cuba, Drake described being seized off a British trader bound for Boston by a Spanish privateer sometime in the late 1720s. Released on the island of Trinidad, Drake made for Puerto Príncipe, in central Cuba, where he hoped to catch a ride to Jamaica and, ultimately, home. But Cuba suited Drake just fine. Finding that he "could get a very comfortable living there by fishing," he decided to remain, and over the course of the next decade he moved with the seasons back and forth between Puerto Príncipe and the eastern towns of Bayamo and Santiago. By the time he was hauled aboard Vernon's ship, Drake had more or less settled down, exchanging a third of his bounty for hunting rights in a spot on Cuba's southern coast just east of Guantánamo Bay.[72]

This Caribbean Leatherstocking knew the Santiago-Guantánamo region as only a hunter-gatherer could. Having fished its rivers and traipsed its fields, Drake could calculate times and measurements down to the hour and even ankle ("farther than which even a dory cannot pass, being only ankle deep"). While debating Spanish targets back in Port Royal, Vernon had learned from another source that a frontal assault on Santiago harbor would be suicidal thanks to the harbor's tortuous, precipitous entrance, which made it easy to protect. But the source described Santiago as vulnerable to a land-based attack, and Drake's testimony convinced Vernon that Guantánamo Bay, forty miles down the coast, would make an ideal staging ground.[73] Emptying into the southwest corner of Guantánamo Bay flowed a significant river (Rio Guantánamo), navigable in twenty-five to thirty feet of water for about three miles, and in over nine feet of water for up to fifteen. From there the advancing army would have to strike out on foot, skirting the mountains that made direct progress up the coast impossible. Drake estimated that a soldier could cover the remaining sixty circuitous miles to Santiago in less than two days. "Very good" in dry weather, the route was passable even when inundated, though the road to Santiago was "for the most part woody." These woods would become a sticking point between Vernon and his army counterpart, General Thomas Wentworth, who feared the woods, as he feared an ambush, and who took cold comfort in Drake's description of a route "so broad that ten Men may very well go a-breast."[74]

Striking in its detail, Drake's testimony is notable too for what it omits: mention of any fortifications at Guantánamo Bay, for instance, or local garrisons, or even significant settlement. A few isolated salt-works and a couple of cattle pens lined the river above where it shoaled. Roughly forty miles from the mouth of the bay lay the little village of Santa Catalina ("an hundred Houses and one Church" inhabited by "Indians and Mulattoes who lived by hunting and raising of Stock").[75] In short, nothing in Drake's report led Vernon to conclude that this territory was anything but ripe for the picking; a few odd farms and a colored village posed no obstacle to the plan crystallizing in his mind for a new American colony.

Vernon arrived at Guantánamo that July with high hopes. What he found exceeded his expectations. It was not simply that Guantánamo afforded ready access to Santiago; nor that the bay could absorb the entire fleet; nor that it offered better protection from tropical storms than Port Royal; nor, finally, that it was ideally situated to safeguard British shipping in the heart of the Caribbean. All of this was true. What put Guantánamo over the top in Vernon's mind was its native splendor: its navigable rivers, rolling hills, and fertile plains.

Vernon spent the first week at Guantánamo Bay unpacking. Though not unnoticed by Spanish authorities, his arrival went unopposed. Spanish defenses in the vicinity of Santiago were light. Just how light became clear after the interception of a packet of letters from the Spanish governor of Santiago to the captain of the local militia acknowledging the British arrival and promising to release arms and ammunition for at most a hundred men. Later testimony from a Spanish captive put the actual number of enemy troops in the area at seventy-five, giving the British a numerical advantage of more than forty to one.[76] The only significant skirmishes of the campaign occurred at the end of the second week, when a scouting party dispatched to confirm Drake's intelligence flushed the Spanish militia from its lair. For two days the Spaniards peppered the invading army from the bushes, after which the Spaniards essentially disappeared. In their wake lay three British casualties (one fatality) and an open road to Santiago.[77]

Yet the British Army never advanced. No amount of intelligence, however favorable, could compel Wentworth forward. Vernon had witnessed such foot-dragging before—at Cartagena, where the army's hesitation before the central citadel effectively halted that campaign. Determined to avoid another such debacle, Vernon spent the next two months trying to cajole his army counterpart, whose irresolution was evident by the second day. "I hope it will please God we shall avoid splitting on the Rock of Discord," the admiral wrote the general, "as I think, if this be but heartily set about, it can never fail of Success."[78] Within a week, Vernon saw so little evidence of heart among the army that he began to fear for the safety of his guide, Drake. "It cannot but be apprehended," Vernon warned a lieutenant, that "there are some might even be glad our Guide should be destroyed."[79] When, after nine days, neither the absence of an enemy nor the establishment of a secure camp proved any inducement to Wentworth, Vernon set off to canvass the local countryside for himself.

Descending the ladder of the *Boyne*, he boarded a longboat and headed up the Guantánamo River, his delight at what he found apparently exaggerated by his fear of losing it. "I thought it the most beautiful Prospect I ever saw," he wrote the Admiralty back at Whitehall, "to row five Leagues up a navigable River, of about a hundred Yards wide all the Way, with green Trees on both Sides appearing like a green Fence." Skirting Wentworth's camp, he crested a hill to come face-to-face with "the finest Plains" in the West Indies, watered "by a River the farthest navigable." Wentworth, meanwhile, occupied a rise along the river, "as beautiful a Situation for a Town as this Country can afford, with a fertile soil behind it."[80] Vernon was a confident, egotistical man, as his eager forging of "victory" medals suggests. Might he have confided to Washington, who remained by his side at Guantánamo Bay, his hope that such a town would one day bear his name? The sources do not say, but the similarity between this site and another back home in Virginia is uncanny and must have left a lasting impression in Washington's mind.

As days leached into weeks and Wentworth's intransigence stiff-

ened, relations between the admiral and the general deteriorated.[81] En
route to Cuba from Jamaica, a navy captain had overheard an army
officer grumbling that "the Army would not land in Cuba"; once landed,
this officer was said to have remarked "that the Army would not move
from the Encampment on the River Side."[82] When, by mid-August,
Wentworth had come to justify his inaction by pointing to a lack of
reinforcements, Vernon called his bluff and dispatched one of his
fleetest ships, the *Sea-Horse*, to the colonies to beat the bushes for
more men.[83] No doubt Wentworth's numbers *were* dwindling; this was
a self-fulfilling prophecy in the face of tropical disease. But talk of reinforcements was a distraction, as Wentworth himself acknowledged
the next month when he allowed that no number of reinforcements
would compel him on to Santiago. Over the ensuing days, excuse followed excuse until the army finally retrained its sights on, of all places,
Cartagena.

Glowing accounts of Guantánamo Bay began to sweep the colonies just as Vernon came to recognize that the campaign was over. In
early autumn 1741, newspapers up and down the Atlantic seaboard
announced almost accurately that "Admiral Vernon was arriv'd at
S. Jago de Cuba, and the Land Forces had got safe ashore at a Village
a small Distance from the City."[84] More detailed descriptions of Guantánamo accompanied the *Sea-Horse* north: "the finest Harbour that
ever I saw," "a pleasant Island, far exceeding all the West Indies that I
have been in," a country laden with "Cattle, Goods, and Horses," "a
place as healthy as Man can wish," "no want of good Beef, Cabaritas,
wild Hogs, Indian Corn in abundance," "Water plenty and pure, as
good as any I have seen among us"—these just some of the images
calculated to distract beleaguered colonists anticipating another long
winter. "Rigg out and make the best of [your] way here," one writer
urged, "for I make no doubt but we shall in a very short time have
quiet possession of the whole Place, and then first come first served;
now or never for a plantation on the island of Cuba."[85]

Most recruiters appealed to individuals' private interests to raise
the new troop levy. Massachusetts's new governor, William Shirley,
saw in this campaign the embodiment of "the publick good." To be
sure, Guantánamo promised land to individuals *and families* "on the
easiest terms yet ever were." But as the "chief mart of Trade in the

British America," Massachusetts had something particular to gain, namely "opening a more extensive, rich and beneficial trade for ourselves in the West Indies, than we ever yet enjoyed"—trade sure to redound to the king's benefit, too.[86] In Shirley's and other pamphlets and proclamations from the second troop drive, the message was all "mission accomplished" and "danger over" as Guantánamo took on the character of a vacation retreat. This would be no new errand into a hostile wilderness. Construction on the new colony proceeded apace, with secure perimeters, cleared roads, and "1000 huts" already in place.[87]

Unfortunately for the Americans and their supporters—for Shirley and Washington, for Vernon and Drake—British land officers did not cling to so generous an understanding of the "publick." Colonial troops overheard the "Europeans," as they called them, protesting being asked "to expose their lives for procuring settlements for the Americans."[88] In a military lacking unified command, the army's opposition to this venture was enough to carry the day. As the odds of delivering this Land of Promise dwindled, Vernon consoled himself with the thought that he had at least understood the Americans correctly. "I think my inclinations have been entirely conformable to what, I believe, was the principal motive of all the American officers engaging in the service," he wrote Whitehall, "the hopes of being settled in the West Indies, and in Cuba preferably to all other places."[89] Weeks of butting heads with Wentworth had left Vernon dispirited and ready to return to higher latitudes. Still, the wistful admiral could do nothing but stand aside as his American dream went up in smoke. "We discerned the huts of the camp to be on fire," he reported on November 16, 1741, "Mr. Wentworth having that morning marched down with his remaining well men, and embarked . . . on board his Majesty's ship the *Grafton*."[90] Cruelly, to Vernon fell the burden of completing the self-immolation. Three weeks later, on December 6, a Sunday, he set fire to a fine new fascine battery at the center of the bay and sailed out of Guantánamo, never to return.[91]

The Americans, by contrast, would be back. Not these Americans, to be sure, not anytime soon, but soon enough—before any rival power (including Spain) could occupy Guantánamo and exploit its riches. Very few of the original American recruits survived the expedition.

Massachusetts sent five hundred troops and returned fifty; Rhode Island sent two hundred troops and returned twenty—figures replicated
throughout the colonies.[92]

Lawrence Washington was among the fortunate to return to the
colonies, thus securing Edward Vernon's place in U.S. history. But
Washington left Cuba with more than a new name for Epsewasson;
a stubborn case of tuberculosis accompanied him home. Latent in
1743, it blossomed by the end of the decade, ultimately killing him
on July 26, 1752, at the unripe age of thirty-three. It was left to Lawrence Washington's half brother, George, to transform Mount Vernon
from a solemn epitaph to a bungled military campaign into a triumphant symbol of a new nation. But the more Mount Vernon became
associated with its new owner, the further its connection to Guantánamo Bay receded, so that, today, Guantánamo's place in early
American history is all but forgotten. Guantánamo was there at the
beginning. It has been there ever since, reflecting, sometimes shaping,
the aspirations and institutions of the people who like to call themselves "Americans" and of the American peoples to whom they have
been so closely and controversially tied.

Cuban sources describe the British retreat from Guantánamo Bay in
November 1741 as the product of a heroic Spanish-Cuban military
campaign.[93] But Francisco Cajigal, Santiago's governor, seems to have
recognized how lucky Spain was that Cuba survived the British occupation intact. The safety of the east, indeed, of Cuba itself, could
never be secure, Cajigal informed Crown officials the next year, so
long as the region remained unpopulated. He commissioned a study of
the bay and its surroundings to determine what could be done to ensure that it not fall into enemy hands again. Among other measures,
Cajigal proposed constructing defenses at the bay, the costs of which
could be borne by exploiting copper deposits back of Santiago. He
praised the fertility of the Guantánamo Basin, and criticized its Creole
landlords for ignoring the agricultural potential of their vast estates,
many of them seemingly abandoned. He also called for the establishment of two towns at strategic locations near the bay, capable of
promoting and maintaining local manufactures and markets while

ensuring the security of the entire region. Like the former governor-general Manzaneda's proposal a half century before, Cajigal's proposition fell on not so much deaf as distracted ears. Santiago was now safe, but the War of Jenkins' Ear dragged on in Europe, drawing the attention and resources of the Crown to matters closer to home.[94]

In ensuing years, others echoed Manzaneda's and Cajigal's calls to populate and develop what the prominent Santiago attorney Nicolas Joseph de Rivera described as "a jewel of the monarchy"—to equally little effect. These proposals illuminate Guantánamo's position in the social fabric of Cuba and anticipate its later uses. Empty, Guantánamo became a void into which Spain and Cuba and even America projected solutions to their pressing problems. Long before refugees from Haiti and Cuba began to crowd the tarmac at the U.S. Naval Base at Guantánamo Bay in the 1990s, Guantánamo functioned as Spain's social safety valve in the New World: as a refuge for displaced settlers from Florida, Santo Domingo, and, eventually, revolutionary Haiti.

In 1757 an informal census of the Guantánamo Basin identified 15 cattle ranches, 24 hog farms, 6 tobacco plantations, a sugar mill, and 419 people in an area of roughly 250 square miles. Formally, most of the land in the region remained the property of a few great lords. The single town mentioned in the census, San Anselmo de los Tiguabos, suffered from disrepair, the destruction of its church unfairly blamed on the British occupation sixteen years before. Like others before him, the author of this tally, Bishop Pedro A. Morell de Santa Cruz, called for the construction of three new towns, an odd—and perhaps particularly Spanish—way of envisioning colonial development. *If we build it they will come.*

After 1757 the Guantánamo region began to stir, at least a little. It did so as a result not of top-down and seemingly artificial projects to create towns "on spec," but of individual initiative. Cuba also got a brief shot in the arm when next the concentrated power of Britain's navy appeared off the coast of Cuba during the Seven Years' War (known to North Americans as the French and Indian War). A year-long British occupation of Havana threw Cuba open to free trade and inspired a short-lived commercial bonanza that gave merchants and the old landed elite a lesson in the limitations of mercantilism they would never forget. Before the British capture of Havana, Cuba's

political elite had always been able to keep colonial policy tilted in
their favor. After the British withdrawal, it was hard to get the genie
back in the bottle, not least because the Crown realized that it would
be the primary beneficiary of commercial reform.

Besides demonstrating the dynamism of free trade, the British occupation of Havana revealed Cuba's continuing vulnerability to rival
attacks. In 1763 the Crown charged Ambrosio de Funes y Villalpando,
conde de Ricla and new governor-general of Cuba, with the task of
fortifying Havana along with strategic sites along the Cuban coastline. Ricla set to work constructing at Havana what would become
upon completion twelve years later the largest fortress in the New
World. He also commissioned a careful study of the island. Based
on the results, Ricla called for the further liberation of commerce,
the encouragement of agricultural production, and the promotion of
white migration to the island. Together these initiatives would create
the economic vitality on which true security and adherence to law
depended.

Ricla's emphasis on *white* migration reflected growing concern
about the most salient effect of the British occupation: an end to the
Asiento, the contract between Britain and Spain giving Spain a monopoly on the African slave trade, which soon transformed Cuba into
the largest slave market in the world. Ricla's desire to whiten Cuba
competed with others' sense that the way to stimulate the Cuban
economy was to unleash the slave trade. While Ricla was reconnoi-
tering Cuba, a Santiago surveyor named Baltasar Díaz de Priego presented the Crown with the first practical plan to promote the island's
eastern economy. The price of Spain's recovering Havana from England in 1763 had been the ceding of Spanish Florida. When Florida became a colony of Britain, many Spanish colonists abandoned
their homes there for Cuba. In Cuba, they sought a place where they
could pursue the things they knew how to do—namely, raise cattle
and cultivate tobacco and other vegetables. To Díaz de Priego, the
Floridians were just what the Guantánamo region needed to move it
toward a market economy. To lure the Floridians east, Díaz de Priego
suggested a series of incentives. For six years the refugees would pay
no taxes. They would be granted the right to buy and trade everything
but tobacco (the province of a Havana syndicate) anywhere in Cuba.

Finally, they would be permitted to import up to three hundred slaves tax-free. None of this could happen, however, unless Guantánamo Bay had suitable port facilities, and Díaz de Priego urged the Crown to construct infrastructure worthy of the bay's natural endowments. Díaz de Priego saw Guantánamo as far more than an auxiliary of Havana or Santiago. Together with Santo Domingo, Puerto Rico, Cartagena, Veracruz, and Havana, Guantánamo would ensure Spanish supremacy in the Caribbean, vanquishing pirates and black marketeers while securing the welfare of the Spain's commercial and naval fleets.[95]

By now readers may have guessed the outcome. Díaz de Priego's vision was never realized. The Floridians did not want to settle in the Guantánamo Basin, where blacks outnumbered whites by more than five to one, and where a diminishing population lived an isolated, bleak, subsistence. But when the eastern economy did advance in the early nineteenth century, it advanced along the lines Díaz de Priego suggested, spurred by the sort of incentives he proposed.[96]

A set of seemingly unconnected political events combined with an atmosphere of intellectual creativity to finally populate the Guantánamo Basin at the turn of the nineteenth century. By the second half of the eighteenth century, more and more politicians, public figures, and businessmen throughout the Spanish Empire had begun to mimic their counterparts in England and France by showing a greater interest in economic and political reform based on rationalized administration and scientific principles. Extended to colonial policies, this bred skepticism of the old mercantilist premise that the surest way to amass wealth was to wrest it from the ground, and a corresponding openness to free trade. Cuba's yearlong flirtation with the market during the British occupation of 1762–63 had planted the seed of interest. In the late eighteenth and early nineteenth centuries, Cuba became a laboratory for imperial reform and the site of demographic and economic transformation. In 1778 the Bourbon monarchy proved its commitment, solidifying the commercial gains by passing the landmark "free trade law."[97]

The new way of thinking spawned new partnerships between former adversaries. The old landed, Spanish-born (peninsular) elite joined forces with a less established, mostly Cuban-born (Creole) class of merchants and entrepreneurs to form commercial societies such as the Economic Society of Friends of the Country (1792), the Royal Economic Society of Havana (1793), and the Royal Havana Chamber of Agriculture and Commerce (1795). These societies popularized market ideas, demanded infrastructure improvements, and helped establish the technical, administrative, and educational institutions associated with market liberalism.[98] Most of this intellectual and commercial activity was centered in Havana and transpired in the west. As always, Santiago and the east lagged behind. Still, the oligarchs of Santiago could not help but notice the new alliances struck and the opportunities created as old estates were divided into sugar, tobacco, and coffee plantations.[99]

As Spain came to regard Cuba and its other colonies as sources of staple agriculture and markets for domestic manufactures, it updated and tightened its administration, but did so finally sensitive to the need to give as well as to take. The giving took the form not just of more favorable trade terms, but also of the introduction into Cuba of a modern professionalized bureaucracy designed to facilitate commerce. The changing worldview coincided with the importation of some seventy thousand slaves in the last third of the eighteenth century to jump-start the Cuban sugar industry. Between 1764 and 1769, Cuban sugar exports increased to seven times the level of the decade before. In the 1770s sugar exports were five times greater than they had been in the 1760s; between 1789 and 1818, they increased almost tenfold. By 1820, Cuba had become Spain's richest colony and the largest sugar exporter in the world. The rise of Cuban sugar brought improvements in infrastructure, new demand for labor and capital, and a host of associated business and industries.[100]

Cuba's economic expansion took place amid a series of dramatic political events that further fed the island's economic development, particularly in the east. In 1776 the outbreak of the American Revolution opened the vast American market to Cuban sugar. But the game changer occurred in 1791, when slaves in the French colony of Saint-Domingue, hitherto the most valuable colony in the world and the leading exporter of sugar, burst their chains. Over the next decade and a half, first Britain and then France would try unsuccessfully to restore slavery in the colony. In the meantime, the black revolution sent French refugees and planters to Cuba in droves, to be followed a few years later by still more refugees when Spain ceded Santo Domingo (eastern Hispaniola) to France, this time uprooting Spanish colonists, who, like the Floridians of 1763, headed straight for Cuba.[101]

In 1803 and continuing thereafter, the old estates of the Guantánamo Basin were dismembered and parceled out to French and Spanish colonists and others on favorable terms, thus opening them to agriculture. In 1817 a royal decree promoted white settlement in Cuba on especially generous terms. In 1818, Spain opened the port of Havana to free trade. Like the Floridians before them, the Spanish refugees from Santo Domingo refused to settle in the long-neglected Guantánamo Basin, and made instead for Mariel and other towns and cities to the west. But with fewer connections and less to lose, the French stayed, and they took advantage of the available land on favorable terms to establish a foundation of commercial agriculture.[102]

While the French refugees from Haiti joined a few Dominican exiles to establish coffee, cotton, and sugar plantations and to lay the foundation for Guantánamo City, the Crown itself commissioned one final study designed to propel the Guantánamo Basin into the modern world. The inspiration for what would come known as La Real Comision de Guantánamo (The Royal Commission of Guantánamo), seems to have come from José Solano, marques de Socorro, captain-general of the Spanish navy and former captain-general of Santo Domingo. Like Díaz de Priego, Solano recognized in Guantánamo a bay every bit the equal of Havana, Veracruz, San Juan, Puerto Bello, and Cartagena. Like Díaz de Priego, Solano advocated assigning Guantánamo Bay a permanent naval squadron, accompanied by ground troops, which could once and for all rid the east of contraband while defending it from enemy attack.

Solano's appeal was hardly new. Still, coming from the man in charge of the Spanish navy, it was difficult to ignore. Its timing was fortuitous, given the recent Spanish cession of Santo Domingo. With Solano's report still ringing in his ears, Spain's prime minister, Manuel

Godoy, looked to Guantánamo as a potential site for the latest round
of refugees. But before settling on Guantánamo, Godoy resolved to
learn more about it. At his urging, King Carlos IV constituted the Royal
Commission, known colloquially as the Mopox Commission, after
Joaquín Beltrán de Santa Cruz, conde de Mopox y Jaruco, the man
selected to carry it out.

In conception, design, and operation, the Mopox Commission reflected the new intellectual climate in Spain. Though associated with
Guantánamo Bay, the commission encompassed all of Cuba, its goal a
scientific accounting of the island's natural resources, including flora
and fauna, soil and minerals, rivers, harbors, and bays. Detailed dia-
grams of proposed canals and fortifications accompanied painstaking
blueprints of new cities and meticulous sketches of plants and animals. With this information, the Crown expected to modernize Cuba
economically, socially, and militarily.[103]

Determined to secure Cuba's borders and exploit its natural resources, the Mopox Commission was no less committed to saving
Cuba from the social conflagration afflicting Haiti. The decades following the British occupation of Havana saw a precipitous rise in
Cuba's slave population, and Spain's military leaders had not been
idle. The impressive fortification of Havana was matched by the dis-
semination across Cuba of trained militias and artillery brigades, acknowledged to be among the most effective in the world. So afraid
were Spanish officials of black insurrection across the Windward Passage that Cuba's captain-general introduced a law in 1795 prohibiting the immigration of "negroes" from foreign colonies. Spain also
contemplated replacing Cuba's African slaves with Indian slaves. The
Mopox Commission took the race problem to heart. The cities it proposed were to be white cities, their populations organized into disciplined militias. It was not for commercial purposes only that the
commission aimed to knit the country together with a fabric of canals,
sea-lanes, and roads. Modern infrastructure would facilitate a rapid
militia response.[104]

The Mopox Commission called for the construction of two cities
located near Guantánamo Bay. The first, La Paz, was to be located on
the Guantánamo River at or near the spot that had so captivated Admiral Vernon on that afternoon in June 1741. The other city, Alcudia,

would lie slightly north and west. Six miles apart, the cities were to be joined by both road and canal and connected by highway to the regional capital at Santiago. The commission called for La Paz and Alcudia to be populated originally with settlers from the Spanish regions of Catalonia and Galicia, as well as from the Canary Islands; these settlers might be joined at a later date by others from within Cuba itself. The commission explicitly enumerated the incentives to be offered prospective settlers, including land, a pair of mules, an ox, a yoke, farming implements, a slave, birds, a hog, the right to exploit local minerals, and finally, a twenty-year grace period on local fees and taxes. To help the settlers establish themselves, each settler would receive two royals (Crown silver currency) per head, reduced to one in the second year. In return, they would be expected to produce basic staple crops for local consumption and to repay the cost of their establishment in Cuba.

"Negroes" were not the only ones to be excluded from citizenship at La Paz and Alcudia. There would be no room for vagabonds or other individuals unable to maintain their end of the bargain. Meanwhile, prizes awaited citizens who excelled in producing coffee, sugar, indigo, honey, and tobacco. To promote commerce and industry on Guantánamo Bay, boatbuilding would be encouraged and individuals with surplus would be granted access to Spain's markets while reaping the benefit of an open commerce in slaves and other provisions.[105]

In elaborate technical sketches never to be realized, Mopox's engineers transformed Guantánamo's naturally open and inviting mouth into a deadly trap. The engineers exploited all of Guantánamo's natural endowments. On the outermost terrace of Windward Point a large battery commanded the Cuban coastline, north and south, affording the bay's defenders ample warning of approaching vessels. Along the mile-long ridge overlooking Windward Point ran a wall, several hundred yards long, connecting three batteries, some four hundred feet above the bay. Halfway along the same side of the entrance lay another large battery atop the thirty-foot terrace, capable of treating enemy vessels to withering fire. Finally, at the north end of the Windward Point, the engineers designed a jetty protruding half a mile into the bay at the end of which sat yet another battery. Beyond the jetty, on Fisherman's Point, sat the major fortification of the bay, comprising an arsenal, storehouses, dikes, troop quarters, and houses for officers' families and servants. Beyond the fort and jutting into the bay was a harbor, protected on four sides and capable of sheltering the largest vessels. Here were the beginnings of a new garrisoned city.[106]

Meanwhile, on Leeward Point, opposite the battery at the end of the Windward jetty, would sit another rampart, smaller than its counterpart only in degree. Across from these two forts, halfway down Hicacal Beach would be yet a third large fort, the three together forming an equilateral triangle of death and destruction. And that was it. The engineers saw no need for other fortifications farther up the harbor. The bay was now impregnable. An ambitious plan, surely, but no more so than that which had made Havana the securest port in the New World in the aftermath of the British occupation of 1762.[107]

Had Spain carried out the commission's plans for Guantánamo Bay, the United States would not occupy it today. But like other, far less ambitious plans to develop the bay that preceded it, the Mopox Commission was never put into effect. The reasons are by now familiar: an overextended Crown committed its resources elsewhere; the refugees from Santo Domingo were unenthusiastic about Guantánamo Bay. Mopox himself actually came out against developing Guantánamo Bay, "despite its importance, on account of the costs that it demands."[108] It would take the investment and machinations of an up-and-rising empire to finally give Guantánamo the economic boost it needed.

2

★

THE NEW FRONTIER

The view from Thomas Jefferson's hilltop home Monticello lends it-self to speculation. "I candidly confess," Jefferson wrote James Mon-roe in October 1823, "that I have ever looked on Cuba as the most interesting addition which could ever be made to our system of states. The control which, with Florida point, this island would give us over the Gulf of Mexico, and the countries, and the isthmus, bordering on it, as well as all those whose waters that flow into it, would fill up the measure of our political well-being."[1] Nestled in the Virginia upcoun-try, its back to the Blue Ridge Mountains, its front gazing down across the piedmont and the valley of the James River, Monticello provided Jefferson a unique perspective from which to appreciate the accom-plishments of the young American republic and anticipate its future wants.

Since the ships of the Virginia Company first arrived off the mouth of the James River in 1607, successive waves of colonists had spread out across the coastal plain, pushing their way past the fall line up into the valleys of the James, York, Rappahannock, and Potomac Rivers, before pausing, momentarily, at the foothills of the Allegheny Moun-tains. Evidence of their labor, and of that of their draft animals and slaves, was plain to see as Jefferson looked off to the east. In two hun-dred years, they had vanquished the Indians, reclaimed a wilderness, secured independence, and planted the seed of empire. And even then, Jefferson might have mused as he strode through Monticello from front to back, they were just getting started.

At the foot of Monticello, plainly visible from the west portico, lay the town of Charlottesville, still under construction, signs of a frontier breached. Beyond Charlottesville rose the Alleghenies, local range of the great Appalachian Mountain chain, which stretched from Georgia to Maine and which, up until the time of Jefferson's birth in 1743, defined the western limit of the colonists' world. To the settled eye, the land west of Monticello looked uninviting, if not impassable. But to Jefferson, as to his father, Peter, like George Washington's father, a surveyor, the Allegheny ridge was but a veil concealing a seemingly infinite, largely unexplored watershed whose valleys and plains fairly shimmered with opportunity.[2]

As a farmer dependent on water to get his produce to market, Jefferson knew rivers. He was born in the shade of the hill that would become Monticello, on the Shadwell estate of his father, one of the first settlers and commissioners of Albemarle County. On its southern edge, Shadwell was bordered by the Rivanna River, along which sat a small mill, built by Peter and later enlarged by Thomas, after Shadwell was incorporated into Monticello in 1794. As the young Thomas watched the milling and floating of his father's crops, one imagines him launching boats of his own design down the Rivanna, destined for the James, the Chesapeake, the Atlantic, and—who knows?—Europe, Africa, or Asia.[3]

Roughly half the rainfall that waters the Allegheny drains to the east. Above Monticello, in Jefferson's day, creeks with names such as Lynches, Moores, Prettys, Redbud, Wolftrap, and Ivy fed the north and south forks of the Rivanna, which, uniting just above Charlottesville, shot the gap between Monticello and Wolfpit, Broadhead, and Lonesome Mountains, before cutting through the fields of Shadwell and Monticello and continuing down to Columbia, where it joined the larger James River and, after clearing the falls at Richmond, meandered through the tidewater before emptying into Chesapeake Bay.

The other half of Allegheny rainfall ends up a thousand miles or more to the south. Several valleys and roughly seventy miles west of Monticello rise the tributaries of the New River, rare among the waterways of what is now the northeastern United States in that it runs due north up the Allegheny Plateau for over a hundred miles before veering west, through the New River Gap (today's Fayetteville, West Virginia), and finally joining the Great Kanawha River on its journey to the Ohio and Mississippi Rivers and ultimately the Gulf of Mexico. Having accompanied his father, the surveyor, on trips to the frontier, Jefferson could describe these western rivers in intimate detail.[4] He understood their relation to the Mississippi watershed and the Gulf of Mexico. And he recognized the promise that the Mississippi and Gulf of Mexico held for the prosperity of the young republic—so long as it controlled Cuba.

Farmer, son of a surveyor, amateur scientist, Jefferson was a systematic thinker. He saw the world in terms of systems, of networks of harmonious and interdependent parts. Ninety miles of ocean could no more separate Cuba from the United States geographically, economically, or politically, in Jefferson's mind, than an apple could be separated from the tree, as John Quincy Adams once put it.[5] Cuba belonged with the United States. Indeed, in a footnote in *Notes on the State of Virginia*, Jefferson surmised that Cuba had once been *part of* the American mainland. "I have often been hurried away by fancy, and led to imagine that what is now the bay of Mexico, was once a champaign country [a plain]; and that from the point or cape of Florida, there was a continued range of mountains through Cuba, Hispaniola, Porto Rico, Martinique, Guadeloupe, Barbados, and Trinidad, till it reached the coast of America, and formed the shores which bounded the ocean, and guarded the country behind." Rocked by some tremendous force, the mountains broke apart, flooding the plain and creating the Gulf of Mexico.[6] Jefferson was not naïve about the reality of political boundaries. As a naturalist, he doubted the durability of man-made boundaries, which, like Spanish Cuba, defied the natural order.

Gazing west from Monticello, then, Jefferson saw an expansive, trans-Appalachian confederation of states shipping its produce down the Ohio and Mississippi Rivers and out the Gulf of Mexico, with Cuba, guardian of the Gulf and Caribbean trade, firmly in American hands. To this point, Jefferson's vision circa 1820 was not that different from the imperial vision of Lawrence Washington and Edward Vernon seventy or eighty years before. They, too, had seen Cuba as the key to opening Caribbean markets to British goods, relieving population pressure along the colonial seaboard, and unlocking the potential of the American interior. But commercial prosperity comprised only half of Jefferson's vision of American empire. The other half was liberty. Liberty, Jefferson and James Madison had come to conclude somewhat paradoxically by 1789, depended on empire, which, by mitigating factionalism and providing for healthy population growth, ensured the virtue and independence of the American citizenry. But what was good for Americans, Jefferson insisted, was likewise worthy of the world. The empire Jefferson envisioned encompassed the liberty of fellow American republics and, indeed, all who suffered the yoke of despotism. Of course, to Jefferson, as to so many of his compatriots north and south, the liberty of white Americans and Europeans was compatible with African slavery. Though Jefferson wrestled with the moral contradictions of slavery to the end of his days, he never doubted that the annexation of Cuba was essential to preserving the "peculiar institution" and southern way of life.

There were similarities and differences, too, between Jefferson's vision of American empire and that of the generation of 1898, which propelled the United States into war with Spain and finally landed Cuba and Guantánamo Bay. At the turn of the twentieth century, Cuba was no less an essential strategic element of an unfolding imperial vision than it had been eighty (or twice eighty) years before. But by then Jefferson's rhetoric of liberty had become hollowed out. In part this was the result of maturing southern slave interests forsaking Jefferson's republicanism in their pursuit of Cuba as a slave state. ("Cuba must be ours," Jefferson Davis announced matter-of-factly in 1848, "to increase the number of slaveholding constituencies."[7]) In part it was a result of apostles of Manifest Destiny inflating Jeffersonian rhetoric to the bursting point. Throw in the blandishments of social Darwinism and the new racial "sciences" and you have a justification for imperial expansion altogether divorced from the reality of colonial relations in the Philippines, say, or Cuba, one that, in comparison to Jefferson's vision of an empire for liberty, seems little more than a case of special pleading.

Which is not to suggest that Jefferson's vision of American empire was devoid of arrogance or presumption, or that it lacked contradictions of its own. The point is not to defend Jefferson but to illuminate the different ends that Cuba and Guantánamo could serve in an unfolding, expanding U.S. political economy. Over nearly four centuries of development, Cuba remains a constant presence. Readers familiar with Edward Vernon's expedition to Cuba in 1741 will not be surprised to learn that Cuba figured centrally in debates about expansion long before expansion meant expansion overseas. Until late in these debates, Guantánamo Bay drops away. But never entirely. When the United States decided finally to move on Cuba in the spring of 1898, it did so through Guantánamo Bay; when, after the Spanish-American War, the United States decided to stay in Cuba, it chose Guantánamo as its forward operating base.

The American Revolution was not a war against empire. As Jefferson made plain in the years leading up to the war and in early drafts of the Declaration of Independence, it was not an aversion to empire itself that compelled Americans to declare independence, but rather, dismay over the king's inability to mediate equitably between the various parts of the British Empire. The king had failed as a neutral arbiter between Parliament and the colonial assemblies. Only when it became clear that there could be no equality in empire did the colonies resolve to pursue equality outside it. They would create an empire of their own.[8]

Creating an empire out of thirteen independent republics, or states (with presumably more to come), was no mean feat. To begin with, empire and republican government were thought to be contradictory. The eighteenth-century French political philosopher Montesquieu was only one in a long line of political thinkers who assumed that republics must be small and independent to be worthy of the name. Empire entailed conquest and the administration of foreign peoples and territories, along with a concentration of power and resources necessary to carry it out. By contrast, self-rule implied not only smallness but also liberty, equality, and living within one's means. The American colonists needed no lesson in the ways that empire eroded liberty and self-government. But what if Britain had misconceived empire? What if, rather than promoting narrow English interests, the Crown had acted impartially, safeguarding the well-being of separate but equal colonies? What if Montesquieu had been wrong?

Such was the logic of many prominent colonists in the years leading up to independence. It was also the burden of much of the writing of Jefferson and fellow Virginian James Madison throughout the founding era. Jefferson and Madison disagreed about the desirability of commercial markets in the new nation. (Jefferson generally endorsed them; Madison regarded them as a source of inequality, corruption, and foreign influence.) But both agreed that empire, rather than eroding republican institutions, could be republicanism's very salvation. More land meant opportunity and independence for the citizen farmers of their agrarian ideal. Land also offered a way to resolve one of the most vexing problems confronting republican governments, namely, the existence of political and/or economic factions, which supposedly eroded citizens' commitment to the public good. Rather than striving futilely to stamp out factionalism, Jefferson and Madison thought to neutralize it by encouraging the proliferation of factions the better to counterbalance one against others—at all levels: local, state, and national. The bigger the nation, the better the odds of preventing the centralization and corruption afflicting Britain.[9]

The American victory in the War of Independence presented Americans with the opportunity to imagine the world anew. No one took to this opportunity more eagerly than Jefferson. The American empire he envisioned would not be the product of conquest carried out by an existing centralized state. Rather, it would be the product of a compact between equal, sovereign, and independent states forged for their mutual benefit. The government of this union would reflect its intended aim, namely, to preserve its members' happiness. Like the individuals who made up these states, the states knew best what was good for them; the more the union promoted states' rights, the stronger, the greater the states' devotion to the union. There was no natural limit to how large this union might grow, but grow it must, as open land was the condition of citizens' virtue and independence.

In 1800, Americans elected Thomas Jefferson president of the United States. Jeffersonian Republicans swept into office, ending the decade-long rule of the Federalist Party and inaugurating what Jefferson liked to refer to as the second American Revolution. Virginia governor James Monroe caught the note of optimism, writing to an English friend that the nation might become again "the patroness of peace, harmony, and liberty."[10] Elevation to the presidency allowed Jefferson to put his ideas into practice, to begin to construct that "pacific system" of equal and reciprocal federated republics that might one day literally cover the globe.[11] Jefferson's own revolution of 1800 coincided with political instability in Spain's New World empire, which would culminate by 1829 in the creation of eight new Central and South American republics. Jefferson included the peoples of these regions in his vision of a great American empire, just as he did the indigenous inhabitants of North America. Join us, he told representatives of the Delaware, Mohican, and Munrie tribes in December 1808; we will teach you how to plow.

For its time, Jefferson's vision of an inclusive, equal, and reciprocal republic of federated states was generous indeed.[12] Enfolded in this union, individuals, including Native Americans, would enjoy the blessings of liberty, security, and property, just as the states, including foreign states, would benefit from reciprocal privileges. But how likely was Jefferson's "pacific system" to usher in the peace, harmony, and liberty that he, Madison, and their fellow Virginian James Monroe envisioned? Suppose Indians rejected the plow. Suppose the new republics of Central and South America, once independent, did not want to become part of the "American system"? How reciprocal was Jefferson's idea of American empire, really?

The electoral landslide that ushered Jefferson into office in 1801 was not the only "revolution" under way in the "American" colonies at the time. A social and political cataclysm did indeed rock the Western Hemisphere at the end of the eighteenth century, but it wasn't the cousins' war fought on the North American continent and known in local circles as the American Revolution. The true American Revolution began in Saint-Domingue in 1791, when half a million slaves, who outnumbered whites and mulattoes by ten to one, burst their shackles and over the course of the next decade and a half repelled the attempts of England and France to return them to bondage, ultimately declaring an independent Haiti in January 1804. The events of what became known as the Haitian Revolution nearly cured Jefferson of his abolitionism—*nearly*, because despite doing everything in his power to undermine the Haitian Republic in its infancy, Jefferson seemed to recognize at heart that the future was with the Haitians.[13]

It is difficult to exaggerate the portent of a successful slave revolution in Jefferson's and other Americans' eyes. Informally established by French buccaneers at the end of the sixteenth century, who took advantage of Spain's neglect of Hispaniola, Saint-Domingue had become by the late eighteenth century the most valuable colony in the world, not only providing Europe with 60 percent of its coffee and 40 percent of its sugar, but also constituting an essential marketplace for U.S. manufacturers and global slave traders alike. The potential spread of slave revolts beyond Haiti terrified southern planters. Haiti conjured visions of a world turned upside down, with the Atlantic economy in ruins and European and American civilization in retreat.[14]

In the 1980s and '90s, fears of Haitians contaminated with HIV/AIDS immigrating to the United States induced U.S. Customs and Immigration officials to set up a refugee camp at Guantánamo Bay, from which most of the Haitians were returned to Haiti. Nearly two centuries earlier, fears of liberal-minded ex-slaves from Haiti washing up on American shores led southern states to adopt laws banning the immigration of Haitians to the United States. In parts of Virginia, and in South Carolina and Georgia, where slaves outnumbered whites, fear of a Saint-Domingue-inspired slave mutiny was hardly an abstraction at the time Jefferson acceded to the presidency. The presidential election of 1800 took place against the backdrop of a foiled slave insurrection in Richmond, Virginia, the previous summer, orchestrated by a slave named Gabriel Prosser, who aimed to capture the local arsenal and arm his fellow bondmen. To slaveholders throughout the South (including Jefferson), Prosser's uprising was a logical extension of developments in the colony still known at that time as Saint-Domingue. Together the two incidents solidified southern opposition to abolitionism, formerly widespread even in the South. What could not be stopped on Saint-Domingue would have to be contained, both by preventing Haitian immigration to the United States and by maintaining an iron grip on slaves, ex-slaves, and all remaining slave societies.[15]

Which is where Cuba and ultimately Guantánamo come in. With

Saint-Domingue ruined for U.S. commerce and the African slave and sugar trades, Cuba emerged as the world's leading sugar producer and the most valuable market for African slaves—driven to a large extent by U.S. investment.

The Mopox Commission was by no means the last high-level call to populate and develop Guantánamo Bay. Continuing waves of white and mulatto refugees from Haiti bearing horror stories of black murder and rapine combined with eastern Cuba's mounting slave population to keep the subject of white settlement in the east on everybody's mind.[16] Well into the nineteenth century, government officials continued to produce census surveys of the bay and basin, while offering generous naturalization terms and other incentives to white foreigners willing to settle in the area. Paradoxically, one of the most attractive incentives, abundant slaves at affordable rates, only exacerbated the perceived racial imbalance in the region. The specter of racial conflagration in Cuba would continue to haunt white planters in Guantánamo and indeed throughout Cuba well into the twentieth century.

French immigrants fit right in, then, in seeing the world in terms of black and white. But their propensity to work, plant, and farm, rather than simply to endorse development schemes, finally set the eastern economy in motion. Unlike their Spanish counterparts, French refugees from Haiti had no social or political connections in Cuba and hence nowhere else to go. The first several waves of French refugees included farmers experienced in coffee production, who helped spur Cuban coffee to an eightfold increase between 1792 and 1804.[17] At Guantánamo, French coffee farmers brought previously ignored land into cultivation, for the first time producing on a scale that exceeded local consumption. Though Spanish politics remained unstable and Crown policies in flux through mid-century, on the whole the French refugees from Haiti benefited from the generous settlement terms and more liberal trade and tax policies adopted by the Bourbons. By the second quarter of the nineteenth century, a real market had emerged in the Guantánamo Basin, not only in coffee and sugar, but in cotton, cocoa, and indigo besides.

Not until 1858 would Guantánamo Bay get a port, at Caimanera, worthy of the name. Until then, any farmers with surplus to trade had to make do with primitive wharf facilities at Matabajo, a site up the Guantánamo River near where the British disembarked in 1741, or at Cerro Guayabo, located on the shore of the inner harbor, farther from the sea. Once afloat, the farmers had to take their goods to Santiago to be traded, as up until 1822, Guantánamo Bay lacked even the fourth-class port status that qualified it for the coasting trade.[18] The establishment of a real port at Caimanera at mid-century confirmed the growing importance of Oriente province as a producer of not only coffee but now sugar. In 1846, eleven primitive mills produced raw sugar mostly for local consumption in the Guantánamo region. By 1852 the region's sugar exports began to grow, doubling by 1858. By 1862, Santiago and Guantánamo together produced 15 percent of Cuban sugar, roughly double what they contributed in 1827.[19] The precipitous rise of the Guantánamo region's agricultural productivity raised eyebrows in the United States, where Francis Badell, the U.S. consular agent in Santiago, noted the fact in his annual report.[20]

The Guantánamo region would finally receive its long-sought town not as a result of a royal commission or the plunking down of a settler population onto an imaginary grid. Rather, over the course of the first few decades of the nineteenth century, a group of French, Catalan, and Creole farmers began to concentrate their commercial and, increasingly, their social activity around an old and important crossroads midway up the Guantánamo Basin between the bay and the fertile valleys to the north, east, and west.[21] What emerged as a humble village of mud (and several brick) houses and a few stores and bakeries in 1820 became, within a generation, an established town of nearly a thousand inhabitants, roughly a third of whom were white. In 1847, Santa Catalina was the center of a regional population estimated at nearly eight thousand, in which slaves and free people of color outnumbered whites approximately seven to one. Successful in launching a city, the French, Catalan, and Creole planters had failed to secure their racial dominance.[22]

Over the next several decades Santa Catalina continued to grow, its importance magnified by the establishment of a rail link between the town and the bay in 1856 and the opening of the bay to free trade two years later, which coincided with the construction of the port of Caimanera. But for all its commercial success, the populating and development of the Guantánamo Basin was no more successful in ridding the region of contraband traffic than it was in rectifying the racial imbalance. In 1817, Spain signed a treaty with England, pledging to bring its slave trade to a halt within three years. Yet between 1816 and 1867 nearly six hundred thousand new slaves arrived in Cuba, many of them carried aboard American ships.

While the Guantánamo region made halting steps toward commercial viability, U.S. leaders were busy charting the young nation's foreign policy. Revolutionary Haiti was only the first in a long line of aspiring American republics to experience the chasm separating Jefferson's and others' noble republican rhetoric from political and economic reality. One can detect the fate awaiting future American republics in Jefferson's comments about recalcitrant Indians from his Second Inaugural Address.

Here was a people "endowed with the faculties and the rights of men, breathing an ardent love of liberty and independence, and occupying a country which left them no desire to be undisturbed." However gallant, they were defenseless in the face of "the stream of overflowing population from other regions," and so ended up "within limits too narrow for the hunter's state." And yet some resist the "liberal" policy adopted by the United States to train them in the skills of husbandry and to furnish them with the necessary tools. Residing among the Indians, Jefferson told the assembled nation, were "interested and crafty individuals . . . who feel themselves something in the present order of things and fear to become nothing in any other," and who, therefore, "inculcate a sanctimonious reverence for the customs of their ancestors." Adverse to reason and afraid of knowledge, such "antiphilosophists" take comfort in their ignorance, exerting "all their faculties to maintain the ascendancy of habit over the duty of improving our reason and obeying its mandates." Jefferson's political heirs would adopt similar language to describe Cubans who resisted American meddling in Cuban affairs.[23]

Jefferson assumed a unitary worldview. Though he admired many

Native American characteristics, when it came time to apportion a continent, Native American characteristics would have to yield to the supposedly universal liberal characteristics on which human progress depended. In a speech to Native American tribes a few years later, Jefferson anticipated the late-nineteenth-century idea of the melting pot with all its cultural presuppositions, assuring the tribes that he looked forward to a day when "your blood and ours united will spread again over the great island."[24] Aware of their "present numbers," Jefferson understood that it would be the Native Americans who did the melting. "Peace and agriculture will raise you up to be what your forefathers were," he assured them, "will prepare you to possess property, to wish to live under regular laws."[25]

On the one hand, then, private property, regular laws, blood lost in our blood, progress; on the other hand, antiphilosophists with a sanctimonious reverence for their ancestors' customs, atavism itself. Here Jefferson expresses the leitmotif of Americans' interaction with other peoples and countries over the course of the past two-hundred-plus years. In the name of liberty and equality and in a spirit of reciprocity, we invite you to join us. If you decline our invitation, we will *make* you join us, though it will be harder for us both. Language first used in addressing Native Americans would be easily adapted to address foreign peoples and nations.[26]

Most Americans of Jefferson's generation could not fathom that a new despotism born and raised in the United States might one day replace the old. Supremely confident that the United States was on God's and history's side, they saw no contradiction in prescribing self-government to others, or in declaring themselves leader of a federated republic of equal states. John Quincy Adams was among the few doubters. Adams had opposed Jefferson's arbitrary takeover of the former French colony of Louisiana.[27] He worried that expansionism was getting out of hand. He was skeptical of calls for U.S. intervention in the Latin American revolutions. And he feared lest America become the "dictatress of the world" (and thereby "no longer be the ruler of her own spirit").[28] But there were two John Quincy Adamses vying for influence in this era: the skeptic and the ardent nationalist. The 1820s belonged to the nationalists—to men such as Jefferson, then nearing the end of his life, and to Jefferson's colleague and fellow Virginian, the young president James Monroe.

On May 4, 1822, a year and a half before announcing the "doctrine" that would forever bear his name, President Monroe delivered a speech to Congress in which he addressed some of the contradictions posed by the empire for liberty, though notably not the question of U.S. imperium over Latin American states. Monroe began by reiterating Jefferson's and Madison's arguments about the benefits of territorial expansion, especially for states. For state governments, Monroe argued, expansion was the means to freedom and security, ensuring both the availability of resources and the room for population growth.

Late the following year, Monroe had the opportunity to refine the parameters of the American imperial system. The catalyst in this process was the British foreign secretary, George Canning, who proposed that the U.S. join with Britain in an alliance ostensibly designed to prohibit Spain's allies (Russia, Prussia, Austria, and France) from intervening on Spain's behalf in the ongoing Latin American revolutions, but which included a disavowal on the part of both Britain and the United States of further imperial ambition in the region. Monroe's advisors, including the previous presidents Madison and Jefferson, were divided. Madison and Jefferson urged Monroe to accept the British overture; John Quincy Adams advised Monroe to reject it. Jefferson thought the question "the most momentous which has ever been offered to my contemplation since that of Independence." If that made America a nation, "this sets our compass and points the course which we are to steer through the ocean of time opening on us." Jefferson reiterated his fundamental belief that the Western Hemisphere comprised a system of its own; the United States must steer clear of European entanglements while keeping Europe out of "cis-Atlantic affairs." Only one nation had the wherewithal to defy this division, Jefferson told Monroe, namely, Britain. By accepting Britain's overture, the United States would attract to its side its most powerful European rival, thereby ensuring the security and integrity of the American system.

What about Jefferson's old dream of one day taking Cuba? In the interest of peace, an aging Jefferson was willing to defer that dream for

the time being. Even Cuba was not worth the cost of war. Cuban independence, America's "second interest" after annexation, could be
won without war, and by this time, late in his career, Jefferson found
empire less compelling than Britain's "peace and friendship."[29] Monroe himself appeared to be leaning away from his old mentor and
toward Adams. "I have always concurred with you in sentiment," he
wrote Jefferson in June 1823,

> that too much importance could not be attached to [Cuba], and that
> we ought if possible to incorporate it into our union, availing ourselves
> of the most favorable moment for it. . . . I consider Cape Florida and
> Cuba, as forming the mouth of the Mississippi, & other rivers, empty-
> ing into the Gulf of Mexico, within our limits, as of the Gulf itself, &
> in consequence that the acquisition of it to our union, was of the
> highest importance to our internal tranquility, as well as to our pros-
> perity and aggrandizement.[30]

Jefferson lost this debate to the younger, more vigorous John
Quincy Adams. Adams convinced Monroe that England's real purpose
in proposing the alliance was not to neutralize France and its allies but
to impede American expansion. Indeed, Canning's proposal threatened the premise of the American system itself by assuming an equality of British and American interests on this side of the Atlantic. Britain
had everything to gain, the United States less than nothing. "We
should at least keep ourselves free to act as emergencies may arise,"
wrote Adams, "and not tie ourselves down to any principle which might
immediately afterwards be brought to bear against ourselves."[31]

A month later, Monroe uttered the sentiment that became the
Monroe Doctrine, but which owed more to Adams's and Jefferson's
thinking than to his own. In his speech to Congress on December 2,
1823, Monroe reiterated the idea of Jefferson, Madison, and others
that Europe and the West constituted two distinct and irreconcilable
"systems" of government. The United States had long since disavowed
any interest in Europe's internal affairs; now it expected Europe likewise to keep out of America's neighborhood. Any "enlightened and
impartial" observer could see that the United States had a keener
interest than Europe in the fate of Latin American states. Monroe

warned Europe that the United States would regard "any attempt on their part to extend their system to any portion of this hemisphere as dangerous to our peace and safety." The United States had, "on great consideration and on just principles," acknowledged the independence of the new Latin American states (except Haiti). It "could not view any interposition for the purpose of oppressing them, or controlling in any other manner their destiny" as anything but an expression of hostility. In warding off Europe, Monroe had no doubt that he spoke for the hemisphere. It beggared belief, Monroe insisted, that left to their own devices "our southern brethren" would adopt the European system "of their own accord."[32]

Lawrence Washington, Benjamin Franklin, Jefferson, the Adamses, Monroe—in short, anybody who thought to capitalize on the resources of the North American continent—understood that the continent was valuable only to the extent that the United States had access to the rivers and seaports that drained it, and that the usefulness of those rivers and seaports, in turn, depended on access to the Gulf of Mexico and the Caribbean Sea. Though the Monroe Doctrine encompassed more than Cuba, Cuba was inspiration enough. "The right to use a thing, comprehends a right to the means necessary to its use," Secretary of State Thomas Jefferson had written the U.S. chargé d'affaires for Spain, William Carmichael, in August 1790, regarding U.S. access to the Spanish port at New Orleans. Jefferson and his successors knew that New Orleans was useless without control of the Gulf of Mexico and Caribbean, and that control of these waters was the province of Cuba. The presence of an enfeebled Spanish empire in Cuba was acceptable to Jefferson and his successors; the advance of France or, especially, England was not. If a hostile power ever thought to use Cuba to deny U.S. merchants access to the Gulf of Mexico and the port of New Orleans, Jefferson warned Carmichael, "there is no saying how far we may be led"; the United States would never forsake its "western citizens" or abandon "their rights."[33]

One of the clearest early elucidations of U.S. policy regarding Cuba came from—no surprise—Secretary of State John Quincy Adams in the spring of 1823. In a note to Hugh Nelson, U.S. minister to Spain,

Adams observed that, despite America's determination to steer wide of
European conflagrations, Europe's "maritime wars" inevitably concerned
the United States, as they took place upon the sea, "the common
property of all." More than that of any other nation, Adams observed,
U.S. well-being relied on that common property; the nation's status as
a neutral among belligerents was bound to create conflicting interests.
At the time Adams wrote, France and Spain were on the verge of war.
Adams worried lest a defeated Spain be put in a position of having to
barter off her few remaining colonies in the New World: Cuba and
Puerto Rico. These islands were nontransferable to any but the United
States, Adams emphasized. They were "natural appendages to the
North American continent," he wrote, "and one of them, Cuba, almost
in sight of our shores, from a multitude of considerations, has become
an object of transcendent importance to the commercial and political
interests of our Union." Cuba's location at the entrance to the Gulf of
Mexico and

> the West Indian seas; the character of its population, its situation
> midway between our southern cost and the island of St. Domingo, . . .
> the nature of its production and of its wants, furnishing the supplies
> and needing the returns of a commerce immensely profitable and mu-
> tually beneficial—give it an importance in the sum of our national
> interests with which that of no other foreign territory can be com-
> pared, and little inferior to that which binds the different members of
> this Union together.

Cuba and the United States, insisted Adams, shared geographical,
commercial, moral, and political interests rooted in nature. Current
developments in the United States, Cuba, and the larger world made
it "scarcely possible to resist the conviction that the annexation of
Cuba to our federal republic will be indispensable to the continuance
and integrity of the Union itself." Of course, Adams understood the
objections of many of his compatriots to extending the American republic overseas. Still, there were "laws of political, as well as physical
gravitation," he wrote, "and if an apple, severed by a tempest from its
native tree, cannot choose but fall to the ground, Cuba, forcibly dis-
joined from its own unnatural connection to Spain, and incapable of

self-support, can gravitate only toward the North American Union, which by the same law of nature, cannot cast her off from its bosom." Like Jefferson three decades earlier in warning Spain to grant the United States access to New Orleans, Adams assured Nelson that America was ready to fight for these *natural* rights. In the interests of U.S. citizens, and now, crucially, the "incapable" Cubans, America could do no less.[34] Thus Jefferson's notion of an empire for liberty—an empire of equal and reciprocal and federated states—began to evolve into a narrower claim about America's natural right to take Cuba, and to govern it on behalf of others not yet ready for self-government.

The United States was not the only American republic interested in Cuba. In the mid-1820s, Mexico and Colombia, two powerful and newly independent states, proposed mounting an expedition to liberate Cuba and Puerto Rico from Spain, thereby finally ridding the hemisphere of the last vestige of the Spanish Empire. U.S. officials did not like the sound of this. In April 1826, Daniel Webster rose in the House of Representatives to weigh in on Mexico, Colombia, and Cuba. Webster declared Cuba unequivocally the "most important point of our foreign relations . . . the hinge on which interesting events may possibly turn." Did Spain have the right to transfer Cuba to another European power? Was there a limit to U.S. rights in the Western Hemisphere? Wasn't the United States, after all, the *universal* nation? Rights, Webster observed, are realized in geographical contexts. The United States enjoyed rights in its own hemisphere that European states plainly did not, and vice versa. "Proximity of position, neighborhood, whatever arguments the power of injuring and annoying, very properly belong to the consideration of all cases of this kind." Jefferson's purchase of Louisiana was a case in point. That action had been based on "convenience," "proximity," and "natural connection." Where some of Webster's colleagues differentiated between a voluntary transfer by Spain of Cuba to another European state and a forcible transfer, Webster recognized "a distinction without a difference." The question came down to whether there was "a danger to our security, or danger, manifest and imminent danger, to our essential rights, and our essential interests." In the case of Cuba, there could be no doubt. Not only had U.S. trade with Cuba come by 1826 to exceed U.S. trade with France ("and all her dependencies"), but also Cuba commanded "the mouth of the Mississippi River. Its occupation by a strong maritime power would be felt, in the first moment of hostility, as far up the Mississippi and the Missouri as our population extends." Moreover, Cuba lay "in the very line of our coastwise traffic, interposed in the very highway between New York and New Orleans." The states of Europe must know—the Latin American republics, too, for that matter—that Cuba was transferable to none but the United States.[35]

U.S. concern about Cuba's fate ebbed in the late 1820s and '30s, when U.S. and European powers informally agreed to maintain the status quo. Meanwhile, the U.S. government pledged to do nothing to encourage Cuban insurrection. In 1830, Spain consented to the seating of a U.S. consul. Despite occasional diplomatic flare-ups, relations between the United States and Spain remained stable enough to encourage American investment in the Cuban sugar and railroad industries. Notably, it was at this time that American shipping gained control of the lucrative Cuban slave trade. A note from the U.S. secretary of state, Edward Livingston, to William Shaler, U.S. consul in Havana, aptly sums up U.S. interests during this era. "The great objects of our Government in relation to Cuba," Livingston advised, "are a free and untrammeled trade, on its present footing, eased of the discriminating duties; to preserve it in the hands of Spain, even at the expense of war; and only in the event of finding that impossible, to look to its annexation to our confederacy." Livingston himself appeared cool on the matter of annexation, not least because of widespread doubts about Cubans' ability to shoulder the burdens of republican government. This was talk for a later day.[36]

In 1846, the United States went to war with Mexico over a border dispute in Texas. It emerged from the war with the New Mexico and California territories, which, along with the recent addition of the Oregon Territory, extended U.S. possessions to the Pacific. Disagreement about the fate of slavery in these new territories culminated in the Civil War. In the immediate aftermath of war with Mexico, many northerners and southerners alike looked to the annexation of Cuba as a means of forestalling, perhaps ending, the sectional controversy.

By the time Americans' attention returned to the subject of Cuban annexation in the late 1840s, Cuba had emerged as one of the world's most valuable colonies and its leading sugar producer. Cuba was also one of the few remaining slave economies and, hence, one of the few remaining markets for what had become after 1831 (when Brazil became the last country formally to outlaw the African slave trade) the trade in contraband slaves. Cuba's black market in slaves peaked in the five-year period between 1840 and 1845, when nearly one hundred thousand slaves were brought ashore, many off U.S. ships. This American bonanza inspired Spain to introduce stiff penalties for slave traders, and over the course of the next fifteen years, fewer than three thousand slaves arrived in Cuba.[37] Whenever the market got tight, slavers looked to Guantánamo, which, as early as the 1820s, had come to the attention of British patrols as a leading depot for contraband.[38]

Beginning in the late eighteenth century, Cuba's economic rise was propelled in part by merchants from the northeastern United States, who were every bit as adamant as southern planters in advocating annexation. The same is true of northern manufacturing and banking interests.[39] To southerners and many northerners alike, physical expansion went hand in hand with the spread of slavery. This was the premise not only of Thomas Jefferson, Andrew Jackson, and Jefferson Davis, but also of James Polk, James Buchanan, and journalist John O'Sullivan, the foremost propagandist of Manifest Destiny. Southerners dominated the call for the annexation of Cuba, but the impetus had plenty of support in the North. By mid-century, the South lagged behind the North in population, jeopardizing its political influence in Washington, D.C., despite rough parity in the U.S. Senate. But the North was highly invested in Cuba, with northerners owning plantations there and northern manufacturers and merchants dependent on Cuban commerce. Before the U.S. Civil War, northerners and southerners salivated over the thought of Cuba; southerners imaged two new slave states cut from Cuba returning balance to the Union; northerners hoped to consolidate and expand their markets. After the Civil War, former southern planters moved to Cuba (and to Brazil) in droves, seeking to revive their fortunes there. Many returned to the United States or sought their fortune elsewhere after the outbreak of the Ten Years' (civil) War in 1868. But those who endured in Cuba triumphed at the war's end as the devastation wrought by the conflict created new opportunities for planters with the capital to invest in Cuba's rapidly consolidating sugar industry—even after slavery was abolished there in 1886.

A principal force behind the renewed interest in Cuba was the Democratic U.S. president James Polk, the man credited with delivering Oregon, California, and New Mexico into U.S. possession. Polk turned his attention to Cuba after John O'Sullivan suggested to the president that the acquisition of Cuba would be the perfect capstone to a remarkable career. Thus began a renewed effort on the part of successive American administrations to acquire Cuba from Spain, which halted only with the outbreak of the American Civil War.[40]

Goaded by O'Sullivan, Polk ordered his secretary of state, James Buchanan, to find out what it would take for Spain to part with Cuba. Buchanan's letter to the U.S. minister in Spain, Romulus M. Saunders, summarizes U.S. thinking about Cuba at this time. The specter of British ambitions in the Caribbean and Cuba haunts Buchanan's note. If Britain ever took control of Cuba, he warned, it could bring U.S. commerce to a halt. Despite endless denials, there could be no doubting Britain's resolve to monopolize the Cuban trade. Parliament knew full well how a British Cuba would transform British commerce while thwarting the commercial ambitions of the United States. On the other hand, a Cuba in U.S. possession would thrust American commerce to the top of the world. "Were Cuba a portion of the United States," Buchanan observed, "it would be difficult to estimate the amount of bread-stuffs, rice, cotton and other agricultural, as well as manufacturing and mechanical productions—of lumber, of the products of our fisheries and of other articles—which would find a market in that island, in exchange for their coffee, sugar, tobacco, and other productions."[41]

Was there ever a riper time for adding Cuba to the American confederation of states? Early worries about overextending the American confederation "seem to have passed away," Buchanan noted. Time had confirmed Madison's and Jefferson's hypothesis that a proliferation of states would strengthen rather than erode the union, binding parts to the whole, the whole to parts. It was not space so much as race that potentially limited the scope of the American empire. But where some

Americans balked at a union with Cuba's "Spanish race," Buchanan thought the problem sufficiently mitigated by an abundance of white Americans ("large holders of property") settled in its midst. As in Louisiana, Cuba's heterogeneous population would be "Americanized" speedily enough. And Cuba's sea-lanes would provide access to the states of the Mississippi River Valley and the Gulf of Mexico, thereby energizing the economies of the "ship-building and navigating states," further binding the sections together. But the benefits of adding Cuba to the Union transcended the United States itself. A Cuba in U.S. possession promised "free trade on a more extended scale than any which the world has ever witnessed," thereby promoting the most "rapid improvement in all that contributes to the welfare and happiness of the human race."[42]

Britain was not the only rival whose ambitions unsettled U.S. officials in this era. In making the case for the annexation of Cuba, Americans invoked Spain's mounting hostility toward the United States. As evidence, U.S. officials pointed to Spain's supposed "Africanization" of Cuba, a charge meant to conjure the nightmare of revolutionary Haiti. Just how Spain went about Africanizing Cuba is not exactly clear, unless talk among Spain's reform-oriented government of ending Cuban slavery constituted such a threat. What is clear is that an illegal and booming slave trade, propelled by U.S. merchants, continued to swell Cuba's black population at mid-century, raising fears among Spanish and foreign businessmen alike that Cuba could go the way of Haiti. The Louisiana legislature formally condemned the Africanization of Cuba.[43]

Mississippi governor John Quitman was among those who took the bait about Cuba going the way of Haiti. As early as 1835, Quitman had begun talking about secession as the surest means to defend the institution of slavery. By the late 1840s he had come to see the annexation of Cuba as a slave state as the means to save the institution of slavery itself while redeeming Cuba from Africanization. Like many of slavery's defenders, Quitman was disinclined to wait for the federal government to act on Cuba. Beginning in the late 1840s he began to keep company with Cuban exiles and militant proslavery advocates in the United States determined to wrest Cuba from Spain.

In early 1850, Quitman was approached by a Venezuelan-born

Cuban exile named Narciso López, who asked the governor to lead a filibustering campaign against Cuba. At this time, *filibuster*, derived originally from a French word for pirate, referred not to the hijacking of political debate but to the overthrow of Latin American states in order to make them safe for the expansion of slavery. With the self-assurance that would later curse the Bay of Pigs invasion, Lopez assured Quitman that Cuba was eager for annexation to the United States, and that the island would virtually roll over upon the filibusterers' arrival. Though tempted, Quitman demurred, offering financial and political support in place of his own leadership.[44]

This was actually López's second attempt at the liberation of Cuba. His first had been thwarted by U.S. president Zachary Taylor, in July 1849, before it was able to set sail. (Private invasions of foreign countries were obviously illegal.) In his second attempt, López made the coast of Cuba, but the expedition did not advance much beyond that. The anticipated Cuban support never materialized, and López was forced to withdraw. Undeterred, he readied yet another expedition, this time offering its command to Jefferson Davis, future president of the Confederacy, and to Robert E. Lee. Worried about staking their political futures on an illegal (and unlikely) expedition, both gentlemen declined, but not before endorsing López's vision of Cuba as a slave state in the American Union. Davis and Lee proved prescient. Like the first expedition, this one never gained the Florida Straits. President Millard Fillmore did not want to antagonize the government of Spain. The next expedition would be López's last. Launched in August 1851, it penetrated the Cuban coastline, but fell apart shortly thereafter. López was caught and executed along with fifty members of his filibustering crew, among them the Mexican-American War veteran William Crittenden.[45]

The aims of curbing Britain's colonial appetite and beating back Spain's insults while preventing Cuba's Africanization gained new currency in the administration of President Franklin Pierce. A native of New Hampshire, Pierce ascended to the presidency in 1853 believing that a vigorous foreign policy might deflect the mounting sectional animosity tearing the union apart. After a series of failed attempts by the American minister to Spain, Pierre Soulé, to persuade Spain to sell Cuba to the United States, Pierce ordered Soulé to convene a meeting of his fellow ministers to Britain and France (James Buchanan and John Mason, respectively) to devise a strategy by which the United States could finally acquire Cuba.

The three ministers convened in the autumn of 1854 at Ostend, Belgium. There they produced what became known as the Ostend Manifesto, a classified document that when leaked to the press caused an uproar of condemnation at home and abroad. Most of the manifesto restated old themes: "It must be clear to every reflecting mind that, from the peculiarity of its geographical position, and the considerations attended on it, Cuba is as necessary to the North American republic as any of its present members, and that it belongs naturally to the great family of States of which the Union is the providential nursery." The three ministers treated audiences to a lesson in geography: "The natural and main outlet to the products of this entire population, the highway of their direct intercourse with the Atlantic and the Pacific States, can never be secure, but must ever be endangered whilst Cuba is a dependency of a distant power in whose possession it has proved to be a source of constant annoyance and embarrassment to their interests."[46]

Still, there was much that was new in the manifesto, too, most significant, perhaps, the ministers' suggestion that they, as *Americans*, knew best the interests not just of the United States but of Spain besides. "We firmly believe that, in the progress of human events, the time has arrived when the vital interests of Spain are as seriously involved in the sale, as those of the United States in the purchase, of the island."[47] To be sure, such presumption had imbued American rhetoric since before the Revolution. But rarely had rhetoric been directly translated into policy. The consequences of such thinking were ominous. After presuming to know Spain's interests (and Cuba's value) better than Spain, and after offering Spain "a price for Cuba far beyond its present value," and after then being refused, the United States couldn't help but ask: "Does Cuba, in the possession of Spain, seriously endanger our internal peace, and the existence of our cherished Union?" Should the answer be yes, then "every law, human and divine," justified the United States' taking Cuba from Spain on the same grounds that justified a person "tearing down the burning house of his neighbor if there were no other means of preventing the flames from destroying his own."[48]

As if a feckless Spain incapable of maintaining the status quo weren't grounds enough, there still loomed the specter of Africanization. "We should . . . be recreant to our duty, be unworthy of our gallant forefathers, and commit base treason against our posterity, should we permit Cuba to be Africanized and become a second St. Domingo, with all its attendant horrors to the white race." Current conditions in Cuba appeared to be "rapidly tending towards such a catastrophe."[49]

Leaked to the public, the Ostend Manifesto became the subject of controversy, at home and abroad, and was quickly repudiated by the Pierce administration. Soulé himself shouldered much of the blame and ultimately resigned. Still, if ahead of the field in his expansionist zeal, Soulé was only slightly so. This was the heyday of Manifest Destiny, and there were other Soulés anticipating the annexation of Cuba with equal urgency. George Fitzugh, for example, one of the leading apologists of slavery, saw in Cuban annexation "the richest and most increased commerce that ever dazzled the cupidity of men." In the epic struggle about to begin, American merchants—those "apostles of republicanism"—would once and for all vanquish the placemen of Spain's "greedy Queen."[50]

Though mounting sectional controversy would gradually make the Pierce administration cool to filibustering, in his first year in office, the president approached John Quitman, López's old sponsor, about leading an filibustering expedition. No longer governor of Mississippi, Quitman agreed, and between July 1853 and the following May, he amassed a small arsenal and army of men for an attack on Cuba. Only the uproar between free-soil and pro-slavery advocates sparked by the Kansas-Nebraska Act in 1854, which repealed the Missouri Compromise and allowed settlers in those territories to determine their fate, induced Pierce to withdraw government support for the expedition. Quitman continued to plan into 1855.

By this time, England and France had joined Spain in protest. It was one thing for these American filibustering expeditions to be the work of a few proslavery zealots. It was another thing entirely for them to be sponsored by the U.S. government. Wasn't that the definition of war? One vigilant British resident of Adams County, Ohio, thought so. In a letter to the British foreign secretary, W. H. Holderness warned of "an expedition of immense magnitude now on foot in the United States for the subjugation of Cuba. General [John A.] Quitman is at the head of it. It is secretly organized, chiefly throughout the Slave States. General Quitman proposes raising 200,000 men, of which I have been informed that 150,000 are enrolled already." Though the expedition was apparently the work of southerners, Holderness had no doubt that the U.S. government was aware of it. His information was dependable, he insisted; it came "from one who has been among the conspirators, and has seen their arms." What was his motivation for coming forward? Only "to prevent, if possible, the consummation of as dark a piece of villainy as can disgrace the 19th century, to be carried out under the hypocritical pretext of enlarging the area of freedom."[51] By this time, England and France had dispatched warships to Havana, to protect Spanish Cuba from American aggression.

Two of the most intriguing filibustering plans for Cuba never advanced beyond the planning stage. The first was the work of William Walker, an ambitious, if not megalomaniacal, native of Tennessee who wanted to extend the American republic southward into Central America. In 1853, Walker tried and failed to establish an independent state in Baja California. In May 1855 he led a band of U.S. and Latin American mercenaries to Nicaragua, then in the midst of civil war. In September of that year he defeated the Nicaraguan army in a pitched battle; in October he captured the city of Grenada. By May 1855 he had set himself up as the puppet of a new political regime that won recognition of the outgoing Pierce administration. The next year, Walker was "elected" president of Nicaragua, at which point he relegalized slavery (abolished there in 1824) and undertook an Americanization campaign.

Walker's ambition did not stop there. From Nicaragua he hoped to establish a federation of five Central American republics that would include Cuba. But by this point, Spain and Costa Rica had had enough. Despite the new Buchanan administration's recognition of Walker's regime, Spain and Costa Rica moved on the man from Tennessee, who ended up fleeing into the arms of the U.S. Navy, who spirited him home to the United States.[52]

Walker's ambitious plans for Central America and Cuba received close scrutiny from what appears at first glance to have been an unlikely source: the African American black nationalist philosopher Martin

Delany. Unlikely, that is, because Delany scrutinized Walker and the other filibusterers not simply to oppose their effort to infinitely extend the scope (and life) of slavery, but also to emulate them, in black form: to liberate Cuba from Spain and complete its "Africanization." But for Delany, too, Cuba was just the beginning. Just as Nicaragua in Walker's mind was to serve as the focus of a new southern slaveholding republic, so Cuba would occupy the heart of a prospective confederation of African–Latin American states. Long ambivalent about projects to re-colonize free African Americans to Africa, Delany saw black Cuba and a black confederation in Latin America as an ideal solution to the prob-lem of U.S. racism. He rejected the notion that blacks and whites could coexist in the United States, but he did not want blacks to "return" to Africa. In the end, Delany was no less blind to the imperialism of his project—no more sensitive to the individuality of the actual Cuban or Latin American peoples—than the others who went before him.[53]

After 1854 and the uproar over the Kansas-Nebraska Act, the new Republican Party wasn't alone in believing that the containment of slavery would put it on the road to ultimate extinction.[54] Southern pro-ponents of slavery agreed with them. Southerners saw their political influence in Washington diminish as slavery was excluded from part of the territory taken from Mexico. As beleaguered defenders of slavery came to see Cuba as the salvation of slavery and the southern way of life, the debate over Cuban annexation betrayed signs of the sectional polarization of the national political parties that was finally breaking the nation apart. Democrats generally advocated the annexation of Cuba as a slave state; Whigs (-cum-Republicans) generally opposed it.[55]

In November 1857 a correspondent for the New York *Weekly Herald* witnessed "over three hundred young negroes in excellent health" be-ing off-loaded at Guantánamo. One day, the correspondent specu-lated, this "beautiful" and "capacious" harbor was likely to become "the center of a large and active [and presumably legal] commerce"; for now, it remained a "favorite harbor for the off landing of cargoes of negroes from Africa, as [its] numerous bays and inlets surrounded and separated from each other by high hills enable the slavers to discharge their cargoes in perfect security." In this case, the writer suggested, the traffic transpired with full knowledge—indeed, collusion—of the district governor and local commander, whose forces corralled the slaves, exacted a fee, then sent them on their way. Within days, the slaves were said to be at work building a new railway for an English merchant named Thomas Brook.[56]

On the eve of the American Civil War, U.S. traders seemed to be ramping up their traffic in slaves, as if anticipating an interruption in the trade. In July 1860 *The Chicago Tribune* reported that its sources in "Guantánamo, Cuba, assert that ten or twelve American vessels have landed over 5,000 negroes on the island within the last six weeks."[57] A few years later, Abraham Lincoln's naval secretary, Gideon Welles, contemplated occupying Guantánamo Bay as a coaling base to help enforce the Union blockade of the South. Whether the Union navy could have succeeded in curbing the *American* traffic in slaves at Guantánamo Bay is impossible to say, but the thought of such a show-down *there* is intriguing.[58] In fact, the outbreak of the Civil War de-flected pro-annexation sentiment in the United States, when formerly pro-annexationist enthusiasts in the Confederacy found themselves in the uncomfortable position of having to throw themselves at the mercy of Spain for recognition of the Confederacy and access to Spanish ports. After the Civil War, many former southern planters moved to Cuba (and to Brazil), seeking to revive their fortunes there.

It was not the U.S. Civil War but the Ten Years' War in Cuba (1868–1878) that effectively ended the slave trade and precipitated the formal abolition of Cuban slavery in 1886. The Ten Years' War was Cuba's first war of independence, and like so many Cuban revolts and insurrections, it arose in the east, more precisely in the western region of Oriente province, to the west of Santiago and Guantánamo Bay, where Creole planters had grown old waiting for Spain's promises of liberal reform to improve their lives. From the very beginning of the war, the revolutionaries faced an intractable dilemma of needing both to marshal into its army Cuba's restive slave population and to retain the sympathy of the majority of Creole planters without whose sup-port the revolution was sure to fail. In the end, military necessity over-whelmed political strategy. Marshaling the slaves of eastern Cuba into their ranks, the revolutionaries alienated planters across the island, so that the spirit of independence never caught on.[59]

In the region around Santiago and Guantánamo, planters who did not ally themselves with the rebels had their fields destroyed, their crops burned, their slaves freed. The coffee and sugar economies of the region, just hitting their stride, would take years to recover, and even then in unrecognizable form. Many of the war's original leaders were ambivalent about the destruction. But as the revolution ran on and became a war of attrition, older, white Creole leaders were pushed aside, to be replaced by younger men of mixed blood, less ambivalent about the economic and political system they laid to waste. The French planters of the Guantánamo Basin had seen this before. Eastern Cuba had become Haiti. Their world crumbled around them as Cuba descended into racial conflagration.[60]

Meanwhile, many U.S. planters who had abandoned the American South for Cuba after the Union victory returned to the United States in 1868. But those who endured in Cuba triumphed at the war's end as the devastation wrought by the conflict created new opportunities for planters with the capital to invest in Cuba's rapidly consolidating sugar industry. Meanwhile, the Grant administration, in office for eight out of the ten years of the war in Cuba, muddled through, alternately threatening Spain and resisting the calls of Cuban partisans in the United States for recognition first of belligerent rights, then of Cuban independence. To Grant, Cuba remained "a friendly nation," one "whose sympathy and friendship in the struggling infancy of [America's] own existence must ever be remembered with gratitude." Intervention would wait a quarter century.[61]

The Ten Years' War in Cuba, though confined largely to the east, crippled Cuban industry and commerce. As in the aftermath of most wars, the first to recover were individuals and businesses with surplus capital to invest, and in 1880s Cuba this meant above all American businessmen, who took advantage of the depressed Cuban economy to consolidate and recapitalize once-small sugar, coffee, tobacco, cocoa, and indigo plantations. Big was in. "The tendency of modern times is toward consolidation," remarked Massachusetts senator Henry Cabot Lodge in March 1895. Lodge spoke to justify U.S. imperialism and

America's absorption of smaller states such as Cuba, which were a thing of "the past and have no future."[62] But he might just as well have been referring to the smaller farms of Cuba (and the United States) at the time when Cubans needed them most. If bad for Cubans, post–Ten Years' War Cuba was good for U.S. investors, tamping down annexationist sentiment in the United States. By 1896, American investment in Cuban sugar and mining exceeded $50 million. Ripe for American investment, Cuba was also a good market for the United States, whose exports to Cuba exceeded $105 million by 1894.[63]

The consolidation and recapitalization of the Cuban economy mimicked developments in the United States in the aftermath of the American Civil War. Industrialization proceeded apace, spurred by improvements in communications and infrastructure and the arrival of millions of immigrants desperate for work. These were simultaneously exhilarating and anxious times, full of opportunity but also uncertainty, as the nation became further and further enmeshed in a global economy whose subtleties were not always easy to discern. Like other ambitious countries at this time, the United States thought to stabilize its economy and quell anxiety by venturing out into the world. Truly, the would-be world empire had come of age at an opportune time. Its warehouses were full of goods, its factories hungry for resources. Its writers and statesmen were poised for adventure and imbued with a sense of mission. Its rivals were curious, expectant, not precisely sure what to make of the ambitious young republic. When the American historian Frederick Jackson Turner announced the "closing" of the American frontier in 1894, Theodore Roosevelt, Henry Cabot Lodge, Albert Beveridge, Elihu Root, and John Hay, among others, heeded Turner's essay like a starting gun, charging onto the public stage and laying the ideological groundwork for new imperial adventures.

When so-called anti-imperialists protested that republics do not lend themselves to empire, Roosevelt and company replied with a resounding *Hogwash!* What, after all, had the United States been doing to the Indians on this very continent lo these many years? On the frontier, American settlers confronted an indigenous population that had not owned that land and thus had no claims worthy of respect, Roosevelt argued. The U.S. government could hardly have treated the Indians as individuals with attendant civil rights. Indians were "warlike and bloodthirsty," living lives "but a few degrees less meaningless, squalid, and ferocious than that of the wild beasts with whom they held joint ownership." In the face of such savagery, neither "the rules of international morality" nor the nation's founding principles applied. Like the defenders of the Indians before them, anti-imperialists were not only sentimental but dangerously naïve. "To withdraw from the contest of civilization because of the fact that there are attendant cruelties," Roosevelt observed, "is, in my opinion, utterly unworthy of a great people." All Americans benefited from Western conquest, all were implicated in the violence. "The rude, fierce settler who drives the savage from the land lays all of civilized mankind under debt to him." American was to Indian as Boer to Zulu, Cossack to Tartar, New Zealander to Maori: in "each case the victor, horrible though many of his deeds are, has laid deep the foundation for the future greatness of a mighty people."[64]

In Captain Alfred Thayer Mahan, a naval officer who hated nothing so much as to go to sea, the propagandists of empire found a bard.[65] Twice president of the U.S. Naval War College at Newport, Rhode Island, Mahan was one of the world's foremost authorities on naval power at a time when the term *naval power* could be said to be redundant. Mahan shared many of the assumptions about American nationhood just described: a century of isolation had come to an end, liberty and empire were compatible, the United States had a right to appropriate distant territory for strategic interests, U.S. commercial expansion would benefit the entire world.[66] But where many nineteenth-century Americans underemphasized the conflict entailed in American global expansion, Mahan took conflict for granted, insisting that the nation be prepared for it. When, around 1890, he began to write his influential essays on the history of naval warfare, he became convinced that the nation was decidedly *un*prepared. The nation needed not just ships, coastal defenses, and overseas bases— though it needed those in spades—but also an education in the role of sea power in promoting and maintaining national prosperity in an industrial age.

Two premises, closely related, undergirded Mahan's writing on naval policy: first, that "control of the seas, and especially . . . the great lines drawn by national interest or national commerce, is the chief among the merely material elements in the power and prosperity of nations"; second, that "communications are . . . the most vital and determining element in strategy, military or naval." Though blessed internally by two coasts and a river system with few rivals on earth, the United States was woefully underrepresented in the region that mattered most: the Caribbean Basin, which Mahan described as "one of the greatest nerve centers of the whole body of European civilization."[67]

Never was control of the sea-lanes more important than at the end of the nineteenth century, when industrial production in many Western countries threatened to outpace consumption, forcing those countries to turn outward for markets and resources. To the list of familiar rivals Britain and France, there was now added Germany and, significantly, the rising continent of "Asia," whose commercial ambition remained yet unmitigated by Christian values. Though the nineteenth century had seen advances in international law designed to curb global conflict, law remained, according to Mahan, an inadequate resource in a competitive environment whose ultimate arbiter was force.

Complicating matters immensely for the United States was the prospect of a new canal across the Isthmus of Panama. The Caribbean Basin and Pacific islands were already "dangerous germs of quarrel," Mahan observed. Connecting the Atlantic and Pacific, Europe and Asia, the opening of an isthmian canal promised to convert a "now comparatively deserted nook of the ocean" into something "like the Red Sea, a great thoroughfare of shipping" sure to attract "the interest and ambition of maritime nations." In its current state of "military and naval preparation," Mahan warned, the "piercing of the Isthmus" by rival powers could be "nothing but a disaster." America had neither the navy nor the coastal defense proportional to its interests in the region. Nor did it have, as others had, "positions, either within or on the borders of the Caribbean, which not only possess great natural advantages for control of that sea, but have received and are receiving that artificial strength and armament which will make them practically impregnable."[68]

More than America's well-being was at stake here. Mahan thought of the world's oceans and sea-lanes as a global "commons," over which spread the blessings of prosperity, liberty, and Christianity. As a nation whose shores were washed by two of these great seas, and which sat just north of the prospective isthmus, the United States had the responsibility to maintain public order. The commons needed a policeman, and the United States was the only country qualified geographically, politically, and racially for the job. First, Americans would have to get over their hang-up about overseas possessions. Americans could acquire such possessions "righteously," Mahan felt sure, but acquire them it must. And not just a few but many. Only under U.S. control could an isthmian canal "knit together the whole system of American states," thereby advancing "by thousands of miles the frontiers of European civilization."[69]

How different seems this body of thought from the candid desire for land and plunder that sped Massachusetts recruits to Guantánamo more than a century and a half earlier. The philosophical roots of the ideology of liberal empire precede Vernon's trip to Cuba. But the ideology coalesced in the aftermath of the American Revolution, as the nation's founders worked to reconcile the ideals of liberty and self-government with the imperative of imperial expansion.

By the end of the nineteenth century, the United States and Spain looked to be on very different historical trajectories. Beginning in the late eighteenth century and continuing through the nineteenth, Spain suffered loss after loss of its once vast colonial possessions, so that by the end of the nineteenth century, Spain had only Cuba, Puerto Rico, the Philippines, and a few insignificant Pacific island chains left. The chipping away of Spain's global empire coincided with a century's political upheaval during which Spain endured occupation, restoration, and revolution, culminating in fragile constitutional reform. It did not take the fall of Cuba and the final remnants of empire in the summer of 1898 to inspire soul-searching among Spanish writers and artists, but the cultural movement that blossomed in late-nineteenth-century Spain would be forever stamped *la generación noventa y ocho* (the Generation of '98). The work of this generation is distinguished by, among other things, candor and introspection. Far from bemoaning the loss of imperial status, Spain's writers and artists welcomed the opportunity for reflection and self-criticism.

There were voices of candor and introspection among America's *generación noventa y ocho*, too. But they tended to be drowned out by louder voices touting the arrival of a powerful new nation on the block. Cut from imperial cloth, the United States has been an empire from its inception. British subjects such as Lawrence Washington and Thomas Jefferson's father, Peter, took for granted the colonists' expansion across the North American continent and understood its global implications. Still, if steeped in empire, late-nineteenth-century Americans sensed that they were on the brink of something new. A youthful nation stood poised to take its place among the company of men, and there was no shortage of chest pounding and triumphalism on the part of U.S. political, cultural, and religious leaders.

For centuries the Spanish Crown had ignored calls by local Cuban authorities to populate and fortify Guantánamo Bay. When, at the beginning of the nineteenth century, French refugees from Santo Domingo combined with a few enterprising natives of Catalonia to establish a town on their own, the Crown finally recognized it. But as before, it did nothing to prepare the bay to withstand an enemy attack. And so it happened that four centuries after Columbus turned up his nose at Guantánamo Bay, Captain George Watson Sumner, commander of a U.S. Navy vessel fittingly named after Genoa's first son, entered the bay in early February 1895 to conduct a geological survey. The USS *Columbia* would remain in Guantánamo for days—completely without permission or, apparently, even the knowledge of Spanish officials. And this in the first days of what would become the Cuban War of Independence. Meanwhile, as the *Columbia*'s engineers went dutifully about the task of measuring the bay, her officers began a tradition that would extend until the coming of Fidel Castro: they went on liberty to the home of an American sugar baron up the Guantánamo Basin. *The New York Times* could barely conceal its delight at this breach of Spanish security. The Crown itself was not amused. The *Columbia*'s visit did not bode well for Spanish defenses supposedly in a state of "unusual watchfulness."[70]

What were the Americans doing there? They did not say. Instead, the U.S. State Department told Spanish officials that a telegrapher's cipher error had brought the *Columbia* to Guantánamo; the ship was supposed to have been plumbing the waters of Bluefields Harbour, Nicaragua, some five hundred miles away. The *Columbia* would depart immediately and all would be rectified. Rectified, perhaps, but not redeemed. Captain Sumner left Guantánamo with more than fond memories of smooth rum and sweet cigars. Detailed drawings and measurements of the bay accompanied the *Columbia's* return to the United States. These drawings and measurements came in handy three years later when, in June 1898, the Americans arrived off the mouth of Guantánamo Bay and fired the shots that announced the nation's arrival as an imperial power.

3

INDEPENDENCE DAY

Camp McCalla, Guantánamo Bay, June 11, 1898. The U.S. occupation is going swimmingly. Some of the marines are on the beach taking a bath. Yesterday's landing was "as easy as placing a Sunday school picnic," reports *The New York Times*. Twenty-four hours later and still no enemy in sight. Which comes as a relief to Lieutenant Colonel Robert W. Huntington, who commands the first American troops to set foot on Cuban soil in over a century. Huntington has been ordered to seize and hold Guantánamo Bay. The navy wants it as a coaling station to support its blockade of Santiago Harbor. The army wants it as a beachhead for a ground assault on Santiago itself. In the absence of an enemy, Huntington may be excused for giving his troops a break before fully digging in. They've been trolling the Florida Straits for over a month, beneath a blistering sun, clad head to toe in wool, surviving on hardtack and stale water, and sleeping in quarters so rank they may fairly be compared with stables. Truly these men deserve a dip.

But Huntington has left the camp exposed, and a fury of gunfire erupts from thickets surrounding the U.S. position. The so-called picnic comes to a crashing end, along with the lives of two young Marines and the innocence of an entire battalion. Fortunately, reports the *New York Journal*, Huntington's recruits respond like veterans. "Up from the sea came running a line of naked men, grabbing their carbines and falling into place as Colonel Huntington issued his orders." Together

with the rest, the bathers sprawl on the ground, then plunge downhill
in the direction of the Spanish fire. "There was no fun in this for the
naked men," the *Journal* allows, "but they held their places and charged
away with the others, the bushes scratching them and the insects fes-
tering their nakedness." With the Spaniards on the run, the bathers
return to fetch their clothes.[1]

Spain has made its presence known and for the next three nights
will test the resolve of the intruders as it has seldom been tested before. Of all the battles of this war, journalist Stephen Crane will later
recall, "none were so hard on the nerves, none more strained the courage so near the panic point, as those swift nights in Camp McCalla."
By now the marines had thrown up breastworks, but they remain
pinned down with their backs against the sea. The ensuing standoff
generates a hideous cacophony as U.S. pistols, rifles, field guns, and
ships' cannon combine with the malignant howl of the Spanish Mauser.
Huntington and his lieutenants recognize an untenable situation.
When Cuban scouts report that the Spaniards are operating from a
base at Cuzco Well, two miles over the hills along the Cuban coastline, a call goes out for volunteers to take the battle to the enemy. The
response is overwhelming. Scores of marines are turned away.[2]

The next morning, two hundred marines led by fifty Cubans disap-
pear into the chaparral. The procession advances without incident, as
if undetected by the Spanish host. But the Cubans know otherwise.
Those melodic "coos" come not from doves but from enemy pickets
tracking the intruders' progress toward Cuzco Well. There the Spaniards lie in wait, locked, loaded, and concealed in underbrush as the
raiding party appears over a nearby ridge. The Mausers uncork, and
the marines hit the dirt, guns blazing. Once more fire and brimstone
choke the air as the barranca succumbs to a stupefying roar. At first
the Spaniards benefit from their position. But the marines enjoy a
boon the Spaniards lack: six huge guns mounted atop the USS *Dolphin*, which has paralleled the procession up the coast. A little artful
signaling on the part of a U.S. soldier is all that separates the Spaniards from their doom. Up pops a young marine whose job requires
only that he stand astride the ridge, his form and flag outlined against
the sky, gesturing to the *Dolphin* while the pride of Spain unloads on
him. Courage, heroism, sacrifice, valor—these are the common cur-

rency of war. This signalman's act requires a language all its own. The *Dolphin*'s gunners take their mark. The Spaniards are blown to pieces. The U.S. occupation of Guantánamo Bay begins.

What began as the Cuban War of Independence ended a few short years later as the Spanish-American War. The Cuban dream of "Cuba Libre"—a Cuba free and independent of outside rule—fueled the insurrection. But Cuba Libre did not sit well with many Americans. For over a century, U.S. officials had looked on Cuba as a "natural addition to its system of states," as Thomas Jefferson put it back in 1823. Americans had resisted the temptation to seize Cuba, confident that Spain was capable of maintaining law and order conducive to U.S. commercial exploitation of the island. Most Americans had no faith that Cuba could govern itself. When the battle against Spain appeared to be turning Cuba's way, the United States hastily intervened, promising to grant Cubans the independence they had all but won themselves.

Like most wars, the Cuban War of Independence had its proximate cause in a previous conflict, in this case the Ten Years' War against Spain (1868–1878), which came to an end with the controversial Pact of Zanjón (named after a town in eastern Cuba). By the terms of the pact, Cuban separatists agreed to lay down their arms in exchange for the promise of liberal reforms and amnesty for all who had taken part in the insurgency. Many separatists violently opposed the peace agreement. Those who endorsed it did so only out of grudging acknowledgment that their current campaign was unlikely to succeed. Few saw the settlement as a long-term solution. Barely had the pact been signed when separatist general Calixto García, exiled in New York, devised plans for a new invasion of Cuba. Like its predecessor, La Guerra Chiquita (or the Little War, 1879–80), as García's latest uprising became known, did not achieve its ends. But García's labor was not in vain. Cuba Libre needed political as well as military organization, and with the help of a young maverick named José Martí, García established the Cuban Revolutionary Party, which imbued the movement with the nationalist vision and organizational discipline it previously lacked. With Martí as its guiding light, and taking advantage of an economic downturn in the mid-1880s, the Cuban Revolutionary Party galvanized disgruntled Cubans (at home and abroad) into a formidable political and military coalition. When liberal reforms and economic recovery in the early 1890s yielded to political reaction and more economic hardship, Martí and his followers struck, declaring Cuban independence in *el grito de Baire* (the shout of Baire) on February 24, 1895.[3]

"REVOLTS IN CUBA," proclaimed *The Philadelphia Inquirer* three days later. "SEVERAL REVOLUTIONARY PARTIES ON THE ISLAND HAVE RISEN IN ARMS." U.S. readers followed the insurrection with rapt attention. Cuba's governor-general declared martial law; leading separatists and conspirators were arrested throughout the island; other separatists fled to the United States; Spain patrolled the Cuban coastline searching for filibusters; suspicious activity was reported in Tampa and Key West.[4] U.S. newspapers had covered Cuban insurrections before. But this one seemed to be broader based and, in the words of the *Sioux City* (Iowa) *Journal*, promised to be "THE BLOODIEST YET." Few papers expected the insurrection to succeed, but many noted its careful orchestration, as well as the talent of the charismatic Martí and general Máximo Gómez, a native of Santo Domingo and veteran of the Ten Years' War. The previous month, Martí had left New York for Santo Domingo, where he met up with Gómez before heading for Cuba in the wake of three thousand trained and armed men. As a symbol of their confidence, the revolutionaries launched the latest uprising simultaneously in Santiago province, near Guantánamo Bay, and in Matanzas, just east of Havana.[5]

For tactical reasons, Gómez, Martí, and their lieutenants did not arrive in Cuba until April, leading newspapers skeptical about an independent Cuba to doubt the insurrection's odds. *The New York Times* went so far as to mock its leadership. "CUBAN REBELS PENITENT," ran a column out of Havana. "Those Who Were Fierce in New-York Are Like Doves Elsewhere." "GOMEZ AND MARTI ARE INVISIBLE." With insurgent troops "fleeing from the military," the *Times* concluded, Cuban independence didn't "stand a chance." Over the ensuing months, the *Times* drew on evidence channeled by Spanish authorities to confirm the revolution's demise. "CUBAN INSURGENTS SUBDUED," the paper announced in early March. "The military commander of Guantánamo reports that several members of [Cuban general] Pedro Perez's band have surrendered to the authorities. The officials of the district assert that the rebel force there numbers 180 men, who are poorly armed, and are unable to do much fighting."[6]

Like U.S. journalists, the Spanish government did not expect much from the latest violence. In Washington, D.C., the Spanish ambassador told New Orleans's *Daily Picayune* that Spain's thirty thousand troops in Cuba were "sufficient to meet any probable emergency." He also suggested that Spain would exploit U.S. business interests in Cuba to quash American support for the insurrection. U.S. businesses had just begun to benefit from relaxed duties on U.S. goods bound for Cuba, he observed; surely they would persuade the American government to stem the flow of money and arms to the rebels from Cuban sympathizers in the United States.[7]

In Cuba itself, the latest uprising was greeted with equanimity. Boston planter Edwin Atkins, for one, regarded the violence as a mere escalation of the banditry that had plagued planter communities since the economic downturn a decade earlier. A Bostonian by birth, Atkins was the largest American landlord in Cuba. He owned a vast sugar plantation in south-central Cuba named Soledad, near the port of Cienfuegos. Soledad functioned as a sugar *central*, grinding cane not only from its own fields, some of which were farmed by tenants, but also from the fields of neighboring farmers, to the tune of 120,000 tons of cane per year. In high season, 1,200 employees ("specimens from fifteen different countries," in Atkins's words) worked the Soledad estate, its 12,000 acres knit together by 22 miles of private railway.[8] A little over half of Soledad's land was devoted to sugar production, the rest to raising cattle. Soledad was by no means unusual in the capital-intensive sugar industry of late-nineteenth-century Cuba. By the early 1890s it was surrounded by American-owned estates sprinkled throughout Cienfuegos and neighboring Trinidad provinces. The Americans comprised quite a "colony," Atkins wrote in a reminiscence of life in Cuba; they "liked to meet at Soledad where they knew they could find rooms and were sure of a welcome."[9]

Atkins came to Cuba to make money. Like many in the planter community, he was frustrated by Spain's erratic trade policy, which made it hard to run a business. When war erupted, Atkins declared himself "autonomist"—that is, in favor of political and economic rights for Cuba within the umbrella of the Spanish empire. In the initial months of the conflict, Atkins attempted to steer a middle way between the insurgents and Spanish authorities. For a while, such a way seemed possible, as neither side stood to benefit from alienating American interests. After the initial flare-up in Matanzas, the violence retreated east, and by April 1895, journalists across Cuba were declaring the insurgency all but over. Only "small bands" of "mostly negroes" with "very poor" arms and "utterly incapable leaders" continued to fight on, *The New York Times* reported. In June, a planter friend wrote Atkins that as far as he could "judge, the war on this island will be of no consequence, and will soon come to an end."[10]

But the war did not come to an end. Led by deceptively capable leaders, the insurgents weathered Spain's initial counterattack, and as the insurrection lasted, enthusiasm mounted in the United States, where friends of Cuba Libre continued to recruit troops, raise money, and funnel weapons to Cuba. So great was pro-Cuban support in towns and cities up and down the American seaboard that even the *Times* acknowledged what amounted to a popular mobilization in the United States. "Steamships leaving [Havana] for Key West, Tampa, New-York, New-Orleans, and Mexico are crowded with passengers," the paper noted. "Many young men of the best families are joining the insurgents, and students are leaving college for the same purpose."[11] By June 1895 evidence of private American interference in Cuba had become so overt that President Cleveland felt obligated to denounce it. After all, the president chided, Spain was "a power with which the United States are and desire to remain on terms of peace and amity."[12] It was one thing for the American government to imagine a Cuba free of Spanish rule; it was another thing entirely for the Cubans to want to govern the island by themselves.

Emboldened by success at home and sympathy abroad, the insurrection swept out of the east in the summer of 1895. That July an incendiary announcement from Liberation Army headquarters sent Atkins and other planters scurrying to beat their plowshares into swords. "Whereas all exploitations of any product whatsoever are aids and resources to the Government that we are fighting," General Gómez announced, "it is resolved . . . that the introduction of articles of commerce, as well as beef and cattle, into the towns occupied by the enemy, is absolutely prohibited. The sugar plantations will stop their labors, and whosoever shall attempt to grind the crop notwithstanding this order, will have their cane burned and their buildings demolished." Those who thought "to profit from the present situation of affairs . . . shall be considered as an enemy, treated as a traitor, and tried as such in case of his capture."

It took a couple of months for the rebel forces to reach Cienfuegos, that ominously named land of "one hundred fires." Atkins defied the general's order and farmed that summer. He ground cane that autumn, too, describing journalists' accounts of upheaval in central Cuba as "exaggerated." Still, Atkins himself soon abandoned Cuba for his home in Belmont, Massachusetts, where he received news in October that Gómez had "invaded the villas," making matters "now serious." By the end of November, Atkins's fields were ablaze, payback, he later learned, for his efforts to convince the Cleveland administration not to recognize the insurgency. But the reason hardly mattered. That same month, a second proclamation from Gómez authorized the complete and total destruction of all plantations, irrespective of their owners' allegiances, including fields, outbuildings, and railroads.[13] Cuba was bound for total war.

Gomez's success in taking the battle to the heart of Cuba brought turnover atop the Spanish chain of command. In February 1896, Valeriano Weyler replaced Arsenio Martínez Campos as captain-general of Cuba. Like Martínez Campos, Weyler was a veteran of the Ten Years' War, and is said to have greeted his latest appointment with the cryptic remark that "war should be answered with war."[14] Long before Weyler arrived in Havana, Cubans interpreted his appointment "as a prophesy of a reign of blood and terror." In the last war, Weyler had distinguished himself by "cruelty to women and defenseless prisoners"; in this war, sources predicted, he would alienate even the United States by abusing anyone "unfortunate enough to fall under suspicion."[15] He did not disappoint. Within days, he began corralling peasants into concentration camps while destroying the fields they left behind. Within months, he had so alienated even American interests on the island that a collection of U.S. businessmen, Atkins in the lead, called on President Cleveland to intervene on the side of the insurgents.[16]

U.S. newspapers reflected the drastic change in fortunes. Papers that had once brimmed with tales of insurgent license now bristled with reports of American suffering at Spanish hands. Americans were being driven from "their homes," reported *The* (New York) *World*, "the torch applied to their belongings, and their employees, Cubans and mulattoes, killed before their very eyes." Individuals under suspicion "have been brutally carried away and thrust unceremoniously into prison."[17]

In Weyler the press corps met a subject whose cruelty matched its own penchant for hyperbole. Under Weyler, every peasant became a rebel sympathizer, every planter or "autonomist" an enemy of Spain. As Weyler tightened restrictions on the press and civilian populations in cities, Cuban civic life ground to a halt. Weyler's clampdown did nothing to end the insurrection, of course; less than a year after his arrival in Cuba, the number of rebel troops in the country had swollen from a mere three thousand at the start of the conflict to fifty thousand. By the following year, the war had reached a stalemate, with Weyler controlling the cities and Gómez patrolling the countryside.[18] Neither place could be considered much of a prize. Cities aren't really cities without the freedoms Weyler denied. Meanwhile, the countryside had been thoroughly ravaged, first by the rebel campaign against the planters, then by Weyler's persecution of the peasants. Still, stalemate favored the underdogs. And when another year went by with Spain unable to end the insurrection, even formally staunch Spanish interests began, in the words of one American official, to "wish and pray for annexation to the United States."[19]

If the United States intended to intervene in the Cuban War of Independence, it would have to hurry. By winter 1897–98, the war turned decidedly in favor of the insurgents. Once confined to the countryside, the insurrection began to target cities, and Spanish troops more or less threw down their arms. "Spanish forces seldom sally forth in the east," reported Emory W. Fenn, a filibustering American fighting with the Cuban Army, just as U.S. forces prepared to join the war. "In order to fight, the Cubans were obliged to attack fortified towns. With the exception of the large cities on the seaboard, and a few large inland towns, the entire eastern part of Cuba was free and might truthfully be called 'Cuba Libre.'"[20] Just a month or two earlier, Gómez himself declared the conflict "dead" and the enemy "crushed," and for the first time claimed to see an end to the fighting.[21]

Despite popular support for the insurrection in the United States, the Cleveland administration remained cool to the idea of intervention from the first. In early December 1896, President Cleveland delivered a speech on the Cuban conflict to Congress. He began by acknowledging the calls for intervention. He conceded that the United States had an interest in the war more than merely "sentimental" or "philanthropic." Some $30–$50 million in U.S. capital was tied up in Cuban railroad, mining, sugar, and other industries, and U.S.-Cuban trade had reached nearly $100 million on the eve of the war. The president also noted the inconvenience and expense the U.S. government faced in having to defend American property owners suffering damages in Cuba, all the while meeting its legal obligation to stem the flow of arms and money to the insurgents.

These interests and inconveniences, together with "considerations of philanthropy and humanity," generated various calls for the U.S. government to accord the insurgents belligerent rights, to recognize Cuban independence, to intervene in the conflict, or to buy Cuba from Spain. Cleveland insisted that all such actions were either impractical or unworthy of a nation that desired "nothing so much as to live in amity with all the world," and whose "ample and diversified domains satisfy all possible longings for territory, preclude dreams of conquest, and prevent any casting of covetous eyes upon neighboring regions, however attractive." Secure in its principles, institutions, and resources, the United States would continue to demonstrate "restraint," notwithstanding the evidence of Spanish atrocities.

Cleveland's hopes for Cuba shaded his analysis of the situation. Spain had begun to rethink its Cuban policies, the president insisted; it was ready to exchange real autonomy for an end to the insurrection. Surely autonomy was consistent with "all the reasonable objects of the insurrection," and indeed "all rational requirements of her Spanish subjects." Besides, Cubans would need time to "test their capacity for self-government," something autonomy, not independence, would facilitate.

Still, American patience had its limits. The void of law and order in Cuba grew costlier by the day. Should the contest further "degenerate into a strife which means nothing more than the useless sacrifice of human life and the utter destruction of the very subject matter of the conflict," the president warned, then American "obligations to the sovereignty of Spain will be superseded by higher obligations which we can hardly hesitate to recognize and discharge." Cleveland cautioned Congress that the United States must avoid behavior that could precipitate a war, while acknowledging that there may come a time when "considerations of American interests, along with considerations of humanity and a desire to see a rich and fertile country, intimately related to us, saved from complete devastation" would compel him to intervene.[22]

In his speech to Congress, Cleveland presumed to speak on behalf of the insurgents, distinguishing their rational demands (autonomy) from their irrational ones (independence). It took a few months for Máximo Gómez, the insurgent general, to respond. By early 1897, Gómez explained, the insurgents sought not so much U.S. recognition (much less U.S. intervention) as U.S. influence on Spain to halt the slaughter of innocents. Of course the civilized world differed on the merits of the insurgent cause; but the civilian toll of the war threatened the ideals of humanity itself, of which the United States had traditionally been "so noble an exemplar." The insurgent leadership had fully expected mercilessness from the country that had expelled the Jews and Moors, unleashed the Inquisition, annihilated the Native Americans, and butchered South American revolutionaries. But "not to pause at the holy and venerated hearth, personification of all most peaceful and noble; nor at women, emblem of weakness; nor at children, overwhelming symbol of inoffensive innocence"—these were offenses beyond the capacity, one might have thought, of even Spain. Would the United States really do nothing, Gómez demanded, as these atrocities continued?

For over a century, U.S. statesmen had referred to a set of hemispheric interests that distinguished "American" peoples and republics from their European counterparts, a perspective immortalized in the Monroe Doctrine. Gómez challenged the United States to make good on a century's worth of rhetoric. It was not enough to prevent "the usurpation of American territories" without defending "the people of America against European ambitions"—not enough to "protect American soil and leave its helpless dwellers exposed to the cruelties of a sanguinary and despotic European power." A revised Monroe Doctrine, based on a genuine and reciprocal understanding of a hemispheric public good, could be the blueprint for a true confederation of American states. Expanded "to the defense of the principles which animate modern civilization," this Cuban Jefferson suggested, such a doctrine might "form an integral part of the culture and life of the American people."[23]

In November 1896, Americans elected Republican William McKinley president of the United States after a vigorous election campaign in which questions of foreign policy and events in Cuba scarcely came up. In his inauguration speech the following March, McKinley managed barely a paragraph on overseas developments. "We want no war of conquest," the new president told the nation. "We must avoid the temptation of territorial aggression. War should never be entered upon until every agency of peace has failed; peace is preferable to war in almost every contingency." By appearances, anyway, McKinley planned to carry on the policies of his predecessor, whose only intervention in the Cuban conflict had been to try to stop the flow of money and arms to the insurgents.

Through late 1897 talk of U.S. intervention in Cuba remained hypothetical. On New Year's Eve, a correspondent of *The New York Herald* visited General Gómez in his camp, as if to size up the year's events and anticipate the year ahead. Asked whether he *still* opposed U.S. intervention in the conflict, Gómez replied not *necessarily*, so long as intervention did not mean "arbitrary annexation." With this distinction, Gómez struck preemptively at those who said that Cubans were incapable of self-government. How could anyone be sure just what Cubans or anybody else was capable of before they had been given the opportunity to prove themselves? In the meantime, annexation interested Gómez no more than autonomy. "Our object is independence," the general declared; "we have among us young men who have sacrificed everything to this sacred cause." The aging general confessed to having "but one object in life, and this is to see the flag of Cuba supreme from Cape Maisí to San Antonio." Again anticipating later events, Gómez worried lest the Cubans "be robbed of any share in the honor of the expulsion of the Spaniards," while at the same time expressing confidence that "the people of the United States will never balk us in this, our hour of victory."[24]

Had Gómez known the plans for Cuba being formulated in the U.S. War Department as the year drew to a close, he would have been mortified. While President McKinley struggled to maintain the formal neutrality established by his predecessor, his military officials were preparing for what they had come to regard as the nation's inevitable entry into war. The planning and execution of this war differed dramatically. U.S. strategists anticipated no "splendid little war," as Secretary of State John Hay would later put it, but a long and bloody battle for Cuba that would begin in the east and culminate in the west with an assault on the Cuban capital, Havana. If taxing militarily, a protracted campaign would serve the purpose of creating a clean slate in Cuba, allowing the United States to remake Cuba in its own image, which the slave revolution had precluded in Haiti.

American plans for Cuba were the subject of a letter from U.S. undersecretary of war Joseph C. Breckenridge to the commander of the U.S. Army, Lieutenant General Nelson A. Miles, dated December 7, 1897. U.S. military planners expected to begin the war not in Puerto Rico, where Spanish defenses were considerably lighter and where a supposedly sympathetic population eagerly anticipated annexation to the United States. It is the job of the military to keep the nation safe, and just as racial conflagration was on everybody's mind in late-eighteenth-century Cuba, so it remained on Americans' minds a century later. U.S. military planners sought to expel Spain from Puerto Rico not as an end in itself, Breckenridge informed Miles, but to establish Puerto Rico as a colony for African Americans, thereby once and for all resolving the nation's "internal racial conflict." With its "cosmopolitan" and "peace loving" inhabitants, Breckenridge suggested, Puerto Rico could be taken with "relatively mild measures." Miles should steer clear of population centers and respect "all the laws between civilized and Christian nations."[25]

Cuba was another story. Comprised of "whites, blacks, Asians and people who are a mixture of these races," Cuba's population was "indolent and apathetic," "indifferent to religion," at once "immoral" and impassioned, possessed of only "a vague notion of what is right and wrong." Absorbing such a people into the American federation "would be sheer madness." The army would first have to "clean up the country, even if this means using the methods Divine Providence used on the cities of Sodom and Gomorrah." Miles must "destroy everything in our cannons' range," Breckenridge announced; he must "impose a harsh blockade so that hunger and its constant companion, disease, undermine the peaceful population and decimate the Cuban army." First fighting with the Spanish, Miles should force the Cubans to take "dangerous and desperate measures." Then taking Cuba's side, the United States must precipitate "a phase of indeterminate duration" during which an independent government would alienate autonomists and Spaniards, thus creating conflict and unrest and jeopardizing the Cuban government's ability "to meet our demands and the commitments made to us."

In short, Breckenridge concluded, U.S. military policy in Cuba "must always be to support the weaker against the stronger, until we have obtained the extermination of them both, in order to annex the Pearl of the Antilles." With the likely start date of the operation the following October, Breckenridge urged Miles to "tie up the slightest detail . . . in case we find ourselves in the need to precipitate events."

Breckenridge need not have worried. An insult and an explosion catapulted the United States into the Cuban conflict more swiftly than the War Department had anticipated and, it turns out, could be ready for. On February 11, 1898, the pro-intervention *New York Journal* greeted readers with a letter from Enrique Dupuy de Lôme, Spain's minister to Washington, to a confidant back home describing the U.S. president as a "weak and popularity-seeking . . . hack politician." Though probably few Americans found Dupuy de Lôme's remarks to be "THE WORST INSULT TO THE UNITED STATES IN ITS HISTORY," as the *Journal* put it, it was an insult nonetheless. When coupled with the explosion of the battleship *Maine* in Havana Harbor four days later, the de Lôme letter brought cries for intervention to a fever pitch. In a nation eager for martial adventure, it did not take an inquiry to reveal the source of the *Maine*'s demise. "The Maine was sunk by an act of dirty treachery," Theodore Roosevelt, assistant secretary of the navy, wrote a friend the following day. The *Journal*, meanwhile, blamed "AN ENEMY'S SECRET INFERNAL MACHINE."[26]

McKinley did not want to go to war. If there was ever a time for the president to prove Dupuy de Lôme wrong, this was it. He wasn't up to it. Over the course of the next few weeks, McKinley struggled to retain control of U.S. foreign policy as his opportunistic young assistant secretary of war dispatched Admiral Dewey to the Philippines, as Congress passed a $50 million war appropriation (without a dissenting vote), and as Spanish general Ramón Blanco y Erenas suspended hostilities in Cuba. On April 11 the president petitioned Congress for authorization to intervene in Cuba. On April 19, Congress passed its war resolution, which the president signed the next day. On April 21 the president ordered a naval blockade of Cuba. On April 25 the United States declared war on Spain.[27]

Apart from the war declaration itself, the most significant aspect of these preliminaries went virtually unnoticed. Attached to the Congress's War Resolution was a legislative rider introduced by Senator Henry M. Teller (R-Colo.), thereafter known as the Teller Amendment, which in one sentence repudiated a century of U.S. policy toward Cuba. Clause one of the resolution asserted Cuba's independence. Clause two demanded Spain's withdrawal from Cuba. Clause three authorized the U.S. president to use the military to effect these ends. Then came the kicker: "The United States hereby disclaims any disposition or intention to exercise sovereignty, jurisdiction, or control over said Island except for the pacification thereof, and asserts its determination, when that is accomplished, to leave the government and control of the Island to its people."

Historians disagree about how exactly to account for the Teller Amendment. Its passage followed the withdrawal of a more radical resolution granting immediate recognition to the revolutionary government, suggesting that a bargain had been struck.[28] Senator Teller himself hailed from the state of Colorado, home to a lucrative sugar beet industry already reeling from increased European competition; the introduction of Cuban sugar into the U.S. sugar market duty-free could potentially have ruined U.S. beet growers.[29] Then there was the roughly $1 million in cash that Tomás Estrada y Palma, exiled leader of the Cuban Revolutionary Party in New York, handed to Samuel Janney, a Cuban lobbyist in Washington, D.C., to distribute among U.S. congressmen as he saw fit.[30] Finally, there was widespread and sincere support for Cuba Libre among the American people and some of their elected officials.[31] Whatever the explanation, there could be no doubting the amendment's effect: by appearances, anyway, for the first time in U.S. history, American officials had elevated the cause of Cuban independence above American interests on the island. Americans were heading down to Cuba to help remove the Spanish. With that mission accomplished they would leave Cuba in the hands of its people. Gazing northward from Revolutionary Army headquarters, Gómez must have found the Teller Amendment too good to be true.

On March 24, 1898, seeking "to secure a lucrative position and better" himself, a young man named Frank Keeler left a job in Down East Maine, bound for Boston, Massachusetts, aboard a steamer named the *City of Bangor*.[32] In fair winds and following seas, Keeler arrived in Boston the next day, just as the city began to stir. After securing a place to stay, he set off to explore Boston's neighborhoods; with "plenty of money" in his pocket, he could afford to put off the hunt for work for at least a couple of days.[33]

Like cities and towns across the United States that spring, Boston buzzed with talk of war. Due out the afternoon of Keeler's arrival was a U.S. Navy report on the cause of the explosion of the battleship *Maine* in Havana Harbor the previous month. Few doubted that the report would conclude that Spain was responsible, or that it would lead to war. The *Boston Journal* reported that President McKinley believed that a peaceful end to the Cuban War of Independence was imminent, but that column shared space with news of naval mobilization up and down the eastern seaboard and a headline announcing ominously, "SPANISH TORPEDO FLEET COMES."[34]

By day, Keeler strolled Boston's neighborhoods. By night, he shuttled between Tremont Temple and the Grand Opera House, where audiences were treated to theater suited to wartime: *Julius Caesar*, *Spartacus*, and the more whimsical naval yarn *Spitfire*. Bostonians were selling their private yachts to the government for use as transports. The Springfield Armory was working round the clock to turn out thousands of new rifles. Preparations were under way for the fortification of Boston Harbor and Narragansett Bay. War was very much in the air.[35]

A few days after arriving in Boston, Keeler found himself taking in the bustle at the Charlestown Navy Yard, across the channel from Boston's crowded North End. "It was there I saw the Marines at drill," Keeler wrote in his diary. "It was a fine sight, their neat uniforms, their manly appearance impressed me." Friendless in a new city, Keeler was seduced by the marines' "home life at the barracks." He couldn't stay away. Returning to the yard a few days later, he once more "watched the drill of the Marines. It was grand," he wrote. "Fate had decided that I should be a Marine."[36]

As Keeler enlisted in the marines that spring, young men throughout the nation confronted the vexing question of whether to enroll in the army. In late April 1898, Robert Huntington Jr. wrote a letter to his father seeking advice about what to do. Robert Huntington Sr. must have seemed a likely source of clever counsel. Huntington was a Civil War veteran and a Marine Corps lieutenant soon to be promoted to lieutenant colonel, the very man who would oversee the landing of the U.S. Marines at Guantánamo Bay. "I do not think I would go for adventures in this war," the father cautioned the son. "Going to war in almost any part of the US would be better, I would say, than Cuba in summer . . . nothing less than high principle ought to carry a man into this fight." Wanting such principle, Bobby took his dad's advice and spent the summer shuttling between apartments in New York City and Hartford, Connecticut, and the family cottage on New Hampshire's exclusive Squam Lake.[37]

With no one to turn to for advice ("I had not been home for five years. If killed there would be no one to mourn"), Frank Keeler found himself tethered to what turned out to be a deeply ambivalent commander as marines from across the northeastern United States converged on the Brooklyn Navy Yard.[38] In his letter to Bobby, Colonel Huntington confessed that he thought the Cubans "not worth fighting for. At least I do not think they would be much improvement on the Spaniards." Only later would Huntington's ambivalence compromise the welfare of his troops; for now, Keeler and his fellow marines were buoyed by the martial euphoria that brought crowds thronging to observe the marines at drill. Who was thinking about the *Cubans* anyway? It was war for war's sake that inspired the roars and whistles that spirited Keeler and his fellow marines out "the main gate of the Barracks down Flushing Avenue to the gate of the Navy Yard, and thence through the Yard to the *Panther*," the converted passenger steamer that would carry the marines south. After a jubilant send-off, the *Panther* pulled out into New York Harbor, groaning under a load of "mosquito netting, woolen and linen clothing, heavy and light weight underwear, three months' supply of provision, wheelbarrows, pushcarts, pickaxes, shovels, barbed-wire cutters, wall and shelter tents, and a full supply of medical stores," not to mention guns and ammunition.[39]

Euphoria soon gave way to the drudgery of a prolonged deployment. Many of the young enlistees had never been to sea. A rough baptism on the first leg of the journey to Hampton Roads, Virginia, was nothing compared to the punishment meted the *Panther* off Cape Hatteras, where a spring tempest tossed the overloaded steamer "like a wash-tub," and where "every man and the Colonel's horse were sick."[40] The marines' introduction to sea life was made more taxing by the jealousy of their navy hosts, who resented having to share their ship with landlubbers. When the *Panther*'s captain was not confining the marines "like cattle" to half the main deck, the first officer busied them with menial chores typically reserved for sailors.

On April 30, the marines arrived off Key West, in what Keeler described as "lovely sea and weather." Anything is better than a stomach in a roiling sea, and if the Florida sun seemed a blessing at first, it soon combined with monotony and mistreatment to raise the marines' blood pressure to the boiling point. Had Huntington been more forceful, he might have defended his men from the *Panther*'s crew. But, he confessed to Bobby, he was past his prime and more than a little halfhearted in taking up his latest commission. "Have been sick (grippe and malaria) and have not been on shore," he reported. "As one grows older they had as soon somebody else went. Of course this ought to be my chance, but I think I am all of ten years' too old for this business."[41]

As days in the scorching heat became weeks, and with their commander down with fever, the marines became the playthings of the *Panther*'s officers. "Should we ever set down for a moment some officer would order us to another part of the ship," Keeler complained, "then another would order us back. If a dozen of us ever got together at one time they would turn the hose on us." All the while, the marines "could not say a word only mind like cattle." Had the treatment lasted another week, Keeler imagined, "there would have been a mutiny and the officers would have been thrown overboard."[42] Huntington confirmed Keeler's account of the mistreatment. "The Captain and Executive Officer did not treat us well," he remarked, "and under the regulations he commands everyone on board and my men were punished without my advice and against my protest in more than one case." One of the men got ten days in "double irons" in a small room belowdecks simply for playing cards.

Weeks after leaving Brooklyn, Keeler lamented being "given no chance for a bath since leaving the barracks and food was bad. We had hard tack and canned corn-beef or canned corn beef and hard tack just as we like." This they washed down with distilled water "so warm we had to work hard to drink it." Mornings, the marines went ashore to perform "fierce drills" in blazing sun and full uniform. Journalists assigned to the military staging areas in Florida reported taxing conditions. "With the thermometer at ninety-eight in the shade . . . the U.S. troops sweat night and day in their cowhide boots, thick flannel shirts and winter trousers." Details of the troops' living conditions were so bad, another journalist remarked, "if I started to tell the truth at all . . . it would open up a hell of an outcry from all the families of the boys who have volunteered."[43] Still, Keeler and his fellow marines were better off aboard the *Panther* than in Tampa with the army, where the soldiers received meat canned five years earlier, at the time of the Sino-Japanese War.[44]

After three and a half weeks at anchor aboard the *Panther*, the marines received orders to disembark to a nearby campground, their relief at escaping the *Panther*'s crew tempered by the drudgery of having to unload (and later reload) the thousands of pounds of guns, ammunition, lumber, and other equipment that would accompany them to Cuba. Never mind the nuisance of mosquitoes and flies. Outside the clutches of the *Panther*'s captain, the marines turned out to be unruly. "I hope I get a hold on the men," Huntington wrote Bobby. "They have little idea of obeying orders and perhaps they may improve some."

Though they worked hard, "they stole lots out of the ship"; some "steal anything they can lay [their] hands upon."[45]

Four weeks of these appalling conditions did not sit well with the marines. Like Keeler, many had enlisted in the war in a pique of patriotism. Unflattering, often racialized images of Spanish troops abounded in newspaper and periodical cartoons, depicting Spaniards as dark, almost black, and barbarous. Desperate for a fight, the marines settled for the nearest thing they could find to the diabolical Spaniard. When "a nigro shot and killed a sailor" in the town of Key West, Keeler reported, the marines greeted it as the opening salvo of the Spanish-American War. Refusing to leave the matter to the local sheriff, "75 Marines on liberty . . . armed themselves with ropes, clubs, knives, and revolvers" and marched on the jail where the suspect sat in custody. Only an official guard dispatched from the marines' camp managed to prevent a lynching. It was past time to sail for Cuba.[46]

Clearing Key West on the afternoon of June 7, 1898, Colonel Huntington could not be sure exactly where in Cuba he and his marines were headed. But Spain's new captain-general, Ramón Blanco, thought he had a good idea. In April that year, Blanco warned his commander in eastern Cuba, Arsenio Linares y Pombo, to expect the Americans to come ashore along the southeast coast. Blanco ordered Linares to fortify Guantánamo Bay and to reinforce Santiago. The calls of Spanish officials to fortify Guantánamo Bay had not ended with the populating of the basin at the beginning of the nineteenth century. Before Blanco's, the latest warning to be ignored had been that of Captain-General Arsenio Martínez Campos y Antón, who had dispatched a team of engineers and artillery experts to Guantánamo in the wake of the USS *Columbia*'s visit in February 1895. By the late nineteenth century, Guantánamo Bay had strategic value as more than a potential staging ground for an attack on Santiago. French telegraph lines connecting Cuba to Jamaica and Haiti stretched across the mouth of the bay, and a French telegraph station sat atop Fisherman's Point, just inside the southeastern entrance to the harbor. To Campos, as to a long line of Spanish officials before him, Guantánamo presented an obvious, and vulnerable, target.[47]

Predictably, Campos's plans went unheeded, leaving Linares to fortify Guantánamo virtually from scratch while holding back increasingly confident Cuban forces. The best Campos could do that spring was to refurbish an old battery of smooth-bore guns on Toro Cay, at the center top of the outer harbor, and erect two blockhouses, one on Windward Point, at the southeast corner of the bay, the other at the port of Caimanera, at the western entrance to the inner harbor. Conceding the outer harbor, Linares mined the mouth of the inner harbor.[48] As for the rest of the bay's defenses, that fell to the gunship *Sandoval* and its plucky commander, Lieutenant Teniente de Navio Scandella, who for over two months played cat and mouse with the largest ships in the U.S. Navy.

By early June 1898, Spain had nearly 200,000 troops in Cuba, though these were by no means fresh. Roughly 36,500 Spanish troops were dispersed throughout Santiago province, with about 6,000 stationed at Guantánamo City, under the command of General Felix Pareja. Some 300 patrolled the immediate perimeter of Guantánamo Bay. At the bay, Spain had established headquarters at Cuzco Well, near Windward Point, site of the only known source of freshwater at the outer harbor. Meanwhile, confronting Pareja and his 6,000 troops at Guantánamo City was Cuba's First Division, 1,000 strong, under the command of General Pedro A. Pérez.[49]

On the night of June 9, 1898, the *Panther* rounded Punto Maisí, the southeastern tip of Cuba, and entered the Windward Passage. There it collided with a U.S. transport named *Scorpion*, nearly cutting the *Scorpion* in half. Despite this hiccup, by midmorning of the next day, the *Panther* arrived at a rendezvous with the U.S. fleet off Santiago, where it reported to Rear Admiral William T. Sampson. Charles L. McCawley, a captain in Huntington's command, remembered the rendezvous as "most picturesque. In front of the harbor, lying one inside the other in two half circles, were assembled the two splendid squadrons of Admiral Sampson and Commodore Schley, comprising the flower of the navy." Meanwhile, "Morro Castle and Socapa Battery loomed up before us four miles away, and the dark green hills of Cuba were spread out before us to the east and the west as far as the eye could see."

This proved to be the extent of the marines' sightseeing. The sailors whom the marines joined that day off Santiago had long since ceased to regard the Cuban coastline as picturesque. They had been blockading the island since April 21, two days after the U.S. Congress passed its war resolution. That day, U.S. Navy secretary John D. Long named Sampson commander in chief of the U.S. naval fleet on the North Atlantic Station, promoting him to rear admiral and ordering him to Cuba. Long also charged Sampson with locating and observing the Spanish fleet under the command of Pascual Cervera y Topete, last seen off Cape Verde and known to be headed for the Caribbean Sea.

On May 12 one of Sampson's cruisers spotted the Spaniards leaving the French port of Martinique, where they had tried unsuccessfully to recoal (the French policy of neutrality prohibited the fueling of warships). Three days later, they were reported to be at Curaçao, the Dutch colony off the coast of today's Venezuela. There Cervera met a slightly warmer reception and attained coal sufficient to carry him to Cuba. A week later, May 19, Cervera stole unobserved into Santiago Harbor, where Cuban informants caught up to him the following day. Still, conflicting reports had Cervera in other harbors along Cuba's southern coast, and for over a week U.S. naval officials bickered about his exact whereabouts while Sampson searched frantically to find him. Cervera, all the while, stayed put in Santiago, creating confusion about his ultimate destination.

The very day Cervera arrived at Santiago, the U.S. Navy fought its first engagement in the Cuba campaign, just down the coast, at Guantánamo Bay. Since long before the war broke out, Sampson had been eyeing the telegraph cables at Santiago and Guantánamo Bay. Amid the confusion over Cervera's whereabouts, Secretary Long ordered the USS *St. Louis*, under the command of Casper F. Goodrich, to Guantánamo to cut the French cable and thus sever communications between Cuba and the outside world.[50] The *St. Louis* was greeted by the Spanish gunship *Sandoval*, which boasted heavier guns than the converted passenger liner. Rather than risk his ship, Goodrich withdrew, vowing to return to Guantánamo with proper equipment and protection. If less than auspicious, this debut in Cuba nonetheless provided crucial information about Spanish defenses in the region. Notwithstanding the presence of the gallant *Sandoval*, Goodrich reported, Guantánamo Bay was exposed and vulnerable.[51]

The Spanish fleet that tucked into Santiago on May 19 was nearly out of coal. Nothing so confirms the demise of the Spanish Empire in the New World than the fact of Cervera's having to throw himself upon the French (in vain) and the Dutch (nearly so) for fuel upon arriving in what had once been a Spanish sea. "Fuel is the life of modern naval warfare," Admiral Mahan wrote just the previous year. "Without it the modern monsters of the deep die of inanition. Around it, therefore, cluster some of the most important considerations of naval strategy."[52] For Mahan, as no doubt for Cervera, fuel was synonymous with naval bases. Any navy that expected to operate overseas needed secure bases and a ready supply of coal.

The U.S. fleet did not venture far from home before testing Mahan's thesis. Havana lies a mere ninety miles off Key West, Santiago de Cuba a little farther. The problem of getting coal to the U.S. ships blockading the coast of Cuba gave fits to the Navy Department as early as the first week. "Get colliers to Sampson as soon as possible," Secretary Long ordered Commodore Winfield Scott Schley, Sampson's second in command, on April 28, 1898. But transferring coal from colliers to naval vessels is difficult work in calm seas. In rough seas, the giant steel hulls clang together like oversized chimes, making the work dangerous, often impossible. The seas around Cuba are seldom calm. That April and May, Cuban waters were particularly unsettled, lending the challenge of coaling decided urgency.

"Expect difficulty here will be to coal from colliers in the constant heavy swell," Schley wired Long off Cienfuegos at the end of May; the presence of Spanish mines "is easy compared with this one, so far from base." If Schley was unusually cautious about coaling in rough water, he was not alone. One commander after another was forced to abandon the blockade and return home for coal. Ships forced to abandon the blockade for fuel could not simply pop back to Key West. After the St. Louis failed in its attempt to cut the cable at Guantánamo, Captain Goodrich requested permission to make a quick run to New York Harbor "to coal and refit." He promised to be back "in ten days or so from the date of leaving St. Thomas," ready for "three or four weeks' duty with the fleet."[53]

The problem of coaling, combined with the navy's failure to locate the Spanish fleet, left Long exasperated by the end of May. He ordered Schley to tap his reserves of "ingenuity and perseverance" to "surmount difficulties regarding coaling." This was, after all, a crucial time, "and the Department relies upon you to give quick information as to Cervera's presence and to be all ready for concerted action with the army." It was inconceivable to Long that this was happening just off the U.S. coastline. Finally fed up with Schley's lack of ingenuity, and certain now that Cervera was indeed at Santiago, Long asked Schley whether he couldn't "take possession of Guantánamo" and "occupy [it] as a coaling station?"[54] Long repeated the question to Sampson that same day. "Consider if you could seize Guantánamo and occupy [it] as a coaling station." Guantánamo would be far preferable for this purpose, Long realized, than any of the other options— "Gonaives Channel, Mole, Haiti, Porto Nipe, Cuba, or elsewhere." While Schley took advantage of a break in the weather to coal several of his gunboats at sea, hardly a long-term solution, Sampson and Long exchanged a very different pair of cables. "Think I can occupy Guantánamo," Sampson wrote confidently. "Captain Goodrich reports Guantánamo very weak," Long replied; "the seizure of, immediately, is recommended."[55]

On June 7, 1898, Captain Goodrich returned to Guantánamo Bay to deliver on his vow to cut the cable between Santiago, Guantánamo, Jamaica, and Haiti. This time the Spanish gunboat *Sandoval* proved no match for Goodrich's escorts, the *Marblehead* and the *Yankee*. As the *Sandoval* steamed out of Caimanera to meet the *St. Louis*, the *Marblehead* and the *Yankee* opened fire, sending the intrepid Spanish gunboat scurrying back to its nest. This left the single blockhouse above Fisherman's Point to face the U.S. cannon on its own. Within minutes, the Spanish guards at Fisherman's Point were driven off and the blockhouse destroyed, leaving the U.S. vessels in sole possession of the outer harbor. Goodrich succeeded in cutting the telegraph cable. By doing so, he interrupted communication between the six thousand Spanish troops around Guantánamo City and the regional command in Santiago. Troops of the Cuban general Pedro Pérez's First Regiment controlled all ground traffic between the eastern cities. So light was Spain's presence in the area that Captain B. H. McCalla, commander of the *Marblehead*, dismissed the *Yankee* to rejoin the blockade down the coast.[56]

With the navy in command of the outer harbor at Guantánamo, and with Spain's defenses in the vicinity apparently so light, Admiral Sampson worried that a protracted deployment of the U.S. Army would result in a missed opportunity. His messages to Washington recall Admiral Vernon's letters to the British Admiralty back in the summer of 1741. "Again, I urge the [Navy] department to expedite the arrival of troops for Santiago de Cuba," Sampson wrote in early June. "Army should be here now." In lieu of the army came the next best thing: Huntington's marines, with 22 marine officers, 623 enlisted men, 645 troops in all. On the morning of June 10, as the *Panther* pulled up to the blockade off Santiago, Sampson redirected it immediately to join Captain McCalla at Guantánamo Bay.

Upon arriving at Guantánamo Bay in 1741, British troops had to go out of their way to stir up an enemy, which, outmanned and underarmed, melted away upon the British arrival. This time, too, the marines seemed to have arrived at a part of Cuba all but abandoned by the Spanish. "We went ashore like innocents," Huntington wrote, "and made a peachy camp and slept well on the tenth." Frank Keeler remembered being astounded by the nonchalance of Huntington and his staff. "While we were stacking arms and unloading the ship the Spanish had every chance in the world to close in on us and slaughter or kill everyone," Keeler wrote in his diary. "To think of the risk we went through makes me angry with our Commanding Officers every time I think of it. The Spanish were laying in the bushes all around watching us and they knew every movement we made even to where our sentry were posted." Why the Spaniards didn't end the thing then and there is not clear. A captured Spanish prisoner reported that they'd been ordered not to fire until the Americans had unloaded their equipment. "They were hungry," Keeler wrote, "and wanted our food more than dead Yankees."[57]

The Americans set up camp in a small clearing above Fisherman's Point, on the opposite side of the bay from where they had disembarked a century and a half earlier. Huntington described the clearing in his official report to the marine commandant. "The ridge slopes downward and to the rear from the bay, the space at the top is very small, and all the surrounding country is covered with a thick and al-most impenetrable brush. The position is commanded by a mountain, the ridge of which is about 1,200 yards to the rear."[58] The first night the marines "slept with our clothes on and rifles by our side," Keeler remembered. "Had the Dons surrounded the hill they could have fired upon us with deadly effect, for they could have fired from all sides without hitting their own men."[59]

In hindsight, Huntington's choice of a campground seems inauspi-cious. In Key West, Huntington had proved incapable of checking the abuses of the *Panther* captain; at Guantánamo, he lacked the confi-dence to question the decisions of his superiors. In the three days between occupying the outer harbor and the arrival of the marines, the navy had seen little or no enemy activity along the shores of Guan-tánamo Bay. When the *Panther* pulled in, Captain McCalla directed the marines toward a landing site and campground selected in ad-vance by a colonel in the Cuban Army. McCalla informed Huntington that it was safe to erect tents. As a veteran commander, Huntington might have thanked McCalla for his assistance and proceeded as he had been trained to do: secure a safe landing site, identify a suitable campground, and entrench. A young captain in Huntington's com-mand remembered the colonel declaring the position "faulty" and de-ploying pickets. But that's as far as Huntington's initiative went.

Spain opened fire the following afternoon. "I was looking at my watch," wrote Keeler. "It was just 5 o'clock, Saturday, June 11th, when we received the greatest surprise of our lives." Some of the men were in the water bathing; some "were asleep when the reports of the rifles rung out." As the marines dove for their guns, the "bullets came among [them] like rain." There was no place to hide. "We dodged about trying to find shelter but there was neither trees or big rocks to get behind." U.S. Marine Corps major Henry Clay Cochrane remembered being surprised by the vulnerability of the camp and disappointed in Hun-tington's response to the initial onslaught. When the marines went ashore on June 10, Cochrane remained aboard the *Panther* to oversee the unloading of cargo. He first set foot on land just as the Spaniards

launched their initial attack. Dashing up the hill at the sound of gunfire, Cochrane claims to have found Huntington not leading the counterattack but entirely missing, as if unable to stomach the excitement.
Only after the attack was repulsed, according to Cochrane, did Huntington emerge to assess the damage.

The marines lost two men that first afternoon, privates William
Dunphy and James McColgan. According to Keeler, the two had been
posted like sacrificial lambs, some five hundred yards in front of a
main body of pickets, to the north of camp, in the direction from which
the Spanish fire was sure to come. Again, it did not take a career officer to recognize that Dunphy and McColgan occupied "a very dangerous place . . . down in the valley on a cross road . . . with no chance to
escape."[60] The two had been deliberately murdered at close range.
They "were unspeakably shocking to look at," Captain Charles L. Mc-
Cawley would later recall. "Their faces and the upper parts of their
bodies were literally torn to pieces and it was first thought that they
had been mutilated." Part of a retrieval party, Keeler remembered shiv-
ering at the sight of his two comrades. "Were we to be treated likewise?" he wondered. "Was this Christian warfare?" U.S. newspapers
carried reports of the alleged mutilation, confirming public assumptions about Spanish "barbarism." The rumors of mutilation were later
retracted, and the damage was reported to be the work of the diabolical Mauser.[61]

Beginning the night of June 11, the Spanish treated Huntington's
marines to three straight days without sleep. "I do not know why I did
not expect night attack for we had a flurry in the PM," Colonel Huntington wrote his son, "and we had two men really assassinated . . . but
I did not."[62] "It was not with the pleasantest feelings that we got supper that night," Keeler recalled. Around 9:00 p.m., their supper was
interrupted by gunfire from U.S. pickets stationed now in an orderly
circumference around the marines' exposed ridge. Still, with intimate
knowledge of the nearby terrain, the Spanish were able to penetrate
the marines' flanks, moving into bunkers dug by General Pareja's forces
the day before the Americans arrived. The Spanish shredded the marines' tents, but miraculously none of the men were hit, giving credence
to the emerging sense that the Spanish sharpshooters were misnamed.
"The Spanish troops really shoot awfully," Colonel Huntington re-

marked. "One could hear the bullets humming high in the air while various marks show that our men, although *entre nous* badly scared, shot low and stirred up the dirt and I believe we did kill 17 and probably wounded three times that."[63]

Not all the Spaniards were poor shooters. After several hours' pause they opened up again in earnest, just after midnight. About to head for cover, acting assistant surgeon John Blair Gibbs was struck through the temple from eight hundred yards. Gibbs was the third casualty among Huntington's marines, and his death was felt the keenest. Popular among officers and enlisted men alike, he was the son of a soldier killed with Custer at the Battle of Little Big Horn. A physician with a profitable practice in Manhattan, he had volunteered the minute war was declared, insisting he be sent to Cuba in the company of the first ground troops. It was only the next morning that "we learned with sincere regret that our surgeon Doctor Gibbs and Sergeant Major Good had been killed in the early morning battle," Keeler wrote. "We were all sorry to lose the surgeon for the other one left was no earthly good."[64]

Sunday, June 12, was a busy, somber day at Guantánamo Bay. There were two new bodies to bury in addition to Gibbs's. The Spaniards did all they could to make Gibbs's funeral as grave as possible, punctuating the chaplain's words with gunfire, as if honoring Gibbs with a final military salute.

As fear and fatigue combined with stifling heat to sow bitterness and fray nerves, some of Huntington's lieutenants began to doubt the wisdom of their mission. Two officers approached Colonel Cochrane, second in command to Huntington, asking him to urge Huntington to clear out of Guantánamo Bay. Huntington needed no urging. While Cochrane exploded at the men, Huntington was aboard the *Marblehead*, putting the matter before Captain McCalla. McCalla was no more sympathetic to withdrawal than Cochrane. He ordered Huntington back to camp, assuring him that he'd take perfect care of Huntington's body should he be killed. The issue was dropped and the marines did the next best thing for themselves short of pulling out of Guantánamo Bay. They struck camp, dug real trenches, and added two new field pieces and two automatic guns to their artillery, finally leveling the playing field.[65]

That same afternoon, a series of new arrivals brought a bit of cheer to the marines. First came an American flag, sent from the *Marblehead* to bolster the marines' spirit and remind them why they were fighting. Once rigged to a pole sent from the collier *Abarenda*, the flag would continue to float over the bay until well after hostilities had ended.[66] "Three times three cheers went up from the battalion," wrote Keeler, "and from all the ships in the harbor came back an answering echo. Several of the ships fired a salute and blew their steam whistle. 'The flag up, and up to stay.'"[67]

Next came a bottle of whiskey, in the hand of a journalist, one among a phalanx of newspaper reporters who stormed ashore, relieved to be where the action was after so much idleness in Tampa and Key West.[68] Finally, and most significant, came a detachment of sixty Cubans from the First Army division led by Colonel Enrique Tomas. Well after the war, Tomas remembered signaling the Cubans' arrival at the bay by placing a white horse, backed by a Cuban flag, on Leeward Point, near the mouth to the Guantánamo River. "When the commander of the *Marblehead* saw it, he was to send a boat for us," Tomas recalled. "They must have been watching for the signal, for no sooner had we led the white horse into sight and hoisted the flag, than the boat put out from the ship." Meanwhile, "there was much cannon firing from the Marblehead, and we all knew that when we got into the fight we should have a good chance to strike lusty blows for Cuba."[69]

Keeler remembered taking heart at the sight of the Cubans. "They seemed just as glad to join us as we were to have their assistance." Tomas recalled the gracious welcome afforded the Cubans as they arrived aboard the *Marblehead*. "It was plain they were glad to see us. We were glad to be there, for it meant we got some hot breakfast and hot coffee." McCalla greeted Tomas in French, and distributed clothing and arms to Tomas's men.[70]

Meanwhile, the Spanish did not stand on ceremony; no amount of funerals, flags, field guns, trenches, journalists, whiskey, or Cuban reinforcements would deter them on the evening of June 12. "Several nights without sleep" had made the marines "miserable," Keeler recalled. They "had a presentiment that when the next attack came it would be by as large a force as the Spaniards could get together." When the Spanish did open fire, Keeler believed thousands of Spaniards were arrayed against him, so ear shattering was the noise. "Fully three-thousand rifles cracked as if one man had fired all, and the bullets seemed to come from every direction," he noted. "We were surrounded. You can form no conception as to what the discharge of 3000 rifles mean by night, it makes a fearful racket. We were surprised and in many cases our hair stood on ends. We could not but feel our time had come, but we would make our lives cost them as much as possible."

Keeler was indeed surrounded. He'd been posted along the cliff behind the marines' encampment, between the camp and the bay. So far from the camp itself did Keeler and his fellow pickets appear to the U.S. ships in the harbor that the ships mistook them for Spaniards and were doing everything possible to take them out. "We were laying with our feet to the sea on the bluff," Keeler wrote in his journal, "and 'boom su'e' a shell passed so near that the wind from it took off my hat." Shrapnel from one of the missiles hit Keeler's neighbor. He "had a frightful piece torn out of his leg shattering the flesh down to the bone from hip to knee." Finally, the American ships understood their mistake, "and there was no more firing from the ships that night."

And a long night that was. The Spaniards shot away through the wee hours, leading Keeler to despair of ever seeing the sunrise or his comrades' faces again. "We could not but believe that a greater part of our companions had been killed and could but expect our own lives would [not] be long spared. But we stood, or rather laid, on our ground. There was nothing else to do, for to stand up would mean death."

But the sun came up, and as its slanting rays illuminated the American flag, so recently planted, the roar of gunfire yielded to "cheer after cheer from the ships in the bay." What could it mean? Keeler wondered. "We were unable to guess." But the cheers were for Keeler and his fellow marines. Looking on from the ships, the sailors couldn't imagine how anybody had survived the Spanish onslaught. Much less *everybody*; going out to collect their dead, the marines were amazed there were none to be found. One marine had gone missing, and was later found in the water at the base of the cliff, a bullet in the middle of his chest.

Gratified by the marines' willpower, Captain McCalla himself rowed in from the *Marblehead* to commend the troops. McCalla apologized to Keeler and his fellow pickets for accidentally targeting them. Generous to the Cubans, McCalla was no less generous to the marines. Though "a Naval Officer," Keeler wrote, "he had more regard for the Marines than we were used to receiving. There was not a man in our command who did not like him, and he treated us as gentlemen."[71]

Throughout this war, Spain betrayed an uncanny knack for stealing defeat from the jaws of victory. Had Spain followed up the assault of the night of June 12–13 with an equal or greater onslaught the next day and night, it might have driven the marines from Windward Point. But all remained quiet through the following day and night, leaving the Americans time to devise an end to Spain's harassment. When Cuban scouts explained the pause in the Spanish fire as a break for reinforcements, Huntington and McCalla drew up plans for an assault on Cuzco Well.

With Windward Point cleared of Spaniards, the navy put the bay to good use. Within days of the marines' victory, the *Yankee* could be found coaling comfortably along Hospital Cay in the middle of the outer harbor. Ships needing repair pulled into the coves near Camp McCalla. Enemy ships captured during the siege of Santiago were brought to Guantánamo and held there until the end of hostilities. The base became the navy's favored rendezvous site in the region.

As early as June 10, Spanish general Felix Pareja noticed that the Americans had taken an immediate liking to Guantánamo Bay. "The American squadron in possession of the outer bay has taken it as if for a harbor of rest," Pareja reported in a letter intercepted by a Cuban patrol. "They have anchored as if [at] one of their own ports since the 7th, the day they cut the cables. In the entrance and center of the harbor, I not being able to reach them, they have not again molested me except with two cannon shots on the 8th. It appears from the work that is being done that they are preparing to plant the harbor with mines, or place their ships for disembarkation at Playa del Este, their favorite place."[72]

Playa del Este would indeed become the navy's favorite place at Guantánamo Bay. Located around the corner from Fisherman's Point on the Windward side of the bay, it consisted of a series of protected natural jetties and coves that lent themselves to all manner of port activities. Pareja knew Playa del Este to be the one strategic spot at the outer harbor suited to the disembarkation of Spanish troops. He assured his boss Linares that, should the "Americans abandon port, which I doubt," he would do "everything possible . . . to reestablish communication, to which end I have everything ready."[73] To this day, Playa del Este remains the hub of activity at the now expansive U.S. base.

Though Spain had been driven from Windward Point, the bay itself remained hot through June and into July, with small mobile bands of Spanish pickets taking potshots at U.S. troops from outcroppings above Hicacal Beach and Toro Cay. Weary of the impertinence, McCalla dispatched some of his ships to shell the local port of Caimanera, and through mid-June, the *Texas* and *Suwannee* engaged Spanish snipers at the northern and western perimeters of the outer harbor. Spain retained control of the inner harbor through the armistice.[74]

This last point deserves attention. Unquestionably in command of the outer harbor, and with firepower dwarfing that of the solitary *Sandoval*, the navy might have cleared the region of Spanish troops, occupied the inner harbor, and even pushed the marines on toward Guantánamo City. McCalla declined to do so, judging it wiser not to precipitate a confrontation with the six thousand or so troops of Felix Pareja, who were strung out along a ten-mile ribbon between Caimanera and Guantánamo City. Pareja and his boss Linares expected the Americans to advance on Santiago through Guantánamo Bay, just as Vernon had urged Wentworth to do in 1741. The longer Pareja thought such a move imminent, the longer he remained in place, thereby cheating Linares of reinforcements. The last message Pareja had received from Linares before Captain Goodrich cut the cable line was to hold Guantánamo City no matter the cost.[75]

Herein lay the short-term significance of the marines' accomplishment of holding Guantánamo Bay. Had the marines been driven from the bay, had they retreated (as Huntington appears to have wished), Pareja's troops in Guantánamo City would have had no reason to stay put. Pareja could have broken through the relatively sparse Cuban line separating Guantánamo City from Santiago, thereby ending his isolation and joining forces with Linares. Six thousand more Spanish troops might just have been sufficient to turn the ensuing ground war in Spain's favor.[76]

Cut off from communicating with Linares, Pareja was hardly idle. Between Caimanera and Guantánamo he erected some fifty block-houses—small forts, really, consisting of stone foundations and wooden superstructures. He threw up several more at the Guantánamo City junction of the old Santiago-Baracoa road. He fortified the territory behind the town of Caimanera. Finally, he constructed breastworks and dug trenches around Guantánamo City itself. Meant to contain the Americans, Pareja's work effectively isolated Guantánamo City from the rest of Cuba, at great cost to the local inhabitants. Captain McCalla would later report that, though "the Spanish officers were well fed" at Guantánamo City, the "civilians were starving." Even the troops "had been without quinine for weeks and fifteen or twenty of them were dying every day" of malaria. An indication of just how cut off the towns of eastern Cuba were from one another is given in an Associated Press account of a pirate boat out of Baracoa inadvertently pulling into Guantánamo Bay in July. Apparently its crew had heard nothing of the American arrival.[77]

A graphic report out of Santiago, less isolated than Guantánamo City, conveys a sense of conditions throughout eastern Cuba at about the time the American army arrived. "In the stores many articles were wanting," observed José Muller y Tejeiro, a Spanish army lieutenant, in his diary late that June. There was no flour in Santiago, hence no baking and no bread. There was no milk, "indispensable for the sick and for babies." Though "music continued to play at the Alameda," Santiago's bayside promenade, there was nobody to listen to it, nobody to walk with, nothing to eat. Dead dogs and horses littered the streets, and the city gradually "acquired the stamp of sadness and absence of life which is seen in places into which cholera and plagues carry sorrow and death."[78]

A month later, reports out of Guantánamo City had become so dire that McCalla asked Admiral Sampson to urge his army counterpart, William Shafter, to hasten the work of the Spanish surrender so that food might be delivered to the city's starving inhabitants. In the end, McCalla decided he couldn't wait. Two days before the formal end of hostilities, he sent a launch up the bay waving a white flag and offering

Pareja flour and bacon captured off a Spanish vessel.[79] Sampson himself weighed in a few days later. "There are about 5,000 Spanish soldiers in Guantánamo and Caimanera, 1,700 [one third] of them sick," he wrote navy secretary Long. "There are political prisoners still in jail in Guantánamo [threatened by Sp Volunteers]; . . . steps should be taken in interest of sanitation and humanity." Reluctant to act without authorization, Sampson declared himself "most ready to assist, if desired."[80]

Sampson's and McCalla's willingness to come to the aid of local Cubans reflects the atmosphere of reciprocity and respect that characterized relations between U.S. naval officers and their Cuban counterparts at Guantánamo Bay in those early days of the war. By any measure, the Cuban-American cooperation at the bay had been a notable success. As Máximo Gómez anticipated, the U.S. encounter with the Cubans at Guantánamo Bay and elsewhere during the American intervention, and their accounts home of it, would play a crucial role in shaping U.S. public opinion about Cubans' propensity for self-government— and in determining U.S. policy toward Cuba in the aftermath of the war.

Initial reports were encouraging. After a meeting with the Cuban general in chief, Calixto García, aboard his flagship, *New York*, Admiral Sampson described García as man "of the most pleasant character. He is a large, handsome man, of most frank and engaging manners, and of most soldierly appearance." Arriving off Santiago de Cuba in late May, Sampson's fleet had distributed food, clothing, and weapons to the Cubans, besides "rendering them all assistance possible." Sampson assured Washington that "the returns" for the American aid would be good. "We have the best evidence of this in the activity and courage shown by the Cubans at Guantánamo, and commander McCalla has been most eulogistic in reference to their conduct."[81]

Huntington, if uncomplimentary in his private remarks, publicly praised the Cubans' contribution at Guantánamo Bay. "I suppose native Cubans are not all black," he wrote his son, Bobby, "but 99/100 in the part of the country are, and the average US cannot help regarding them as inferiors and while I do not doubt the wrongs of Cuba I doubt if it was a case for governmental interference unless we were going to take and keep the country."[82] Still, Huntington described the Cubans as "excellent woodsmen and fearless," and ultimately "of the greatest assistance."[83] And, though crediting the success of the assault on Cuzco to U.S. "coolness, skill, and bravery . . . alone," Huntington acknowledged that the "affair was planned by the Cubans," and that had it not been for their arrival at the bay, the demoralizing Spanish attacks on the U.S. camp "might be going on now."[84]

Meanwhile, Keeler himself described the Cubans as "all men of good size, some of them being over six feet in height." The Cubans were proud and appreciative of the warm reception extended them by Captain McCalla and Huntington's marines. "We were glad to see them," Keeler remembered. "It gave us courage when we were able to look upon those who we were fighting for."[85] Finally, even *The New York Times*, though skeptical early on in the war of the Cubans' competence, recognized virtue when it saw it. Evidence from Guantánamo suggested that the Cubans would be a big help in the coming ground war, the *Times* reported. "The insurgent forces, which have been armed and equipped by Capt. McCalla, not only prove to be daring scouts, but brave fighters and good shots with the Lee-Metford rifles. Our own men are warm in their praise, and look for unexpectedly strong co-operation upon the part of the Cuban Army." A day later, according to the *Times*, passengers on board a naval supply ship arriving in Key West reported that "100 Cubans had joined the United States marines when a landing was effected" at Guantánamo Bay. The Cubans had "fought gallantly and rendered great assistance to the Americans, their aid being specially valuable in the work of throwing up entrenchments. The American officers speak highly of the efficiency and bravery of the soldiers."[86]

How dissonant, then, seem the reports of Colonel Herbert H. Sargent, journalist Stephen Crane, and others of the Cuban Army's lack of discipline, professionalism, or commitment at Guantánamo Bay and elsewhere. Despite overwhelming evidence to the contrary, Sargent described Cuban contributions to the defeat of Spain at Santiago as negligible.[87] Cubans did not fight "with desperation and courage." They did not "take the initiative and lead the way in every battle," to

prove that they were "worthy of freedom." Rather, "in only two ways were they of any assistance in this campaign": in providing information and in harassing the Spanish general Federico Escario's column outside Santiago. In short, "taken as a whole, they had neither the discipline nor the courage to close with the enemy and fight until one side or the other was defeated or crushed." García's troops, earlier commended by Sampson, were now reported to have "utterly failed to perform the easy task assigned them." While the fate of Cuba was up in the air, "they stood by, inefficient, inactive. The reward was theirs, but the Americans made the sacrifice."[88]

Sargent's book was not published until 1907, long after the fate of independent Cuba had been sealed in the United States. But there was no shortage of opinion like it in the eyewitness accounts of Stephen Crane and other journalists. In contrast to the sturdy, competent figures of Sampson's and Keeler's accounts, Crane's Cubans were undisciplined and "noisy," "a hard-bitten, undersized lot, most of them negroes, and with the stoop and curious gait of men who had at one time labored in the soil." From Crane's descriptions of the Cubans, one might have gotten the impression that it was they, rather than the Americans, who were joining a contest already three years old, so radically did their dishevelment contrast with the U.S. Marines' noble bearing.[89] "The marines were silent," Crane wrote; "the Cubans were cursing shrilly." In Crane's accounts "toiling, sweating marines" were juxtaposed to "shrill, jumping Cubans." The Cubans were bad shooters: "The Cubans, who cannot hit even the wide, wide world, lapsed into momentary peace."[90] By contrast, "the firing-drill of the marines was splendid. The men reloaded and got up their guns like lightning, but afterwards there was always a rock-like poise as the aim was taken. One noticed it more on account of the Cubans, who used the Lee as if it were a squirt-gun."[91]

Cuban officers were no better than the rank and file. "The entire function of the lieutenant who commanded them in action was to stand back of the line, frenziedly beat his machete through the air, and with incredible rapidity howl: 'Fuego! fuego! fuego! fuego!' He could not possibly have taken time to breathe during the action. His men were meanwhile screaming the most horrible language in a babble."[92] As for daring, that's another matter. Like savages, the Cubans "paid no heed whatever to the Spaniards' volleys, but simply lashed themselves into a delirium that disdained everything."

Crane had counterparts at other papers. One pool reporter described the Cubans' behavior after the allied victory at Cuzco well. "The easy victory put the command in high spirits. The Little Black Cuban warriors waved their machetes and howled curses at the Spaniards in savage fashion. Their firing had been wild throughout, but they all displayed the utmost contempt for the Spanish bullets, apparently being absolutely without fear."[93] Unable and unwilling to secure their own independence, in American eyes, these Cubans were unfit for self-government—just as Gómez had feared.

Discounting the Cubans' contributions to the defeat of Spain, the United States could write Cuba out of the picture. On July 4, 1898, America's Independence Day, Frank Keeler lay at picket duty on a hillside overlooking the outer harbor. Below him, spread out across the water, was arguably the largest collection of U.S. warships ever convened in a single place. "Fifty-five vessels of every description" sat at anchor in the bay, Keeler recalled in his war diary, most of them "fighting ships of the latest type."[94] The fleet had come to Guantánamo for fuel, repair, and, on this day, celebration. The previous day, the U.S. fleet smashed its Spanish adversary off Santiago Harbor, ending a six-week blockade, demonstrating the primacy of U.S. naval power in the region, and virtually ensuring a U.S. victory over Spain.

A mix of motivations had compelled the United States to intervene in the Cuban War of Independence that spring. Some Americans regarded intervention as an opportunity finally to rid the New World of Spanish rule. Some viewed intervention as a means of protecting and promoting U.S. business interests in Cuba. Some saw it as a way to expand U.S. military and commercial influence in the Western Hemisphere. Some, as the only course of action befitting a liberty-loving people in the face of Spain's trampling of Cuban rights. Many Americans held to several or all of these convictions in combination.

Yet, on a day that suggested that Cuba's century-long dream of independence might at long last come true, it was American independence that the navy celebrated at Guantánamo Bay, as if it were the Monroe Doctrine that had been ratified off Santiago Harbor. The display the U.S. fleet put on this Fourth of July "was one of the grandest sights . . . that had ever been witnessed in Cuban waters," Keeler remembered. Just yesterday, these fifty-five warships "had been fighting dogs and had won a victory. Today they were dressed in gala attire, decorated with every bit of bunting on the ship." Begun at noon, the celebration would last throughout the night. At nightfall, "the beautiful sight of the day was surpassed by the electrical display. The big marine battle was over, the celebration was allowable. The thousands of lights on the ships gave them the appearance of a wonderful city that had sprung up from the unknown depths." Only the enthusiastic ribbing by a fellow picket detracted from what Keeler remembered as one of the great pleasures of his life.

But his reverie "didn't or couldn't last." The rising sun revealed the city sunk beneath the waves. In its place, warships: the United States had come to Guantánamo to stay.

4

★

A CRUEL AND AWFUL TRUTH

"I have no doubt," Calixto García wrote to the exiled head of the Cuban Revolutionary Party, "that before the campaign ends, all the people of the United States will be convinced that we do not lack the conditions to govern ourselves."[1] This proved wishful thinking. On July 17, Spain surrendered Santiago to the Americans. On what might have been a day of joyous celebration among victorious allies, Shafter refused to let the Cubans take part in the surrender. When the Cubans complained, the Associated Press ridiculed their disappointment at not having had Santiago "turned over to them to loot and plunder, as they had in succession sacked Daiquiri, Siboney, and El Caney"—none of which was true.

García's son, Brigadier General Carlos García Vélez, remembered a deep sense of foreboding suffusing the Cuban ranks upon learning of Shafter's snubbing of their boss. Just three days before, "the news of the capitulation of Santiago spread about the camps with shouts of joy." Now joy yielded to bewilderment as Cubans "were absolutely excluded from all participation in the surrender of the city." After an "imposing" conversation with Shafter, García spent the night in solitude, so overcome by "apprehensions of the future" that he dared not appear before his men. How could he disclose "the cruel and awful truth . . . that our allies of yesterday with whom we had so willingly and nobly cooperated to overthrow the enemy, not needing our ser-

vices further, had pushed us aside?" As disbelief gave way to "excitement," only García's "extraordinary diplomacy" defused a "dangerous
situation."[2]

García's diplomacy was on full display in a letter to General Shafter
protesting his mistreatment just as the American flag rose over Santiago. Ordered the preceding May to assist the Americans, García had
done his level best. "Until now," he wrote Shafter, "I have been . . . one
of your most faithful subordinates, honoring myself in carrying out
your orders as far as my powers have allowed." Yet, when Santiago fell,
García received news of the event from "persons entirely foreign" to
Shafter's staff. Shafter did not so much as honor García with a "kind
word," inviting him "to represent the Cuban army on that memorable
occasion." Worse, Shafter had left in charge of Santiago the very Spanish officials whom García had been fighting for three years as "enemies
of the independence of Cuba"—officials, García noted, originally appointed by "the Queen of Spain."

García had fully expected the Americans to have "taken possession
of the city, the garrison and forts"; he expected to cooperate with
Shafter to preserve order until the time came for the United States to
fulfill its pledge to "establish in Cuba a free and independent government." What could explain this turn of events? "A rumor too absurd to
be believed," García wrote, "describes the reason of your measures
and of the orders forbidding my army to enter Santiago for fear of massacres and revenge against the Spanish. Allow me, sir, to protest against
even the shadow of such an idea. We are not savages ignoring the rules
of civilized warfare. We are a poor, ragged army, as ragged and poor as
was the army of your forefathers in their noble war of independence,
but like the heroes of Saratoga and Yorktown, we respect our cause too
deeply to disgrace it with barbarism and cowardice."

Referring to Saratoga and Yorktown, García challenged Shafter to
imagine how American patriots would have felt had the French, having
intervened in the American Revolution, refused to allow the Americans to attend the British surrender. Rather than submit to the indig-
nity, García resigned his commission as commander of Cuban forces
at Santiago and rode off over the mountains to continue the fight at
Jiguaní.[3]

Shafter's treatment of García was only the first in a long series of

humiliations that the United States visited on Cuba in the aftermath
of the Cuban War of Independence as it tried to reconcile its pledge,
as stated in the Teller Amendment, "to leave the government and control of the island to its people" with the centuries-old conviction that
Cuba was essential to the security and prosperity of the United States.
More than the fate of Cuba was at stake here. The defeat of Spain
compelled the United States to confront the tension between its liberal, universal principles and its self-interest. Whether and how it resolved this dilemma would determine not only U.S.-Cuban relations
but also U.S. relations with independent (often weaker) nation-states
throughout the hemisphere and, indeed, the world. Guantánamo Bay
figured crucially in these negotiations. Despite the strong objection of
Cuba, the Americans retained Guantánamo Bay in the aftermath of
the war both as an instrument of control over a nominally independent
Cuba and as a base of U.S. influence in Latin America.

In the autumn of 1898, the United States recapitulated Shafter's snubbing of García on a grand scale. As American and Spanish officials
descended on Paris in early October to work out the details of the
transfer of Spanish sovereignty over Cuba and its other colonial possessions to the United States, not a single Cuban representative could
be spotted in their midst. Like Shafter before it, the U.S. government
simply assumed that Cuba had no role to play in negotiations with
Spain. The next year, as if acknowledging the appearance of unfair-
ness, U.S. secretary of war Elihu B. Root justified Cuba's exclusion
from the peace talks by appealing to the conventions of international
law. "I assume," Root wrote in his annual report, "that all acquisition
of territory under this treaty was the exercise of a power which belonged to the United States, because it was a nation, and for that
reason was endowed with the powers essential to national life."

In the face of international law, García's faith in American support
for Cuban independence appears, in retrospect, quaint. Spain's former colonies were "subject to the complete sovereignty" of the United
States, Root continued; the United States was "controlled by no legal
limitations except those which may be found in the treaty of cession"
between the United States and Spain. America's new possessions

had "no right to [be] treated as states, or to [be] treated as the territories previously held by the United States have been treated." Cubans possessed certain "moral rights," Root acknowledged, among them, the right to be treated "in accordance with the underlying principles of justice and freedom which we have declared in our Constitution."[4]

In justifying the U.S. treatment of Cuba, Root reached back to arguments developed over the course of the preceding century regarding Native Americans. As early as 1834, U.S. Supreme Court chief justice John Marshall referred to American Indians, once considered independent nations with whom the United States negotiated treaties, as "pupils" and "wards" of the state. A succession of Supreme Court cases throughout the second half of the nineteenth century confirmed Indians' dependent status, ultimately re-creating tribes as colonial subjects beneath the sovereignty of the United States.[5]

Like Native American nations before them, Cubans found it difficult to square the U.S. commitment to justice and freedom with the fact of American domination. "There is so much natural anger and grief throughout the island," Máximo Gómez noted in his diary in January 1899, "that the people haven't really been able to celebrate the triumph of the end of their former rulers' power." Gómez thought the U.S. military occupation "too high a price to pay for [America's] spontaneous intervention in the war we waged against Spain for freedom and independence." The occupation was "dangerous for the country, mortifying the public spirit and hindering organization in all the branches that, from the outset, should provide solid foundations of the future republic, when everything was entirely the work of all the inhabitants of the island, without distinction of nationality."

American officials dismissed Cuban calls for immediate independence as irrational. Gómez wondered what could be "more rational and fair" than that the owner of a house "be the one to live in it with his family and be the one who furnishes and decorates it as he likes and that he not be forced against his will and inclination to follow the norms and dictates imposed by his neighbor?" Cuba could never have true "moral peace" under a transitional government dominated by the Americans. Imposed by force, such peace was plainly "illegitimate and incompatible with the principles that the entire country has been upholding for so long and in the defense of which half of its sons have given their lives and all of its wealth had been consumed." U.S. bullying of Cuba was sure to extinguish "the last spark of goodwill" between the two peoples.[6]

Cuba's grief contrasted markedly with the triumphalism suffusing the United States as the war drew to a close. The defeat of Spain, the occupation of Cuba, and the annexation of Puerto Rico, Hawaii, Guam, and the Philippines transformed the United States into a global power seemingly overnight. In the public response to these developments, familiar themes of commercial expansion, Manifest Destiny, and empire for liberty took on global dimensions.

"We have just emerged from a short, but momentous war," the educator, editor, and now U.S. postmaster general Charles Emory Smith told an audience at the Chicago Peace Jubilee in October 1898. The war's "transcendent events have spanned the whole wide horizon of this world, and have unveiled a new destiny for this country."[7] The United States had "taken a new position in the great family of nations," had "stepped out upon the broad stage of the world's action," becoming one of its undeniable powers. Not only had the rest of the world learned something new about the young republic, but Americans were coming to appreciate themselves in a new way. War had united North and South, prairie and brownstone, in common cause to uphold the flag and promote a renewed sense of "our national possibilities and national greatness."[8]

To Walter Hines Page, editor of the *Atlantic Monthly*, the U.S. victory over Spain promised to transform a century's talk about liberty and empire into a world historical project. Americans stood "face to face with the sort of problems that have grown up in the management of world-empires," Page marveled. The only question was how Americans would react. Would they "be content with peaceful industry" and their increasingly "indoor life"? Or did there yet "lurk in us the adventurous spirit of our Anglo-Saxon forefathers?" With "no more great enterprises awaiting us at home," it was only natural that Americans should "seek them abroad"—not in wars of conquest, Page cautioned,

but in redeeming Anglo-American civilization from European deca-
dence. American would open the Orient to Western principles and
commerce, thus effecting "one of the greatest changes in human
history."[9]

Like Page, John Henry Barrows, president of Oberlin College, regarded the nation's new colonies as stepping-stones, which, by transporting American institutions to Asia, would thereby "unitize" the
world. To be sure, U.S. interests would be served by the conquest of
Asia; but so, too, would Asian and above all *human* interests. Commerce and liberty were but two sides of a coin whose universal allure
would speed the U.S. "penetration" and "control" of West and East
Indies alike. The twentieth century would be an American century,
Barrows predicted, with U.S. scholars, missionaries, teachers, books,
and businesses overrunning the world. But these were but the means
to the next millennium and a still greater end: "an empire of peace"
with "representatives of brotherly nations" cooperating in "the new
parliament of man."[10]

More than merely compatible, civil liberty, commerce, and American empire were ultimately indistinguishable, according to Chicago
lawyer and businessman Franklin MacVeagh. In America, MacVeagh
insisted, empire found its ideal vehicle: a free and restless workforce
combined with unprecedented natural abundance; here, finally, were
the sources of "universal relations between our nation and the whole
of mankind." The new century would see "no seas without American
ships, and no ports without American goods carried there under our
own flag." Thoughts of America isolating itself had become outdated.
The nation would be great, MacVeagh announced, and "greatness is
interested in all related great things; greatness has relationships, responsibilities, duties, which are on the scale of its own proportions."
Greatness implied involvement "in the activities of all the world together." Like Barrows, MacVeagh viewed America's new empire as the
means to a universal end. The choice Americans confronted was not
between colonies or no colonies; it was between peace or war, cooperation
or conquest, civilization or chaos. The world need not fear. The nation
would remain "the exemplar of free government, the hope of social
progress, and the powerful friend of the oppressed."[11]

All that was missing was God. John Ireland, archbishop of St. Paul, Minnesota, differed from his compatriots only in emphasis by describing the U.S. victory over Spain as "a momentous dispensation from the Master of Men." According to Ireland, the war heralded the arrival of the universal nation to which "no world-interest" was "alien." Our "spirit travels across the seas and mountain ranges to most distant continents and islands." Territories, shipping, conquest—these were but the instruments of democracy, liberty, and self-government. Where these ideals ruled, there America ruled; where they were "not held supreme, America has not reached." Ireland confessed awe, even a certain trepidation, in contemplating the nation's new responsibility "to God and to humanity." America, he warned, "thou failing, democracy and liberty will fail."[12]

The strains of argument on display here—the sense of a new day dawning, the sense of a need for strenuous projects to replace the vanishing American frontier, the sense of commerce as the agent of global harmony, the sense of expansion as divine duty—achieved apotheosis in the speeches and writing of Indiana senator Albert Beveridge. Even more than Theodore Roosevelt, Beveridge emerged as the nation's leading imperial propagandist. Just days after the United States declared war on Spain, Beveridge challenged an audience at Boston's exclusive Middlesex Club to distinguish "events," "the arguments of God," from "words," "the arguments of man." With their liberal principles and economic institutions, Americans were "the allies of events and the comrades of tendency in the great day of which the dawn is breaking." Embarked on its new "imperial career," the United States would harness untapped labor, idle capital, and congealed industry around the world to save civilization and redeem humanity.[13] The nation's power, principles, and divine sanction authorized the United States to go out into the world, Beveridge told an Indiana audience later the same fall. To be sure, by opening new markets to American farmers and factories, and by securing new resources for American manufactures, the nation was destined to dominate "the imperial trade of the entire world." But it would do so in a public manner befitting "the sovereign power of the earth."[14]

Not all Americans were as sanguine as Beveridge and the others about the implications of the U.S. victory over Spain. To William Jennings Bryan, the Democratic Party presidential candidate in 1896 and a veteran of the recent war, the prospect of empire represented a radical departure from a century of republican rectitude. U.S. victory over Spain left the nation on the horns of a grave dilemma, Bryan warned an audience convened to commemorate George Washington's birthday in February 1899. "The ancient doctrine of imperialism, banished from our land more than a century ago, has recrossed the Atlantic and challenged democracy to mortal combat upon American soil." The founding fathers had aimed to secure liberty for themselves and their posterity despite regional and economic differences; their successors upheld "self-government as the controlling national idea" and avoided "entangling alliances." Sure in their understanding of their neighbor to the north, Cubans had appealed to the United States to free them from Spanish tyranny, and in the name of liberty and self-government Americans had done so. "Have the people so changed within a few short months," Bryan wondered, that they would now force on others the "system of government against which the colonists protested with fire and sword?" Surely, this was not what America was about.

What America was about, Bryan insisted, was the selfless promotion of liberty and prosperity. A product of all the world's great civilizations combined, the United States had transcended them all—and, indeed, transcended nationhood itself. "During its brief existence it has exerted upon the human race an influence more potent for good than all the other nations of the earth combined, and it has exerted that influence without use of sword or Gatling gun." Where "Anglo-Saxon civilization has taught the individual to protect his own rights, American civilization will teach him to respect the rights of others." Where the former taught self-interest, the latter will propagate the commandment "Thou shall love thy neighbor as thyself."[15]

Ostensibly Bryan differed markedly from proponents of American imperialism. But his "love thy neighbor as thyself" bears striking resemblance to the universalism of his imperialist counterparts, whose logic blinded Americans to the prospect that theirs was not the only way to decorate a house, as Gómez put it, that justice, liberty, and self-government could take different forms in different places according to local customs and conditions. Only by learning to love their neighbors on their neighbors' own terms could Americans promote the ends of true self-determination and self-government that Bryan ostensibly defended.

It has taken a century or more for the apologists of American empire to begin to come to terms with the alienating effects of U.S. triumphalism on global sentiment. Slower still has been the ability of liberals such as Bryan to acknowledge that the nineteenth-century America they mythologized differed little in its logic from the imperialism they opposed. Only by ignoring the insatiable appetite for land, markets, and resources of a liberal political economy, only by overlooking the conquest of a continent (never mind a century of saber rattling over Cuba), could Bryan make the claim that Americans had intervened in Cuba simply "to aid a neighboring people, struggling to be free." With friends like Bryan, Cuba needed no enemies. One way or the other, the Americans would come. Cubans had plenty to say about the Americans' arrival, but their protests went largely unheard in a nation swaying to the two-part harmony of imperialism and anti-imperialism.

Though few of these men exercised political power, their views were shared by those who directed U.S.-Cuban policy in the aftermath of the Spanish-American War. In the spring of 1907, for example, future president Woodrow Wilson (still celebrated today as a man of peace) observed that "since trade ignored national boundaries and the manufacturer insists on having the world as a market, the flag of his nation must follow him, and the door of the nations which are closed to him must be battered down." It was the duty of elected officials to ensure that "concessions obtained by financiers . . . be safeguarded . . . even if the sovereignty of unwilling nations be outraged in the process," Wilson argued. "Colonies must be obtained or planted, in order that no useful corner of the world may be overlooked or left unused."[16]

Against this backdrop, U.S. control over Cuba and the retaining of Guantánamo Bay was inevitable, notwithstanding the Teller Amendment. Cuban independence would be tolerated to the extent that it was consistent with U.S. interests. Only the details remained to be worked out. As Gómez feared and García experienced firsthand, this process of adjusting Cuban expectations to U.S. norms began long before the war was over. After the war, proponents of U.S. control over

Cuba made their case in earnest, first insisting that Cubans were unfit for self-government, then arguing that American control over Cuba was fully consistent with the pledge of the Teller Amendment to leave Cuba to its own devices.

The armistice brought no end to the contest to define the Cuban people in terms suitable to U.S. aims. Unusual only in its detail is the report of *Boston Herald* journalist Herbert Pelham Williams published by Page's *Atlantic Monthly* in June 1899. After the war, Williams walked from Santiago de Cuba to Havana, a distance of some six hundred miles, in order to get a feel for the state of the country. Hence Williams claimed to be something of an authority on Cuban conditions and Cubans' character.

Above all, Williams began, Americans must face the fact that Cubans were essentially "'children.' The word describes them almost exactly. Ignorance, delight in seeing or owning pretty trifles, curiosity, the tendency to tell an untruth whenever telling the truth may have unpleasant results, cruelty, wanton destruction of inanimate things which have obstacles in their path, fondness for personal adornment, intense desire for praise, and a weakness for showing off,—these are the attributes of children." As such, Cubans needed nothing so much as a firm hand. Unfortunately, U.S. policy in Cuba had been anything but firm, thanks in part to Teller. As a result, Cubans responded as children would: pursuing their selfish interests without any concern for the greater good.[17]

Yet all was not lost. Children were pliant, and Cubans "malleable to a surprising degree," Williams observed. "Like children and unlike savages, almost anything can be made of them." This only made a firm and consistent U.S. policy all the more imperative. "Under suitable government, education, treatment, and guidance," Cubans might be "developed and uplifted to an extent amounting to transformation." Indeed, so "extreme" was their "teachableness, and their quickness to adopt new habits of mind and action" that Williams thought it "not impossible" that Cubans might one day "be fit for citizenship."

But first, several Cuban characteristics would have to be expunged. One was Cubans' "cheerful contentment," one of their "worst traits."

Contented people, everybody knows, make bad capitalists and worse
laborers. So contented were Cubans in their daily lives that they never
ventured beyond "two or three leagues" (eight to twelve miles) from
home, thus disqualifying themselves as a mobile workforce. Another
salient characteristic of Cubans was their propensity to lie. "It is often
hard to tell whether a Cuban lies to you from ignorance or from mal-
ice," Williams observed. "Here the absence of a moral sense becomes
apparent. With the Cuban, lying is a matter, not of right, but of policy,
his shortsightedness preventing him from perceiving that to-day's advantage may be tomorrow's loss"—again, not the stuff of contracts.[18]

If Cubans' childlikeness, contentment, and shortsightedness made
them dubious material for capitalism, hadn't they at least earned the
right of self-rule by fighting for it? "It is generally admitted," wrote one
critic of U.S. colonialism, "that a people who fight strenuously for liberty against powerful oppressors deserve to obtain it; and that such a
people should be presumed, till the contrary is proved, to be fit to possess it."[19] This is perhaps so as a general principle, Williams argued,
but not in the case of Cuba, where Cubans' descriptions of their military feats and "the glorious victories of their somewhat mythical army,"
while not "intentional, deliberate, cold-blooded lies," were nonetheless "monstrous inventions." Intolerably vain, Cubans were susceptible to the notion "that there was once a band of men worthy to be
called a Cuban army, and that they fought battles." In reality, "there
were merely little companies of starving stragglers, who sometimes
fired their two cartridges apiece from ambush at Spanish scouting parties, and then scattered." Then again, Cubans' refusal to confront the
Spaniards in open battle was only to be expected in a people "to some
degree like a race of slaves."[20]

Clinical in his dismantling of Cuban character, Williams attributed
it to Spanish rule, thus leaving open Cuba's future, at least a crack.
Cubans would have to quit their misbehavior and banish their ingratitude, both of which frustrated the "disinterested" Americans. Above
all, Cubans would have to get to work. Sounding much like the conquistadors who preceded him by four centuries, Williams couldn't
imagine why unemployed men would eschew jobs in the mines of the
Guantánamo Basin, for example. "Left to themselves, the Cubans

would never develop their country,—not in centuries." It wasn't so much that Cubans were "shiftless; every man of them can shift for himself so long as he stays in the country. The trouble is that it is so easy to get along and have plenty to eat without doing much work." Such a people might make "good servants," but they could not be expected "to be masters of themselves or of anybody else."

Good Cubans knew this. Indeed, Williams insisted, all Cubans "whose convictions deserve respect"—namely, merchants, shopkeepers, and men of property—earnestly advocated "permanent American control" of the country. Only the "half-barbarous rabble," many of them "negroes," still clung "to the old fetish of 'Cuba Libre.'" If America sailed away, the latter would murder the former, just as García and his men had allegedly desired to do to the Spanish at the conclusion of the war. By contrast to the Cubans, the Spanish enemy in Cuba possessed all the capitalist virtues. Spaniards were "men of honesty, industry, and stamina, [who] kept the stores and owned most of the property." Here was material Americans could work with. Cubans, on the other hand? "Cuba under a republic would be a very unsatisfactory place to Americans."[21]

It was the job of Major General Leonard Wood, military governor of Santiago province from 1899 to 1900, and of Cuba generally between 1900 and 1902, to make republican Cuba *satisfactory* to U.S. economic interests. Wood interpreted this challenge much the way his Spanish predecessors had: transforming Cubans into a disciplined and compliant workforce. In an essay published in the journal *North American Review* in May 1899, Wood described the steps he was taking in Santiago province to prepare the local population (30 percent of whom were black or "colored," and whom Williams would describe as "scum, the refuse of the island"[22]) not so much for self-government as for contract labor. In transforming Cubans into a labor force, Wood was aided greatly by the widespread poverty that pervaded the region even before the Americans arrived. "The condition of the people in Cuba today is one of extreme poverty, and in many provinces great suffering for want of food," Wood reported. He denied the charges of Williams and others that the Cubans were too lazy to work. On the contrary, he noted, Cubans "are not only willing but anxious to work. The problem has never

been one of finding workers, but of giving work to those who wished it."
Throughout Santiago province, and indeed the entire country, every
element of infrastructure needed rebuilding, from highways and railroads to bridges and telegraph lines, villages and towns, schools and
municipal lines, water and sewer facilities. "Great sections" of the country had "been absolutely destroyed by war."[23]

Sympathetic to Cuba's plight, Wood recognized an opportunity.
Not a penny would he waste on food that had not been earned through
labor or on projects unrelated to public infrastructure. Cuba was to be
made safe for business. "We have been able to open up many of the
main roads, put the towns in order, and, in fact, scatter the people over
the country in honest labor on public works, in return for which they
have received either a daily wage of seventy-five cents or fifty cents
and a ration." To regions of the province suffering, like Guantánamo,
from "great destitution," Wood dispatched his officials "with money
and authority to start needed public works." The net effect of these
interventions was a people "gone back to work in one way or another."
Cubans remained "desperately poor," but Wood's staff reported "no
starvation, and, generally speaking, a quiet, contented condition of the
people."[24]

What accounted for Wood's success? The trick, he explained, was
to provide the Cubans with "only just enough to make it possible for
the people to re-establish themselves upon the most economical basis."
Economy was everything to Wood and the Americans, both an end in
itself and the means to the end. There was no incentive like scarcity.
"Economy has been insisted on, and it has been impressed upon them
that, no matter how limited their income may be, they must try to adapt
themselves to it." The lesson seemed to be having the desired effect.
Rather than these policies being "narrowing, they have had a very beneficial effect on the people, who are beginning to realize that there is a
certain satisfaction and independence to be gained by paying their own
way." Such policies could not help but produce "permanent good results." Doubters had only to consult U.S. history to recall that "some of
our best and ablest men have sprung from the very poorest families,
and their development under conditions of the greatest hardships and
adversity has tended to foster the very qualities which have made them

successful in later life." In postwar Cuba, putting food on the table constituted the strenuous life.[25]

You want order in Cuba? Wood demanded. Create "an army of workmen." Give men work, pay them leanly, steer them toward tasks of "public character," and you will "open the country once more to commerce." Of course, Cuba needed supporting institutions—education based on "our own system" ("intelligent and uniformly progressive methods of teaching"). Municipal government, too. Sounding much like the Frenchman Alexis de Tocqueville describing American democracy in the 1830s, Wood praised local Cuban governments not so much for their efficiency as for the habits self-government instilled. "Of course, we cannot expect a people who have never had a hand in governing themselves, to take hold of the situation with the same grasp and clearness which we should expect [from ourselves]."[26] But Cubans were doing quite nicely, given the recent war. Though they remained intemperate and emotional, the Cubans would succeed, Wood concluded, and America "would give up control of [Cuban] affairs."[27]

Compared with Williams's denigration of the Cuban character, Wood's report of stability and order in postwar Santiago province comes as a relief. But Cubans themselves scarcely recognized the country that Wood described. Most Cubans did not want to be "Americanized," as Wood suggested in *Century Magazine* in August 1899. Nor did they see themselves as needy recipients of American "gifts" such as "honest government." Nor did they think they lacked virtues conducive to "self-government and control."[28] Indeed, Horatio Rubens, American counsel to the Cuban Revolutionary Party, asked in April 1898 how, if Cubans were so bereft of virtue, intelligence, leadership, and discipline, had they managed to bring Spain to its knees just as the United States joined the war?

Writing in the *North American Review*, Rubens aimed to familiarize American readers to the Cuban campaign for independence and to counter the assertions of Edwin Atkins and others that the movement was essentially an oversized race riot confined mostly to the east. Such was not at all the case, Rubens explained. "Professionals and businessmen, engineers, and men of leisure flocked from the cities to the insurgent standard, leaving their families behind them. The country people applied for admission to the ranks in great numbers, until the leaders decided to take no man unless he could be armed with a rifle."[29] From the first, the revolutionary movement was characterized by professionalism and organization. During the first year of the war, provincial delegates adopted a constitution and elected officers of the revolutionary government for a term of two years. President and vice president met in council with secretaries of war, foreign affairs, treasury, and the interior. Undersecretaries and provincial governors were also appointed, and the island was divided into administrative districts of local self-government called prefectures.[30]

A common argument in the United States against an independent Cuba was that it would inevitably become indebted to other (i.e., European) countries, thus inviting foreign intervention in Cuban affairs detrimental to U.S. interests. Rubens insisted that long before the United States joined the war, the Cuban revolutionary government had anticipated this danger, taking "the utmost care" to "avoid the creation of liabilities." Another argument favored by opponents of Cuban independence was that Cuba, so long ground beneath the yoke of Spanish tyranny, could not comprehend the mechanisms of self-government. Again, not so, Rubens reported. In revolutionary Cuba, not only was the military "subordinate to the civil government," but a carefully adjusted pay scale provided for "the speedy disbandment of the army when the war ends, by enabling its members to return immediately to their peaceful pursuits, and placing a considerable sum in circulation." After the war, the revolutionary government expected to have to borrow money to disperse tools and agricultural implements among the population; it foresaw no difficulty in this regard, "as the credit of the island had been kept unpledged."[31]

The revolutionary government proved itself a government of laws, not men, in the autumn of 1897, electing a new executive and assembly as stipulated by the constitution. It also took steps to ensure a smooth transition to peacetime, mandating "an immediate general election of a new government" by universal male suffrage. To U.S. skeptics who doubted the stability of a government forced by exigency to move its capital during the war, Rubens countered with the reminder that "our own revolutionary government" similarly had been forced to move its headquarters during the American Revolution.

Moreover, Cuba's government moved not for safety reasons but for logistics: in order to expedite conferences between the military and political leadership.[32]

Cultural institutions—newspapers, schools, political societies—the revolutionary government boasted too, especially in the east, where revolutionary control was total but for a few cities and towns. On and on Rubens went: Was it the guerilla tactics that bothered skeptics? Those General Gómez had adopted out of necessity, facing an army outnumbering him five to one. Were Cuban leaders untutored? They had successfully employed tactics used by the German cavalry in the Franco-Prussian War.[33] It was not Cubans who had demonstrated incompetence but Spain. By the time the United States joined the war, Spain's army was demoralized, physically and psychologically; its "struggle to retain Cuba had been gigantic," Rubens remarked, "but it has been badly directed." By contrast, Cubans had demonstrated "good judgment in retaining and husbanding" scarce resources and in exploiting their enemy's weaknesses. A "people capable of such organization, civil and military, and of fighting a European power to a standstill," or better, "without a navy and at first utterly unarmed, have surely given sufficient promise of capability of self-government."[34]

In his diary entry of January 1899, Máximo Gómez lamented that the U.S. expropriation of Cuba's victory over Spain had robbed Cubans and Spaniards alike of the opportunity to part respectfully. "I had dreamed of peace with Spain," Gómez wrote; "I hoped to bid farewell with respect to the brave Spanish soldiers with whom we always met, face to face, on the field of battle. The words peace and freedom should inspire only love and fraternity on the morning of concord between those who were combatants the night before; but, with their guardianship imposed by force, the Americans have turned the Cubans' victorious joy to bitterness and haven't sweetened the grief of the vanquished."[35]

Graver still, the Americans' treatment of the Cuban forces deprived them of a sense of closure. What should the Cubans make of an armistice concluded entirely without their consent? So long as it looked like Cubans had merely exchanged one set of rulers for another, in what sense could this war truly be declared over? In the Guantánamo region, the traditional bastion of Cuban radicalism, many Cuban soldiers concluded that the war was not over, and for months after the armistice that August something less than peace pervaded the region. In early October 1898, General Calixto García, commander of Cuban forces in the east, refused to recognize the legitimacy of the U.S. military government, thus leading hundreds of his former soldiers to refuse to surrender their arms.[36] A week later, Máximo Gómez, García's boss, resigned his commission as general in chief of Cuban forces in protest of the revolutionary authorities' passive submission to U.S. military occupation of Santiago province. Only under pressure from colleagues in the revolutionary government did Gómez and García agree to urge their junior colleagues at Guantánamo Bay to disarm. Many of the Cuban soldiers hadn't been paid, and there was talk among the Americans of exchanging guns for money.[37]

Pedro Pérez was among the last Cuban generals to capitulate at Guantánamo. Through October and into November, he refused to disband his army, unsettling both U.S. military officials and local planters, who hoped to salvage what little they might of the year's crops. Only the intervention of Leonard Wood defused a tense situation. Pérez wanted a concession from the Americans to allow his men to retain their weapons in exchange for service as a provincial police force. Wood denied the request but appointed Pérez mayor of Guantánamo City, while dispatching food to his hungry men.[38] When Calixto García, the most irreconcilable of Cuba's generals, died unexpectedly while on a trip to Washington, D.C., in early December, high-level resistance to the U.S. occupation came to an end.

Yet disgruntlement smoldered in the Guantánamo region into the next year. By Christmas 1898, it had been given a name: Francisco Valiente, a colonel in García's ranks. This Cuban Robin Hood was said to be leading a band of not-so-merry men on the outskirts of Guantánamo City, terrorizing local planters and bringing to a standstill what little cane grinding occurred. Only the arrival of U.S. troops led by Colonel Henry Ray allowed the grinding to resume. U.S. troops stayed around to guard some twenty-three plantations around Guantánamo alone as Ray remained perplexed by the Cubans' motivations.[39] Leonard Wood, then military governor of Santiago province, thought that

Ray exaggerated both the number and the significance of the Cuban brigands.[40] Still, the Americans had an answer to Valiente and his associates: "They will be followed by a force of cavalry and persistently pursued," readers of the (Portland) *Morning Oregonian* were assured. "The same general method will be observed as has been followed in dealing with the Indians on the plains and mountains of the West." Valiente and his followers would be "cured" of their recalcitrance; it was just a matter of time.[41]

While the U.S. Army maintained a fragile peace in the interior, the U.S. Navy continued to use and enjoy Guantánamo Bay. Beginning in the spring of 1899 and continuing through the summer, the USS *Eagle* made Guantánamo Bay its home, charting the harbor and nearby Cuban waters without arousing local passions. In February 1902, Rear Admiral Francis Higginson led his Atlantic squadron into Guantánamo Bay, where he found fellow officer Robley Evans, captain of the USS *Iowa*, ensconced at the bay in the company of a band of U.S. cavalry and "some very fine horses." Evidently, the Americans had the run of the place. "We were very well received at Guantánamo," Higginson assured Leonard Wood. "We visited Guantánamo [City] also Soledad"— a large U.S. sugar estate—"and saw the sugar mills, and then to Mrs. Brooks' orphan school where they sang for us. The next day we had all the children aboard the *Kearsage* [the commander's headquarters at the bay] where the band played for them. They played games and sang, and had a most delightful time."[42]

The prospect of acquiring the bay from Cuba and converting it to a U.S. base continued to delight naval officers, Higginson assured Wood. Higginson himself was "impatient to see the work commence there. Strategically it is without price," he observed, "covering routes to the Isthmus, and tactically there is nothing I have seen equal to it—possessing a large exterior harbor for vessels and an interior one for the location of docks and machine shops, with narrow passages separating the two basins quite capable of efficient defense." Higginson lamented that the navy was not in a position where it could petition Congress for a million dollars to begin work at once. The only challenge that he foresaw concerned the question of "how much land around the water and how far back from the edge of the water [the navy should] ask for."[43]

The U.S. military occupation of Cuba formally began on January 1, 1899. For the first year and a half, the United States concentrated its efforts on curbing disease, improving sanitation, creating municipal governments, rebuilding infrastructure, building schools, and generally repairing the damage inflicted by a relatively short but brutal three-year war that had torn the country apart. Though no U.S. law restrained the McKinley administration from recognizing the Cuban revolutionary government at the conclusion of the war and transferring authority to it, the United States waited nearly two years before convening a Cuban constitutional convention. Leonard Wood, promoted to military governor of Cuba in 1899, consistently delivered only the rosiest accounts of U.S.-Cuban relations during the military occupation. By contrast, U.S. and Cuban journalists reported mounting Cuban frustration at U.S. policy virtually from the beginning. Looking back on the first two years of the U.S. occupation, journalist Albert G. Robinson acknowledged the efficient work of American officials in addressing sanitation and infrastructure, but noted that these were not problems topmost in Cubans' minds (indeed, "the doing of them was a cause of discontent rather than satisfaction"). If anything, Robinson reported, Wood was less popular among the Cubans than his less competent predecessor, General John Brooke, an observation that deserves attention, given the dissonance between Wood's descriptions of Cuban opinion during the negotiations over the terms of U.S. withdrawal from Cuba and actual Cuban sentiment. It apparently never occurred to Wood that in face-to-face discussions, Cubans might be telling him what they thought he wanted to hear.[44]

By the summer of 1900, U.S. officials felt confident enough about conditions in Cuba to begin the process of forming a Cuban government. Since the start of the U.S. military occupation, four general elections had been held in Cuba "in an orderly and tranquil manner," Wood remarked in an annual report. The Cuban population was supporting itself "without any assistance from the State," leading Wood to conclude that "there must be something in the people themselves to have brought about this result and to have rendered these changes possible." Having observed Cubans since the start of the U.S. occupation, Wood could confidently describe them as "orderly and obedient, and in sympathy with law and order."[45] It was time to begin the process of transferring government to the Cubans themselves. Who could argue with that?

On July 25 Wood issued an order calling for the election of delegates to a convention to be held in the Cuban capital, Havana, on the first Monday of November 1900, "to frame and adopt a constitution for the people of Cuba, and, as a part thereof, to provide for and agree with the Government of the United States upon the relations which ought to exist between that Government and the Government of Cuba, and to provide for the election by the people of officers under such constitution and the transfer of government to the officers so elected."[46] This prompted an immediate firestorm. As the Cubans recognized, a convention elected to draw up a constitution had no authority to determine questions of political relations. That was rightly the prerogative of a duly elected government. When widespread protest against the wording of the order on the part of individuals and the major political parties threatened to derail the selection of delegates, Wood assured the Cubans that the United States would modify the language, and the election of delegates proceeded.

In November, Wood formally opened the constitutional convention with another order that met part though not all of the delegates' original objections. They would still be expected to treat the subject of U.S.-Cuban relations, but now Wood stipulated that this topic could be taken up *after* the constitution itself was framed and adopted, and then on terms suitable to the Cubans *themselves*. As journalist Robinson later observed, this distinction, though seemingly minor, was the cause of much anti-Cuban sentiment in the United States later that spring, when critics charged the delegates with ignoring U.S.-Cuban relations in the constitution, just as Wood himself had authorized them to do. This proved Cubans' lack of gratitude, many complained, and revealed Cuba as unprepared to be left on its own. As if ignoring the ambiguity, Wood himself lectured the delegates about the fine points of self-government, just as they set to work. In "true representative government," Wood observed, "every representative of the people, in whatever office, confines himself strictly within the limits of his defined powers." The delegates to the constitutional convention had "no duty and no authority to take part in the present government of the island." And yet, by continuing to insist that the convention take up the matter of U.S.-Cuban relations even after the constitution itself was framed, Wood was asking the Cuban delegates to exceed their mandate.[47] Moreover, the degree of Cuba's liberty to define its relations with the occupying power remained decidedly ambiguous. The U.S. government would, of course, have something to say about these relations, too, Wood cautioned. Still he never doubted the result: "a final and authoritative agreement between the people of the two countries" to promote "their common interests."[48]

Over the course of the next six months, it became clear that Cuba's interest and America's interest were diametrically opposed. The Cubans wanted to realize the dream of Cuba Libre. The Americans wanted to undo the damage of the Teller Amendment, which pledged the United States to "leave the government and control of the Island to its people," thus apparently repudiating a century and a half of U.S. thinking about Cuba.[49] By the terms of Teller, the United States would withdraw "absolutely" upon the establishment of an independent Cuban government (an interpretation "commonly accepted in both countries"). From Secretary of War Root's perspective, the U.S. Congress had presented President McKinley with an intractable dilemma: he could comply with a literal reading of the Teller Resolution and abandon American interests in Cuba, or alienate the Cubans and divide the American people. Congress had created this mess, Root insisted; Congress should clean it up. If the United States was going to have to force Cuba to recognize America's unique interests there, Root wanted this done "not by a divided government or in the exercise of a doubtful right or as the subject of an internal dispute, but with the whole united power of the nation, in its different branches of government standing behind the demands."[50]

Still, to most observers it wasn't clear exactly what authority Congress exercised on the subject of Cuban independence. As the *Pawtucket* (Rhode Island) *Times* remarked, Cuba was neither a dependency, a protectorate, nor a colony of the United States. "It is to be a free and independent nation, yet its constitution must be submitted to the United States for approval." Could the United States accept part of the constitution while demanding changes? "Nobody knows what the rights of Congress are in the matter," the paper acknowledged, "because never before has Congress been called upon to act in a similar case. There are no precedents. The way has to be pioneered . . . without chart or compass."[51] Ordinarily relations between countries are negotiated by treaty. But suppose an "arrogant" Cuba should "decline to enter into treaty relations with the United States and assume to manage its own affairs without regard to the United States"? Then the United States would have to force its will on the new republic; wasn't there something that could be done now to preempt such a regrettable course of action?[52]

The *Pawtucket Times* quoted a "prominent Republican senator" (likely Orville H. Platt, chairman of the Senate Foreign Relations Committee) surmising that the Cuban constitution "might contain an article by which the suzerainty of the United States" over Cuba's relations with "the rest of the world could be acknowledged." The same could be done for the question of a U.S. naval station, about which, Wood pointed out, the Cubans were "particularly touchy."[53] The key would be to reassure the Cubans that the point of these measures was not to diminish Cuba's independence in any way, nor to interfere in Cuba's internal affairs, but simply to promote the prosperity of both countries. This was an "extremely complicated" problem that would have to be managed "with great delicacy."[54]

Delicacy was not America's stock-in-trade. On February 11, 1901, delegates to the Cuban Constitutional Convention accepted and signed the new Cuban constitution, thus freeing themselves to take up the question of U.S.-Cuban relations. The previous month, the ever-optimistic Wood had assured Root that casual conversations with many of the delegates suggested that Cubans would define relations between the two countries in terms suitable to the United States. Unwilling to take Wood's word for granted, Root wrote Wood a letter spelling out the administration's position on U.S.-Cuban relations in characteristic detail. Root ordered Wood to remind the convention that the U.S. Congress, not the executive, had ultimate authority on the subject of relations, so that any conversations between Wood and the delegates up to that date were nonbinding. Wood was also to remind the delegates that the United States took seriously its duty under U.S. and international law to secure conditions in Cuba conducive to individual property rights and the fulfillment of international obligations, and to promote a Cuban government adequate to those ends. Finally, Root reiterated America's commitment, articulated "in varying but always uncompromising and unmistakable terms" since the nation's founding, to ensure that no new foreign power ever laid a hand on Cuba.

Happily, Root observed, America's and Cuba's interests jibed perfectly, for "the condition which we deem essential for our own interests is the condition for which Cuba has been struggling, and which the duty we have assumed towards Cuba on Cuban grounds and for Cuban interests requires." It was simply unthinkable, Root emphasized, that having expended so much blood and treasure, the United States would emerge "through the constitution of the new government, by inadvertence or otherwise, . . . in a worse condition in regard to [its] own vital interests" than it was before the war. Hence President McKinley's talk in December 1899 of the United States maintaining ties of "singular intimacy" with Cuba, and the administration's refusal to expose the island "to the vicissitudes" confronting naturally rich but politically weak states. It was, after all, to secure such singular ties that the administration had convened the Cuban Constitutional Convention in the first place.

Lest the Cubans (or the perpetually sunny Wood himself) miss the gist of these remarks, Root provided him with a list of provisions that "the people of Cuba should desire" to incorporate in the Constitution. Cuba was to agree not to enter into treaties or negotiations with foreign powers without U.S. consent. Cuba was not to amass public debt that exceeded the "ordinary revenue" of the nation. Cuba was expected to grant the United States the right to intervene at will in Cuban affairs to maintain life, liberty, and property and Cuban independence. Cuba was to sign off on all the acts of the U.S. military government. Finally, Cuba was to furnish the United States with land for naval stations. This list of demands became the basis of the Platt Amendment, a legislative rider appended to the U.S. Army Appropriation Act of March 1901, which the United States obliged the Cuban Constitutional Convention to incorporate into the new constitution. So much for Wood's assurances of November 1900 that the constitution and the question of relations were separate matters and that the Americans would leave the defining of U.S.-Cuban relations to the Cubans themselves.

One can fault Wood his optimism and still sympathize with the unpalatable task he faced in informing the delegates that Cuba Libre was essentially dead. No wonder that one of his first acts upon receiving Root's instructions was to flee Havana. On February 15 he set out on a hunting expedition to nearby Batabano, a trip apparently scheduled before the arrival of Root's latest order. Rather than canceling his trip to break the news to the delegates with due solemnity, Wood took its leaders for a proverbial ride, ordering Domingo Méndez Capote and Diego Tamayo, presidents, respectively, of the Constitutional Convention and the newly appointed Committee on Relations, to accompany him. As usual, Wood thought the expedition a smashing success.[55] The Cubans felt otherwise.[56]

Only Wood could have been surprised that the delegates greeted these affronts with disappointment and disdain. In the wee hours of February 27 the Cuban Committee on Relations issued its report. It began by recalling the days just before the trip to Batabano, when the delegates expected that their work "would be as easy as it would be brief." The Cuban nation's gratitude to the United States was indeed palpable, and the delegates were ready to acknowledge eternal "ties of the most intimate and fraternal friendship" between the two nations, "inasmuch as there is not a glimmer of the slightest opposition between their legitimate interests, nor possible the least disparity in their reasonable aspirations." Then came Root's (and Wood's) interventions. The committee now realized it would have to "proceed with greater care, since the matter had to be considered under a different aspect." The McKinley administration had introduced "something new."[57]

Far from renouncing its right to proceed as originally authorized by Wood's orders of July and especially November 1900, the committee proceeded with, if anything, more resolve. What had begun as an *opinion* would become an argument as the Cubans turned Root's language back on him. Root's order had referred to what the Cuban delegates *ought to desire* to be incorporated into the Cuban constitution. But who knew Cuban desires better than the Cubans themselves? "We are the delegates of the people of Cuba," the committee wrote, as if talking to a child. "On this account our primordial duty consists in interpreting the will and heeding the interests of our country." Had not Root himself acknowledged that only the U.S. Congress possessed the power to state definitively the American perspective on relations? Thus, weren't Root's terms simply the "opinion of the executive department"? In light of this qualification, the committee reiterated its authority "to accept or not accept" Root's stipulations—"to choose from among them what seems proper to us, and to add to, amend, or substitute them, in conformity with the dictates of our conscience." It also confirmed the delegates' belief that no further statement on U.S.-Cuban relations was necessary. "The interests of both countries are preserved, as far as human foresight will reach, with the precepts of the constitution we have just adopted for the Republic of Cuba."[58]

The delegates had always imagined it their duty to make Cuba independent of all nations, "the great and noble American nation included." Were Cuba to accede to the demand that it acquire U.S. consent for its international policies; were it to accede to the United States the right to intervene at will in Cuba's internal affairs; were it to grant the United States the right to acquire naval bases, Cuba might "seem independent of the rest of the world" while being in fact dependent on the United States. And truly, what were the Americans so concerned about? As realized in the new constitution and in policies newly announced, Cuba was politically and economically on a firm footing. Liberal constitutional protections ensured the sanctity of life and property even—nay, especially—for foreign individuals.

So plain were these facts that the commission was tempted to respond to Washington's recent overtures with the simple statement that the end of Cuban independence had been attained. Out of respect for Washington and in a spirit of generosity toward the Americans, the committee urged their fellow delegates to adopt the following five declarations into the new Cuban constitution: First, Cuba would not compromise its independence or national integrity by means of treaty, convention, or territorial cession. Second, Cuba would not allow other nations to use its territory as a base of attack against the United States. Third, Cuba would abide by the terms of the Treaty of Paris regarding the protection of life and property. Fourth, Cuba would approve the acts of the U.S. military government. Fifth, Cuba would negotiate a mutually beneficial trade agreement with the United States. With these provisions, Cuban delegates aimed to assure the McKinley administration that they were prepared to maintain Cuba's independence at all costs, and to live "in peace with all the world, orderly and pacifically governing ourselves, and being to the United States a brotherly, deferent, and thankful people."[59]

But there was one demand they rejected: naval bases. Before Wood took the Cuban leaders on his hunting trip, most Cubans had apparently been prepared to *lease* the Americans a coaling station or two. Root's suggestion, forwarded to the Cubans by Wood, that the United States should "acquire and hold the title to land for naval stations" had so alarmed the Cuban Committee on Relations that they omitted mention of the naval bases altogether.[60] But it wasn't just bases the United States would insist on. Root had intended the Cubans to adopt his suggestions whole hog, and when they declined to do so, he sent Wood the slightly enlarged list of demands that would become the Platt Amendment. The Platt Amendment essentially reiterated Root's previous five demands, simply moving the fifth clause about naval stations to number seven, while inserting as clauses five and six statements about sanitation and the future of the Isle of Pines (an island traditionally considered to be part of Cuba whose fate would be decided later). Also added was an eighth clause obliging Cuba to embody the foregoing seven clauses into a permanent treaty with the United States.

The Cubans first received word of the new terms on February 27, the day the Cuban Committee on Relations proclaimed its own *desires* about U.S.-Cuban relations and before the Platt Amendment had become law. It didn't take a U.S. Senate vote approving the Platt Amendment on March 1 to plunge Cuba into a political uproar somehow unanticipated in the United States. Predictably, Wood assured Root that both the Cuban Constitutional Assembly and the population at large had no real objections to Platt Amendment demands. "The general feeling in the country is excellent," Wood wrote Root on March 4, just three days after the Platt Amendment became U.S. law, "and the proposed relations have inspired confidence in the responsible and conservative element of all parties." At bottom, the Cubans were "willing to do what we want them to do."[61]

When Cubans objected to the proposal, Wood could come up with no more compelling explanation than that their leaders were emotional, cowardly, hysterical, irresponsible, unprincipled, ignorant, ungrateful, and, above all, of modest financial means; the list went on.[62] Wood was hardly alone in denigrating Cubans critical of U.S. policy, as if riches were a prerequisite of self-government, submissiveness its cardinal virtue, and dissent unpatriotic. Wood's and Root's misreading of Cuban sentiment caught many Americans by surprise. In Congress, not a few of Platt's initial supporters insisted that they would never have voted for the amendment had they known that the majority of Cubans were opposed to ceding independence to the United States.[63]

In Havana, Cubans greeted news that Platt had become U.S. law with protests outside the Martí Theater, home to the Cuban Constitutional Convention. The anti-American protest combined with a strike by stevedores and harbor lighters to lend the capital city a decidedly incendiary air. Inside the Martí Theater, delegates debated how to respond to the latest American aggression. Radicals wanted to throw Platt back in the Americans' lap and shut down the convention. Moderates proposed suspending the convention for a couple of weeks so delegates could return to their districts to consult the people. In the end, conservatives prevailed on a majority to stay in session, while referring the convention's response to the Committee on Relations.

In the time that elapsed between Senate passage of the Platt Amendment on March 1 and the committee's response, which came out on March 26, U.S. periodicals and audiences weighed in on Platt's relative merits. Predictably, discussion focused on clauses three and seven, the first of which authorized the United States to intervene at will in Cuban affairs, the second of which provided naval bases, and which together, everybody agreed, restricted Cuba's sovereignty.

To critics such as *The State*, a Democratic newspaper out of Columbia, South Carolina, Platt was a "dastardly act" obviously designed to "coerce the Cubans into relinquishing the essentials of sovereignty and independence which this government solemnly pledged to them three years ago." As if still smarting from the Union occupation of the South after the American Civil War, the formerly pro-annexationist

State castigated the McKinley administration's deployment of military force to overawe a democratic and constitutional process. The delegates to the Cuban Constitutional Convention, the paper argued, lacked authority to curtail Cuba's sovereignty or part with any of its land. Precisely for this reason the Committee on Relations had been silent on the subject of naval bases in its original report. Any "intelligent reader" would concede, as the Cubans put it, that U.S. bases in Cuba "militate against the independence which both parties desire to preserve." Rhetorical skill and logic, never mind right, lay entirely on the side of Cuba.

Platt's critics were not altruistic. Indeed, it was America that *The State* was actually worried about. In breaking its promise to Cuba—"in putting a pistol to the head of its protégé and demanding compensation for a volunteered kindness"—the United States disgraced itself in the eyes of the world "for generations to come." The paper lamented, "The loss and the humiliation are ours. The penalty will be ours—the penalty of national faithlessness which hereafter may well cause every people in the world to withhold all trust from 'lying America.'"[64]

But many Americans were unwilling to concede logic to the Cubans. Opposition to Platt, *The New York Times* argued in early February, derived from misunderstanding of the terms *sovereignty* and *independence* themselves. Inadequate understanding of the these words "led, on the one hand, to extravagant notions of the future political status of Cuba, and on the other to weak and foolish arguments for a partial or complete repudiation of the pledge of the Teller resolution." Sovereignty was perfectly compatible with a degree of U.S. control over Cuba. Without question, sovereignty entailed the right of a people to form a government, establish laws, and regulate their country's internal affairs. But sovereignty did not imply the right of a state to do whatever it so pleased. Just as the liberty of an individual was subject to the liberty of others, so the sovereignty of a state was "subject to the general peace and public order of nations."[65]

But who got to define *public*? The *Times* didn't flinch in assigning that right to the United States. Just as in Europe, for example, the sovereignty of individual states was subject to the "concert of Europe," so in the Western Hemisphere states were answerable to an analogous system. "The peace of Europe is the law of Europe," the *Times* observed. "The law is enforced by the concert—the Great Powers acting together. Any act that endangers peace contravenes the law of the public system and the concert may take jurisdiction." This hemisphere, too, possessed such a public system; it just so happened that responsibility for that system fell entirely to the United States (on account of its "indisputable primacy"). While not assuming to regulate inter-American relations or determine "territorial arrangements" here, the United States absolutely forbade new European expansion here. In other words, the Monroe Doctrine *was* the public system of the Western Hemisphere; "the peace of the United States" was its "law." Cuba would enjoy sovereignty "subject to this law," though whether Cuba would be expected to make concessions to the United States not conceded to by, say, Chile or Brazil, remained to be worked out.[66]

If the *Times*'s equating of Western Hemispheric law to "the peace of the United States" seems audacious, to put it mildly, the editors were only stating definitively sentiment that American officials had expressed since the founding era. Cuba's "interests and the interests of the United States are identical," the *Times* put it a week or so later; they "will be served and protected by the same measures."[67] The presumption of the claim that U.S. interests were the public law of the hemisphere to which other nations' sovereignty would be held accountable was matched only by its hubris. Does Cuba wish to erect coast defenses, build ships of war, maintain armies, and maintain a big public debt to pay for these luxuries of greatness? the *Times* demanded. "Is it her purpose to seek admission into the family of great nations with the full privilege to sue and be sued, to make war and get whipped?" Or would Cuba prove sensible and commit its fate to the "infinitely more effective, the amply sufficient, guarantee" of U.S. national policy? These were rhetorical questions. The choice wasn't Cuba's to make. Though Cuba might do as it pleased with its constitution, in its relations with the United States, recognition of U.S. rights and "common interests" must "necessarily find a place."[68]

By the end of March, the Cuban committee assigned to devise a response to the Platt Amendment issued not one but five reports.[69] The most detailed and most popular was that of Juan Gualberto Gómez (no relation to Máximo), veteran of all three Cuban wars of independence since 1868, including La Guerra Chiquita, during which he was captured and imprisoned in Spain.[70] Having struggled so long for Cuban sovereignty, Gómez was dismayed to see it whittled away at the hands of Platt, which would only make Cubans "a vassal people." Like many critics, Gomez focused on clauses three, six, and seven, which granted the United States the right to intervene at will in Cuban affairs, separated the Isle of Pines from Cuba, and demanded that Cuba sell or lease land for naval stations.

In authorizing the United States to intervene in Cuba's affairs, Gomez observed, Platt bestowed a right that the U.S. Constitution did not grant the federal government vis-à-vis the individual states. To concede that right would be like handing a stranger the keys to your house, allowing him to enter as he pleased, at any hour of day or night, whether for good or ill. A government that conceded such a right wasn't worthy of the name, and could be nothing more than a docile instrument of a "foreign and irresponsible power." Moreover, clause three's expressed aim to ensure in Cuba a government capable of protecting life, liberty, and property was simply redundant. For what was the purpose of government if not èxactly that? It didn't take a treaty between the United States and Spain to justify U.S. intervention in the Cuban War of Independence. To insist that Cuba grant the United States the right to intervene in what amounted to a treaty would "dishonor future Cuban governments before they were born, condemning them to inferiority so humiliating that no Cuban would agree to take part in them."[71]

As for the contention that Platt was consistent with Cuban sovereignty since it was Cuban sovereignty that Platt aimed to protect, Gómez replied simply that no nation could be considered sovereign whose internal affairs were subject to review by another nation. Lest skeptics doubt Gómez's authority on questions of politics, he cited three world-renowned theorists who defined sovereignty as ultimate, unlimited, and inalienable power. The Platt Amendment, by making "the dictates of the United States the supreme power in the land," plainly violated the Teller Amendment's pledge to leave Cuba in the hands of its people. A Cuba under the Platt Amendment "could only inappropriately be called the Republic of Cuba."[72]

Gómez argued that there was no separating clause three from clause seven—on naval stations—"the most vulgar of the provisions," and "absolutely unacceptable." In the first place, there were "the moral considerations that prompt us to look with unshakeable repugnance at the idea of foreign strongholds installed on our coasts." Then came the plain fact that American bases could only bring conflict to Cuba, both between Americans and Cubans themselves and between Americans, Cubans, and any third party that the United States engaged from Cuban shores. As if anticipating the Cuban Missile Crisis, Gómez feared that Cuba would become a site of political hostility originating elsewhere, thereby "inexorably drawing us into conflict not of our own making and in which we have no stake."[73]

In short, American bases in Cuba would increase rather than decrease the likelihood of conflict on the island. It wasn't Cuba but America that seemed most likely to plunge the nation into international war. Cuba had no international problems (its "great desire is for peace"). Peace is what Cuba had been promised by the congressional resolution of April 1898 and the Teller Amendment. Once promising, the future of Cuba was now uncertain, Gómez lamented, and "one can't help but see dark horizons and sad prospects for our country."[74] No wonder, then, that "of all the clauses of the Platt Amendment, none so injures the sentiments of the country, or displeases the people as that which refers to the selling or leasing of land for naval stations. The shout 'No coaling stations' is the dominant one in all the popular demonstrations against the Platt Amendment." Gómez and his colleagues on the Committee of Relations could not "help but take note of this popular sentiment." As obnoxious as was clause three, clause seven was worse. It "involves not only the mutilation of our home, but a permanent threat to our internal peace."[75]

Gomez's report on the Platt Amendment won the support of a majority of Cuban delegates and the Cuban public at large, bringing discussion to a standstill. In early April, Wood solicited from Root a statement clarifying the terms of intervention entailed in clause three, which, along with seven, was the biggest stumbling block for Cuban delegates. "You are authorized to state officially that in the view of the President the intervention described in the third clause of the Platt Amendment is not synonymous with intermeddling or interference

with the affairs of the Cuban government," Root wrote back, but rather
"the formal action of the government of the United States, based upon
just and substantial grounds, for the preservation of Cuban independence," the protection of life, liberty, and property, and so on.[76] Meeting none of Gomez's objections, Root's response accomplished nothing
so much as convincing the delegates that if they really wanted to be
heard they would have to travel to Washington themselves.

On April 24 a delegation of Cubans arrived in Washington, D.C.,
to address the question of U.S.-Cuban relations face-to-face with U.S.
administration officials. Greeted courteously by President McKinley,
the Cuban delegation spent most of its time with Secretary Root. Root
repeated what he had written before. Platt was intended to maintain
rather than erode Cuban independence. It merely confirmed by law
what the Monroe Doctrine had long asserted by proclamation: that
the United States would not allow European states to compromise the
independence of Cuba. Root never addressed the Cubans' concern
that Platt would make Cuba subservient to the United States, thereby
impeding international recognition of Cuban independence.[77] For
that Root had no acceptable answer.

Asked if the naval bases were really essential, Root replied that
indeed they were, both for the good of Cuba and for the United States.
Cuba might have a navy of its own one day, the secretary allowed, but
never would that navy be strong enough to defend Cuba against the
navies of Europe. Moreover, even a country such as Italy made alliances with stronger powers to safeguard its independence. The United
States sought only a few strategic positions from which to defend both
parties. The bases would never be adapted to other uses. Suppose
another country intended to attack Cuba or the United States, Root
argued; they would have to begin by taking Cuba, and Cuba had no
means to defend itself. U.S. bases in Cuba conferred no right to the
United States to intervene in Cuban affairs, nor to diminish its independence, but exactly the opposite: to ensure Cuba's independence.
The United States had similar treaties with other sovereign nations,
Root observed. Never, he promised, would the U.S. sites be a point of
departure for U.S. intervention in the interior of Cuba.[78]

Impressed by Root's patience in answering their questions and flat-
tered by a state dinner and elaborate lunches, the Cuban delegates

departed Washington feeling "strongly supported" by American officials, though without having moved the McKinley administration a
millimeter in their direction.[79] The emptiness of Root's responses
would be appreciated only later. He promised, for instance, that the
United States would never intervene in Cuba via Guantánamo Bay,
something it did repeatedly in the first three decades of the naval
base's existence. Root's refrain that the purpose of Platt was to promote Cuban independence and his references to other nations having
similar treaties only obscured Platt's coercion. In the end, he fell back
on coercion itself: this was simply not an arrangement Cuba was free
to reject. Passed by Congress in March 1901, Platt was American law.
It must become Cuban law before the United States would end its
occupation of Cuba.

On May 28, a little over three weeks after receiving the report of
the delegation to Washington, the Cuban Constitutional Convention
voted on the Platt Amendment. In a 15–14 vote, the convention endorsed the majority report of the Cuban Committee on Relations,
which accepted the Platt amendment with qualifications based on the
delegates' recent discussions with Root. To Platt's simple wording in
clause seven, that "the government of Cuba will sell or lease to the
United States lands necessary for coaling or naval stations at certain
specified points to be agreed upon with the President of the United
States," the Cubans added, "for the sole purpose of defending American waters" from foreign aggression. At first, U.S. officials and periodicals greeted the Cuban vote with relief. Upon reading the fine print,
however, Wood quickly informed the delegates that their qualifications were unacceptable. The law passed by Congress authorized
McKinley to withdraw the military from Cuba after the Cuban Constitutional Convention had adopted the Platt Amendment into the
new Cuban constitution, Root reminded Wood to remind the Cuban
delegates. The Cubans themselves had no say in the matter. It was all
or nothing for Cuba: Platt as originally worded or continued U.S. military occupation.[80]

On June 12 the Cuban Constitutional Convention adopted the
Platt Amendment, unamended, in a 16–11 vote. Compared with the
uproar Platt had generated in February and March, its final passage
was greeted by an ominous calm. "FREE BY CHRISTMAS," ran a head-

line in the *Grand Rapids* (Michigan) *Press*. "Cuban Independence Is Now at Hand." If Cubans did not know otherwise, Leonard Wood certainly did. "There is, of course, little or no real independence left Cuba under the Platt Amendment," Wood wrote the new American president, Theodore Roosevelt, in October 1901. "The more sensible Cubans realize this and feel that the only consistent thing now is to seek annexation."[81]

5

★

GUANTÁNAMO BLUES

"How many know that the United States has a plant of extraordinary value and efficiency at the Bay of Guantánamo?" Herbert Corey asked readers of *National Geographic* in June 1921. "Or what it means to the Atlantic fleet each year?" Corey, a veteran travel writer, acknowledged that until recently he certainly had not. Oh, he "had a vague idea that the fleet each winter visited a cactus-bordered beach on which the men walked for health's sake, and that from time to time it went outside for practice." And he had heard talk of towns near the naval base where a fellow could enjoy a good drink and then some without having to duck federal agents (1921 was the second year of Prohibition, and Americans were thirsty). But Corey had also heard that a trip to Guantánamo wasn't worth the trouble. "The background to the picture was always bare white sand and cruelly hard sunlight and scrubby bushes, with a restless surf beating at an inhospitable strand."[1] Such was hardly the case, Corey discovered while accompanying the Atlantic Fleet on its winter cruise. It was as if the navy had been trying to suppress news of a good thing.

By June 1921, when Corey's piece came out, the events that briefly made Guantánamo Bay a household name back in the steamy summer of 1898 were twenty-three years old and had well-nigh been forgotten. Over the course of those intervening years, the base slowly expanded, so that by the time Corey paid his visit to Guantánamo Bay, it housed roughly eleven hundred marines and laborers on a regular basis and could accommodate up to twenty thousand sailors when the fleet pulled in. Still, compared with the base of Admiral Mahan's dreams, Guantánamo remained underdeveloped. Its most touted feature was a rifle range capable of engaging upward of three hundred men at once. An old golf course had been converted into a training facility for new seaplanes. There was a launching ground for dirigibles. There were roads, "pleasant walks and charming gardens." There were hospitals, clubhouses, canteens, tennis and handball courts. And there were baseball diamonds—ten of them—with more on the way.[2]

Between December 1903 and June 1921 one would have had to be a pretty close reader to keep up with developments at Guantánamo Bay—a fan of naval appropriations hearings, perhaps, or a follower of ships' movements. News of Guantánamo reached the United States during the 1912 "racial insurrection," when marines left the base to protect U.S. property and restore order; and again in 1916 as political tension rose in the Dominican Republic and Guantánamo swelled with marines bound for the American intervention there. Still, Corey might as well have been introducing Americans to a new place. He was certainly introducing them to a new thing: the colonization of the nation's overseas bases, and the cultural contact and social interaction that this entailed.

Joining the crew of the USS *Black Hawk* in the late autumn of 1920, Corey surprised the ship's commander by being more interested in ships than in sailors. "A navy isn't ships," the commander chided. "A navy is the men." His attention properly directed, Corey began to focus on the navy's "production of personnel of extraordinary intelligence." At sea, "the American is made into an excellent sailor, as a matter of course," Corey acknowledged, "but it is likewise the navy's effort to make him into a better American" that really counted. To this end, sailors were educated, introduced to foreign ports, well fed, well clothed, and physically and morally "guarded." The sailor's life at sea paid political as well as martial dividends. "Upon his return to civilian life he has attained a higher and more intelligent standard of citizenship."[3]

Just as the world would know Americans by the behavior of their sailor ambassadors, so Americans would come to know the world by these cultural encounters. In one photograph accompanying Corey's story, white sailors in white uniforms "barter with natives in one of the West Indies," the sailors' arms laden with fruits and vegetables, as if confirming Mahan's belief that the navy was not only the protector but also the point man of American overseas commerce. The message here was not only one of a power disparity, with white male sailors from U.S. gunships juxtaposed against black female marketers from a barter economy; there were goods to be had, but also an economy to transform, the local labor force already in place. The American-male-versus-colonial-female juxtaposition suggested another form of exchange that remained inchoate in this image, and with which Guantánamo would become quietly synonymous: prostitution. The coincidence of what look like yuca or other tubers scattered in front of avocados or other egg-shaped fruit seems more than a little contrived.

The contrast of Americans to natives, whites to blacks, civilization to savagery, capitalist to barter economy—with the valorization it implied—was susceptible to a kind of internal critique or inversion. In its proper place, civilization is all well and good, but these sailors were supposed to be steeling themselves for battle. To prepare for battle, they would have to become not only tougher but darker. Beneath a photograph of sailors amusing themselves on a Guantánamo beach reads a caption: "It is here that the enlisted man begins in earnest to lose the pallor, the narrow shoulders, the white knobs, and bony angles of the civilian and to take on the saddle-colored coat of tan and other attributes of husky health."[4] What a relief to see elbows "sharp as boat-hooks" and forearms "puny and pale as the stems of clay pipes" yield to "blotches of bright and inflammatory red upon their shoulders." There was "virtue in sunburn."[5]

At Guantánamo, and more specifically at the nearby port of Cai-manera, just outside the northern limit of the U.S. base, the husky health of the Atlantic fleet confronts its sable Cuban counterpart for an extended stay. Where a pigsty installed on the U.S. base inspires "fond recollections" of "wistful" sailors ("there is something homey and comfortable under this Cuban sun about the grunt of a Duroc Red lady whose children are gathering sustenance while she sleeps in the shade"[6]), the streets of Caimanera "assail the nostrils" with "one thousand assorted smells." In Caimanera, "small dogs sleep in the sun or scratch themselves with an irritated vigor rarely manifested by other dwellers of the town." Meanwhile, "little naked gourd-shaped babies permeate the principal thoroughfares and make excellent mudpies between showers."

Why endure the squalid town? Alcohol. It's still 1921, after all, and "'Sis's Place' and 'The Two Sisters' and 'The American Bar' woo thirsty callers by a display of backbars stacked with bottles. There are no fronts to the saloons," writes Corey, "so that one pauses on the pavement, so to speak, to wet an arid whistle." Many of Caimanera's bars sit on pilings out over the water. Nearby, "on their verandas," also over the water, "one sees dark-skinned women, dressed in flowing white, languidly fanning themselves as the ship's barge pulls in." The bars, the water, the nearby Guantánamo River, the languid locals—all call to mind "Conrad's African backgrounds." Everything has such "a remote and exotic air." As if succumbing to temptation, Corey seems relieved to encounter "the black and green badge of the [U.S. Navy] shore patrol," mistaking its presence as evidence that the nearby streets and alleys of Caimanera "are emphatically out of bounds."

At the time of Corey's visit, only officers, not enlisted men, enjoyed the liberty of Caimanera. To extend Corey's Conrad analogy, they play the part of Marlow to the Cubans' Kurtz; there is a desperation to the officers' imbibing that clashes with the exotic, as if Prohibition could last twelve more years. Arriving at five o'clock, the officers depart by six, their calls for drinks causing their Cuban hosts to "rain perspiration from their dark brows as they shake 'em up." And "so it goes down the dingy, dusty, sometimes flagrantly muddy street, with its weird multitude of vicious odors." The Cubans and Americans regard one another with bemusement. "It is not the Cuban temperament to hurry so over a handful of drinks. Nor does the Cuban need to hurry. Big negroes, with the strong features of the Arab, look one squarely in the eye."[7]

A booze-soaked outpost, its tawdrier side lurking just offstage— this is not the Guantánamo of navy mythology. Yet it is the salient feature of virtually all journalistic and eyewitness accounts of the U.S. naval base from the 1920s until the coming of Castro, which ended U.S. "liberty" tours of Cuban villages and towns around the base. Most of these narratives describe these cultural encounters as innocent. The boys just want to have fun. Long after the inconvenience of the venereal disease has passed, the memories endure.

At the close of the nineteenth century, historian Frederick Jackson Turner warned Americans that the frontier was filling up. The opportunity and prosperity Americans had come to take for granted on the continent must now be won overseas. In the aftermath of the Cuban War of "Independence," Americans of all stripes flocked to Cuba as if hearkening to Turner's warning. No sector of Cuban commerce and industry was left untouched: real estate, agriculture, mining, finance, engineering, construction, education, the professions, gambling, prostitution, and so on were all overrun by opportunistic Americans who arrived in Cuba often with extended families in tow. It is hard to exaggerate the scale of the migration. By 1905 some thirteen thousand Americans had bought land in Cuba valued at $50 million. By 1919 forty-four thousand Americans had moved there, prompting one southern journal to remark, "Little by little the whole island is passing into the hands of American citizens." And why not? In U.S. journals and newspapers, Cuba was depicted as "a land of perpetual sunshine, flowing with milk and honey," "an all-the-year-round country" with "no unproductive season."[8]

Oriente province, the least developed region of Cuba, was the target of intense foreign investment. After the War of Independence, the development of Oriente proceeded at an exhilarating pace, spurred by U.S. entrepreneurs who at long last responded to the calls of the early Americans who first sang Guantánamo's praises. Historians describe the Americanization of Oriente in terms of an "invasion." Much of this invasion took place in the Guantánamo Basin, where low population combined with cheap real estate to set off a land rush.[9]

In the first decade after independence, U.S. capital investment in Cuba soared from $80 million to $220 million; by 1923 it had reached $1.3 billion, over half of which was devoted to sugar. Much of this sugar capitalization happened in Oriente, which by the third decade of the new century had become Cuba's second most populous province and its second leading sugar producer. Between 1907 and 1919, when

Cuba's population increased by slightly over 40 percent, Guantánamo's rose by an astounding 60 percent. By 1929, foreign sugar growers, most of them American, owned 64 percent of Oriente province.[10] Three quarters of foreign investment in Oriente was devoted to sugar production, which by the second decade of the century pushed aside smaller homegrown industries such as coffee and tobacco, displacing local farmers and workers and replacing them with cheaper Haitian, Jamaican, and West Indian labor. Coming so quickly on the heels of what was supposed to have been Cuban independence, the social upheaval entailed in transforming Oriente into Cuba's leading sugar-producing region would have been untenable but for Platt and the proximity of the new U.S. naval base at Guantánamo Bay. Together, the two acted as an insurance policy for U.S. and foreign businesses, maintaining order and tamping down agitation for political and economic reform. It took nearly half a century for Guantánamo to become the place of Admiral Mahan's dreams. In the meantime, it functioned quite efficiently as American capital's private guard not only in Cuba but throughout the Caribbean region.

"The difficulty of our colonial possessions [is] beginning to weigh heavily on our deliberations," U.S. navy secretary John Long confided in his diary at the Paris peace talks in December 1898. "What an immense task it is to change our whole system of government in Cuba." On the one hand, Long recognized that the United States "must establish naval stations" on the island; on the other hand, he knew that seizing Cuban land would violate America's promise to leave Cuba to its own devices at the end of the war with Spain. Wary of alienating the Cuban and American public, the McKinley administration refused to take up the matter of naval stations in the Treaty of Paris. What was a navy secretary of an up-and-coming liberal empire to do?[11]

Enlist the help of his subordinates. Before the United States intervened in the Cuban War of Independence, Alfred Mahan had been in the minority in calling insistently for overseas bases. By the end of the war in August 1898, very few Americans did not concede that overseas bases had become a necessity. With the war barely drawing to a close, government officials were debating which offshore coaling stations the

United States ought to acquire, tacit acknowledgment that Americans were ready to forsake what Senator Henry Cabot Lodge called the nation's "blundering" policy of isolation.[12]

Passing the Naval War Board's findings on to Secretary Long, Admiral Mahan suggested that there were two regions in the world where U.S. and foreign interests were sure to collide: the Pacific Ocean and the Caribbean Sea. To safeguard U.S. access to the increasingly lucrative Asian trade, the board recommended establishing coaling stations at Guam, Manila, Hawaii, and Samoa; to control Pacific Ocean access to the much-anticipated isthmian canal, it suggested occupying Ports Culebra and La Union in Costa Rica and El Salvador, respectively. In the Caribbean, meanwhile, the board urged the establishment of stations at San Juan, Puerto Rico, and in eastern Cuba (at either Santiago de Cuba or Guantánamo Bay). "The Caribbean Sea is one of the most interesting and vital regions in the world to the United States, considered from the point of view of commerce and of war," the board remarked; "there our interests may be most seriously interrupted by hostile navies in time of war."[13]

In the Caribbean, nothing was more important than controlling the Windward Passage. "No solution to the problem of coaling and naval stations can be considered satisfactory which does not provide for military safety upon that route," the board observed. As potential sites of U.S. stations along the Windward Passage, both Santiago and Guantánamo had their advantages. Santiago, with its narrow channel, was easily defensible. Guantánamo, with its generous entrance, would be easy to escape in the event of enemy attack. Santiago was well sheltered. Guantánamo could accommodate a whole fleet of ships.[14]

So began a long debate about the virtues of Guantánamo Bay, not only compared with Santiago de Cuba and other Cuban harbors, but among Guantánamo and other locations throughout the Caribbean Sea and the Gulf of Mexico and along the eastern seaboard of the United States. Had the debate remained within the limits of the naval community, it would quickly have resolved in Guantánamo's favor. Along with New York and Norfolk harbors, Guantánamo was generally acknowledged to be an invaluable strategic asset among experienced naval personnel. But the debate didn't remain intramural. Politicians, too, would have their say. U.S. bases provided jobs and income to host communities whose representatives in Washington did not want naval funding moved offshore. In negotiations about naval appropriations in the first decade and a half of the twentieth century, U.S. politicians seized on the slightest pretext to deny Guantánamo the funding required to make it a fully functioning naval base, with a fuel depot, dry docks, machine shops, ample living quarters, and appropriate defenses. Instead, sustained by discretionary funding channeled to the station by the secretary of the navy, Guantánamo became a limited coaling and emergency repair facility—useful to the navy as a rendezvous site for the fleet and as a jumping-off point in Cuba, but hardly the springboard of the forceful new naval strategy envisioned by Mahan, Roosevelt, and Henry Cabot Lodge.

The U.S. Navy never really abandoned Guantánamo Bay in the aftermath of the Spanish-American War. But the U.S. occupation of Guantánamo became official in October 1903, when the Cuban Senate ratified a treaty leasing forty-five square miles of territory at the outer harbor to the United States, as stipulated in the Platt Amendment. The treaty included the leasing of Bahia Honda in northwest Cuba, a site the navy never developed.[15] From the first, navy officials and President Roosevelt himself were dissatisfied with the amount of land conceded by Cuba. Even an unseasoned observer could see that it was surrounded by higher land. As early as December 1900, naval officials had requested that Cuba concede a ten-mile radius focused on the old Spanish battery at the top (or north) of the outer harbor on South Toro Cay, which the navy expected to become the heart of the U.S. station. The three-hundred-odd square miles of territory within that radius included the local foothills of the Sierra Maestra and Nipe-Sagua-Baracoa mountains, and would allow the navy to command the high ground surrounding Toro Cay. It also encompassed access to the freshwater of the Guantánamo, Guaso, and Yateras rivers, the absence of which in the land allotted to the navy proved nettlesome for years to come.

If three hundred square miles seems an unreasonable request on the part of navy officials, their concern about the defensibility of the base was vindicated in February 1904, when the Japanese successfully captured the Russian naval bastion at Port Arthur, Manchuria. It wasn't so much that Port Arthur and Guantánamo were analogous in their degree of vulnerability to potential enemies; Port Arthur was infinitely more exposed. Rather, the apparent susceptibility of Guantánamo to a land-based attack was all the fodder that jealous congressmen needed to withhold support for Guantánamo over the course of the next ten years. Meanwhile, naval officials did everything they could both to quell fears about Guantánamo's vulnerability and expand the territory of the base. When political instability in Cuba in 1905–1906 provoked a second U.S. military occupation lasting three years, naval officers thought the time might be ripe for simply seizing more land. President Roosevelt and Elihu Root, now secretary of state, refused to endorse the suggestion, sensitive to America's deteriorating reputation throughout the region.[16]

Talk of expanding the base continued through January 1914, when mounting hostilities in Europe deflected attention away from Cuba. In the waning days of the Taft administration, U.S. and Cuban officials signed a treaty, never ratified or implemented, that would have afforded the base the much-coveted high ground surrounding Toro Cay as well as a freshwater source at the Yateras River. Meanwhile, naval and congressional officials continued to debate the merits of Guantánamo versus existing naval installations along the eastern seaboard and throughout the Caribbean Sea and the Gulf of Mexico.

Congress's reluctance to fund a full-fledged naval base in the first decade of the U.S. occupation did not detract from the base's usefulness. On May 21, 1912, *The New York Times* reported that a "Negro" insurrection on the island of Cuba threatened American lives and property.[17] The revolt seems to have had its origin in disgruntlement among Afro-Cubans who had seen their position in Cuba decline in the aftermath of independence. Prominent in the revolutionary movements of the nineteenth century, Cuban blacks were denied full participation in Cuban society during and after the U.S. military occupation. In 1902, for instance, the United States banned black Cubans from a new Artillery Corps; when convening the Cuban Constitutional Convention in autumn 1900, Leonard Wood tried to exclude black Cubans from participating in the electoral process. The "illiterate mass of people" had no business participating in the democratic process, Wood declared, equating illiteracy with "the sons and daughters of Africans imported into the island as slaves."[18]

Discrimination persisted into the Cuban republic and through the second U.S. military occupation of 1906–1909, when U.S. troops returned to Cuba to quash an uprising ignited by the corruption and incompetence of the so-called Moderate Party of President Estrada y Palma. In response to the discrimination, a group of Cuban blacks left the Liberal Party to form the Partido Independiente de Color (PIC), whose exclusive-sounding name belied its ambition for broad social, especially working-class, reform. In the 1908 national election, the PIC fared miserably, proving itself unable to compete with the patronage of the mainstream political parties. When, by 1910, the PIC appeared likely to erode black support among the mainstream Liberal and Conservative constituencies, the parties passed a law outlawing single-race political institutions. PIC's members were harassed and arrested, its political organs banned. The PIC members preferred "to be blacks rather than Cubans," one editorial writer warned. The new nation had no place for such "racists." The PIC, meanwhile, appealed to the United States to intervene under the Platt Amendment, something the new Taft administration was not ready to do.[19]

Excluded from political participation and unable to air its grievances, the PIC took matters into its own hands in May 1912. The way to get the United States' attention, Cubans had learned back in 1906, was to create social upheaval threatening to U.S. property. And so the PIC began to destroy U.S. and foreign property throughout Cuba, but especially in Oriente province, in the vicinity of Guantánamo Bay.

As early as February 1912, U.S. representatives in Cuba had begun closely following the behavior of PIC leader Evaristo Estenoz, a "troublesome negro."[20] On May 23, U.S. secretary of state Philander Knox ordered his ambassador to Cuba to warn the Cuban government that the U.S. Marines were on the way to Guantánamo, in response to U.S. property being seized and employees of U.S. plantations threatened. The U.S. government took these steps not to intervene in Cuban affairs, Knox insisted, but simply to protect American lives and property.[21] And to goad Cuban officials to action. The next day, U.S. ambassador A. M. Beaupré informed his boss that three battleships with 250 marines each had arrived at Guantánamo, making "a very good impression" on Cuban officials, if not on the rebels themselves. Cuban officials had finally assigned guards to the vulnerable American businesses, calming American fears considerably. Tellingly, a day later, Beaupré confessed ignorance about the rebels' motivation. "It is difficult to say," he remarked, "what the moral effect the presence of [the American] ships will have upon the irresponsible negroes." Sizing up the insurrection, Beaupré could say only that it seemed "to be organized and directed by some unknown interest, it being highly probable that the negroes at the head of the Independent Party would be capable of engineering a movement on this scale. The negroes now in revolt are of a very ignorant class."[22]

Beaupré claimed that Cuban officials welcomed the arrival of the U.S. fleet, fully recognizing the distinction between U.S. intervention in Cuba and the protection of U.S. property. A letter from Cuban president José Miguel Gómez to U.S. president William Howard Taft suggests otherwise. That was a distinction without a difference, Gómez wrote Taft. To Cuba, the arrival of the U.S. forces smacked of intervention,

> and the natural development of events, once these foreign troops landed, would accentuate that character, it is my duty to inform you that a determination of this serious character alarms and injures the feelings of a people loving and jealous of their independence, above all when such measures were not even decided upon by previous agreement between both Governments, which places the Government of Cuba in a humiliating inferiority through a neglect of its national rights, causing it discredit within and without the country.[23]

The Cuban military itself was quite prepared to "annihilate" the "negroes" itself.

In reply, Taft told Gómez that the United States appreciated Cuba's resolve, and that the ships had sailed to Cuba merely in case of necessity. Gómez responded in turn that the United States was most welcome to observe events in Cuba. Any deployment of U.S. forces should only follow an agreement of both parties.[24] In a note to Beaupré, Secretary of State Knox distinguished American intervention in Cuba from police action to protect U.S. property; the government would never consult Cuba on that.[25] As they had during the so-called negotiations over the Platt Amendment, U.S. officials continued to talk past their Cuban counterparts. Meanwhile, with marines itching for action aboard battleships anchored at Guantánamo Bay, Secretary Knox became increasingly forthright in dictating the number and location of *Cuban* troops to be dispersed around the Cuban countryside to protect U.S. and foreign planters.[26]

On June 6, 1912, *The New York Times* announced that American marines had come ashore at the Cuban port of Caimanera, just outside the boundary of the U.S. base. From there they fanned out up the Guantánamo Basin, taking positions around the U.S. estates. Meanwhile, more marines were headed to Cuba from Key West. The larger strategy, according to the *Times*, was to station an American battleship in each of the major towns along Cuba's southern coastline, "with the idea that the crew of a thousand bluejackets [sailors] will impress the negroes with the fact that the power of the United States is nearby, and that further acts of lawlessness on their part will lead to their ultimate punishment." The sailors were to be granted "liberal shore leave, so that the negroes as they come into the towns to get supplies may see them and carry back word to their associates that the forces of the 'North Americans' have arrived and are on the alert."[27]

With the U.S. Marines guarding American property, Cuban forces were now free to take the battle to the "troublesome negroes," which they did with ruthless efficiency. It was bad enough that Afro-Cubans threatened foreign property; their "diabolical assaults upon the honor of white women" were beyond the pale. With marines providing cover, the Cuban military, joined by white vigilantes, massacred black Cubans, ultimately claiming between three and six thousand lives. The vengeance loosed upon the rebels seems out of proportion to their crimes, and calls to mind the violence against African Americans during Reconstruction, when the sanctity of white womanhood was reported to have been similarly imperiled.[28]

Ultimately, the United States was satisfied with the way things turned out. "I beg to express my thorough conviction," Beaupré wrote his boss, "that the sending of troops was fully warranted by the situation, that the effect of their visit was salutary, and their withdrawal at this time would be a serious mistake." There was mopping up to do. And then there was the instability in states within sailing distance from Guantánamo, such as black Haiti and the nearby Dominican Republic.[29]

In May 1916, in the face of political and social instability in the Dominican Republic, seven hundred marines deployed to the capital, Santo Domingo, to begin an eight-year occupation. Like earlier interventions in Cuba, this occupation handsomely benefited U.S. commercial interests on the island. U.S. sugar producers, for example, increased their holdings nearly twofold, elevating their share of Dominican sugar production to 80 percent by the time U.S. forces pulled out. The occupations of the Dominican Republic and Cuba would become a model for future U.S. policy in Haiti and throughout Latin America for decades to come.[30]

In November 1916, Cuban president Mario García Menocal, a member of the Conservative Party, won reelection in a poll in which the number of votes exceeded the number of voters. Liberals protested, prompting Cuba's Supreme Court to schedule a second vote for the following February. But on the eve of the second election, Liberals revolted and took up arms under the leadership of José Miguel Gómez, like most politicians of this era, a veteran of the War of Independence. By February 1917, the U.S. government was on the verge of declaring war on Germany, and expected a pacified Cuba to serve as a first line of defense of U.S. interests in the Caribbean Sea and Gulf of Mexico. As a result, the United States supported President Menocal against the rebels, despite the rebels' considerable backing in the United States and among some American interests in Oriente province.[31]

In mid-February, the U.S. Navy commander at Guantánamo Bay became embroiled in negotiations between Cuban and rebel forces over the fate of the harbor at Santiago de Cuba, which the rebels controlled and threatened to block by sinking vessels across its mouth. As the self-appointed representative of U.S. business interests in the area, Captain Dudley W. Knox did not want to see the harbor closed to U.S. commerce. Knox convinced the rebels to refrain from shutting down the harbor at Santiago in exchange for a promise that the Cuban warships would not force the entrance. Knox's initiative, undertaken without authorization from Washington, won the enmity of U.S. consular and State Department officials, who supported Menocal against the rebels, with whom they refused to negotiate. Knox returned to Guantánamo after several days. In the ensuing weeks, rebel forces, increasingly desperate and hard-pressed, began to do as Cuban political minorities before them had done in Oriente province, namely, threatening U.S. property in the hopes of triggering a full-scale U.S. occupation of Cuba under the Platt Amendment.[32]

But with war against Germany all but inevitable, the U.S. government had its hands full. President Wilson ordered marines from the naval base to guard American and foreign property, while sending sailors from American warships into Santiago, Guantánamo City, and other eastern towns. The presence of U.S. troops in eastern Cuba bolstered weak Cuban government forces. Again, with the Americans guarding their backs, the Cuban Army was able to confine the rebels to an increasingly diminishing area, so that by midsummer 1917, the rebellion was essentially smothered. But not before thousands of U.S. troops had been dispersed throughout southeastern Cuba for the second time in a decade, allowing the corrupt Menocal to be inaugurated for a second term.[33]

The social unrest that gripped Oriente province in the first two decades of the twentieth century reflected structural defects in Cuban society traceable to the encomienda system of land and labor distribution introduced onto the island by early colonial Spain. From the arrival of Diego Velázquez in 1511 through the seizure of American assets at the time of the Cuban Revolution, the Cuban economy was dominated by absentee landlords who regarded Cuba as a source of status and wealth rather than as a home. The dissolution of the great cattle estates at the end of the eighteenth century and the simultaneous opening of Cuba to foreign trade gave rise not to the diversified and indigenous free market economy that Havana's Creole merchants and entrepreneurs anticipated, but to a capital-intensive, foreign-owned, export-oriented sugar monoculture based on plantation slavery and supplemented with Chinese indentured servants.

The U.S. hijacking of Cuban independence exaggerated these structural flaws. In contrast to the American patriots' expropriation of British Loyalist property during the American Revolution, the United States allowed no nationalization or redistribution of peninsular (Spanish) or Creole property at the end of the "Spanish-American War." On the contrary, Spanish loyalists, "peninsulares," Creoles, Europeans, and Americans retained their property and political and economic influence. In the cases of the few Spaniards or foreigners who did abandon their property during or after the war, an absence of Cuban capital and credit inhibited the disbursement of property to the Cuban people. In fact, in the aftermath of independence, foreign control of Cuba's economy expanded while Cubans remained essentially sidelined.[34]

The ravaging of the Cuban countryside during the war provided the opportunity to decentralize Cuban agriculture. One can imagine the proliferation across Cuba of small and midsize farms producing diversified goods for both local and global markets. But this flew in the face of both U.S. and foreign capital interests in Cuba, as well as global trends. Big is in, Henry Cabot Lodge had announced back in 1895, in reference to America's new interest in overseas colonies. But Lodge might just as well have been talking about agriculture and industry. The three went handsomely together. Leonard Wood's first aim as military governor of Cuba was to get the Cuban economy up and running. Wood's administration underwrote the recapitalization of Cuban agriculture and industry on an ever-larger scale, creating insurmountable barriers to entry for Cuban farmers shy of capital. In his letter to Shafter of July 1898, Cuban general Calixto García expressed dismay that Shafter would leave Spanish officials in charge of Santiago at the end of the war. Something similar happened throughout the Cuban economy. In Cuba's emerging industrial sector, for example, the influence of Spanish merchants and entrepreneurs actually *expanded* in the first three decades after Cuban independence. By 1927, foreigners owned two-thirds of Cuba's general stores, Spaniards themselves roughly 50 percent. Similarly, Spaniards dominated the professions, education, and the clergy.[35]

The result was a Cuban economy from which the Cuban middle class was virtually excluded. The lower classes were welcome, but only as laborers. Not even the old Cuban planter elite, small as it was, remained in power. Having tied its fate to the cause of autonomy under Spain, it had no standing when the old political regime fell.[36] American and foreign investors were ready to fill the void. In the fertile central province of Camagüey, for example, some seven thousand Americans possessed land titles; in nearby Sancti Spiritus, Americans owned seven-eighths of the land. By 1906 it is estimated that the United States owned 15 percent of Cuba. Put another way, roughly 60 percent of rural property in Cuba was in the possession of foreign companies. Some 15 percent was owned by Spanish residents, leaving approximately 15 percent of Cuban land to Cubans. Similar imbalance prevailed across the Cuban economy, including mining, transportation, and utilities, and the manufacturing, banking, and finance industries.[37]

The effect on Cuban morale was devastating. For two generations, Cuban patriots had struggled for control of Cuba. Victory in the War of Independence had brought them nothing. When social alienation bred political upheaval over the fall and winter of 1905–1906, disgruntled Cuban politicians solicited U.S. intervention. If initially reluctant, the Roosevelt administration was at the ready. "I am so angry with that infernal little Cuban republic that I would like to wipe its people off the face of the earth," Roosevelt told his confidant Whitelaw Reid the following September. "All we have wanted from them is that they would behave themselves and be prosperous and happy so that we would not have to interfere."[38] U.S. policy had made that impossible.

In the immediate aftermath of war, U.S. officials granted favorable tariff concessions to (largely U.S.- and foreign-based) Cuban sugar producers in exchange for reciprocal benefits for U.S. manufacturers. The cheap U.S.-manufactured goods undercut a nascent Cuban manufacturing sector already suffering from a shortage of investment capital. Naturally, the defects of the sugar monoculture influenced the plight of Cuban labor. In boom times, the sugar industry employed a mostly African- and Chinese-derived labor pool on a seasonal basis and under highly exploitative conditions. In slack times, laid-off sugar workers joined a large pool of under- and unemployed workers.

The structural flaws in Cuba's economy affected Cuban politics. With Cuban sugar production dominated by foreigners, and lacking an industrial base, Cuban elites turned to politics as the surest way to make a living. Government became the instrument not for solving the nation's problems but for distributing political spoils. By the 1920s, as the federal bureaucracy (and payroll) swelled to unimaginable levels, Cuba became a welfare state—for Cuban elites—channeling scarce resources into the pockets of professional politicians.[39]

In the early twentieth century the fate of Cuba's ruling political parties depended on maintaining the good graces of the United States, always ready to intervene under Platt to protect U.S. business interests. More than anything, this meant maintaining law and order, no mean feat in the midst of economic hardship and rampant corruption. It would take Cuba years to descend to the level of political violence that characterized the intimidation and violence (*gangsterismo*) of the 1940s and '50s; but by the mid-1920s, dissident labor leaders were literally being fed to sharks as Cuba's poor confronted the unpalatable choice of participating in the violence as the arm of the ruling party or risking becoming victims of the violence itself.[40]

Like the political parties, the Cuban military had a great stake in maintaining the status quo. U.S. intervention jeopardized Cuban Army legitimacy, making the army a force of political stability at the expense of fair elections and political and economic reform. Beginning in the 1910s, when President Mario García Menocal responded to a wave of labor unrest by unleashing the army on workers, the Cuban Army was never far offstage. Far from stabilizing Cuban politics, the rising influence of the army contributed to the social volatility, adding deadly force to an already explosive relationship between government and labor. Despite their differences, the ruling party and the army agreed on maintaining a pliant workforce. In the second decade of the twentieth century, Cuban agricultural and industrial workers began to protest living and working conditions with increasing regularity and forcefulness. With the United States fiercely opposed to even minimal labor concessions (a minimum wage, for instance, or a majority Cuban labor force), Cuban politicians refused to negotiate with workers, which only added to worker unrest.[41]

By the 1920s, opposition to the Platt Amendment was becoming increasingly widespread among Cubans and Americans alike. For their part, U.S. officials were becoming fed up with Cuban manipulation of an instrument designed to maintain U.S. hegemony, and which threatened to embroil the United States permanently in Cuba's dysfunctional politics. It was Cuba's money the United States wanted, not its reins of government. Meanwhile, Cuban nationalists denounced U.S. meddling in Cuban affairs to greater effect, forcing the ruling parties to acknowledge Platt's cost to their political legitimacy. Finally, Platt had lost its only indigenous support among the Cuban bourgeoisie, who had come to regard it as the principal impediment to agricultural diversification and the promotion of domestic manufacturing. Foreign-owned and exploitative, sugar became—like Platt itself—a focus of nationalist opposition to the United States.

Just a few years after Herbert Corey's sojourn at Guantánamo, writer K. C. McIntosh described Caimanera to readers of the popular magazine *American Mercury*. "A rickety wooden building like a squat barn built on piles over the whispering, greenish water; a long, battered mahogany bar; a hundred white and gold uniforms at white-topped tables that are littered with remnants of salad and fried chicken, and are sloppy with beer-froth and the chill sweat of highball glasses. A hundred grinning black faces at the wide glassless windows on the street side."[42] The walls of the bars of Caimanera, like the fence marking the boundary of the U.S. naval base, separated Americans and Cubans along lines of nationality, class, race, and gender. But the walls had windows, and the windows were "open," and through those openings U.S. sailors and their Cuban hosts came to know one another in the first few decades of the twentieth century. Like the fence itself, those windows facilitated all manner of border crossings that blurred, while not ultimately obliterating, the differences that distinguished Americans from their Cuban hosts.

Like Corey's Guantánamo, McIntosh's is distinguished first and foremost by race. Besides the "hundred grinning black faces" at the windows of Caimanera, the Guantánamo base was populated by "Chinese coolies" working at the direction of "a brown Cuban foreman."[43] A few of the local bars were owned by whites, but all were staffed by Cubans—by Manuel, Pablo, Pepe, Jim, and Chico. Different grades of officers drank in different places: the higher the grade, the closer to the base. Time was of the essence. At Caimanera, Peanut Mary, a Jamaican, sold peanuts and evidently a little more to the Americans, her gender providing a competitive advantage over her rival, a "thin brown urchin."[44]

U.S. sailors worked as well as drank at Guantánamo Bay. Long before the base became home to the Navy's Fleet Training Group in 1943, it was used to put the fleet through its paces. Visits to local watering holes followed exhausting days of drilling and target practice at sea. But the same cannot be said for women at the base. When the fleet is out, McIntosh reports, the base falls quiet, and if the heat allows, the navy wives may be found "riding lazy ponies over the hill to call on the ladies of the Marines Corps." On the base itself, "there is just enough tennis to keep in condition, just enough swimming to keep moderately cool, just enough bridge of an evening to exhaust the conversation of your neighbors, and an occasional ride up the bay for a cocktail on Pablo's back gallery or a cold bottle of beer in Jimmy Beauzay's or O'Brien's."[45]

The arrival of the fleet brings "a broad smile [to] every face in the station," though the ladies grow "impatient" and "protest violently" when naval business disturbs their plans of "dinners and dances." When the women complain to the officers—"You haven't been to see me yet! You've forgotten me entirely"—the men mutter fake apologies. "Doesn't the woman know he's busy and tired," McIntosh demands. "Drill today, drill tomorrow. God send Saturday without a casualty."[46]

From the early years, the naval base did not take kindly to criticism. When, a few years after McIntosh's visit, the wife of naval officer at Guantánamo published an anonymous exposé about sex and drinking on the base, the piece was officially banned. Looking back on the incident twenty-three years later, the base commander, author of the one "official" history of the base, concluded that the article presented "a distorted picture of life at Guantánamo with the Fleet present."[47] The banning of the article and its dismissal by a respected chronicler suggest, to the contrary, that the author hit her mark.

"I am strong for naval disarmament," begins "a Navy Wife," author of "Guantánamo Blues: A Taste of Tropical Fruits of Prohibition," published in *Liberty Magazine* in April 1930. "If they took the arms off our really charming American naval officers, the admirals couldn't pet, the captains and commanders couldn't drink, the lieutenants couldn't ever become cave men, and the pink-cheeked ensigns couldn't—well, they'd *have* to keep their hands to themselves for the very good reason they wouldn't have any hands!" The context of this critique was not only a male-to-female ratio on the base reminiscent of early colonial America (between twenty and forty to one, depending on the whereabouts of the fleet), but also a naval administration striving to stave off a cultural revolution sweeping the United States that threatened conventional gender and racial norms. In the "New Navy" that emerged at the turn of the twentieth century, the 1920s-era New Woman met her match. A certain degree of frivolity, even flamboyance, was welcome among the women at Guantánamo Bay, but not so behavior that questioned the established social order.[48] At Guantánamo Bay, even the homeliest maiden was fair game, so long as "she was round in the right places. There is no true feminine vanity on a foreign naval station," the Navy Wife reports.[49] And no true feminism.

Like many in or married to the navy, the author had heard exotic accounts of life at Guantánamo Bay. "Cuba sounded romantic," she recalls; "it was the fleet's winter base. There would be dancing, swimming, sailing, horse-back riding, and all the other things I love." And then there was the allure of "the tropics," with the "palm trees, white sand, sparkling sunshine, masses of flowers with heavy perfume, funny brown natives, and jungles." She'd heard the stories: "Perhaps I'd even have a beau! . . . a romantic young bachelor" with "a past," a trifle "cynical and grim; soured on life so that he needed sweetening." Only later did she realize that "a wise government never sends a bachelor to such a post as Guantánamo, which is on the fringes of things"; only later did she learn of the "'foreign duty suicides' . . . tucked away in the secret archives of the Navy Department in Washington."[50]

The writer arrived at the base via train from Havana to nearby Caimanera. By the late 1920s, Caimanera boasted a daytime population of roughly 2,500. It was "a tiny ramshackle town with mostly dirt streets and unpainted tumble-down board hovels in its so-called residential section." Its nearby commercial quarter comprised "saloons, gambling houses, a red light district, and a few shops that carry both vegetables and native curios." Caimanera's economy was driven by the base. Navy stewards procured supplies there. Officers were permitted to visit the town in the afternoons and on weekends. The navy spawned "a large liquor trade," the author reports, in what seems to have been an understatement. (One authority estimated the annual value of the liquor trade at $500,000 "preprohibition wholesale.")[51]

The red-light district was staffed by "twenty regular prostitutes . . . officially listed by local authorities." But, like the alcohol, prostitutes were stocked in anticipation of the fleet. With Santiago and other local towns offering up their sisters and daughters, the number of prostitutes in Caimanera rose into the sixties, with more available at other towns around the bay. Here (and only here), the author pulled her punches. "In justice to our men," she wrote, apparently in reference to the base's *resident* officer corps, "I must say that they are clean enough and fastidious enough to leave the native women pretty much alone. I scarcely need add that nature's own penalty for licentiousness is more severe in the tropics than in the temperate zones." It was the job of four "native policemen" and a "boatswain's mate on permanent duty" to keep the lid on Caimanera. Though technically subject to the laws of Cuba, legal transgressions involving American sailors were dealt with back at the base.[52]

In 1930, living quarters at the naval base were a far cry from the cushy suburbs they have become today. The author describes arriving at "a double row of small frame bungalows, all exactly alike." Her bungalow was distinguished from the others by "a small white cross" with her husband's name on it. ("It looked just as if he had been buried there.") Did she like it? her husband wanted to know. "Our own men built it." Taking in the simple structure, with its two-foot walls painted gunboat green and its sides constructed entirely of screen, she could only reply, "The porch is very nice," but "where is the house?" With marines on constant patrol around the neighborhood, she "undressed in the cupboard."

The next day began the author's initiation into the spouses' sorority at the naval base. Like initiations everywhere, this involved no small amount of alcohol. "The senior commander's wife was giving a dinner party. There was a rumor that I was to be the guest of honor." Arriving home the afternoon of the party, her husband found his wife "lying on the bed with the immodesty a tropical afternoon permits, resting from a strenuous morning of tennis." Hurry up, she was ordered; "the cocktail boat leaves at four thirty." Mystified, she learned that, though most household closets were neatly stacked with liquor, open drinking on government property was frowned upon. Hence base dinner parties began in Caimanera, at Pepe's, "the 'unofficial' officers' bar."

Function trumped form in the cafés of Caimanera. Pepe's was "a small, picturesque but smelly shed which might have been put together in a movie studio for a Mexican melodrama. There was no art in the arrangement of the hundreds of bottles that lined the bar shelves." Tables, a small dance floor, greasy-aproned waiters who "leered at their immaculate customers as if fully aware of the petty subterfuge to which an American was reduced in order to exercise a personal liberty." If life at Guantánamo is any indication, Prohibition produced world-class drinkers, experts in the art of the immediate and sustained elevation of blood alcohol levels. At Pepe's, rounds (plural) of daiquiris preceded whiskey (beer for most of the women), and finally rounds, again, of cognac—all of it designed to enable "the guests to keep their jazz throughout the coming party."[53]

Her initiation was successful, the writer discovered. ("I learned more about it the next day when the usual post-mortems were held.") It came off, she later learned, according to regulation. "Each family had one colored servant," who labored alongside "Wong, an obliging Chinaman . . . always on hire from a native restaurant." Surely it wasn't the food that made these parties, as there was only so much even the inventive Wong could do with canned corn, soup, peas, beef, sometimes chicken, mashed potatoes, stuffed tomatoes, saltines, ice cream, fruit cocktail, black coffee, and other staples purchased at the local commissary. "Wong and the coffee cups, loud ribald conversations about nothing, the same faces, tramp of the sentry's feet outside, an inescapable smell of stale paint, flashing gold stripes on the officers' costumes, the buzz and thud of tropical insects against the screens, an occasional bugle call from the station ship anchored in the roadstead . . ." Welcome to Guantánamo Bay.[54]

The author was lucky to reach Guantánamo on the eve of the arrival of the fleet, which elevated the local population from between one and two thousand to ten to twenty thousand people, thus giving navy wives something to talk about. "Our little post turned out en masse and waved frantically as the miles-long column of grey vessels swung in from the Caribbean and steamed slowly up their anchorage abreast our quarters." One by one, fifty destroyers, twelve cruisers, six battleships, and countless tenders and supply ships came to rest in the bay. "The heart of every woman among us beat a little faster at the long white lines of men drawn up on the decks of the warships—men who had left their women thousands of miles north and were now, in a sense, at our disposal."[55]

As the parties began, it soon became clear just who was at *whose* disposal. From the first, the author recalls, the fleet dances were a "nightmare," notwithstanding the three daiquiris prescribed by a devoted husband. What exactly husbands thought they were doing towing their wives along to dances is far from clear; what they were in fact doing was serving them up, and there proved to be no shortage of rivals eager to compete for them.

"'Where have you been all my life, you wonderful girl?' For a moment I am not sure whether the voice is that of the hot and handsome lieutenant who is my partner or of one of the three or four jiggling dancers who hem me in on either side. They all smell of commissary soap and their voices are all a little hoarse from too much rum." If tedious, most of this game is harmless. Some is not—at least it didn't seem so to the author, and perhaps it was her willingness to say so, to break the code of silence, that raised the pique of early censors at the bay. "Before I can reply I am snatched away by powerful arms. No apology or chivalrous request for my permission to dance with a new partner; just a violent seizure, as if I were to be the victim of a rape." More blandishments, a too-tight squeeze, an offer to go outside. Only the intervention of an equally boorish lieutenant takes her mind off the violence. But not for long. Another offer. An unwanted kiss. Again, "the idea of rape comes to me. With a woman's instinct I realize that I am protected only by the thin shred of circumstance which lies in the proximity of so many others. I must not dare get outside the circle of light and moving white figures." She succeeds, and "a good deal of indiscriminate kissing" draws this carnival to a close.[56]

But where to go for relief? For a time, the author tried eschewing the parties altogether. This only exposed her to charges of being "selective," a reprimand suggesting both snobbishness and promiscuity. ("I was accused of stealing the high-rankers and giving them a better time than the elder women could.") Only when her diffidence began to jeopardize her husband's standing did the author swallow her pride and rejoin the social circuit. Mercifully, she won the sympathy of a true navy veteran, a senior officer's wife, who advised her to imbibe the minimal amount of alcohol required to help her "stand the life."[57]

During Prohibition, class—or, to the navy, "grade"—distinctions prohibited the enlisted men from visiting Cuban towns around the base. Why? the author wanted to know. Because, replied an officer in a position to know, "we Americans don't know how to drink." Clearly they were out of practice. "An officer manages to get away with it because if he goes too far his whole career is wrecked; whereas the enlisted man has very little to lose but his microscopic pay." Still, supply is slave to demand, and local Cubans proved ingenious at getting alcohol onto U.S. ships. This commerce, common wherever the navy dropped anchor, was said to be Cuba's greatest source of income.[58]

Tedious, offensive, sometimes threatening as it was, life for the wives during fleet visits was vastly preferable to life with the fleet put to sea. With "no daily papers, no real news except a few items that sifted in by radio," and "few books," daily existence at the base was reduced to morning bridge games, afternoon sports, and the ubiquitous dinner parties. No wonder a navy wife took up writing. With little to differentiate themselves from one another, wives fell back on invidious distinctions of rank. "Even the servants caught the spirit of the post," the author notes. "One morning my maid burst out with: 'You ought to have a better rug, ma'am. Mrs. Smith's husband is only a lieutenant, and her rugs are twice as nice as yours.'" When one wife phoned the commissary to request a certain cut of steak, she was greeted by a "Sorry, madam, but we haven't much meat this month and your husband doesn't rate that cut." It was enough to drive a person to drink.[59]

What did the Cubans make of all this? The "respectable ones," those bold enough to declare themselves, did not approve of American ways. But Cubans were tolerant and far from critical. As one put it to the author, "I wouldn't be surprised if we behaved the same way, were conditions reversed, and were there prohibition in Cuba and liquor in America." In all, Cubans viewed the American sailor as "a splendid chap at heart." They were proud that their nation provided "such joyful relief from intolerable conditions in the United States."[60]

In fact, many Cubans were far from proud of the social dynamics in the towns surrounding the U.S. base. The year "Guantánamo Blues" appeared, Gerardo Castellanos, a celebrated Cuban geographer, published a record of a leisurely trip through the Cuban countryside from Remates de Guane, in far northwest Cuba, to Guantánamo, in the southeast, the culmination of a lifelong dream. Fully two-thirds of the book is devoted to the Guantánamo region, including the U.S. naval base and its immediate surroundings.[61] Much of Castellanos's book confirms the account of the Navy Wife. But he goes beyond her to provide a wrenching portrait of the base as seen from the other side.

"We come to the US Naval Station," Castellanos writes. "It's very early. Since leaving Guantánamo, I have enjoyed a beautiful view of one of the saltworks of the Guaso River." Abundant waterfowl and attentive fishermen decorate the scenery. Approaching the outer harbor, Castellanos crosses "a deserted beach," really a dry sea, with no sign of habitation or life. Finally, he arrives at Caimanera, the "local customs office and entry point of the sea-faring trade." Originally a maritime town, Castellanos explains, Caimanera has profited in recent years from the traffic in liquor and troops associated with the Yankee base. By 1930, alcohol had become a fabulous business in Caimanera, the source of many a rapid fortune. Indeed, so full of liquor are some of the bars and cafés of Caimanera that they seem more like "warehouses" than restaurants. Arriving in the early morning, Castellanos fails to note the sex traffic, but there are other trades in town "no less profitable" than liquor, such as the sale of perfumes and tobacco, and "the famous souvenirs," curios and postcards depicting the Cuban landscape.

Castellanos is no less critical of Caimanera's shoddiness than Corey, McIntosh, or the Navy Wife. Nor is he any less conscious of race. He arrives at an hour when one would expect to see local businesses stirring to life. But "commercial activity is negligible." And not just because Caimanera is a city of the night, but because Castellanos visits at a time when the fleet has put to sea, taking with it the town's means of subsistence. In its wake? Nothing but a couple of "black Jamaicans" and two or three drunks, who look to Castellanos "like Yankees."

From the base's inception at the turn of the twentieth century, the navy insisted that it was a great boon to the local Cuban economy. Yet, curiously, Castellanos notes, for all the business the base generated, Caimanera itself remained woefully undeveloped. This sets Castellanos ruminating about all the money being literally flushed down the toilet. *Someone* may be benefiting from the U.S. propensity to "drink to the point of intoxication," but by the looks of things, it isn't the people of Caimanera. Nor is it the American sailors themselves, who typically squander over half a million dollars per year. More than merely wasteful, this industry is socially insidious, turning Cubans everywhere into potential "patrons" for U.S. clients. In Caimanera, U.S. and Cubans come to know each other at their predatory worst. The one or two Cuban policeman on hand cannot possibly maintain law and order, and from time to time the town succumbs to a "state of siege." In these showdowns, the hosts suffer a distinct handicap, as everyone knows that detaining an American sailor could spark a diplomatic crisis. The guests, meanwhile, revel in their immunity.

Castellanos wrote at a time when a moratorium on liberty party visits to Guantánamo City was just coming to an end. Historically, Guantánamo City competed with Caimanera for fleet business, and, like Caimanera, it never flourished so much as when the fleet was in. But in the mid-1920s, the cost of property damage in Guantánamo City forced Cuban bars and restaurants to raise their prices, making them a target of American hostility. This hostility, in turn, forced U.S. naval officials to declare Guantánamo City out of bounds, thus contributing to Caimanera's boom.[62]

From Caimanera, Castellanos pushes on toward the U.S. naval base, his early morning reverie long since soured by the social and economic inequality he encounters. The need to solicit the U.S. Navy's permission to travel through Cuban waters does nothing to improve his mood. Though the Americans formally control only the outer harbor, he notes, "in fact, the entire bay with its customs facility falls under American domination." Castellanos enters U.S. territory, his self-consciousness on high alert. "We have taken one of the channels that crosses into the naval station. Perched on one of the buoys is an enormous bird. It eyes us curiously as we continue on, sheltered by our flag, as if our little boat were a child's plaything."

Past the warehouses of the Guantánamo Sugar Company, past the shoreline of the U.S. base "where typical American bungalows sit atop steep cliffs," past the landing field at Hicacal Beach, past the commotion of the never-ending dredging work, Castellanos advances. He pauses before another beach, this one "situated at the foot of the residence of the base commander where floats an American flag, striped symbol of the North American imperial republic." Each star represents an American state, Castellanos muses, "but among these great stars are asteroids that the world doesn't see—symbols of peoples suffering the yoke of American imperialism. I looked then at my pretty little standard and I wondered whether I too was supposed to tip my hat to this strange flag."[63]

From the water, the base looks deceptively benign. There is scarcely any movement. No sign of warships, only a few barges huddled alongside the wharves. There are no visible fortifications, "as if the Americans recognize that fixed armaments require constant attention and are ineffective in certain situations." In short, Castellanos concludes, the naval station is nothing but a great fueling depot for boats and warplanes. Therein lies its signal importance in extending the reach of American military and commercial influence throughout the Caribbean. In the event of an attack, the station could be defended by a few simple measures or abandoned altogether. The base "costs the US virtually nothing." It costs Castellanos his pride.

Before heading back to Caimanera, Castellanos makes a final stop at El Deseo, a tiny village in Cuban territory on the outskirts of Caimanera. El Deseo returns Castellanos to the subject of alcohol. Approaching the wharves that skirt the village, Castellanos is surprised to find several American launches tied up to a pier. One of the boats is particularly fancy, evidently the property of the base commander. Live jazz and murmured conversation float over the water. At the foot of one of the wharves sits a small café with an outdoor terrace and dance floor. On a large counter along one wall of the café "shimmer a rainbow of liquor bottles." Seated at tables are groups of men and women drinking an assortment of cocktails. "There is much merriment," Castellanos observes. "Swollen faces, the smell of alcohol. From the orchestra, one Yankee air after another." All patrons are residents of the naval base. Officers of every grade mix together, from the lowest to the commandant. The dress is informal. "Almost nobody wears their stripes." Some wear T-shirts, others swimming trunks. The ladies appear "saturated" in alcohol. Castellanos is astounded by this "representation of the Yankee Navy." Here it is only midafternoon.

Only the commandant maintains his distance, "upholding the laws of his country." Meanwhile, one of the ladies approaches Castellanos and speaks to him in "correct Castilian." An officer joins the author's table and accepts a drink. "Another officer, as if jealous, pretends to discharge his revolver" at Castellanos's companion, a local judge. The chief of the naval station converses with everyone, dances, but still holds back. "But I know the ropes," Castellanos writes; "the more the goat backs away, the worse the charge."

The charge comes, but only after some unseen signal silences the band and draws the happy hour to a close. The Americans all carry off at least one hidden bottle as the commandant looks the other way. The "drunks and drinkers" depart, but the commandant lingers. "Now it's his turn," Castellanos notes. "I look at him and he smiles slyly. He is drinking. Another follows. And another. His cheeks flush." Castellanos departs for Caimanera.[64]

Not all the Americans' socializing at Guantánamo involved overindulgence in alcohol and women. Guantánamo featured plenty of wholesome recreation, too, as the Navy Wife reports, such as golf and tennis, swimming and riding, baseball and volleyball, and hiking trips into the local mountains, where waterfalls and caves caught the Americans' attention. Though the base infrastructure remained largely unchanged between the wars, the opportunities for recreation constantly expanded, so that by World War II, Guantánamo had become synonymous with play.

Part of the credit for this is owed to Admiral Charles M. Cooke, who took command of the base in June 1934, six months after Prohibition came to an end. Up until Admiral Cooke's appointment, his daughter Maynard remembers, "the station was considered a graveyard tour for any officer sent to be commandant." For many years, "under the command of a series of officers unhappy with being stuck in this backwater," the base had gone "downhill." Cooke was charged with bringing the base "up to snuff," a mission he understood to include not just making the facility war-ready but improving base morale.[65]

Cooke liked parties. One Halloween, he transformed the officers' club into a haunted house, taking pains to order well in advance some sixty black-and-orange clown costumes, complete with headgear and black masks. A hit with the children, who were allowed to preview the haunted house before being hauled off to bed, the party was a smash with base personnel, who relished the social inversion that anonymity afforded. Cooke was also known for constructing an open-air pavilion, complete with concrete floor, thatched roof, and an icebox, on the crest of John Paul Jones Hill, the highest elevation at the base. Called Mountain House by the locals, the pavilion provided officers and their wives a dazzling view from which to catch the sunset as they wet their whistle, and sometimes spent the night.[66]

At the beginning of the century, journalist Frank Carpenter described the area surrounding the Guantánamo naval base to readers of the *Boston Sunday Globe*. In the lowlands of the Guantánamo Basin, surrounding the U.S. base, were some "large plantations of sugar owned by Americans, and coffee grows well on the hills." This part of Cuba was "especially healthy," Carpenter reported, "and it was at one time a sort of Newport for the rich sugar and coffee men of the eastern end." One planter supposedly "had an avenue running from his residence to the sea shore. The road was covered with shells and was lined with lemon and orange trees."[67]

By the time Cooke arrived at Guantánamo, the sugar industry had become a victim of the Great Depression, but also of global competition from the rise of the sugar beet industry. If no longer a second Newport by 1934, the surrounding countryside still boasted plenty of opportunities for amusement as well as a few luxurious estates, one of them owned by William "Shorty" Osment, administrator general of the U.S.-owned and -operated Guantánamo and Western Railroad Company, headquartered at Guantánamo City. Cooke befriended U.S. and foreign planters throughout the basin, but he grew particularly close to Osment, with the Cookes visiting Osment at his estate outside Boquerón and Osment traveling to the base for parties at the officers' club.[68] Osment owned a private rail line, which connected his estate to the town of Boquerón. On this track he mounted what Cubans called a *sequena*, an American automobile converted to run on rails. Cooke's daughter, Maynard, remembers riding this "car" into Osment's estate, overrun with peacocks.[69]

Amid the laid-back atmosphere that was 1930s Guantánamo, Cooke had no problem mixing naval business with pleasure. His tenure at Guantánamo coincided with a growing sense of urgency about the base water supply, which in 1934 arrived there in railroad tanks via Guantánamo City and the Guaso River. In 1934, political instability in Cuba combined with enduring uneasiness over the base's dependence on an outside water source to inspire a series of studies about an alternative water source. As most of the proposals involved tapping resources in Cuba, Cooke thought it prudent to examine the proposed sites for himself. On such trips, he was delighted to tap the hospitality of his friend Osment, bringing along not only his wife but a handful of officers and their wives, to a maximum of eight guests.[70] As a foreign businessman operating in a historically volatile region of Cuba during a period of political instability, Osment found it only natural to ingratiate himself with the base commander. Besides furnishing Mrs. Cooke and her daughter with horses, Osment provided souvenirs of his guests' visits.[71] He quartered Cooke and his friends during diplomatic stopovers in Guantánamo City, and he kept Cooke stocked with Cuban cigars.[72]

It is no wonder that Cooke preferred to stay with Shorty Osment on his visits to Guantánamo City rather than at local establishments. In March 1938 the popular Cuban journal *Bohemia* ran an article exposing the U.S. claim that the base propped up the nearby Cuban economy. The article contrasted "Caimanera," the Cuban name for the U.S. base, with the nearby city of Guantánamo, the "sewer of Cuba," where shameless politicians pursued their self-interest in a "stagnant, hedonistic, dirty, and desolate" place. Spotlessly clean and neatly laid out, the base shimmered with energy and purpose, its "luxurious profusion of lights" illuminating a way of life distinctly foreign to the Cuban workers arriving there. Whereas the base overflowed with flowering gardens and snapped with colorful flags, Guantánamo City languished in a state of despondency and boredom, eliciting nothing so much as a large yawn. At once dull and decadent, its citizens failed to even notice the squalor in which they had sunk. Oh, there were still a few well-off Cubans who distracted themselves with the fantasy of marrying their daughters off to American officers and thereby lightening their family's darker skin. But they were but further evidence of a city unable to help itself and shoulder the responsibility required of real improvement.[73]

An enthusiastic guest, Cooke was also a generous host. In March 1935 a yacht named *Cachalot*, with nine family members aboard, radioed the U.S. naval base for permission to ride out a March northeaster in Guantánamo Bay. Permission granted, *Cachalot* was scudding along Cuba's bleak southeast coastline when it was met by a friendly naval escort dispatched by Commander Cooke. Just before dark, Jane Hartge remembers, *Chachalot* entered "the huge bay studded with warships of every size and armor"—"war clouds were rising across the world" at the time. Never mind the threat of war; as *Chachalot* bobbed gratefully at her "designated anchorage in the midst of all this pomp and circumstance . . . alongside came a gleaming brass and macramé spangled 'barge' with invitation from the commanding officer and his lady to our 'party' to come ashore for cocktails." As so often at Guantanamo, cocktails led to more cocktails, then to dinner and an outdoor cinema, at which Cooke and his guests were greeted like royalty, with "the entire audience standing."[74]

In times of crisis, Cooke's generosity extended to his Caribbean neighbors. A few months after *Chachalot*'s visit, Cooke had just completed a Navy Day address when he was handed an urgent telegraph from his bosses in Washington, D.C.:

COMMUNICATE DIRECT WITH CHARGE DAFFAIRES US EMBASSY AT PORTAUPRINCE AND ASCERTAIN EXTENT OF ASSISTANCE REQUIRED

PERIOD STATE DEPARTMENT STATES THAT FOOD SUPPLIES AND
MEDICAL ASSISTANCE ARE NECESSARY PERIOD FURNISH ALL POS-
SIBLE ASSISTANCE UTILIZING WOODCOCK AND INFORM OPNAV OF
GENERAL CONDITIONS AND ASSISTANCE REQUIRED BEYOND YOUR
FACILITIES.

On October 23, a slow-moving hurricane churned up the Windward Passage after inundating Jamaica and claiming the life of an
eleven-year-old boy. The day before, *The New York Times* reported
"heavy rains in Haiti" and described communities across the region
hunkering down. At the Guantánamo naval station, residents were
ushered into hillside bunkers, while Cuba evacuated the towns of Caimanera and Boqueron.

Washington followed developments in the waters south of Cuba
closely. That very day, President Franklin Roosevelt was returning from
a fishing trip aboard the presidential yacht *Houston*, just hours ahead of
the mounting storm. President Roosevelt was not the only one scurrying for cover. Aboard his three-hundred-foot steamer *Alva*, William K.
Vanderbilt was making desperately for Fort Pierce, Florida, in the company of his wife, Rosamund, his daughter, Muriel, and *Alva*'s forty-two-
person crew. With means of escape, the president, the commodore, and
U.S. base personnel were all spared when the hurricane came ashore in
the vicinity of Guantánamo Bay. But Haitians living on the southern
peninsula, west of the capital, Port-au-Prince, weren't so lucky. On October 25, news reached the naval station of flooding in Haiti accompanied by "great loss of life." Someone broached the idea of outfitting the
Guantánamo station ship USS *Woodcock* for emergency relief, but no
orders followed, and the base continued on with its work.

Then came the tales of horror, of whole villages washed down the
Grand Anse River, of thousands of bodies flushed out to sea near the
town of Jacmel. In the Anse Valley, Cooke later reported, "the floods
came up about midnight October 21–22, and filled the valley floor
from twenty to seventy feet, sweeping houses, people, chickens, hogs,
cattle and goats out to sea." Survivors were found clinging to trees,
having "lost everything including their clothes." In one village, eight
out of four hundred inhabitants survived. With the Haitians' homes
went all means of subsistence. Wells were contaminated, sewage ex-

posed, crops ruined. Had there been any medicine in the worst-hit villages, there was scarcely anyone left to administer it. In some towns, nobody remained to bury the dead.

It took five days for the scale of the calamity to register in Port-au-Prince. With roads impassable and electrical and telegraph lines cut, the southwest peninsula was completely shut off. News of the disaster reached the capital only after a cargo ship sailing up the Windward Passage encountered a raft of bodies and debris bobbing off the Haitian coast.

Once alerted to the crisis, the Guantánamo naval station sprang into action. On Monday, October 29, the *Woodcock*, laden with rice, beans, and disinfectant, cleared Guantánamo harbor, Commander Cooke himself at the helm. Arriving in Haiti the next morning, the *Woodcock* offloaded supplies at the port of Jeremie, near the mouth of the Anse River, then proceeded on to the capital. In Port-au-Prince, Cooke was met by Haitian government officials, including the sister of President Sténio Vincent. After welcoming the Haitians aboard, the *Woodcock* set off to deliver lumber, medicine, and other necessities to the stricken villages. By Friday, November 2, Cooke and his crew had returned to Guantánamo Bay, their humanitarian mission complete, in its wake a palpable feeling of goodwill.[75]

By the eve of World War II, Cuba was suffering through a nearly two-decade-long cycle of personality-based politics, in which capricious and self-serving individuals retained power by means of favoritism and intimidation. In 1925, Cubans elected Gerardo Machado president. An industrialist and former general in the Liberation Army, Machado ran on a reform platform, advocating, among other things, tariffs to promote Cuban industry, new infrastructure, and improvements in education and health care. Without the effects of the Great Depression, Machado's attempt to diversify the Cuban economy would have been difficult; despite the falling value of sugar production worldwide, sugar remained the primary source of Cuban capital. But the Depression ravaged Cuban sugar, robbing the new government of the resources required for political and social reform. When Machado responded to the inevitable strikes and antigovernment protests with violence and rigged elections, Cuba succumbed to armed conflict. Underemployed youths, intellectuals, professionals, and students faced off against an increasingly powerful army. The outcome was never in doubt, but the effect was insidious. The government resorted to political repression and physical brutality to crush the dissidents. The rebels hit back with kidnapping, assassination, and terror.

So long as the unrest did not threaten American businesses, U.S. administrations were happy to sit back and do nothing. By 1933 the violence began to erode profits, forcing President Roosevelt to dispatch the diplomat Sumner Welles to Cuba to try to reach an accommodation between Machado, now a dictator, and the old political elite. Machado agreed to a U.S. demand to restore at least the trappings of constitutional government. Meanwhile, Cuban Communists, labor activists, and others denounced U.S. meddling. As the unrest continued, the United States asked Machado to resign. He refused, but ultimately fell victim to further chaos generated by a general strike. Amid the political and social upheaval, the United States tried to orchestrate the appointment of Carlos Manuel de Céspedes to the presidency. This time Cubans said no, and greeted the elevation of Céspedes with violence against officials of the old Machado regime.[76]

In place of Céspedes, Cuba's enlisted officers and university students elevated Ramón Grau to the presidency, along with the radical labor activist Antonio Guiteras as prime minister—this, in direct defiance of U.S. officials, the Cuban officer corps, Cuban political elites, and, above all, the presuppositions of Platt. If unlikely to last, the Grau-Guiteras coalition was unequivocal in its insistence that Cuba determine its own political and economic fortune. The economy would be geared toward national production and consumption. Labor would be granted, among other things, a minimum wage, an eight-hour workday, worker compensation, collective bargaining, and a requirement that at least 50 percent of the labor force be Cuban-born. Perhaps most important, the new government promised land reform.[77]

Despite remarkable successes in advancing much of its reform agenda, the opportunistic pairing of Grau, a moderate, with Guiteras, a radical, could not last. Difficult to maintain under any circumstances, the coalition collapsed after four months in office, the victim of U.S., Cuban Army, and conservative opposition, as well as militant labor activism. The U.S. government never recognized the Grau-Guiteras government. Instead, Ambassador Welles tapped Fulgencio Batista to take over the reins of government. A sergeant in the Cuban Army, and one of the leaders of the enlisted officers' coup, Batista impressed U.S. officials with his ability to neutralize the old officer corps while clamping down on labor unrest. Here was a man the U.S. government could work with.[78]

And work with Batista (and his puppet, President Carlos Mendieta) the United States did, abrogating the now nettlesome Platt Amendment in May 1934 in exchange for an open-ended lease of the Guantánamo naval base. Though less coerced than the original lease, the new lease was hardly negotiated between equal partners, as U.S. officials would later claim. It came on the heels not only of the U.S. elevation of Batista to power but also of passage of the Jones-Cooligan Act, which pledged the United States to a large annual purchase of Cuban sugar. In short, Batista could hardly have said no to the naval base, even had he wanted to.[79]

Under Batista, the Cuban Army replaced the old political class as the true force in Cuban politics. Once aligned to labor radicals, Batista crushed the militant labor movement in 1935, assassinating Antonio Guiteras as he attempted to leave the country. Which is not to say that Batista was anticommunist or antilabor. An army man, Batista couldn't stand disorder. Indeed, he needed the backing of organized labor and even the Communist Party to legitimate his rule. In 1938 he approved the reemergence of the old Partido Comunista de Cuba as the Partido Unión Revolucionario (PUR), which collaborated with the government in exchange for control of Cuban trade unions. For the next eight years, Cuban presidents maintained close relations with PUR, relying on its support to bolster fragile governing coalitions.[80]

Batista endorsed much of the political agenda proposed by nationalist parties since the 1920s, including the establishment of a national bank, a program for agricultural diversification, profit sharing in the sugar industry, land distribution, and the advancement of public health and education. In 1940, he summoned a constitutional convention to which all parties were welcome. The convention led to the restoration of constitutional democracy in Cuba, and produced two consecutive legitimate and undisputed elections in Cuba, utterly unprecedented, the first of which Batista won.[81]

U.S. influence remained strong in Cuba throughout Batista's rise and consolidation of power, though it was subtler, less overt than in had once been. The sugar industry recovered during World War II, thanks partly to the continued trade reciprocity with the United States. At the same time, the Cuban labor movement began to flourish, with labor managing to pass a series of modest reforms focusing on employment protection, evidence of the fragility of Cuba's ruling coalition.[82]

For nearly two decades between the end of World War I and the saber rattling that preceded World War II, little changed at the naval base besides the cast of characters and the establishment of new social diversions for officers and their families. The war altered this. In 1938, President Roosevelt appointed a commission to examine the nation's state of military readiness. The so-called Hepburn Board, named after its chairman, Arthur J. Hepburn, picked up pretty much where Admiral Mahan's Navy Board had left off over a generation earlier: the United States was vulnerable to German incursion in the Caribbean, among other places. The board recommended developing the nation's defenses throughout the Caribbean and especially at Guantánamo Bay.

In the summer of 1940 the U.S. Navy hired the private contracting firm Frederick Snare Corporation, based in New York City but with offices scattered throughout Cuba and Latin America, to undertake a $37 million upgrade of the naval base. The project included an independent and fully functioning marine base, new airstrips on both sides of the bay, ammunition magazines, a school and chapel, and still more recreational facilities. The work was undertaken with great urgency. By 1943, when the work pace eased, some ten thousand Cubans, Jamaicans, and West Indians labored on the base alongside four thousand U.S. servicemen and civilians. The vast labor force transformed life not only at the base but also in the local Cuban communities as workers throughout eastern Cuba showed up seeking work.

From the start, labor relations between Snare and the Cuban labor force, now enjoying the benefits of its enhanced status, were fraught with conflict and charges of exploitation against a private contractor that claimed immunity from both U.S. and Cuban labor standards and laws. The U.S. military and Snare executives saw only radicalism and eventually communism in the escalating complaints. For nearly a decade the navy successfully resisted calls from Cuban workers to allow labor representation on the base. By 1950 the navy gave in, partly to neutralize a growing Communist presence in the region.

Meanwhile, as the Hepburn Board predicted, the Caribbean Sea became a theater of submarine warfare, with Germany targeting not only merchant ships bound for Europe in the North Atlantic but also commercial traffic between the Panama Canal and the port of New York. In February 1942 alone, Germany sank 28 Allied vessels comprising some 93,000 tons of shipping. That year 257 ships went down in the Caribbean alone. A year later, the numbers began to improve as the naval base became the linchpin in a convoy system that stretched from the Panama Canal to New York. In 1943 only twenty-two ships were sunk; the following year a mere two. During the war, commercial and naval traffic through the bay dramatically increased, with Guantánamo becoming a bustling seaport second in volume of traffic along the eastern seaboard only to New York Harbor itself.

The World War II expansion created the footprint of office buildings, warehouses, jetties, airstrips, magazines, and residential neighborhoods still visible today. The base that Cuban labor built in World War II now stretches for three miles from the southwest corner of Windward Point along the southeast shoreline of the outer harbor, past the many jetties that extend their fingers into the bay, and on toward the salt flats that mark the northeast corner of the base. The new construction included thousands of temporary housing units but also comfortable, if modest, stand-alone suburban-style homes. Back from the shoreline and extending up into the hills, streets were laid and neighborhoods planted that in the rainy season, when water turns the hills from brown to green, resembles suburban California.

On July 30, 2007, the U.S. House of Representatives passed Resolution 121, calling on the government of Japan "to formally acknowledge, apologize, and accept historical responsibility in a clear and unequivocal manner for its Imperial Armed Force's coercion of young women into sexual slavery, known to the world as 'comfort women,' during its colonial and wartime occupation of Asia and the Pacific Islands from the 1930s through the duration of World War II." Japan's abuse of Korean, Chinese, and Filipino women forced into sexual slavery is well documented and needs no amplification here.[83] But how many of the U.S. representatives who voted for the resolution know that, since at least the time of Prohibition, the U.S. Navy condoned and later colluded in a sex traffic of its own in the Cuban towns around Guantánamo Bay? Cuba, like other countries, has a long history of commercial sex; the extracurricular activity between U.S. servicemen and local women in the towns around the naval base in the 1920s only mirrored that between international clients and professional call girls in major cities throughout the "island paradise," especially in Havana, at the same time.[84] Critics may object that the case of Japanese comfort women bears no resemblance to the good old prostitution common around overseas military bases since time immemorial. But that judgment may be better left to Cubans.[85]

By all accounts, an industrialization of the sex trade paralleled the wartime expansion of the naval base. In 1943, Doug White, an enlisted man stationed in Puerto Rico with the Naval Radio Service, was marooned at Guantánamo Bay while awaiting passage back to the United States. Though he has forgotten the name of the place, White visited the little town beyond "the Cuban land gate, which was open to all servicemen" by this time, and where "there was a street solid with bars and bordellos." Sailors such as White had

> to run the gauntlet of posters and warnings about venereal diseases to reach the border, but once there, it was a daily circus until the gate closed at 10:00 p.m. The street was mud, the bars loud, the broads filthy, the rum watered and grossly unsanitary. It was impossible to walk on the street without being snatched into a bar or show, which was usually a front for more pleasurable pursuits in the back room. Awaiting your return, just inside the gate was a building of attended

cubicles. Whether you had dallied or not, you were made to strip and
shower, then were sprayed, scoured, powdered and salved for any souvenirs you might have collected during your Cuban charge.

White visited Guantánamo Bay as part of a convoy crew during World
War II. Convoy crews lived "a grueling existence," he remembers, with
"six hours on duty, six hours off, for weeks on end, with a day off only
at their destinations, usually Rio or Guantánamo." No doubt the men
"greatly appreciated the recreation available both on and off the base
when they reached it."[86]
     Late in the war, William Mills, a twenty-year-old ensign and gun-
nery officer, traveled to Guantánamo Bay aboard the USS LSM-104,
an amphibious landing craft. While at Guantánamo, Mills visited Caimanera. Mills remembers the naval base as "ordinary," the quarters as
"quite comfortable, with full recreational facilities such as swimming
pool, officers' club, etc., all heavily used."[87] Meanwhile Caimanera
lived up to its reputation, Mill reports, "as a large-scale brothel for accommodating 'our boys' in ways Mother never intended. Many of us
enjoyed it, some fully and others only as a curiosity we'd never seen
before." Mills was among the few to admit that he had spent a night at
Caimanera. ("Yes," he volunteered. "Once.")
     "We were carried to Caimanera on Navy LCVPs [landing craft,
vehicle and personnel]," Mills recalls, "where we stepped off already
in the town. I recall only one main street, although doubtless there
were others. The nighttime street was brightly lighted with raucous
music on every hand and open-air 'bars' lining both sides of the street."
Separating Caimanera's bars were "pro stations," small canvas-covered
cubicles "where several sailors simultaneously could enter and, concealed knee to neck from the street, drop the front of their trousers
and inject the contents of a prophylactic tube into their urethras, said
to be a surefire way, postcoital, to avoid VD. I think it was." Mills
doubted that these "remarkably clean" facilities could operate "so efficiently" without formal naval sponsorship. The booths were in "regular use, all in an atmosphere of business as usual." They provoked no
reactions from passersby. By night, anyway, Mills remembers Caimanera having few civilians other than the "working girls" and bartenders,

"all others being uniformed US Navy men." Caimanera's "volatile mixture" was kept in check by Navy "SPs," or shore patrols.

Once inoculated, the U.S. sailors "entered the bar, sat down at a table and ordered (usually) beer. Cuban prostitutes lined the walls of Caimanera's bars, usually seated on single chairs. The surrounding whores assessed their chances and chose accordingly to approach the candidate for business." While not every sailor partook in this ritual, "enough did to maintain high occupancy of the 'business rooms.'" Couples retreated to "very small rooms lining the three inner walls, each with a single door and, inside, a single bed, washstand, and pitcher of water. Occupancy was for a limited time that could be enforced, for those who lingered, by a stern knock on the door by an old woman."

The women, meanwhile, were "typical of their kind." Mills describes "simple folk from a background of third-world [extreme] poverty who cope with a harsh life." Many of these women "responded gratefully to even minimal courtesy or kindness. Contrary to popular opinion I've heard, most will respond sincerely to any credible romantic overture, and yes, that too happened more than you'd think with youthful American soldiers and sailors."[88]

"When you're living in a foreign country," observed Captain Roland Faulk, a navy chaplain well acquainted with the cultural economy of the Guantánamo naval base during the 1940s and '50s, "you want to protect your own troops and not become a victim of the host country's standards."[89] Thus Faulk joined the age-old debate about the relationship between supply and demand in the underground economy by blaming the other side. The occasion of these remarks was an unusually candid interview with the archivist John Mason about prostitution in the U.S. military. Where the navy condoned and indeed facilitated the sex trade in overseas bases, Faulk opposed it on pragmatic as well as moral grounds: not only was prostitution just plain wrong according to the moral code that Faulk had committed his life to defending, but the venereal disease that went with it incapacitated the men.

Visiting Guantánamo Bay in the mid-1940s, Faulk took his concerns to Captain Roscoe H. Hillenkoetter, commander of the USS *Missouri*, who, upon arriving at the bay, dispatched a liberty party to the Cuban town of Caimanera, just outside the boundary of the U.S. base. Caimanera, Faulk warned Hillenkoetter, "had only one purpose for its existence," namely, "prostitution." Like many officers in the navy, Hillenkoetter (later to become director of the Central Intelligence Agency) was unimpressed by Faulk's reservations. But Faulk was not to be deterred. Returning to Guantánamo for an extended stay a few years later, he confronted the base commander, Rear Admiral W. K. Phillips, about the local traffic in sex. "Why can't we put the place out of bounds?" Faulk asked Phillips. The answer was "quite simple," Phillips replied. "We could put it out of bounds but up in Havana the Cuban government would go to our ambassador and lodge a protest. That protest would go back to the American State Department. The State Department would call the secretary of the navy and say, 'What are you doing down there in Cuba? You can't do that.' And so the out of bounds would have to be lifted." What was a proponent of personal responsibility and clean living to do? With Cuba impeding a collective solution, Faulk could only "leave it to the individual man. Preach against it, exhort against it, talk against it, persuade against it. That's about all you could do."[90]

In fact, Faulk did more. Suspicious that the source of the problem was not indeed Cuba—that the navy was "aiding and abetting prostitution" at U.S. bases around the world—Faulk resolved to study venereal disease rates among the sailors at Guantánamo and elsewhere. Evidence from 188 cases of syphilis at Guantánamo led him to surmise that misguided naval policies were encouraging the spread of disease. A larger study later confirmed the evidence from Guantánamo. "One of the first things which caught my attention when I was Fleet Chaplain was the recurring rumor which I heard to the effect that Commanding Officers were requiring men going ashore in the Far East to take with them prophylaxis," Faulk reported. Unable at first to trace the origin of that rule, Faulk discovered "that it was carried in a confidential Operation Order issued by the Fleet Commander." Further investigation into naval involvement in prostitution proved "eye-opening." While naval officials touted the benefits of prophylaxis, infection rates in Pearl Harbor, Hawaii, for example, reached as high as 1,780 infections per 1,000 men per year—nearly 2 infections for every sailor.[91]

There is no reason to think Guantánamo was any different. If anything, Faulk's study suggests that infection rates there may have been higher still. "Your [Cuban] servants are given regular health checks, including the Kahn blood test and chest X-rays," a Guantánamo "Housing Information Manual" assured navy wives relocating to the U.S. base in 1958.[92] Designed to screen individuals for venereal disease, the Kahn blood test would have seemed contraindicated for domestic servants unless the infection rate in eastern Cuba had been extraordinarily high. Just how that piece of information was supposed to comfort young navy wives is not clear.

Internal navy documents corroborate Faulk's hypothesis of the navy's abetting the sex trade. A classified security memo from 1952 remarks that "venereal disease control presents the major health problem encountered at the Base. The only off-Base liberty is in adjacent areas where an unusually high incidence of venereal disease is present, and where there is no choice of proper companionship with the opposite sex for the majority of personnel." In contrast to the base itself, where sailors could choose from a variety of recreational activities, "the only form of entertainment available" in Cuban towns around the base was "drinking and girls." Neither bad policy nor poor decision making was behind the alarming incidents of VD; rather, "low-cost liquor is the cause of 95% of venereal infections," the memo alleged, "as men who, under the influence of alcohol, fail to take advantage of the prophylaxis available."[93]

Faulk's testimony and the evidence from the security memo support Peter Grenquist's suspicion that the robust sex traffic he witnessed at the bay could not have proceeded without high-level support. A junior officer at Guantánamo in the early 1950s, Grenquist suggests that by the time of his visit, the epicenter of the sex traffic had shifted from Caimanera to Guantánamo City, some twelve miles up the Guantánamo Basin. Guantánamo City "had various informal brothels and young freelancers happy to service liberty parties from the base." In order to distance itself from traffic, "the navy permanently stationed a relatively low level second-class pharmacist mate and perhaps a couple of seamen assistants in the city to test the girls for venereal disease." Assigned to Guantánamo City for shore patrol, Grenquist remembers meeting one "enterprising petty officer" whose control of the sex trade was so complete that "the navy had to remove him quietly from his czardom." The word on the street: "graft was a factor."[94]

Twice at Guantánamo—first as a sailor, later as a junior officer with the Fleet Training Group—Hal Sacks remembers Caimanera as "an exotic semitropical area." The inhabitants had little to do and plenty of time on their hands. Children hung out in the streets until midnight; there were carts with roast pig on Cuban bread for five cents. There was "marvelous" Hatuey beer and "sensational" Bacardi rum. So, too, "great chicken, fish, rice, and beans." Like Grenquist, as an officer, Sacks was assigned periodically to shore patrol, which gave him an intimate impression of the local nightlife. His headquarters were near the row of whorehouses that lined the harbor. His job was to chaperone, or "supervise," the extracurricular activity—to make sure that nobody got hurt. "Sometimes there was a problem of guys not paying," Sacks recalls, "sometimes somebody hit someone, including the Cuban women." Sacks remembers that the more or less defenseless Cuban women were always grateful for his help.[95]

One night, Sacks was approached by a young woman in tears; she reported being roughed up by one of the Americans. Sacks offered to escort her home. She lived in a one-room house, very simple, with nothing to distinguish it from her neighbors' lodging except for the red-haired kid asleep on her bed—"not at all Hispanic." Next to the bed, on the nightstand, stood a picture of the boy's father, a "red-headed American marine." "Syphilis wasn't the only reason to wear a condom." At the U.S. base and in the Cuban towns and cities that surrounded it, all sorts of sexual and conjugal alliances were struck. The Sackses lost their first maid of eight months to a U.S. sailor. There was a pecking order among the maids, Sacks reports, with darker Cubans making less money than their lighter-skinned counterparts. For the Sackses' maid, "black and dark," marriage to a young second-class petty officer promised immediate upward mobility. She accompanied him back to the United States and expedited U.S. citizenship.[96]

Other witnesses report similar alliances. Attached to a helicopter squadron at McCalla Field, Rex Lake lived with his young family in Caimanera, at the Oasis Hotel, from the autumn of 1956 through the summer of 1958, a period that coincided with Castro's return to Cuba and subsequent guerilla campaign waged from the nearby Sierra Maestra. Long after the end of World War II, the base population continued to exceed available housing, and it was not unusual for U.S. servicemen and civilians and their families to live in Guantánamo City and Caimanera.

In fact, Lake reports, Caimanera had more than the one street that Mills remember in his recollection of liberty parties off the U.S. base. Though Lake would come to appreciate Caimanera over the course of his two and a half years there, the town didn't make a good first impression. "Except for the main street through town, all the streets of Caimanera were dirt," he writes.

> In the rainy season, they were a sea of mud. Most of the population was terribly poor. One large area of shacks was built on stilts over the water. All garbage, including human waste, was simply dumped out the door or window into the bay. It helped keep the home clean, but the smell from the bay was atrocious. The odor along the little dirt streets from the rotting sewage in the ditches would nearly take your breath away. Children played in these streets and somehow many survived. Typhoid was always a fear for the many American families with small children like ours.[97]

The "one street" in Caimanera that Mill recalls was undoubtedly what others knew as "the District." It was indeed a memorable street. Here is "where all the sailors came to drink and make whoopee with the local girls." For the bargain rate of $2.50, sailors could take their pick of the local talent ("many of whom were very lovely") that spilled out of the bars lining the District's lone thoroughfare. "Unfortunately," Lake notes, "for your $2.50 you could also get a grand case of venereal disease. Gonorrhea was the main attraction, but syphilis ran a close second. To protect its young, healthy sailors, the navy set up a first aid station at the entrance to the District and dispensed free condoms and penicillin pills. This was indeed a strange and unusual life style far from the normalcy of home." As strange as it was unpredictable. Lake knew two sailors from his group "who fell in love and married their prostitutes from the District and took them home to the United States."[98]

By the late 1940s and early '50s, with Prohibition long since over, one didn't have to leave the base to have a drink. As a result, Grenquist reports, a marked change occurred in the social atmosphere at Guantánamo City, where the nightlife quieted significantly.[99] In contrast to the "industrial brothels" that Mill, Sacks, and Lake describe in Caimanera, in Guantánamo City the sex trade moved indoors to people's homes, where Cuban prostitutes and U.S. sailors would sit around in living rooms before hooking up and heading off to do their thing. This trade, though obviously organized, seemed "informal, if not amateurish," Grenquist reports. Typically the U.S. sailors arrived one day and returned to the base early the next day: "There was no illusion" that they were in town "just to have a drink."[100]

Some sailors went out of their way to flout their sexual prowess. In one case, a young "mustang" (a career sailor promoted up through the ranks to officer status) of Falstaffian bearing arrived at the Guantánamo station one morning drinking a beer and evidently "quite pleased with himself." Before arriving at the bay, he was greeted at a local depot by a pair of Cuban girls "who looked like twins." Full of giggles, they waved at him; he toasted them. As the shore patrol in charge, Grenquist couldn't decide if the man had actually spent the night with the women or simply paid them to show up as a means of impressing the others.[101]

It is hard to say what the navy made of this. Grenquist suggests that someone evidently had misgivings, for, though officers could go on liberty parties, too, the navy went out of its way try to keep officers entertained at the base. There they would be paired with "proper, nice Cuban girls from respectable families at Guantánamo City" at base dances at the officers' club. The events resembled "high school proms." Boats arrived with young Cuban women in a "rainbow of pastels." Most did not speak much English, and few officers spoke much Spanish, making these dances exercises in mime. These were *not* enjoyable, Grenquist emphasizes, for either the Cubans or the Americans. For the Cubans at least there was a reward. The young women were allowed to go to the ships' store at the officers' club and shop tax-free. Grenquist could not recall the effect of these abstemious encounters on the young officers. But he concedes that they may have made the officers ripe for a visit to Guantánamo City—to "have their ashes hauled."[102]

In 1950, the journalist Gervasio G. Ruiz traveled to the U.S. base for a story to be published in the travel journal *Carteles*.[103] Ruiz's account suggests that over a decade after *Bohemia* compared Guantánamo City to a sewer, the place had improved, but only a little. When Gerardo Castellanos visited Guantánamo Bay in 1930, Guantánamo City was just opening to U.S. servicemen again after a several-year hiatus; when *Bohemia* sent its correspondent to Guantánamo in 1938, Guantánamo City was once again off-limits, thanks to poor sanitation and its generally unsavory social climate. At the time of Ruiz's visit, the Americans continued to shy away from Guantánamo City, a fact regrettable to the entrepreneur in Ruiz, and something he hoped to rectify. Sanitation improvements were a good start. "Until recently," Ruiz reports, "Guantánamo was a dirty and dusty place, with poor hygiene. Today its streets are paved and can count on a sewer system, which, if not perfectly efficient, offers, at the least, a minimum of health to those who dwell or visit there."

But substandard sanitation was not the only impediment to luring U.S. business back to Guantánamo City. Local opposition to "Yankee imperialism" had made Guantánamo City an unfriendly place. Ruiz confirmed Grenquist's account of base officials importing young women from Guantánamo City's "best" families to spice up Thursday night dances at the officers' club. Sometimes these courtesy visits stoked fierce local opposition, and one particularly belligerent protest forced the base commander to cancel a dance, shelter the young women for the night, and return them by plane directly to Guantánamo City. To Ruiz, the so-called patriotic critics of the base were really "Stalinists" determined "to provoke yet another scandal against Yankee imperialism."

Yet a third cause for American wariness toward Guantánamo City were the hustlers who assaulted American sailors when the trains pulled in from the bayside stations at Caimanera and Boquerón. "No sooner had the sailors set foot in Guantánamo station," Ruiz reports, "than tour guides and ticket sellers and salesmen would converge on them like a plague of locusts to rob them blind." The good citizens of Guantánamo opposed the traffic in alcohol, women, and other contraband, Ruiz insisted. And the base authorities tried to put an end to it. Reluctant to offend the Americans on whom Guantánamo's revitalization would depend, Ruiz did not blame the U.S. sailors, who, though not entirely innocent, "would probably have steered clear of Guantánamo's underworld if it weren't for the encouragement of the local merchants."

If eager to protect the Americans' reputation, Ruiz bent over backward to try to please base officials. Against all the evidence of other eyewitnesses, Ruiz insisted that "one shouldn't confuse the behavior of American troops who pass through the base with the long-term residents and their families." With a population of twelve thousand, the base community propelled the local economy. Base residents got along very well with the Cuban population. So well, in fact, that twenty or so "senoritas guantanameras" had married into the officers' club." The town of Caimanera, meanwhile, was "moribund," totally off-limits to U.S. servicemen.[104]

Ruiz had not expected to visit the naval base; most visitors to Guantánamo Bay were not admitted. But *Carteles* had connections with Antonio Civit Jané, a local doctor and a figure well-known at the base, who introduced Ruiz to Hugh Barr Miller, the head of naval intelligence. "The first thing that struck me," Ruiz reports, describing the base, "was the cleanliness of the place—the roads, the gardens, the buildings, indeed, everything we saw." Fumigation and hygiene machinery abounded, and seemed to be used "without stop for getting rid of mosquitoes and cleaning every last aspect of the place."

As the local intelligence officer, Miller was the liaison between the base and the local Cuban community. At every moment, he told Ruiz, the Americans had tried to demonstrate their fondness for the Cuban people and government. Ruiz asked him when the Americans would lift the ban on travel to Caimanera. As soon as the reasons for it are alleviated, Miller responded.

Like Castellanos before him, Ruiz was also struck by the absence of visible signs of ammunition on base. "On our tour," he writes, "we didn't see a single cannon, nor armaments that disfigured the natural beauty of the place."

Ruiz returned to Guantánamo via Caimanera. In contrast to what he had seen at the base, he found Caimanera desolate and depressing. His encounter with the two Cuban cities and the U.S. base left him pondering what it would take to move eastern Cuba forward. Clearly, force was needed to discourage the "wolves" who preyed on the U.S. visitors. But force alone would never be enough, and Ruiz hoped that Cubans themselves would demonstrate enough pride to get their house in order. As a journalist, Ruiz knew the history of the place. It never occurred to him that the United States might be part of the solution.[105]

6

★

SEEING RED

On the evening of November 3, 1956, a thousand Soviet Army tanks surrounded the Hungarian capital, Budapest, center of an anti-Soviet uprising and home to the new National Government of Imre Nagy. Sparked by a student protest on October 23, the Hungarian Revolution spread rapidly across a nation weary of Communist oppression and suffering prolonged economic stagnation. For a time, things seemed to be going the Hungarians' way. On November 1, *The New York Times* proclaimed "Victory in Hungary"; that same day, Nagy announced that Hungary had withdrawn from the Warsaw Pact. While the *Times* cautioned that "communist despotism" might yet be restored by "Soviet troops," the Soviet Army appeared to be heading for the border, as if acknowledging that the people of Hungary had spoken.[1]

But early in the morning of November 4, Soviet tanks crashed through the center of Budapest, and, amid heavy aerial and artillery bombardment, Soviet troops occupied government ministries and began rounding up revolutionary leaders. Simultaneously, Nagy took to the airwaves, assuring democratic allies that his government remained in power, while appealing desperately for their help. Within several hours, he had taken cover in the Yugoslav embassy as the *Times* announced, not quite accurately, that "Soviet Attacks Hungary, Seizes Nagy."[2] It took a fortnight for Soviet officials actually to get their hands on Nagy, whom they executed in June 1958. By November 10, the revolution was essentially over. In its wake, some 2,500 Hungarians were dead and 200,000 more bound for exile.

Six thousand miles away, at Guantánamo Bay, Cuba, Charles Ryan, the nineteen-year-old son of a navy hospital corpsman, followed the events in Hungary with rapt attention. Like young men and women throughout the world, Ryan quickened to media accounts describing the Hungarians' valor and likening them to America's founding fathers. As a young man in search of a calling, Ryan was inspired by the Hungarians' commitment to liberal democracy in the face of the most powerful army in the world—all of which made America's tepid response to the Soviet assault bitterly disappointing. Through CIA-operated Radio Free Europe, the Eisenhower administration had spurred on the Hungarians, even suggesting that the United States would come to their assistance in the face of Soviet aggression.[3] But the American government did nothing once the Soviets mobilized, in effect offering up the students for slaughter. Over the course of the ensuing days and weeks, as *Time* magazine named an anonymous "Hungarian Freedom Fighter" its Man of the Year, Ryan struggled unsuccessfully to get the Hungarian Revolution off his mind.[4]

In the autumn of 1956, a kid drinking beer on a beach at Guantánamo Bay, Cuba, with sympathy for peoples suffering oppression did not need to venture far to embroil himself in revolution. Four years earlier, Fulgencio Batista, the self-styled custodian of Cuban law and order, had launched his second military coup. The coup gave rise not only to a dictatorship more interested in rewarding cronies and pleasing foreign business interests than in addressing Cuba's problems, but also to a host of dissident political groups determined to restore constitutional democracy. Batista did not introduce corruption to Cuba, but under him, corruption reached unprecedented heights, as Cuban politicians entered into an unholy alliance with U.S. gangsters, corporations, and political and law enforcement officials to keep the island safe for capitalist exploitation. The eight years of Batista's final reign saw a burst of commercial development across the country that featured the construction of hotel-casinos and private resorts geared to Cuba's exploding gambling and sex trades, along with the infrastructure required to bring foreign clients to the tables (and beds). With Batista at the helm, Cuba was up for sale, and U.S. investments in Cuban sugar, oil, financial, and other industries soared from $142 million in 1946 to just shy of $1 billion by 1959. Surely some people were making money from what one historian has labeled this "capitalist Shangri-La," but it wasn't ordinary Cubans. Ordinary Cubans provided the services and labor that kept Batista and the notorious U.S. mob boss Meyer Lansky and his associates in business. Cubans who thought to complain about the moral and political bankrupting of the country were brutally suppressed.[5]

If sheltered from the most insidious effects of Batista rule, the Guantánamo naval base was not immune to it. Ryan could sense the weight of Batista's bullying on the faces of Cuban laborers who commuted to the base each day, many of whom he came to know as friends. And he experienced Batista's bullying firsthand on his many excursions off the base.[6]

Sympathetic to the Cubans' plight, Ryan joined the Cuban resistance quite by accident. Only slowly did he come to learn that the ammunition he purchased at the Guantánamo gun shop and turned over to Cubans off the base was bound not for the hunting lodge of this or that Cuban friend, as he had been led to believe, but for a weapons cache being accumulated by one of several local resistance factions. At first Ryan's smuggling of arms and ammunition had little to do with Fidel Castro, who didn't return to Cuba until early December 1956. But Castro's arrival along the southeast coast lent the opposition a focus it had previously lacked. Secluded in the Sierra Maestra, and desperate for weapons and ammunition, Castro's lieutenants canvassed the local territory for support, finding it in unlikely places—at the Guantánamo naval base, for instance—and in the affable, apparently directionless Ryan. When the cry for ammunition yielded to a call to arms in February 1957, Ryan led two teenage drinking buddies from the base up into the mountains of the Sierra Maestra, where the spirit of Hungary—to Ryan, the spirit of America—lived on in the resistance movement of Fidel Castro.

Ryan's story complicates the received notion of Guantánamo Bay as a bastion of political reaction in cold-war Cuba. As an isolated imperial enclave of the United States, the naval base spawned unpredictable political alliances as well as uninhibited social behavior. At the very moment when Batista was digging in his heels, supported by $16 million per year in U.S. military aid, many U.S. Navy officers and their families were passing food, money, and ammunition to the Cuban resistance. By the early 1960s, Fidel Castro would become the focus of U.S.-Cuban cold-war recrimination. But the cold war long preceded Castro's rise to power in Cuba. After World War II, Castro was a mildly anti-American member of Eduardo Chibás's nationalist Orthodox Party (with a soft spot for Americans themselves); as late as April 1959, Castro sought recognition from Eisenhower officials for his revolution. Haunted by the specter of communism in Latin America, Eisenhower mistook Castro's nationalism for Marxism, ultimately denying him recognition and radically curtailing America's purchase of Cuban sugar—Cuba's (and Castro's) lifeline. Castro concluded that he had no choice but to seek the support of the Soviet Union. As a result, by the early 1960s a climate of hostility and brinkmanship displaced the low-level reciprocity between some Cubans and Americans at the U.S. base personified by Charles Ryan. But that result was hardly inevitable at the time Charles Ryan and his buddies took to the hills.

The Cuban government's opportunistic courtship of Communists did not last beyond necessity. In the 1946 midterm election, President Ramón Grau's Auténtico Party won a majority of both houses of Congress, making the Communist Party, reorganized once more as the Partido Socialista Popular (PSP), dispensable. With the cold war heating up, and President Grau determined to ingratiate himself to U.S. and Cuban businessmen, the government purged Communists from the major trade confederation (the Confederación de Trabajadores de Cuba, or CTC), which promptly joined officials from the American Federation of Labor in talks about how to combat Communist influence in Latin America. Auténtico's banishing of Communists from the CTC had the unintended consequence of making Cuban communism more radical and more anti-American than it had been since the early 1930s.[7]

But the big story in Cuba in the aftermath of World War II was less the split in labor ranks between conservatives and radicals than the

bloating of government bureaucracy—national, provincial, municipal—along with escalating political corruption. By 1950, 11 percent of
Cuban workers held government positions, which consumed a stag-
gering 80 percent of the federal budget. Elected president in 1948,
Carlos Prío Socarrás, a genial if uninspiring man, was more concerned
with securing government posts for his family and friends than protecting the country from the armed gangs that terrorized the population, often at the behest of local politicians.[8]

Into this breach came Batista once more. In March 1952, he deposed Prío, setting aside that fall's scheduled presidential election
while restoring order. As always, U.S. and Cuban capital responded to
the restoration of order favorably. Parties opposed to Batista's suspending of elections were unable to reconcile their differences. This opposition included a young member of the new Ortodoxo, or Orthodox,
Party named Fidel Castro, who on July 26, 1953, the hundredth anniversary of José Martí's birth, led a futile assault on the Moncada
Barracks at Santiago de Cuba. The assault was a dismal failure, and
resulted in the capture, torture, and death of many of the young insur-
rectionaries. Still, the cause endured, thanks partly to Batista's over-
reaction, and the date of the attack, the Twenty-sixth of July, became
the name of the revolutionary movement waged by Castro against Batista from the mountains surrounding the naval base.[9]

Meanwhile, labor and other dissident groups who opposed Batista
were met with brutal force. An attack on the Matanzas Barracks, outside Havana, in 1956 followed an unsuccessful military coup the preceding year. In March 1957 a student group based in Havana stormed
the presidential palace in an attempt to assassinate Batista. Though
these efforts all failed, they succeeded in gradually rallying Batista opponents into a loose coalition finally oriented around Fidel Castro,
who returned to Cuba in December 1956 aboard a ship named *Granma*.
This loose coalition issued a joint communiqué calling for the return
of civil government and a program of liberal social and economic reforms. By this time, Batista was deaf to calls for liberal reform. By
1958 even his U.S. sponsor had become alienated by his increasingly
brutal tactics, prompting the U.S. government to suspend military aid.
By midsummer 1958, Cuba was in a state of social, economic, and

political collapse, and the immediate future, at least, seemed to belong to Castro.[10]

Just as in Cuba proper, the cold war came to the naval base itself long before the rise of Castro. The surge of Cuban and other foreign labor on the base associated with World War II expansion had the potential to promote a sense both of reciprocity (jobs for Cubans!) and of suspicion (who could be sure that the workers weren't Communists?). The wave of hiring coincided with a series of political reforms in Cuba protecting workers' rights. On the U.S. base, American officials historically opposed labor protections, as they typically made the local workforce less exploitable and more expensive. As the cold-war tensions mounted across the Caribbean, naval officials came to interpret all but the most modest labor demands as evidence of Communist activity.

Complicating labor relations on the base, much of the hiring was done not by the U.S. Navy itself but by contractors such as the Frederick Snare Corporation, whose responsibility to U.S. and Cuban labor laws was ambiguous at best. Like the contractors themselves, the U.S. Navy exploited the ambiguity to keep costs down. Hence there evolved at the naval base a multitiered system of labor rights and labor compensation, with U.S. civil service employees at the top and Cuban maids and part-time Cuban and West Indian labor at the bottom.[11] Snare was skilled in manipulating the distinction between part-time employees, to whom it owed virtually nothing, and full-time employees, to whom it potentially owed a lot. Snare hired part-timers whenever possible, thereby further cutting costs. The company was no more sympathetic than the U.S. government to criticism of its labor policies; like the U.S. government, it tended to equate criticism with communism, contributing to a growing blacklist of workers unwelcome on the base.[12]

The navy and private contractors were also skilled at manipulating racial distinctions to divide workers and drive down wages. U.S. officers and their wives paid dark-skinned maids less than they paid light-skinned maids, just as American sailors generally paid less for dark-skinned prostitutes than for light-skinned prostitutes. In the early 1940s a premium on English-speaking ability dramatically raised the currency of West Indian labor on the base. In exchange for their loyalty, naval officials protected West Indian workers from having to confirm their foreign status with Cuban authorities, and reserved for them the most desired jobs. The elevated status of West Indian labor inevitably created tension with their Cuban counterparts. Such preferential treatment tapped into latent resentment dating back to the importation of Chinese indentured servants in the mid-nineteenth century. Though Africans and Chinese were originally imported to work on the sugar, coffee, and tobacco plantations, the seasonal and cyclical nature of these industries left labor markets flooded with foreign workers who competed with Cubans for scarce jobs. There was hardly a labor platform in Cuba that did not include a demand that the Cuban workforce be at least 50 percent native-born.[13]

When Fulgencio Batista rose to power in the 1930s, he did so partly thanks to an alliance with moderate labor elements, which lent his government popular legitimacy. In 1938 he allied himself with a reformed Communist Party and the new Cuban Workers' Confederation (Confederación de Trabajadores de Cuba, or CTC). With Batista's backing, and widespread popular support, the CTC managed to pass a series of reforms in 1940 that dramatically improved the plight of Cuban labor. Though wary of Communist influence, the United States put up with the reforms in exchange for Cuban cooperation in World War II.

By 1943 the United States had begun to anticipate the need to curb Communist influence in Cuba and throughout Latin America. One vehicle of U.S. anticommunism was the American Federation of Labor, which worked in tandem with the U.S. State Department to promote a moderate, pro-business labor movement in the region.[14] The concessions won by Cuban labor in the early 1940s were not recognized on the U.S. base, and in 1940–1941, a series of incidents demonstrated the vulnerability of unprotected Cuban workers. In one notable example, a Cuban worker named Lino Rodríguez Grenot was unceremoniously beaten by a U.S. Navy officer and tossed into the harbor at Caimanera while attempting to board a boat filled with Cuban workers bound for the naval base. Rodríguez died in plain view of a host of Cuban and American eyewitnesses among whom there was no uncertainty about what had happened. But there was indeed uncertainty about who had legal jurisdiction over the case: Americans or Cubans? Had officials concluded that Rodríguez had died in Cuban waters, then according to the lease agreement by which the U.S. Navy occupied Guantánamo Bay, the case would have had to be tried in a Cuban courtroom, a prospect the navy naturally found unpalatable. But if Rodríguez had died while on a U.S. vessel, in this case the navy launch that ferried Cuban workers to the base, then the navy would retain jurisdiction over the case, and the alleged perpetrator would be given a court-martial. This is what the navy argued, ultimately exonerating Rodríguez's murderer of charges of manslaughter, to the enduring chagrin of local Cuban people.[15]

Several subsequent cases confirmed the appearance of American impunity at the bay. In the wake of an unexplained shooting of a Cuban worker by an American sentry, the base commander told a U.S. consular official that "the US government is in no way responsible nor liable for the criminal acts of its employees, including the personnel of the armed forces." This overstated the case, though it is true that few if any of the Americans accused of mistreating Cuban workers were found guilty. Meanwhile, the Cuban government was in no position to protest the appearance of injustice. Indeed, in some of these cases, it went out of its way to keep the lid on Cuban reaction.[16]

It took the outbreak of the cold war to bring labor representation to Cuban and foreign workers on the U.S. base. This seeming paradox is explained by logic similar to that which helped promote civil rights reform in 1950s America: it was a means to deflate Soviet propaganda that American society was racist and unfriendly to workers. The way to combat Communist influence in Cuba, representatives of the American Federation of Labor told U.S. officials, was to encourage the moderate labor movement both in Cuba and on the naval base. The timing seemed propitious. The recent consolidation of political power by the increasingly conservative Auténtico Party of Cuban president Ramón Grau led to a government-wide purge of Communists from the CTC. Though the Americans refused to concede to "unions" on the base, they allowed workers to form "employee groups," which, in exchange for forfeiting the right to strike, were granted an eight-hour day, workers' compensation, and pensions, concessions that by the late 1940s could hardly be considered radical. Notably, workers hired by private contractors, usually on a part-time basis, continued to receive no security at all.[17]

Alert for signs of Communist influence and infiltration, U.S. naval officials at Guantánamo began to recognize it in the many inevitable incidents of petty crime on the base, and resolved to bring the perpetrators to justice. By the terms of the original lease agreement, Cuban fugitives apprehended on the U.S. base were to be returned to Cuban territory for prosecution, just as U.S. fugitives apprehended in Cuba were supposed to be returned to the U.S. base. When Cuban courts demonstrated a persistent lack of will to hold Cubans responsible for crimes committed on the naval base, U.S. officials took the law into their own hands. Claiming the authority of the Uniform Code of Military Justice, they began detaining alleged criminals on the base.[18]

In the autumn of 1954 one of these detentions got out of hand. A Cuban named Lorenzo Salomon Deer was suspected of pilfering cigarettes from the Navy Exchange. Navy officials detained Deer for a fortnight, allegedly beating him and making him stand for hours on end. Deer accused the navy of torture, and a navy official conceded that the treatment of Deer had been extreme. Deer signed a confession of guilt, and served time in jail in Santiago. The navy's alleged mistreatment of him sparked outrage in local Cuban communities. The base union leaders vented their dismay in the local papers, on the radio, and in correspondence with government officials back in the United States. "We could not conceive that in a naval establishment of the most powerful nation in the world, champion of democracy, things like this could happen," the leaders wrote in language eerily resonant of post-9/11. The leaders' eloquence earned them dismissal from the naval base. Worse, it jeopardized the union's standing at the base more generally, where officials had only grudgingly conceded to labor representation in the first place and then only to the extent that it did nothing to threaten navy authority.[19]

Predictably, the firing of the labor leaders did little to mollify local outrage at alleged abuse on the base, or the demand of base workers to be treated with dignity. Indeed, the more suspicious that base officials became of Cuban workers and the more hostility they demonstrated toward the labor leadership, the more they came to resemble the Batista dictatorship itself—with whom, not so incidentally, the U.S. government was in close communication. The base workers wanted nothing so much as justice, the fired labor leaders reminded U.S. officials, an end that had nothing whatsoever to do with communism. "It is not by caressing the RED DEVILS that peace for the civilized world will be achieved; no, it is by practicing SOCIAL JUSTICE; it is by practicing the magnificent postulates of democracy, of which our employers boast themselves to be the champions when in reality the only thing they do is to show their contempt for the things which are really vital to the greatness and sovereignty of countries." The workers were no less "enemies of Iron Curtains" than the Americans themselves, "but we are also enemies of any type of oppression harming human dignity," they pointedly announced, especially "the dignity of the country we belong to." They were the "REAL DEMOCRATS."[20]

By the mid-1950s, "real democrats" committed to the "dignity" of Cuba were not welcome on the U.S. base. The U.S. occupation of Guantánamo Bay had never been about promoting Cuban interests. And it was not about to become so in 1954 or 1955, when communism appeared to be on the march in Latin America, and when Fulgencio Batista was all that prevented communism from washing up on American shores.

Charles Ryan and his family arrived at Guantánamo Bay in mid-1956, amid mounting hostility between base officials and the local Cuban labor movement. Ryan's dad worked in Vector Control, the department responsible for combating infectious diseases. As the base health inspector, Ryan Sr. was responsible for ensuring the cleanliness of food provision and preparation. This work kept him in constant contact with the local Cuban community, which provided the base with all sorts of merchandise, fresh fruits and vegetables, and occasionally meat, poultry, and seafood. Ryan remembers accompanying his mother to the wharves where the Cubans unloaded their produce. Small, dark, and attractive, Ryan's mother looked more Latin than her native Irish. The Cubans flirted with her, Ryan recalls, often filling her bags while refusing her money—an attempt, her husband cautioned, to get in the good graces of the sanitation commissioner.[21]

The long history of anti-Americanism in Cuba in the wake of the Platt Amendment, the record of U.S. exploitation of labor on the base and throughout Cuba generally, and the increasing suspicion of Cuban activists bred by the cold war made for difficult social relations. The formal hostility masked countless opportunities for and instances of kindness. Open-minded and gregarious, Ryan got to know many of the Cuban and foreign workers. Generous to the Cubans, he found they were generous to him, frequently engaging him in conversation and giving him rides in their cars and trucks.

When he arrived at Guantánamo, Ryan was not your average navy brat. For one thing, he was nineteen years old, older than many of the sailors at the base (the minimum enlistment age at the time was seventeen), and a member of the U.S. Navy Reserve. Isolated today, Guantánamo was just as isolated then. What was a nineteen-year-old doing following his family to Cuba? Cuba was a nice place, Ryan remembers his dad telling him. Ryan could join his parents and younger brother at Guantánamo so long as he returned to high school, from which he had dropped out a few years back. To sweeten the deal, Ryan's dad pledged to give his son a weekly allowance and all the freedom a young man could ask for—so long as he did not date the girls at William T. Sampson School. Ryan's father had himself a deal. A lack of girls, according to the word in navy circles, was not a problem at the place U.S. Marines fondly referred to as "git' mo'."[22]

For a nineteen-year-old maverick, Ryan got along well with his father. He joined his dad on hunting trips to the Yateras River, source since 1934 of the base water supply, which meandered from the mountains to the sea just a few miles east of the northeast gate. Ryan remembers sliding down slick rocks at the river's edge. He also occasionally accompanied his father on work trips into Cuba, once in the company of a team of medical workers helping to alleviate an outbreak of cholera. Despite cautioning his wife about exploiting the kindness of the Cuban merchants, Ryan's dad was not beyond exploiting his

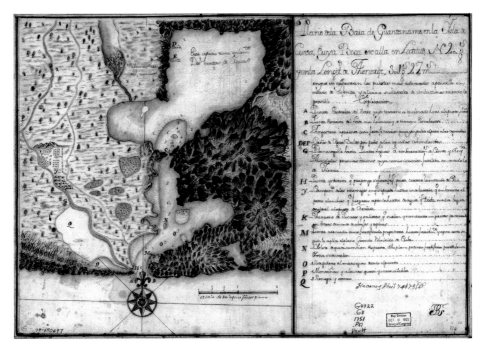

Admiral Edward Vernon was not alone in thinking Guantánamo Bay—shown here in a 1751 Spanish map—"the finest harbor in the West Indies," with "room for all the shipping in the Thames." The Americans, too, he was quick to report, "begin to look on it as the Land of Promise already." (Library of Congress)

left: Vernon reminded his superiors back home that his estimation of Guantánamo's virtues was based on unrivaled knowledge of the Indies. (National Museum of the Royal Navy)

above right: An experienced politician as well as a seasoned sailor, Vernon was drawn to the more cultivated Americans, and to one in particular: Lawrence Washington, a twenty-three-year-old captain in one of the Virginia companies. (Courtesy of the Mount Vernon Ladies' Association)

above left: "We went ashore like innocents," Lieutenant Colonel Robert W. Huntington (right) wrote of the June 1898 landing at Guantánamo, "and made a peachy camp and slept well on the tenth." (Library of Congress)

above right: Marine encampment, Guantánamo Bay, June 1898: "The Spanish were laying in the bushes all around watching us and they knew every movement we made even to where our sentry were posted." (Library of Congress)

below: An American flag, sent from the warship *Marblehead* to bolster the marines' spirits and remind them why they were fighting, hoisted at Guantánamo on June 12, 1898 (Library of Congress)

"There is, of course, little or no real independence left Cuba under the Platt Amendment," Governor Leonard Wood wrote to the new American president, Theodore Roosevelt, in October 1901. (Library of Congress)

According to U.S. Secretary of War Elihu B. Root, Spain's former colonies were "subject to the complete sovereignty" of the United States, which was "controlled by no legal limitations except those which may be found in the treaty of cession." (Library of Congress)

"We are not savages ignoring the rules of civilized warfare," pleaded the Cuban general Calixto García. "We are a poor, ragged army as ragged and poor as was the army of your forefathers in their noble war of independence, but like the heroes of Saratoga and Yorktown, we respect our cause too deeply to disgrace it with barbarism and cowardice." (Library of Congress)

Compared with the base of Admiral Alfred Mahan's dreams, Guantánamo remained underde-veloped. Its most touted feature was a rifle range capable of engaging upward of three hundred men at once. (Library of Congress)

Marine campsite, Deer Point. News of Guantánamo reached the United States during the 1912 "racial insurrection." (Corbis)

In a 1921 *National Geographic* profile of the base, Herbert Corey wrote, "It is here that the enlisted man begins in earnest to lose the pallor, the narrow shoulders, the white knobs, and bony angles of the civilian and to take on the saddle-colored coat of tan and other attributes of husky health." (Corbis)

above: In Guantánamo City, the bars, the water, the nearby Guantánamo River, the languid locals—all call to mind "Conrad's African backgrounds." Everything has "a remote and exotic air." (Corbis)

below: The future chairman of the Joint Chiefs of Staff Arleigh Burke (rear, beer raised) leads a liberty party in Guantánamo City. Prohibition produced world-class drinkers, experts in the art of the immediate and sustained elevation of blood alcohol levels. (Naval Historical Foundation)

The fleet dances at this dance hall in Caimanera were a "nightmare," according to one navy wife in 1930.

Pepe's bar at Caimanera was "a small, picturesque but smelly shed which might have been put together in a movie studio for a Mexican melodrama."

"The heart of every woman among us beat a little faster at the long white lines of men drawn up on the decks of the warships—men who had left their women thousands of miles north and were now, in a sense, at our disposal." (Corbis)

above: By the 1950s, the base had become an idyllic American community. One resident proclaimed, "It's very safe for people here. It's safe for kids. There's no crime; there's no drugs." (Hank Walker/Getty Images)

left: Family memberships at the base golf club cost four dollars per month. If swimming, golf, and picnicking weren't their thing, wives could amuse themselves at bowling, tennis, horseback riding, baseball, softball, basketball, volleyball, cycling, archery, sailing, boating, hunting, fishing, roller-skating, or horseshoes. (Hank Walker/Getty Images)

"We lieutenants and our growing families lived in what can best be termed 'genteel poverty.'"
(Hank Walker/Getty Images)

The navy long argued that the base was a boon to the local Cuban economy. These photos from nearby Caimanera in the 1960s offer a different story. (Courtesy of Rex Lake)

above: On February 17, 1957, Charles Ryan and his two friends left the base and headed for Fidel Castro's camp in the Sierra Maestra. (Time/Life)

below: Ryan, pictured in the rear with a straw hat, called Castro's band "a strange little group. They were very disciplined, never raising their voices above a whisper." (Courtesy of Charles Ryan)

Tents on the tarmac, Haitian refugee camp, Guantánamo, 1992 (William F. Campbell/Homefire Productions)

Confined for days on end in small camps, with limited social contact and little to keep them busy, the Haitians soon began to feel like prisoners. (William F. Campbell/ Homefire Productions)

"In the camps," one witness reported, "there are thousands of us. Children everywhere. There is so much confusion. Nobody knows what's happening." (William F. Campbell/Homefire Productions)

Boredom and restlessness, the bane of many a detention operation, proved a challenge from the beginning. (William F. Campbell/Homefire Productions)

above: Continued mistreatment of the Qur'an prompted the detainees themselves to propose a solution: we'll surrender our Qur'ans to you, so long as you cease abusing them. (Louie Palu/Zuma Press)

below: A detainee prays in his cell at Camp Six. (Louis Palu/Zuma Press)

An interrogation chamber at Camp Five (Louis Palu/Zuma Press)

A group of prisioners at evening prayers. In the third year of Barack Obama's presidency, almost two hundred prisioners remain at Guantánamo. (Louis Palu/Zuma Press)

own connections when opportunity arose. In one notable example, Ryan did the grunt work for a rum-running operation his dad launched, collecting and recycling empty gallon Coke syrup jugs from the neighborhoods around the base. Into these jugs, Ryan would pour rum from barrels delivered to his family's house by Cuban workers. The boxes would then be hoisted into the holds of navy planes destined for Jacksonville, Key West, and Panama City. Ryan's dad bought the rum for $1.25 a gallon and unloaded it for $2.50 a gallon, not a bad profit, so long as he could maintain an adequate supply. Supply didn't seem to be a problem. So awash did Jacksonville become in cheap Guantánamo rum that the admiral there wrote his counterpart in Cuba to complain. "Stop throwing so many parties," the commander at Guantánamo shot back, "and you'll stop receiving so much rum!"

Social life at the base was pleasant if unremarkable, according to Ryan. Outdoor movie theaters were its focus. The base had seven outdoor theaters in 1956, the pride of which was Mainside, situated near the officers' club on Deer Point, one of the fingers of land that jutted out into the bay from the eastern shoreline, which was frequented by singles, couples, and officers and their families. Ryan made a name for himself among his teenage peers by revitalizing and later presiding over the teenage club. Situated in an old Quonset hut on Marine Point, just down Sherman Avenue from Deer Point, the teenage club was moribund when Ryan arrived on the premises. He called a meeting, solicited ideas for improvements, and suggested that the navy would happily help the kids transform the place into a youth center. By the time Ryan and the Navy Seabees were done, the hut had a new veranda complete with trellis, live plants, comfortable chairs, and a snack bar with its own cook—"a Jamaican, who doubled as a chaperone, and who turned out the best burgers on the base." Kids started coming to the club every night. A movie, a burger, home by eleven—parents loved it as much as the kids. They knew where their kids were at all times and could imagine, or so they thought, what they were doing. This was a nice crowd, Ryan remembers, and a fun place. On New Year's Eve 1956, Ryan organized a party. Tickets to the gala event cost one dollar for couples, two dollars for singles, the better to bring in a crowd. Parents shared the chaperone duty, hour by hour, and the kids made it straight through to breakfast, when the navy, delighted by the spirit, "sent over a kitchen staff and plenty of bacon" to sizzle in the New Year.

Poised between youth and adulthood, and living simultaneously in the United States and Cuba, Charles Ryan relished his liminal status at the bay. Having accompanied his family on different posts around the world, he welcomed the unfamiliar and took pride in his independence both on and off the naval base. Not long after arriving at the base in the summer of 1956, he befriended a young Cuban named Julio Valdez, a worker at the Navy Exchange. The two struck up a casual friendship, and it wasn't long before Valdez asked Ryan if he could procure a case of .22-caliber bullets for his grandfather's hunting lodge in Cuba. There was nothing unusual in that, Ryan remembers thinking; hunting was popular in southeast Cuba. Like Ryan's dad, navy chiefs and officers regularly spent weekends traipsing local plantations in search of wild boar and deer. It was no big thing to take along guns and ammunition. Shotguns, .30-06s, Colt .45s—all were readily available at the gun shop at the Navy Exchange. (If you didn't find what you liked there, you could have it made to order.) Like food at the commissary, guns and ammo cost next to nothing on a military base in that day; the .22-caliber bullets Ryan smuggled out cost a penny apiece.

Only gradually did Ryan discover the true destination of the stuff he passed along. This was a very small operation with only ten Cubans involved, besides Ryan himself. He came to know the Cubans, and they came to trust him, naturally, through friendships forged in Cuban ranches, rural homes, and local bars where Ryan spent his weekends. "I went everywhere in Oriente province," Ryan boasts. He would leave home Friday and return Sunday night. "For the record," he observed, "Cubans with little or no money don't live in trash hovels. They live in homes with different generations mixed together—grandma, great-grandma, parents, children. They reserved a special room for guests' visits," he continues; "they had dignity and didn't mind or apologize when I showed up." Ryan spent the most time on Julio Valdez's grandfather's farm. It was via the intimacy of these visits that Valdez came to trust the American, eventually revealing the existence of the network of which he was a part. "Even this was not overt," Ryan emphasizes, "but subtle. I've got a couple guns I'd like to get off the base,"

Valdez would tell him. "Can you help me?" Ryan asked few questions. Subtlety was the modus operandi and key to the success of the Cuban resistance, and the reason Ryan never got caught. On these trips off the base, he came to appreciate the burden of Batista's dictatorship on ordinary Cubans, for whom the government did less than nothing, and on whom it preyed shamelessly for its venal existence.

Valdez was not a drinker, but he accompanied Ryan to parties and bars and dances in Guantánamo City, where the friends would listen to live music or catch a movie. "I was dark," Ryan reports, "with dark hair. I wore Cuban clothes; there were not a lot of Americans hanging out in this part of Cuba. In Havana, yes, but not in Oriente." Culturally sensitive, Ryan fit right in. Conversation between him and his buddies was not overtly political. He could goad his friends into complaining about Batista, but they were on the whole amazingly discreet. There were pro-labor, anti-Batista, and anti-American protests in Guantánamo City, but Ryan's friends did not participate in them. They were careful to stay out of the limelight, as if saving themselves for something bigger. "This wasn't about Castro," Ryan emphasizes. "Castro wasn't even in Cuba yet. We didn't know whom we were working for. There was a revolution; there were many revolutionary groups; that was it." If Valdez knew that Castro was bound for southeast Cuba, he never let on.

Just as Ryan's Cuban friends bided their time before openly including him in their gunrunning, so Ryan carefully cultivated the two American youngsters he would escort into the hills. Victor Buehlman was seventeen, the son of a navy commander; Michael Garvey was fifteen, the son of a navy chief. Less worldly, less curious than Ryan, Buehlman and Garvey had something Ryan lacked: size and strength. Ryan remembers looking out for them. "I set them up," he recalls. "I was the first to insist that Michael get his poor vision fixed." The boys would drink beer together on the base's beaches. They easily passed for young sailors, and together the three friends began to dabble in the forbidden fruit of nearby Caimanera, their sexual exploits creating among them something of a sacred bond. Still, "I didn't bring them in right away," Ryan reports. "I had to find out their sympathies."

Convinced, finally, that he could trust the two, Ryan described his contribution to the resistance. "Look, you guys," he told them. "You're not doing well in school. Want to have some adventure?" They began by helping Ryan run guns off the base. Victor had a convertible, whose canvas top they lowered, filling the folds with rifles. Sometimes they would smuggle out parts of guns to be reassembled later. On one run, they concealed weapons in fifty-gallon flour drums. Another time they concealed the guns in grease. With their automobile loaded, the boys passed through checkpoints manned by Batista's soldiers. One particular checkpoint, in front of the police station in Guantánamo City, Ryan thought might be his last. The police ran mirrors under the car, searching for contraband. Once they seized his ID. But, however suspicious, they never caught him.

In part, Ryan owed his success to his understanding of the soft spots of customs officials and guards on both sides of the fence. Navy regulations stipulated that members of the Navy Exchange could purchase up to two cartons of cigarettes per day. And just so much whiskey. On smuggling missions, the boys would deliberately flaunt the cigarettes and whiskey to distract attention from the more precious contraband. When found by American guards to be over the daily ration of tobacco and alcohol, Ryan came up with a lame excuse ultimately ameliorated by his turning over the cigarettes and liquor. This worked in Cuba no less than on the base. "The pushier the guards," Ryan remembers, "the more we surrendered. But we were never threatened."

Some of these gun runs Ryan had to do on his own. More than once, he ducked out on dates at the teenage club and headed down to the boat basin below Marine Point, where he was a familiar face and where, outfitted by the Cuban staff with bait and fishing tackle, he would motor to a rendezvous point with a small arsenal of rifles laid out along the floor of his boat. From the boat basin, he headed for the mangrove swamps along the northern boundary of the U.S. base, clad in a bathing suit, his friends still swinging to music back at the club. Ducking into disguised breaks in the wall of mangroves, he proceeded in silence until a few coos and whistles confirmed he had hit his mark.

He saw interesting things while carrying out these missions along the fence line. On one trip he stumbled upon a group of marine guards who, one after another, scaled the fence via a tree notched with footholds in order to gain access to Cuban prostitutes from the nearby town of Boquerón. In all of this the thing that seemed the most amazing to Ryan was that word never got out. "We were normal students," he observes, by which he means regular old gossiping kids. "And yet we never talked about it with our friends. There was no bragging."

By February 1957, two months after arriving in Oriente province, Castro's band of eighteen men was in dire straits up in the hills of the Sierra Maestra. Initial wonder at their mere survival had long since worn off, and little distinguished these insurgents from the many like-minded cells around the country. A betting man asked to select the resistance group most likely to topple Batista would not have put his money on Castro. Short on uniforms, equipment, arms, and food, Castro was also desperately in need of men. That month, Frank País, a native of Oriente and an agent of Castro's since the previous year, put out a call for individuals willing to join the insurgents.

Ryan, Buehlman, and Garvey, among others, answered País's call. On February 17, 1957, the three boys left the base and headed for Castro's camp in the Sierra Maestra. With Batista's men combing the area, they took a circuitous root, traveling first to Santiago, then to Manzanillo, then to the mountains, accompanied by forty-nine Cuban recruits.[23] Ryan remembers being astounded by what they found there. The first thing that struck him was the simplicity of the rebels' supply chain. Castro's band was being kept alive by a network of primitive stores supplied by mules from nearby towns bearing rice, beans, butter, sardines, milk, lantern oil, and the like. The peasants and their mules were Castro's lifeline. Why Batista did not think to isolate those mule trains, Ryan could never understand. Batista's troops proceeded only as far as they could make it by truck, as if afraid to test the loyalty of the peasants.

If it hadn't been for the campesinos, Ryan suggests, Castro's band of "city slickers" would never have lasted. On first arriving in the mountains, Castro and his few survivors were not any more at home there than their pursuers. If there remains any doubt about the sincerity of Castro's sympathy for the peasants, Ryan observed, it should have long since been dispelled by the very fact of their coming to his rescue. From the peasants, the rebels learned to light fires in the rain, to make fires that did not smoke, and to preserve and transport embers—fire, along with water, the sine qua non of outdoor survival. Compared to Batista's troops, Castro and company were veritable Boy Scouts. One evening, Ryan and his fellow insurgents awoke to a cacophony of gunfire just across the valley from where they lay concealed. The gunfire was directed not at their camp but at a nearby hillside that they knew to be abandoned. "What the hell were they up to?" the rebels wanted to know. Out of their element and simply terrified, the government forces were shooting at random. When next Batista's forces returned to the mountains, they did so by air, dropping bombs on peasant communities, further alienating the local population.

Castro's band was "a strange little group," Ryan reports. They were very disciplined, never raising their voices above a whisper. "They didn't curse. They didn't drink. They ate little. They smoked cigars. They thought of themselves as guerillas more than rebels"—the word *rebel* suggests a casualness their professionalism belied. Castro had a way with people, Ryan remembers. He got along as naturally with campesinos as he did with intellectuals, professionals, and students. The peasants of the Sierra Maestra trusted him implicitly, as he didn't condescend to or bully them—unless he had a reason to. With traitors, Castro was merciless. By contrast, Che Guevara couldn't disguise his elitism. Che is famous for his equal treatment of the peasants and for stoicism in the face of injury, most of which Ryan dismisses as "bogus"—"as anyone familiar with Che would have known." Still, Fidel and Che got along like robbers. Both were well-read and happy to talk ideas late into the night. Che regaled Fidel with proposals for agricultural reform; Fidel taught Che the art of guerilla warfare. Buehlman remembers Camilo Cienfuegos, Castro's most trusted assistant, with particular fondness. Celia Sánchez, Raúl Castro—all were there accompanied by the three boys. With pride and a hint of wistfulness, Ryan recalls smoking in his twentieth birthday with fine cigars in the company of Castro, Guevara, and Cienfuegos.

Once in the mountains, the boys marched. And marched. And

marched. It took a while for news of their flight from the base to reach the United States. On March 8 *The New York Times* reported "3 U.S. Youths Missing" from the Guantánamo naval base.[24] At the end of that month, the paper announced the "U.S. Studying Case of 3 Youths in Cuba."[25] The Batista government denied that the boys were in the mountains with the rebels; indeed, Batista insisted that there were no rebels left in the mountains for the boys to join. The boys were in Havana, Batista declared, or perhaps in Miami.[26] Thus it was with some embarrassment that Batista was forced to admit his error when, two weeks later, two teams of journalists from the United States (one from *Time*, the other from CBS News) met and interviewed the rebel leader, along with the three boys. Later, CBS News correspondent Robert Taber and the three boys became the object of scorn for allegedly legitimating Castro's resistance, and presumably underwriting fifty years of Communist oppression in Cuba. That scorn is misplaced. Castro was not a Communist, Ryan and Buehlman insist. There were Communists in his ranks—Che Guevara among them—but that was a fact of the resistance movement by 1956–57, not evidence of Castro's political aims at the time.

Bigger and burlier than Ryan, Buehlman and Garvey lacked his commitment. Seventeen and fifteen years old, respectively, they were technically minors, and when Taber suggested that he usher them back to the base, Castro and the two teenagers agreed. Back they went, then, in early May 1957, just over a fortnight before Ryan got his first taste of combat in a successful raid on the rural guard outpost at El Uvero.

Ryan remained with Castro's forces through that summer. In October 1957 he was called to headquarters, where one of Castro's lieutenants presented him with a fateful choice. "From this spot lead two trails," the man told Ryan. "Up this trail comes Andrew St. George," the Hungarian freedom fighter turned *Life* correspondent, "who we think is CIA, and who is coming to interview you for a story; you could be famous. At the end of this trail, on the other hand, lies a boatload of guns in Brooklyn, New York, collected for us, and which we need dearly. That trail can get you out of the mountains, out of Cuba, and away from Batista's agents, who, if they catch you, will tear you to pieces." Ryan, never much of a student, didn't like allegories. "I asked Castro's assistant to spit it out; to tell me what he wanted me to do." What "we want you to do," the man explained, "is to get to New York City. The July 26 movement lies in pieces. Contact them. Tell them to forget their petty disagreements, and come together. There is only one government in exile. Then go to New York and get the guns. You know the mountains; you've been here the longest; you can get back to us."

Thus began for Ryan an infinitely more dangerous mission than remaining with Castro in the Sierra Maestra. Just to get out of Cuba, via Guantánamo Bay, entailed tapping the resources of a network of Castro sympathizers that stretched from Pico Turquino, atop the Sierra Maestra, to Manzanillo, Bayamo, Santiago, Guantánamo, and finally New York. "I walked for days," Ryan recalls. "I was hidden in walls. I was disguised as a cowboy, dressed in double-seated mauve pants, cowboy boots, with hair and mustache trimmed day to day according to local styles." The climax of the journey was the final leg to Santiago, where Ryan played the part of a Cuban dentist, seated in the back of a car with a wife on one side, a child on the other, dressed in a suit, immaculately coiffed, sailing through one roadblock after another, until he arrived at the residence of the U.S. consul, of all people, who fed him, regaled him, and ultimately transferred him to the naval base. The U.S. consul was a regular visitor to the base, where he exercised all matter of official duties, from marrying American sailors to local Cuban girls, to ensuring the legitimacy of the ubiquitous real estate and business transactions involving Americans from the base, to investigating accusations of U.S. torture of a sailor who went mad after being forbidden to travel to Caimanera to marry his prostitute.

By the time Ryan returned to the U.S. naval base, seven months after departing, Buehlman and Garvey and their families had long since shipped out. Ryan's parents awaited him in Jacksonville, Florida. Ryan remembers being interviewed for a meager five minutes at the base, after which he was taken to directly to the airport, under tight guard, dressed in a suit, white shirt, and dark glasses. Only the Cubans on the base knew his identity. More than anything, he remembers wanting a cigar. The guards weren't authorized to give him anything. Then a disturbance broke out in an adjacent hangar at the airport, and with the guards distracted, a case of Churchills sailed across the waxed floor, in his honor, a wink from the Cubans sealing the deal with thanks. Ryan was escorted onto an empty C-47 transport plane, where the pilot and copilot, ignorant of his identity, befriended him, and next to whom he sat, side by side, as the plane flew low over the water following the underwater cable all the way to Jacksonville.

While Ryan was in the mountains, his father told an interviewer that he would be happy if his younger son were as committed to a cause as his older one, and as ready to follow a dream. Like his son, Ryan's dad spoke Spanish, knew the local countryside, was friends with many Cubans, and hence had not feared for Ryan's life. Privately, Ryan's dad didn't speak much about his son's time with the rebels, though Ryan himself does not doubt that his mountain sojourn effectively sealed his father's career. Charles Sr. never received another promotion.

Arriving in Jacksonville in October 1957, Ryan was detained by Naval Intelligence, who copied the letter that Castro had given him ("Ryan is my representative in the United States") before turning him over to his parents. He did not remain long at home. Short on money, sick ("with every kind of parasite"), he made straight for New York, where he began speaking and raising money for the Cuban resistance.

Ryan did not like his time in New York. The revolutionary community in Brooklyn lacked the circumspection he had come to take for granted in Cuba. ("For seven months in the mountains I never spoke above a whisper.") He was easily recognizable on the streets, where his presence would elicit pro-Castro and anti-Batista exclamations, all but making impossible the gun (and money) running that had brought him to New York. Only the FBI's own naïveté consoled him. "They stood out worse than I did," Ryan reports. "In 1957, FBI agents looked like U.S. Marines in civilian clothes." Ryan spent much of his time simply trying to keep the Cubans quiet. "When that boat full of guns sails," he warned them, "we're going to get picked up." And so the Cuban supporters and their boat full of guns did, just out of Galveston, Texas. By which time Ryan had long since jumped ship. "The Cubans in the U.S. were not together mentally," Ryan recalls. "And everywhere I looked I saw FBI." And so he faced another choice. He could continue making speeches and raising money among the zealots in New York, or he could go back to Cuba, where he had never felt so comfortable and where his life had taken on meaning that it had previously lacked. Ryan returned to Cuba.

It is tempting to conclude that Ryan's gun running out of the U.S. naval base kept Castro going at a time when he was all but destitute of arms. Ryan rejects the notion. "The thing Victor, Michael, and I delivered to the Revolution was publicity at an opportune time." "You guys got us $5,000,000 worth of publicity for nothing," Castro told Ryan. "We couldn't have paid an ad agency for that."[27]

In June 1958, Raúl Castro, brother of Fidel and one of the leaders of the Twenty-sixth of July Movement, captured a busload of U.S. Marines on liberty off the U.S. base, taking them to the scene of an alleged government massacre of Cuban peasants. The kidnapping coincided with a Cuban military offensive against Castro's rebels, which included a bombing and defoliation campaign in the Sierra Maestra Mountains. Raúl Castro justified the kidnapping as retaliation for the U.S. Navy's allowing Batista's bombers to refuel at the base, which, if true, would have violated a U.S. arms embargo of Cuba instituted on March 14.[28] The previous night, Commander Hal Sacks, on shore patrol at Guantánamo City, remembers his busload of sailors and marines being shot at by rebels as it returned to the base; one of the Americans was slightly wounded. In his report of the incident, Sacks warned navy officials against allowing future liberty parties until the violence in eastern Cuba subsided.

Sacks's superiors ignored the warning. The next night, June 28, Raúl Castro's forces seized twenty-seven U.S. sailors and marines returning from Guantánamo City to the base—until this day the last U.S. liberty party in Cuba. Two days later, Castro contacted the U.S. ambassador, Earl Smith, promising to release his U.S. and Canadian captives if the United States stopped providing military equipment, including spare parts, to Batista, and stopped allowing his pilots to refuel on the navy base. Meanwhile, that same day, the commander of the naval base, Admiral R. B. Ellis, wrote a memo to Chief of Naval Operations Arleigh Burke outlining U.S. options. Among the actions considered were an airlift of several hundred marines to Guantánamo "accompanied by full fanfare," a roundup of the base's many Cuban workers sympathetic to Castro and their relinquishment to Cuban authorities, a threat to support Batista's forces against the resistance, and finally a threat to bar Cuban employees from the base. The last three options were likely to backfire on a base already unpopular among many Cubans; the first was likely to be ineffectual.[29]

While U.S. officials in Guantánamo Bay and Washington reacted with shock at the kidnapping, Americans on the ground in Caimanera found it less of a surprise. From his home at the Oasis Hotel, Rex Lake, for one, had witnessed a notable increase in the size of the Cuban Army presence in the towns around the bay. Surely, amid what was becoming an increasingly bitter struggle, an outside occupying military force allied to the Cuban government while harboring some sympathy for the rebels was unlikely to be able to remain above the fray. As early as the spring of 1957, Lake reports, "the political situation was heating up in Cuba," so much so that American servicemen and their families living in Caimanera were "confined to our homes in the evening and a navy boat stood by at the local pier to take us to the base if any hostilities began between the rebel and government forces." Nor was it "unusual to hear gunfire during the night and the electricity was continually going off because the rebels were cutting the power lines outside of town."[30]

Summer 1957 saw a palpable escalation in the civil war. With the fourth anniversary of Castro's failed assault on the Moncada Barracks outside Santiago approaching, naval officials warned families such as the Lakes to be on alert in town and to be ready to evacuate to the base if necessary. Sure enough, on July 26, Lake reports, "a young child" attending a movie in Guantánamo City "was given a bag . . . which was supposed to be filled with candy. The bag blew up in the theater, killing the child and injuring some other people." At the same time, "unknown forces also blew out the front of the post office." The next month "a labor strike was called by the rebels and all stores in Caimanera were padlocked in support," leading Cuban Army troops to force open the doors, as if to force local citizens to break ranks with the rebels. While the Lakes and other American families remained shuttered at home, gunfire became a regular feature of summer nights—and not just of the nights. "Soldiers fired shots over the heads of a crowd of people at our local market place, just one block from the house," Lake recalls. "We were seeing more soldiers coming into town than usual. The Cuban navy headquarters just 1/2 block from our apartment was reinforced with four new machine guns and piles of sandbags out in front of their building." Barricades went up all over the little town. "On August 7, three bodies were found in the local cemetery, supposedly killed by the rebels. One soldier shot another soldier to death about 200 feet from where Janice [Lake's wife] was having her hair cut and a bus ran a roadblock set up by the rebels and was shot full of holes."[31]

By April 1958, with violence mounting in the towns around the bay, the U.S. Navy recalled servicemen living in Guantánamo City to the U.S. base, sending their families stateside. In Caimanera itself, evacuation remained an option through April 13, when, Lake reports, the violence literally came home. "The day started out calmly enough." Then, "at 7:15, I was sitting at the dining room table writing a letter and Janice was playing with Terry and Kenny in the living room near the front door. The door was open because of the hot tropical evening. Without warning, the rat-a-tat-tat of a submachine gun broke the stillness of the evening. Instantly, it was joined by another and another, then by shotguns, rifles and hand grenades." Momentarily frozen in disbelief, Lake was "brought back to reality" by "an exploding hand grenade near the back entrance to our apartment." Stuffing his family under a bed, he was greeted minutes later by a gun barrel moving through his newly demolished back door. "Instantly, I threw up my hands and yelled 'Americano,'" he reports. "I was forced back into the bedroom which soon became crowded with heavily armed men wearing arm bands which read '26 de Julio'"—emblem of the Castro resistance. "Then I understood what was taking place. This was the rebel war charge of Castro's forces. . . . Our apartment was near Batista's local naval headquarters and these men of Castro's rebel forces were using our apartment to stage their attack. In broken English, one of the soldiers told us not to be frightened." In the end, the Lakes' apartment "proved to be too exposed for [the rebels'] purposes," and they withdrew, ultimately defeating the government forces in a two-hour battle.[32]

Caught by surprise at the kidnapping of U.S. servicemen, American officials were in no position to do much about it. Raúl Castro's accusation that the United States was still providing arms to Batista months after the embargo was supposed to have gone into effect was proved by a U.S. requisition form dated May 28 for rocket heads and fuses bound for Batista. Forced to acknowledge the transfer of arms, the State Department insisted that it was meant to replace an earlier shipment made in error, before the embargo went into effect. The rebels also possessed photographic evidence of a Cuban military aircraft refueling at the base, prompting the State Department to make yet another confession: Yes, we did let one Cuban military plane refuel on account of its being low on fuel.[33]

Meanwhile, Castro's men paraded the hostages, along with Park Wollam, U.S. consul at Santiago, around the Sierra Maestra, showing them incontrovertible proof of the damage wrought by Batista's planes. Wollam had gone up into the mountains to negotiate the hostages' release. Among the evidence the hostages were shown were fragments of U.S.-manufactured bombs and the burn victims of napalm firebombing.[34] In a note to Havana, Consul Wollam lent credence to the rebels' claims of civilian persecution at the hands of government forces. "The Cuban bombing affects mainly civilian population," Wollam wrote U.S. ambassador Earl Smith. "Rebels themselves have lost few men by this but claim that many civilians have suffered. . . . Populace generally afraid of planes and I can realize why after being subject to a similar incident in vicinity of a small church." Indeed, Wollam conceded, the Cuban Army had "been its own worst enemy."[35]

U.S. officials were forced to concede to the rebels' terms: "(A) No more shipment of arms. (B) Complete assurance that naval base will not be used for supplying arms and munitions. (C) An observer to assure compliance" with the arms embargo.[36] If there was an upside to all of this, it was that the contact between Wollam and the rebels allowed the Americans to take the measure of the rebels' Communist sympathies. "Rebels claim program based on Jose Marti but it is not clearly defined and they mainly have fanatic determination get rid of Batista. Believe probably some Communist influence although Castro volunteered at length that the movement was not." Castro had said the same to Charles Ryan. An American familiar with the rebels was informed that they consisted of "people of all stripes." Wollam did "not think at this moment that movement is definitely Communist but probably subject infiltration [*sic*]."[37]

By July 8 the rebels had released sixteen civilian hostages, leaving them with thirty military personnel and four civilians, thirty-four out of the original fifty hostages held. As the days became weeks, U.S. officials grew increasingly frustrated at the standoff, none more so than Arleigh Burke. "It is my opinion," Burke wrote the Joint Chiefs of Staff, "that so long as the hostages provide the insurgents protection from air attack, they will not be released, or released one or two at a time over a protracted period." Meanwhile, "the prestige of the U.S. throughout Latin America has been seriously damaged"—damage that Burke viewed as "almost irreparable if strong measures" weren't taken soon to secure the release of the U.S. personnel.[38] Burke wasn't the only one talking tough. A few days later, after Fidel Castro, operating in a distant part of Oriente province, agreed to intervene with his brother and demand the release of the hostages, Ambassador Smith worried that, barring some show of force on the part of the United States, the Castros would continue to take hostages. By rebel standards, this had been a complete success. The kidnappers "have accomplished their immediate objectives," Smith noted: "(A) Gained publicity (B) Being able to deal directly with the US (C) Suspend air and military action on part of GOC [Government of Cuba]."

By mid-July, the returns to the Twenty-sixth of July Movement of favorable publicity and a cessation of Cuban government bombing began to be outweighed by the exasperation of U.S. officials, many of whom were ready to free the hostages by force. Sensing the turn in U.S. sentiment, Fidel Castro ordered his brother to release the American military personnel. On July 18 Raúl Castro finally did so, and all returned safely to the U.S. base.

U.S. opposition to Fidel Castro's ascendancy was not simply a product of anticommunism. In the wrong hands, democracy could be as dangerous as communism, and was thought to be its antecedent. Such was the premise behind the CIA-orchestrated coup that deposed Jacobo Árbenz Guzmán, the democratically elected president of Guatemala, in June 1954. "Spaniards have many talents," Vice President Richard Nixon informed the National Security Council early the next year; "government was not among them." A few years later, Nixon told the same audience that Latin America's embrace of democracy was not necessarily a welcome thing. For states "lacking in maturity," Nixon observed, democracy "may not always be . . . the best of all possible courses." John Foster Dulles, Eisenhower's secretary of state, shared Nixon's alarm at the "tremendous surge in the direction of popular government by peoples who have practically no capacity for self-government and indeed are like children in facing this problem." Nations that made a premature leap to "self-government directly out of a semi-colonial status [provide] Communists with an ideal situation to exploit."[39]

Throughout the summer and fall of 1958, as the Cuban resistance endured and as Batista proved helpless to crush it, the U.S. State Department and National Security Council (NSC) returned with increasing frequency to the conundrum of whether Castro was or wasn't a Communist.[40] In general, the farther American officials were from the fighting in eastern Cuba, the more prone they were to view the Cuban resistance through the prism of communism. This was inevitable. Touring the towns and villages of Oriente province from his base in Santiago, Park Wollam could see for himself the psychological and physical effects of Batista's dictatorship and bombing campaign. The suffering was real, popular frustration justified. So, too, Cubans' hostility toward U.S. support for the Batista regime. Wollam recognized that, seen through a local prism, the resistance could not be reduced to communism, notwithstanding the presence of avowed Communists in its midst.

Wollam himself had gone out of his way to support the resistance. Just a year before Raúl Castro's kidnapping of American GIs, while Charles Ryan was still in the mountains, Wollam arranged for Léster Rodríguez, a Castro lieutenant, to receive safe passage from the Sierra Maestra to the U.S. base and ultimately on to Mexico City, in exchange for a pledge by Castro's forces to stop using the base as a source of weapons and ammunition. Wollam personally transported Rodríguez to the naval base in the trunk of his car, past checkpoints manned by Batista's soldiers. Meanwhile, the smuggling of arms to the rebels continued.[41]

By contrast, from Havana, where Ambassador Smith enjoyed a regular audience with Batista, and from Washington, where criticism of the United States was equated with communism and where dictators such as Batista in Cuba and Duvalier in Haiti were thought to be all that stood between communism and the eastern seaboard of the United States, mere contact with Communists was enough to disqualify Castro for U.S. recognition. A few days before the release of the hostages in late July 1958, Smith boasted to Lansing of maintaining "a pleasant relationship with Batista, [who] has always tried to accede to my requests." Naturally, Batista was upset by "the many acts, which he considers to have been unfriendly, on our part," Smith explained. If Washington was going to insist that the American ambassador negotiate with the Castro brothers for the hostages' release, thereby granting them de facto recognition, he, Smith, hoped that Washington would show Batista "some act of good faith before we press him again." Smith thought "the delivery to Batista of a wing of T-28" combat training jets would have just the right effect.[42] Three days later, Smith went further, urging Washington to rethink the arms embargo against Batista. Just "because we do not approve of dictators," Smith observed, "let us not unwillingly give aid to those in league with communism." Here Smith made a significant leap. Released U.S. hostages had described their kidnappers as "extremely religious, anti-Communist and ultra supernationalist."[43] Either way, by December 1958, the Eisenhower administration concluded that Castro must be stopped. At a December 23 meeting of the NSC, CIA director Allen W. Dulles "added that we ought to prevent a Castro victory," Secretary S. Everett Gleason confided in his notes. "The President believed this was the first time that statement had been made in" that forum.[44]

There was, of course, precedent for U.S. intervention in a Cuban revolutionary war. In April 1898, with Máximo Gómez's Liberation Army on the verge of victory over Spain, the United States intervened in the Cuban War of Independence, thus supposedly saving Cuba from itself. But if Dulles and company meant to prevent a Castro victory, they would have to hurry. After repelling Operación Verano, a government offensive in the summer of 1958, Castro's forces abandoned the eastern mountains and moved into central Cuba, where they were greeted by enthusiastic crowds. By late December they arrived at the outskirts of the city of Santa Clara, less than two hundred miles east of Havana. Here, over the course of four days, between December 28 and 31, Che Guevara led just under three hundred rebel troops into what proved to be the largest and last pitched battle of the revolution. Aided by a cache of weapons and ammunitions captured from a government train, Guevara routed a force far superior in arms and manpower, much of which capitulated without a fight. In the wee hours of the New Year, Batista fled Cuba for the Dominican Republic, never to return. Within a week, the Revolutionary army arrived in Havana, jubilant and flush with state-of-the-art government weaponry captured at Santa Clara the week before.[45]

The Eisenhower administration spent much of the next two years trying to get a bead on Castro (as late as June 1960, a National Intelligence Estimate conceded that it was "unable to answer the simplified question 'Is Castro himself a Communist?'").[46] At stake was nearly $1 billion in U.S. investment in Cuba. U.S. businesses produced 40 percent of Cuba's sugar; owned two out of three of Cuba's oil refineries, 90 percent of its public utilities, and half of its railroads and mines; and, through the likes of Meyer Lansky and his mob associates, dominated Cuban tourism. Cuba, in turn, counted on a U.S. sugar subsidy worth $150 million, which constituted 80 percent of its foreign exchange.[47] When, on January 9, 1959, U.S. national security officials first broached the question of how Castro's rise would affect the status of the Guantánamo naval base, they assumed Castro would do nothing to jeopardize the two nations' intimate relationship so long as the United States still held the chips in Cuba.[48]

By May 1959, Castro had begun to put that assumption to doubt. As early as February, Castro set aside the 1940 constitution that had once restored democratic government and to whose resurrection he had once committed himself. In March he reduced rents by 50 percent, thereby signaling to foreign and domestic property owners an end to the status quo. In April, while on a trip to Washington, D.C., he alarmed U.S. officials by never bringing up the subject of U.S. aid, as if he did not need it. In May he introduced an agricultural reform bill that limited farm holdings to under a thousand acres, directly threatening U.S. sugar producers on the island, some of whom owned 400,000-plus-acre estates. Confronted by these and other develop-ments centralizing and nationalizing Cuba's politics, industry, and services while targeting foreign businesses and upper-class Cubans, Cubans began to depart for the United States as early as June 1959, just as moderates abandoned Castro's government. Meanwhile, Castro steeled himself for battle, creating the citizen militia that galvanized the lower classes in defense of the revolution.[49] Just over a year after first raising the subject of intervening in Cuba to stop the revolution, the CIA director, Dulles, called for Castro's overthrow. Castro was a "madman," President Eisenhower declared in January 1960; he "is go-ing wild and harming the whole American structure."[50]

From January 1960, when Dulles and Eisenhower decided that Castro must be overthrown, to President Kennedy's pledge not to intervene in Cuba, which precipitated the withdrawal of Russian missiles from Cuba in October 1962, U.S. officials' sense of the strategic value of the Guantánamo naval base underwent a curious evolution. In the first year and a half or so after Castro's rise, U.S. officials appear to have been genuinely concerned that Castro might attack the base. By September 1960 that concern yielded to a conviction that should he do so, U.S. forces would go "all the way to Santiago," as Joint Chief of Staff Arleigh Burke put it. Not to be outdone, Undersecretary of State for Political Affairs Livingston T. Merchant remarked that if Castro attacked Guantánamo, "that's it—we are at war. We would move on Havana."

No sooner had Burke and his associates come to realize Guan-tánamo's potential value as bait than they were forced to acknowledge that Castro was not so stupid as to invite an American invasion. At the very meeting in which Burke and Undersecretary Merchant first raised the rhetoric on Guantánamo, the participants were informed that the State Department considered a Cuban attack on the base unlikely. Guantánamo was too valuable to Castro as a source of anti-American propaganda.[51] In that case, U.S. intelligence and military officials would have to precipitate a Cuban attack on Guantánamo or conjure one up on their own. "We should stage an attack on Guantánamo," Secretary of State Christian Herter told President Eisenhower on November 1, 1960. Contemplating cutting off diplomatic relations with the Castro government, Eisenhower himself argued that "the quicker we do it, the more tempted Castro might be to actually attack Guantánamo," a prospect that intrigued the president, who would then have had the provocation to depose Castro "with force."[52]

The evolution of U.S. thinking on Guantánamo is also plain in the minutes of the National Security Council. In March 1960, National Security Council officials spoke uncertainly about Guantánamo's status. Confident that the United States occupied the base legally, Eisenhower officials were less certain of political support at the United Nations should Castro ask the Americans to leave; typically the United States did not like to occupy the territory of another nation without the host nation's consent. Moreover, at this stage in the getting-to-know-you with Castro, U.S. officials could not be sure that Castro wouldn't target the base. While Admiral Burke was confident that American marines could repel an armed attack on Guantánamo, he was less sure about the integrity of the water supply, which was piped in from the nearby Yateras River.[53]

Throughout this period, the naval base served as a barometer of U.S.-Cuban relations. As early as January 9, 1959, just a few days after the Revolutionary Army's triumphant arrival in the capital, a meeting of U.S. national security officials acknowledged that the revolutionary turn in Cuba had clouded the future of the base. At a minimum, the officials concluded, Castro was likely to want to renegotiate the lease as well as to end the apparent discrimination against Cuban workers. Still, they did not expect Castro to threaten the base and thereby jeopardize the two nations' intimate economic relationship.

The extent to which the naval base was involved in U.S. plans for what became known as the Bay of Pigs invasion remained underreported for years. When Admiral Lyman Lemnitzer wondered aloud in March 1961 if the Cuban exiles training in Guatemala might be moved to Guantánamo Bay, he was informed by Admiral Robert Dennison, commander in chief of the Atlantic Fleet, that the base was not suitable for such purposes—first, because Cuba controlled the local high ground surrounding the bay, hence secrecy at Guantánamo was impossible; and second, because the navy did not want to compromise its legal position at the bay. Still, if secrecy at Guantánamo was out of the question, Guantánamo could still be useful in backing up covert actions in Cuba, especially if, as the administration seemed to hope, Cuba struck back somehow at the United States. In the days leading up to the Bay of Pigs, Dennison pledged to have ready all the ships, planes, and combat troops necessary to overthrow the Cuban government should the opportunity arise. And so, in the weeks preceding the operation's launch, Guantánamo bustled with activity not seen since World War II.

But Guantánamo had a role in the Bay of Pigs invasion unacknowl-edged until relatively recently. Unbeknownst to President Kennedy, simultaneous with the training of Cuban exiles in Guatemala, another band of 260 Cuban exiles, under the leadership of the former rebel army commander and now CIA agent Higinio Días Ane, was prepar-ing off the South Carolina coast for an attack on the city of Baracoa, on the southeastern tip of Cuba, intended to distract the Cuban military in advance of the main invasion force. From Baracoa, the group was to proceed to the naval base and, disguised as Cuban Army troops, pro-voke the base into launching an attack on Cuba. What happened to this second "invasion" is not exactly clear; it remains a blurry sideshow in the bigger fiasco.[54]

In his letter to President Kennedy in March 1961, special advisor Arthur M. Schlesinger had tried to warn the president that illegal, ill-advised, and amateurish plans to undermine the Cuban leader could only backfire, galvanizing support for Castro in Latin America and throughout the world while eroding the young president's moral au-thority. But the embarrassment of the Bay of Pigs made the president and his administration more determined than ever. July 26, 1961, marked the eighth anniversary of Fidel Castro's attack on the Mon-cada Barracks. To coincide with that anniversary, the CIA planned an operation code-named Patty (sometimes Patty Candela), which in-cluded the double assassination of Fidel and Raúl Castro, along with a staged attack on the Guantánamo naval base aimed to provoke a full-scale U.S. response.

The navy's injunction against using the naval base to train a covert Cuban exile force or to launch an unprovoked assault on Cuba did not extend to cultivating intelligence contacts in Oriente province or even sheltering Cuban exiles on the base. Besides the assassination of the two Castros, Operation Patty called for the firing of four mortar shells toward the U.S. base from Cuban territory, with one more mortar fired at a Cuban military post near the base, *as if* originating from the U.S. base. The plan also included the arming by the naval base of local Cubans friendly to the United States, who, again disguised as government forces, would help precipitate the American counterattack. Then, a real war having been triggered, the local Cubans could join the liberators in "restoring" democratic rule to Cuba. Like so many other bungled U.S. operations against the Castro government, the Cubans saw this coming. The leaders of the program were arrested in possession of two 57-millimeter cannons, four bazookas, twenty-three Garand rifles, and an assortment of grenades and ammunition. To this seized cache was later added thirty-five Springfield rifles, a 60-millimeter mortar, one .30-caliber machine gun, twelve M-3 submachine guns, two M-1 carbines, and still more ammunition and grenades, all apparently a product of naval base largesse.[55]

It was not long after this that Cuba filed a formal complaint against the Guantánamo naval base at the United Nations, accusing the United States of using the base as a launchpad for attacks in Cuba. "I shall not descend to reply," said Ambassador Adlai Stevenson in response, "to the argument that the United States base at Guantánamo Bay, which exists by virtue of a valid treaty between the two countries and which has been there for 60 years, is directed against Cuba and . . . the Western Hemisphere and that it is harboring mercenaries for an attack." Such "charges are not only false but absurd. The whole history of this century is eloquent testimony that this installation has been maintained for the defense of the hemisphere and not for attack on the hemisphere." Looking back years later on his time in charge of Guantánamo and the Atlantic Fleet, Admiral Dennison observed that Guantánamo's role in the region was as "a benevolent presence, surely.

Nobody in his right mind would think we were down there for purposes of conquering somebody or taking over countries."[56]

In the summer of 1961, Kennedy authorized Operation Mongoose, a
multifaceted program to remove the Castros from power. This time
Guantánamo featured prominently in the planning of espionage designed to inspire yet another retaliatory strike by Cuban forces on the
base, which would in turn justify a full-scale American response.

In late 1961, President Kennedy met at the White House with his
brother, the attorney general Robert F. Kennedy, Secretary of Defense
Robert McNamara, and General Edward Lansdale, chairman of the
Joint Chiefs of Staff. The purpose of the meeting was to take stock of
the Cuban situation. By all appearances, the situation was becoming
more dire by the day, as Castro's grip on power was tightening and
as the United States seemed to be at a loss to do anything about it.
From that meeting emerged the conviction that deposing Castro would
be the "top priority in the United States Government" in the new year.
Just the day before, President Kennedy had told his brother that "the
final chapter on Cuba has not been written." Where Castro was concerned, "all else is secondary—no time, money, effort, or manpower is
to be spared."[57]

By early the next year, the attorney general was passing out assign-
ments for Operation Mongoose.[58] In February, Assistant Secretary of
Defense for Special Operations Lansdale reviewed plans designed to
"lure or provoke Castro, or an uncontrollable subordinate, into an
overt hostile reaction against the United States; a reaction which
would in turn create the justification for the US to not only retaliate
but destroy Castro with speed, force and determination." One operation, code-named Bingo, called for the U.S. military to use so-called
snakes, or U.S. and exiled Cuban forces planted "outside the confines
of the Guantánamo Base," to "simulate an actual fire-fight," which
would give the appearance that the base was under attack. This simulated attack would then inspire a true counterattack, during which the
U.S. base "could disgorge military force in sufficient number to sustain itself until other forces, which had been previously alerted, could

attack in other areas." Properly carried out, "the above could overthrow the Cuban Government in a matter of hours."[59]

It is hard to know how literally this and other optimistic plans for
Castro's overthrow were greeted by top Kennedy administration officials. Their willingness to sign off on the Bay of Pigs fiasco suggests a
credulous audience. Operation Bingo was just one in a long list of
proposed maneuvers designed to bring down Castro that included,
among other dubious programs, Operation Good Times, which aimed
to sow doubts about Castro's populism by raining down on the Cuban
countryside doctored photographs depicting "an obese Castro with
two beauties in any situation desired, ostensibly within a room in the
Castro residence, lavishly furnished, and a table brimming over with
the most delectable Cuban food with an underlying caption (appropri-
ately Cuban) such as 'My ration is different.'" A surefire spark to counterrevolution.

Operation Bingo was meant to convince the Cuban government
that a U.S. attack was imminent, in part by evacuating "selected civilians, including dependents," from Guantánamo and replacing them
with a battalion of marines.[60] This was as nothing compared to what
the Joint Chiefs of Staff had in mind for Guantánamo by the middle
of March. A list of "pretexts to justify US military intervention in Cuba"
included an elaborate register of potential actions undertaken at or
near the naval base. "A series of well coordinated incidents will be
planned to take place in and around Guantánamo to give genuine appearance of being done by hostile Cuban forces," chairman of the
Joint Chiefs of Staff Lemnitzer informed Secretary of Defense Robert
McNamara. Among ideas intended to create the appearance of a
"credible [Cuban] attack" on the naval base, Lemnitzer noted the following: "Land friendly Cuban in uniform 'over-the-fence' to stage attack on base"; "capture Cuban (friendly) saboteurs inside the base";
"start riots near the base main gate (friendly Cubans)." Not all the
ideas were so benign: "Blow up ammunition inside the base; start
fires"; "burn aircraft on air base (sabotage)"; "lob mortar shells from
outside of base into base. Some damage to installations"; "capture assault teams approaching from the sea or vicinity of Guantánamo City";
"capture militia group which storms the base"; "sabotage ship in har-

bor; large fires—naphthalene"; "sink ship near harbor entrance. Conduct funerals for mock-victims (may be in lieu of (10))."

That wasn't all. "A 'Remember the Maine' incident could be arranged," Lemnitzer informed his boss, adding intriguing fuel to undying conspiracy theorizing: "a. We could blow up a US ship in Guantánamo Bay and blame Cuba. b. We could blow up a drone (unmanned) vessel anywhere in the Cuban waters. We could arrange to cause such incident in the vicinity of Havana or Santiago as a spectacular result of Cuban attack from air or sea, or both." When the Cuban military investigated the presence of hostile Cuban aircraft or naval vessels in the area, it would lend credence to U.S. accusations. And of course "the US could follow up with an air/sea rescue operation covered by US fighters to 'evacuate' remaining members of the non-existent crew. Casualty lists in US newspapers would cause a helpful wave of national indignation."

This was an administration willing to play hardball; the sluices having been opened, the ideas kept coming: "We could sink a boatload of Cubans en route to Florida (real or simulated). We could foster attempts on lives of Cuban refugees in the United States even to the extent of wounding in instances to be widely publicized." Auto-terrorism? "Exploding a few plastic bombs in carefully chosen spots, the arrest of Cuban agents and the release of prepared documents substantiating Cuban involvement also would be helpful in projecting the idea of an irresponsible government." And on and on it went: simulated hijacking of a U.S. plane; simulated shooting down over Cuba of a U.S. airliner filled with college students on vacation. What alternative was there, given the fact that U.S. intelligence had determined that "a credible internal revolt is impossible of attainment during the next 9–10 months?" Clearly, it was up to the United States "to develop a Cuban 'provocation' as justification for positive US military action."[61]

By August 1962 the U.S. State Department and the CIA contemplated for the first time using Guantánamo to mount covert operations into Cuba. Up to this point the Defense Department had shied away from such requests due to the fact of Guantánamo's exposure to Cuban surveillance and to naval officials' reluctance to compromise the navy's legal standing there. In mid-month, Lemnitzer and CIA director John McCone expressed deep reservations about implicating

Guantánamo; a week later, Secretary of State Dean Rusk raised the subject of using Guantánamo for covert operations, with vigorous opposition from the Joint Chiefs of Staff.[62] As best is known, this is the closest Guantánamo came to being the launchpad of U.S. military activity in Cuba between January 1, 1959, when Castro rose to power, and November 1, 1962, the end of the Cuban Missile Crisis.

The Cuban Missile Crisis began in midsummer 1962, when U.S. intelligence officials began to notice large shipments of Soviet military cargo being unloaded in Cuba. Accompanying the armaments were literally thousands of passengers presumed to be Soviet-bloc military personnel, along with heavy construction and communications equipment. Before long, new roads were being laid in isolated areas and new military installations thrown up. "What the construction activity involves is not yet known," an intelligence memorandum confessed in late August. But activity in the vicinity of Matanzas, just west of Havana, suggested, among other possibilities, "the initial phases of construction of a SAM[surface-to-air missile]-equipped air defense system."[63] U.S. uncertainty about what exactly was going on in Cuba was exacerbated by a monthlong pause in CIA-operated U-2 surveillance flights due to several controversial incidents in Asia. When aerial surveillance of Cuba resumed in mid-October, it revealed a host of SAM sites, to be sure, but also the installation of medium- and intermediate-range ballistic missiles capable of delivering nuclear warheads anywhere in the continental United States.

The history of the Cuban Missile Crisis is well known.[64] Less known is the fact that the Soviets directed nuclear missiles not only at the continental United States but also at Guantánamo itself. The United States would not comprehend the existential threat facing the base until fifty years later, when it was revealed by the journalist Michael Dobbs. Guantánamo officials reported unusual movements throughout eastern Cuba and in the vicinity of the bay as early as August 24. "Persistent reports from numerous sources indicates [sic] extensive military construction is in progress in restricted area" northwest of the naval base, the navy warned the State Department. One thousand or so Russian and Czech military personnel were at work on a

missile site amid great security and secrecy. The navy also described
Chinese and Soviet nationals off-loading dozens of rockets in nearby
Cuban ports and transporting them to selected towns ringing Guan-
tánamo Bay.[65]

Again, U.S. intelligence officials were not sure how to read this.
They never imagined that conventional, much less nuclear, missiles
would be pointed at the naval base. They consistently argued that the
biggest threat to the base came not from Russian arms just arrived in
Cuba but from Castro himself. Indeed, they had expected the Soviets
to act as a restraint on Castro's "designs on Guantánamo."[66] On September 7, CIA director McCone learned from a Cuban source that
the Communists were making preparations for the "'complete destruction' of the Guantánamo Base in the event of [a U.S.] attack on
Cuba." But the report made no mention that such an attack would be
carried out by nuclear weapons.[67] Meanwhile, reports of a military
buildup throughout Cuba in general, and more specifically in the region around the naval base, continued to flow from the base commander to Washington throughout September.[68]

News that the Soviets were installing nuclear warheads in Cuba
reached the president on October 16. Beginning with a White House
meeting that evening and continuing over the course of the next week,
top national security officials contemplated a range of responses, from
a full-scale military invasion of Cuba—favored by the Joint Chiefs of
Staff—to targeted bombardment of missile and military sites, to a naval quarantine of the Cuban coast. Any form of U.S. military attack
was at a minimum sure to provoke a strike at the naval base, everybody
agreed, prompting General Maxwell Taylor, newly appointed chairman of the Joint Chiefs of Staff, to order the evacuation of dependents
on October 22. Meanwhile, the thought of using the base to bait Castro into war persisted. "One other thing is whether, uh, we should also
think of, uh, uh, whether there is some other way we can get involved
in through, uh, Guantánamo Bay, or something," Attorney General
Robert Kennedy stammered at the first meeting of national security
officials on October 16, "or whether there's some ship that, you know,
sink the Maine again or something."[69]

It was at this time that a high-level U.S. administration official first
broached the idea of returning Guantánamo to Cuba—as a negotiat-

ing ploy. What if the United States agreed not only to withdraw Jupiter missiles from Turkey and Italy but also to "limit our use of Guantánamo to a specified limited time?" Secretary of Defense Robert McNamara wondered. The president seems not to have engaged this question the first time it came up. But when Adlai Stevenson, U.S. delegate to the United Nations, repeated the suggestion minutes later, the president is reported to have "sharply rejected the thought of surrendering our base at Guantánamo in the present situation." Relinquishing Guantánamo would only "convey to the world that we had been frightened into abandoning our position."[70] The president repeated the sentiment the next day after Stevenson once again suggested that the United States consider Guantánamo as a bargaining chip. Again, the president wouldn't hear of it; that would only reveal the United States "in a state of panic."[71] Thus Guantánamo became a symbol of U.S. resolve to stand up to communism.

"Higher authority has directed the immediate evacuation of all dependents from the Naval Base," a navy handbill informed the local community at 10:00 a.m. on Monday, October 22. Effective immediately, mothers (mostly) were directed to "get your suitcases and children and wait quietly in your front yard when ready"; the "buses are starting their runs now." By 5:00 p.m. the dependents were gone, leaving the base eerily deserted. "No children riding the school buses or playing in the neighborhood; no wives returning from their bridge parties, golf course, bowling alleys or those who were employed, from their offices." Lights were dimmed throughout the base, water rationed. "All went off smoothly," an official report suggests. "No complaints were heard except that the commissary store sold out of TV Dinners the day following the evacuation."[72] Sailors and marines replaced the Guantánamo dependents. At its peak in late October, the military population at the naval base reached just over nine thousand (roughly split between navy and marines) as the base became an "armed garrison."[73]

Armed but defenseless. Even without nuclear weapons trained on the base, the ratcheting up of troops at Guantánamo was purely symbolic, designed to convince local and domestic audiences that the United States would stand up to communism. Surely the president knew what Admiral Dennison himself later acknowledged: surrounded by high ground in Cuban hands, Guantánamo was "undefended and indefensible. I mean here it is in a pocket on the coast, with Cuban hills looking down on it. There's really no way to protect it."[74]

And that was from a conventional attack. The attack planned by the Soviets that autumn involved forty nuclear warheads carrying nuclear payloads of 14 kilotons each (each one roughly the size of the Hiroshima bomb), and capable of striking targets up to 110 miles away. The missiles arrived in eastern Cuba in early October, where they were stored in the village of Mayarí Arriba, thirty-five miles northwest of Guantánamo Bay, high in the San Cristobal Mountains. On Wednesday, October 24, three of the missile launchers loaded with nuclear warheads were moved from Mayarí Arriba to the village of Vilorio, a mere fifteen miles northwest of the U.S. base. On Friday, October 26, just as the missile crisis appeared ready to blow up, the missiles were moved yet again, this time to an abandoned plantation in the village of Filipinas, some ten miles south of Vilorio, in the direction of the Caribbean Sea. In the end the conflict was de-escalated and the missiles withdrawn. A navy film of the evacuation and landing of additional sailors and marines depicts the events of October 1962 in heroic light. Guantánamo had stood up to Castro.[75]

Castro was angry at having been left out of the negotiation that brought the missile crisis to an end. Still, one cannot help but conclude that of the three principal players in the crisis—Kennedy, Khrushchev, and Castro—Castro was the winner. Among other things, Kennedy agreed to respect Cuba's "inviolability" and "sovereignty," and pledged neither "to interfere in its internal affairs" nor to allow U.S. "territory to be used as a bridgehead for the invasion of Cuba." A pledge is a pledge. But were Kennedy to live up to his words, the administration would have a lot of time on its hands.[76]

7

★

THE AMERICAN DREAM

In the autumn of 1956, Lieutenant Andrew Spielman, a navy ento-
mologist and an expert on insect-borne disease, was ordered to report
to the Guantánamo naval base to begin a two-year study on the Hippelates fly, or common eye gnat. "For a number of years," explained a
navy memo, "the pestiferous 'eye-gnat' has created a public welfare
and secondary school health problem at the Naval Base. . . . The problem at Guantánamo has become so acute that the Commander has
requested assistance of the Navy Disease Vector Control Center and
the Bureau of Medicine and Surgery."[1] In a letter to a friend, Spielman
described the situation more plainly: "There is this phenomenon called
the 'Gitmo Wave.' You see people standing in unlikely places and waving at empty air. They are trying to get rid of eye gnats."[2]

Accompanying Spielman on his mission to Guantánamo would be
his wife, Judy. The young couple expected to start a family, and not
long after learning of their assignment, they received a pamphlet in
the mail welcoming them to the base. "This booklet has been prepared
to give you a true picture of life in Guantánamo Bay," announced the
1956 edition. "We are looking forward to your arrival and sincerely
hope that your stay at the Naval Base Guantánamo Bay, Cuba, will be
as pleasant as we have found it."[3]

The pamphlet opened with a detailed description of Cuba's and
Guantánamo's strategic value to the United States, followed by an ac-

count of the region's racial composition. "In race and customs," the pamphlet explained, the local population was "predominantly Spanish." About half of Guantánamo City's population was "white, about one-quarter colored, and the other quarter of mixed descent." The average Cuban was "slender, with small feet and hands, polite, and loves color, music and dancing."[4]

This happy people comprised a ready labor force. "One of the nice luxuries of Guantánamo Bay," the pamphlet continued, "is the fact that domestic help is available." Of course, "as with all good things, a certain amount of responsibility goes hand in hand with this feature of better living." Prospective wives, the pamphlet advised, should expect to be patient when communicating with workers who don't speak the language. They should also expect "a little confusion at first," though most "will be surprised and delighted to find your household running smoothly with the help of your neighbor's English-speaking maid acting as an interpreter."[5]

Newcomers were sure to be surprised by the Cubans' pay scale. "Maids' salaries range from a minimum of $15.00 a month for an untrained person to a maximum of $35.00 a month (plus board) for experienced help." Now, "this may seem ridiculously low," the pamphlet allowed, "and our natural tendency is to spoil them with extra gratuities." But even at the low end (50 cents a day or 6 cents an hour), these wages far exceeded wages off the base.[6] And though "normal human relations require us to be gracious to our employees, it is well to remember that if you allow too much freedom to your maid, you do her a disservice as well as to the next Navy wife who might hire her." Managed correctly, Cuban maids provided "efficient housecleaning, washing, and ironing, as well as child care." They also made good babysitters, "as permanent maids are assigned quarters on the Base when they are available." Further, the most highly paid help could be "expected to do any or all of the cooking if you so desire."[7]

Cuban maids worked eight-hour days. Wives who wanted to extend the workday for chores such as babysitting could expect to pay an additional twenty-five cents an hour, though maids' hours could be adjusted to incorporate babysitting into the normal workday. The same applied to help with "after-hours parties." Cuban maids worked six-day weeks, typically working two weeks straight, then getting two days off. Wives who released their maids on Friday afternoons rather than Saturday mornings were being exceedingly "generous," the pamphlet cautioned, once again putting fellow wives in an uncomfortable position.[8]

The Spielmans' assignment to Guantánamo Bay coincided with a period that people familiar with the base have come to think of as its golden age: between Guantánamo's emergence as a full-blown naval base during World War II and the rise of Fidel Castro, which permanently soured U.S.-Cuban relations and curtailed U.S. access to Cuba.[9] An assignment to Guantánamo Bay put naval and civilian personnel and their families within reach of an American Dream more accessible than at home. Commander Harold Sacks, a young lieutenant at Guantánamo in the late 1950s (and a friend of the Spielmans'), remembers "joyful years" on the base. "We lieutenants and our growing families lived in what can best be termed 'genteel poverty,' in an idyllic 5,000 person 'bungalow colony,' replete with live-in-maid service, dollar prime rib dinners at the Marine Family Restaurant, ten cent happy hours at the Officer's Club, and occasional weekend visits as guests aboard the Navy ships to Ocho Rios, Kingston or Montego Bay, Jamaica, Port au Prince, Haiti, and Panama."[10]

During the 1950s the population of the base swelled to more than fifteen thousand residents.[11] In addition, some three thousand Cubans traveled to the base each day for work, helping to transform this little corner of Cuba into a fair-size American town. With a tight-knit community, traditional values, ample recreational facilities, and cordial relations with its neighbor, the base was thought to represent the best America had to offer, a throwback to the days before civil rights and feminist agitation and political radicalism began to unhinge the United States.

As base residents worked to transform these forty-five square miles into a home away from home, many sensed that they were building more than a navy base; they were erecting a model community. To this day, Guantánamo residents refer to the naval base as a place frozen in time—a modern Mayberry, as a recent commanding officer put it in what has become a standard cliché, after the idealized community of the 1960s sitcom *The Andy Griffith Show*. (For some, the 1950s weren't good enough; these would compare Guantánamo to America in the

1920s.[12]) "It's very safe for people here. It's safe for kids. There's no crime; there's no drugs. They can walk out and go to the McDonald's at 9 at night and you don't worry about it. There's not many places in the world where you can do that."[13]

But a place beyond the reach of social and political upheaval is a place more mythical than real. After all, as another Guantánamo official recently acknowledged, 1950s America was a nation "of walls, divisions, and hostility, of exploitation and prejudice."[14] In their tenure at Guantánamo Bay, the Spielmans and Sackses came to appreciate firsthand the base's many virtues. But their acknowledgment of its virtues did not blind them to its limitations, or to the tension inherent in what remained an American imperial project in Cuba. The American Dream that was 1950s Guantánamo was a particular kind of dream, a class-conscious, color-coded, gender-sensitive dream that entailed its share of exploitation and coercion as well as opportunity and good fun. No one set foot on the Guantánamo naval base who hadn't been approved by the commanding officer, making it the ultimate gated community.

The Andy Griffith Show did not come on air until October 1960, just one month before the U.S. presidential election and just as relations between Fidel Castro and the United States had deteriorated beyond repair. Coinciding with the base's diminishing strategic significance, Guantánamo's new symbolic importance gave the base a new lease on life, quieting calls by Ambassador Adlai Stevenson and others to return the base to Cuba. But with Cuba closed to American tourists, life at Guantánamo would never be the same. As Americans remained pinned down on the base, the glowing reports of life at Guantánamo came to seem halfhearted, if not forced. The myth of Mayberry grew in tandem with the base's isolation, its authority discernible in the way it blinded Americans to the true history of the base and to the larger imperial project of which the base remained an integral part.

The Spielmans arrived at Guantánamo Bay in April 1957 with Judy five months pregnant. That year, Cuba was suffering the final throes of Batista's dictatorship, with Castro's revolutionary forces alternately dodging and engaging government troops throughout Oriente province, often in close proximity to Guantánamo Bay. With no family housing available on the base, the Spielmans moved into a home in Guantánamo City, against the advice of a base official, who warned Andrew Spielman that he would be the only U.S. officer there. Judy Spielman remembers Guantánamo City as an unhappy, dirty, and dilapidated place with little in the way of industry besides a few cigar factories and whorehouses catering to U.S. demand. Andrew experienced Guantánamo City differently. The city "is really very nice," he wrote his navy supervisor; indeed, Cuba itself was "a nice place."[15]

In many ways, living in Guantánamo City suited Andrew Spielman ideally. Eye gnats are cosmopolitan and ecumenical. Living off base allowed Spielman to extend the compass of his fieldwork, and he ended up laying more insect traps outside the base than inside. "Since I have use of a jeep I have been able to travel over much of Oriente Province in the course of my work," he wrote his supervisor. "I have found the Cuban people to be very helpful and the country beautiful."[16]

Judy Spielman often accompanied her husband on field trips throughout the Guantánamo region. These trips extended the couple's social and cultural horizon as well as Andrew Spielman's investigations, and it wasn't long before the local inhabitants became accustomed to the couple's presence—and invested in Andrew's fieldwork. Cubans contributed anecdotal evidence about the patterns and proclivities of the pest they called "Guasasa," as well as information about the region's ubiquitous mosquitoes.[17] "Many of the local Cubans have been asking about mosquito control here," Spielman wrote his boss. "The managers of the big sugar 'centrals' are quite interested in improving the living conditions around their homes. I have spoken to a few ranchers who likewise expressed much interest."[18] Indeed, so great was local interest in his work that Spielman produced a handout for the Cubans that enabled them to distinguish the different kinds of gnats and mosquitoes from one another. They might think of it as a way of "improving public relations," Spielman observed. "If a man really wants to do something by way of control, I can give him more specific information. If my Spanish improves enough, I might even attempt to translate it."[19]

After a few months in Guantánamo City, the Spielmans moved

onto the naval base. In August 1957, Judy gave birth to the couple's
first son, prompting Andrew to boast, "I am now a real family man: a
wife, a baby, a visiting mother-in-law, and a maid, and all talking at
once."[20] The base itself presented a marked contrast to Guantánamo
City, its cleanliness and creature comforts almost making up for its
provincialism.

Once liberated from household chores, what did Guantánamo
women do? The navy pamphlet suggested that a seemingly infinite
number of activities awaited enthusiastic navy wives. Wives could
shop, recreate, worship, participate in the base's many civic clubs, or
travel.[21] But, by all accounts, recreation was the distinguishing feature of the place. Swimming pools, beaches, and picnic grounds were
readily available, as were two golf courses (eighteen and nine holes, respectively) complete with practice green and clubhouse. Family memberships at the gulf club cost four dollars per month. If swimming,
golf, and picnicking weren't their thing, wives could amuse themselves
at bowling, tennis, horseback riding, baseball, softball, basketball,
volleyball, cycling, archery, sailing, boating, hunting, fishing, roller-
skating, or horseshoes. There were two hobby shops, a library, and four
outdoor theaters, never mind the clubs for sailors. Indeed, the pamphlet marveled, with its "dances, special parties, bingo and the like,"
the base provided "recreation commensurate with the average community of 8–10,000 population and the opportunity for a good time is
here for all to enjoy."

But that wasn't all. For the faithful, Guantánamo offered "both
Catholic and Protestant Chaplains," as well as "a Jewish Chaplain for
special Jewish celebrations." Divine worship, Holy Communion, Ves-
per fellowship, adult and child Bible study, a Protestant chapel choir,
Sunday school—all these were available to military and civilian personnel. The base also sponsored a host of civic institutions—from the
local PTA to the Hospital Volunteers to the Ladies Auxiliary, Toast-
masters, Sojourners, Fellowcrafters, Navy Wives, Transport Volunteers, Altar Guild, Girl Scouts, and Brownies clubs.[22]

Those determined to escape the base could "travel to other islands
in the Caribbean area for a few days of relaxation, sightseeing, and
shopping." In what remained in the late 1950s very much a man's
navy, few of the vessels traveling to Caribbean ports could accommo-

date women; when space or circumstances didn't allow for Caribbean travel, residents could visit destinations within Cuba, such as Havana, Santiago, or Guantánamo City.[23]

And yet all the activities in the world couldn't disguise the monotony of the place, according to Judy Spielman. Sure, there was household help and recreational opportunities on the base; at Guantánamo, naval officers and their families enjoyed a degree of luxury unattainable for most of them back in the United States. But the free time that the Cuban labor provided only underscored the fact that there was little or nothing meaningful for American women to do at Guantánamo Bay. Though Spielman worked in the Guantánamo library, hers was an "isolated, narrow life." With little to do at the base, many navy wives resorted to heavy drinking—and to ignobler pursuits. Spielman remembers "lots of interaction between couples."

The naval base that Judy Spielman came to know was a "two tiered society," with officers and their families enjoying privileges and perks unavailable to the civilian personnel and enlisted men (never mind the local workforce). Any discomfort with this arrangement was diluted in booze-soaked get-togethers at "Oil Point," an exclusive watering hole reserved for officers and their wives.[24]

By the spring of 1958, violence in the Guantánamo area had begun to impinge on Andrew Spielman's fieldwork. In April 1958 he wrote his supervisor a letter, eagerly anticipating his visit. "We are looking forward to your visit this summer. I am sure you will find it enjoyable. This is nice vacation country." Just how much of this nice vacation country the visitor would actually get to see was not yet clear. "If things improve out in Cuba," Spielman wrote, "the trapping runs should be most interesting." Spielman himself hadn't "been able to get off the base" since January, due to local violence. "As you probably know," Spielman wrote, "the Gtmo area has been the scene of an awful lot of fighting. We get periodic stories of mass executions and atrocities" carried out by Batista. "All most discouraging. My poor traps!"[25]

It was only a few months later that Raúl Castro captured the busload of marines on liberty. After the kidnapping, the navy restricted military and civilian personnel to the base. "The political situation in Cuba continues in a very bad state," Spielman wrote a colleague that month. "I am afraid that I may never be able to resume my field work in off base areas. It would be too dangerous." Like his gnat study, the couple's social life shrank intolerably. "The big news of the day in Gtmo," Spielman wrote sarcastically, "is that the commissary is now stocking Chinese Food."[26]

The class, or status, distinctions that irked Judy Spielman were not the only form of social stratification at 1950s Guantánamo. Peter C. Grenquist, a junior officer at the base in the early 1950s, remembers a "19th-century colonial atmosphere" pervading the place, with "all the prejudice and discrimination" that this implied. It was as if Guantánamo officials were determined to "turn back the clock" to the era before the Second and even the First World War, when the various races knew their places.

Hard racial lines distinguished whites, blacks, and "coloreds" (Filipinos and Chinese "coolies") on the base. Indeed, until well into the 1960s, the vast majority of African Americans in the U.S. Navy worked in the Stewards Branch as servants and menial laborers. In 1949 there were 19 black naval officers in the entire U.S. Navy out of an officer corps numbering 45,464 (that is, four thousandths of 1 percent); by 1960 the number of black officers had risen seven times, but black officers still comprised less than 1 percent of the officer corps.[27]

At the officers' club out on Deer Point, Grenquist remembers being waited on by Filipinos and African American "servants" from the United States, including enlisted men serving as steward's mates. "They cleaned our quarters, made our beds, set our tables with linens, served left, picked up right, all the while as we sat in order of rank, with the executive officer at the head of the table."[28] Commander Harold Sacks recalls a racial hierarchy affecting wage laborers on the base: the darker the Cuban waiter or maid, the less the pay. "There was a definite pecking order, from dark to light," Sacks recalls, "in terms of earnings, wages, and expectations."[29]

Evidence from the *Coral Reef*, yearbook of the base's William T. Sampson School, confirms this impression of Guantánamo as a sharply stratified place. In 1958, Andrew and Judy Spielman's first full year on the base, student enrollment at William T. Sampson exceeded eleven hundred students for the first time. By the late 1950s the U.S. population as a whole was approximately 89 percent white and 10 percent black, though in the American South, where many military enlistees originated, the proportion of African Americans was closer to 20 percent. The 1958 *Coral Reef* depicts a school population at least 98 percent white. There was not a single African American or "colored" student in the high school. And though there were black and "colored" American, Cuban, and Jamaican workers on the base, there were no racial minorities among the faculty and administrators of the William T. Sampson School. If the base was a microcosm of the United States, as its residents liked to believe, it was a whiter, more homogeneous nation than the place its residents had left behind.[30]

An all-white Guantánamo was not a product of coincidence. Rather, it reflected conscious U.S. Navy policy dating back to the late nineteenth century. Starting around 1890, just as Mahan, Roosevelt, Lodge, and others began to look outward for bases, architects of the "New Navy" resolved to tap the American heartland for recruits. Shipboard technological innovations had reduced the need for experienced sailors to man the fleet, allowing the navy to eschew the worldly, heterogeneous, and recalcitrant seafaring population typically found in America's ports for the supposedly more moral, more disciplined, manlier, and, above all, whiter population of small-town America. World War I mobilization necessitated the enlistment of African American sailors and even the commissioning of a few black naval officers. But after the war, the navy consciously winnowed the number of African Americans in its ranks, and for a decade starting in 1922 it excluded African Americans from naval recruitment entirely. By the early 1940s, African Americans comprised between 2 and 2.5 percent of enlisted men. In 1949 there were few (literally a handful) of African American naval officers, and virtually all African Americans serving in the navy worked as steward's mates.[31] In 1942 the commandant of the U.S. Marine Corps described the enlistment of African Americans in the navy as "absolutely tragic." What, he wondered, could explain Negroes' determination "to break into a club that doesn't want them?"[32]

Yet, the idea of a New Navy comprised entirely of stolid small-town Anglo-Saxon stock was under assault from the very beginning. It represented a futile attempt to dodge the social and economic forces that threatened inherited Anglo-American assumptions about citizenship, civic identity, and racial and gender roles. By the 1950s the pace of this assault quickened, creating widespread anxiety, spawning political and cultural reaction, and inducing many citizens to run for cover. The U.S. Navy was not immune to these developments, and by the 1950s and early 1960s, African Americans began to infiltrate first the enlisted ranks and then, still more slowly, the officer corps. By the 1970s the navy began to refit its ships to accommodate a small but growing number of women.

As depicted in the *Coral Reef* of 1958, the base at Guantánamo Bay might well be considered the last vestige of the New Navy. There is almost nothing in the yearbook to distinguish the base from the small-town, lily-white community about which the New Navy architects had dreamed. The crown-wearing king and queen of "the Stardust Ball"; the queen and her attendants at the boys' Basketball Crowning; the school sports teams; the Student Council; the National Honor Society; the faculty; the "senior story"; the "when I grow ups"; the "last will and testament"; the first names: Don, Pam, Carol, Diana, Fred, Nancy, Judy, Beverly; the last names: Holloway, Newton, Delfo, Lyman, Williams, Stewart, Hoover, Ilgenfritz—everything about the yearbook suggests a place untouched by the social and cultural upheaval beginning to break over the United States. Only the School Board, consisting of nine officers and a few civilians, gives the game away, revealing that this is not small-town America at all but a mighty American naval base. "We've crossed the river," reads the class epigram; "the ocean lies beyond." That, and a cultural and social sea change for the graduates of the William T. Sampson School, who seem, somehow, inadequately prepared for the complexity of life back in the States. The journalist Tom Miller observed a few decades later in *Esquire*, "It is all very strange for someone approaching fifteen or sixteen to have spent most of her or his life within a forty-five-square-mile compound of leisure. Many remain on the base after high-school graduation as long as their parents remain. It is comparable to some prisoners who are afraid to reenter society after a few years in the pen. They hang out near the jail as a secure and familiar reference point."[33]

In March 1961, *National Geographic* magazine published its second major feature article on the U.S. naval base, the first since the coming of Castro. Journalists clearly welcomed the tension that the Cuban Revolution introduced to the base. They finally had something to write about.[34] *National Geographic* staff writer Jules Billard told the story as a straightforward morality play. The Cuban Revolution not only jeopardized century-long rosy relations at the base, but it also imperiled the American Dream. But neither the base nor the American Dream would yield easily, Billard insists. They would be defended by the base's intrepid soldiers and their unflappable women.

By 1961 the myth of the U.S. naval base as a bastion of American virtue committed to securing both U.S. and Cuban interests was well advanced. The historical revisionism began at the beginning, ignoring the history of U.S. imperialism and the century-long debate in the United States about annexing Cuba. After Fidel Castro's ascendancy, as the base's importance as a symbol of American democracy in a Communist country increased, journalistic accounts juxtaposed the hostility emanating from Communist Cuba to the initial years of the base when it was "hired from a friendly Cuba."[35] The myth continues with the Teller Amendment's disclaimer of U.S. ambition to dominate the newly independent Cuban republic, which works only by ignoring yet another debate, this time over the Platt Amendment. In place of Root's and Wood's open coercion of the Cuban Constitutional Convention, readers learn from Billard that in the immediate aftermath of the Spanish-American War, "the U.S. went whole-heartedly about living up to its high promise and began putting Cuba on its feet as an independent nation." With "Uncle Sam" keeping "a protective arm around his island neighbor," a Cuban republic was born. There followed "a 1903 treaty between the two nations" that conceded not only the right of the United States to occupy Guantánamo Bay, but also the right "to send its troops back whenever needed to smooth out Cuban affairs." The rest, as the saying goes, is history. "For nearly 60 years the base placidly went about its business under the Caribbean sun. Now an unfriendly regime in Cuba wants the U.S. to move out."[36]

The myth is accompanied by carefully selected illustrations. The piece opens with two photographs of U.S. military surveillance of Cuba, one from an aircraft, one from a marine observation post. These are followed a few pages later by a photo of a U.S. helicopter patrolling the base's perimeter. The situation is serious, readers are told, but the Americans have things readily in hand. It is safe to read on.

As in Corey's *National Geographic* piece from 1921, and in other journalistic accounts of the base, the most salient contrast remains that of color. In 1961 dark Cubans continued to work for white Americans. But Castro's rise introduced an air of suspicion into what was once an ideal colonial relationship. ("U.S. citizens should not engage in arguments with Cuban nationals concerning Cuban political affairs," advises a pamphlet prepared for prospective schoolteachers at Guantánamo Bay in 1968, though "the advantages of Democracy as opposed to Communism can be explained"[37]). A photo of Cubans hard at work on the base is juxtaposed with Cuban commuters being frisked by U.S. Marines as they head home, a safeguard that, readers learn, was designed to "discourage pilfering and cigarette smuggling." On the whole, noted H. P. McNeal, the industrial relations officer at the base, "we think the Cubans are loyal employees," though Billard learned that "one union leader has been fired for anti-U.S. statements" and there had been "disciplinary measures taken against other workers."[38] After Castro's arrival, apparently, workers could no longer be trusted.

The dark, virtually all-male Cuban labor force depicted in these pages contrasts markedly to images of white domesticity. In one tableau, entitled "Guantánamo kiddies cherish their own Captain Kangaroo," eight children (all but one towheads) surround Marine Corporal Walter Garwood, host of an entertainment show on the base television. Garwood, aka Cousin Whigby, is dressed for the prairie, in a straw hat, plaid shirt, and dungarees held up by suspenders. The following page offers a lesson in free enterprise and American culture. In one photo, a navy wife, dressed in a white sundress and sandals, purchases vegetables from a darkly clad Cuban farmer. In another, an all-white audience takes in the movie *Bells Are Ringing* on the terrace at the officers' club. Finally, in a third photo, a naval officer unwinds with a Cuban newspaper bearing a picture of Fidel Castro and the headline "Are You with Us or Against Us!" (CON LA PATRIA O CONTRA LA PATRIA!) emblazoned on its front. The disorder gripping Cuba is juxtaposed with the calm of a well-ordered American living room on the U.S. base. Across the room from Dad, in a small inflatable swimming pool, sits a child closely supervised by his mother. Dad is unperturbed, the roles clear.[39]

In 1921, Corey was gently reprimanded by the base commander for mistaking the navy for its ships rather than its men. One way of reading Billard's piece, some forty years later, is that the navy is not just its men but also its women. They remind us what we're fighting for. A year after Billard's trip to Guantánamo Bay, another journalist asked the Defense Department why in the world "Navy wives and children remain in such a political hot spot as Guantánamo Bay." Government policy, came the reply; the military "encourages dependents to accompany servicemen to foreign posts," so long as their presence is consistent with "combat readiness." (In 1962, over half a million servicemen's and civilian employees' dependents resided abroad.[40]) In short, the military expected wives to stand by their men. At Guantánamo, Billard suggests, this is exactly what wives do. In yet another photo, taken alongside a monument at McCalla Hill (where the U.S. Marines first came ashore in June 1898), an officer, clad in dress whites, tosses his child playfully into the air while his wife, no less primly dressed, stands statuesque, one arm resting on a ship's cannon, confidently guarding the scene.[41]

In 1961, no less than in 1930, not everyone found the bay completely to their liking. "For some," Billard observes, "living within the confines of the seven-foot-high chain link fence is like being in an idyllic prison camp—a sort of 'comfortable claustrophobia,' as one seaman's wife described it." With only two stores to choose from, it was "the same old thing day after day." With real work to do, navy officers seemed to find the base less constricting than their wives. One pilot compared the base to an island paradise—"Hawaii with Cubans."[42]

Other articles repeat this tableau with other accents. A year after the National Geographic piece, Parade published a feature on Nell Schwarzenbach, a typical navy wife coming to terms with tense U.S.-Cuban relations at the base.[43] "Mrs. Jeanelle Schwarzenbach, 23, a quiet, attractive mother of four, wakes up every morning threatened by the guns of a hostile, U.S.-hating Cuba," journalist Ed Kiester wrote less than one year after the Bay of Pigs.[44] "Her husband, Lt. (j.g.) Hart "Irish" Schwarzenbach, 25, is a Navy jet flier guarding our isolated naval base here against Fidel Castro's possible aggression." Thus the image of the U.S. naval base as an innocent and embattled enclave in Cuba is updated. "Only two miles from Nell Schwarzenbach's kitchen, we watched sullen Cuban militiamen itchily finger their Red-supplied rifles as they patrolled the barbed-wire-topped fence dividing the base from Cuba proper."

Despite the mounting incidents of U.S.-Cuban hostility at the fence line, "Navy wives like Nell Schwarzenbach are cool and re-laxed. Life perks along perfectly normally. Only the vaguest trace of uneasiness gives away what many must feel." In fact, rumors of a pending military conflagration at the base are overblown, Schwarzen-bach reports. "The fact is, you could live here for weeks and never give a thought to an attack." What's Schwarzenbach's life like? Well, not so "different from life in a suburb of, say, Akron, Ohio. She lives in a four-bedroom, concrete-block, ordinary-looking ranch house, which sits on a street with five other identical ranches." The Schwarzen-bachs' eldest child attends the local nursery school; their younger chil-dren "play in a backyard that might be anywhere."

Though "Navy old-timers" refuse to see Castro's rise as a threat to Guantánamo's "soft living," Kiester's article attests, the backdrop of U.S.-Cuban political tension is palpable. What accounts for it? No U.S. action, to be sure—not the Bay of Pigs invasion, not ongoing CIA efforts to destabilize the current political regime and even assassinate Castro, not long-standing Cuban grievances over what remains America's enduring imperial presence on the island. No. Simply Castro's unaccountable, utterly capricious "threat to reclaim the area" for Cuba.[45]

Like other navy wives featured in journalistic accounts of Guan-tánamo reaching back decades, Nell Schwarzenbach confesses to feeling a bit confined on the naval base. It can seem like a "sunny prison." At Guantánamo, wives "feel cut off from the rest of the world. We get Sunday newspapers from the States and we read the base newspaper. . . . But somehow we feel out of touch with what's go-ing on back home, back there on the 'big green island.'" A few of

Schwarzenbach's peers are more "bitter." If Castro is "such a great liberator," one wonders, "why doesn't he liberate us?" But heck, these are just the offhand remarks of a few wives, and they can readily be ignored.[46]

The tension between the United States and Cuba is manifest not in the persons of the unflappable wives but in their Cuban maids, Kiester suggests. The rise of Castro inconveniences the maids, who are now subjected to harassment and searches as they move to and from their families in Cuba. The maltreatment of them also discomfits Nell Schwarzenbach. She and her husband sorely want to intervene, but "can do nothing to help. If we gave our maid food or extra money for her family, she would only lose it at the gate. All we can do is sympathize." Maids bear the burden of U.S.-Cuban hostility in yet another way. During and just after the Bay of Pigs invasion, Castro unaccountably closed off access to the base.

In Billard's account, there's lots of talk about Castro invading the base. Nell Schwarzenbach has her doubts. "If he should attack, the U.S. would immediately strike back," she says. "I don't think Castro would want to give us that opportunity." Schwarzenbach is more right than she knows. At the time this piece came out, while Castro was doing his best to stay away from Guantánamo, Kennedy administration officials were contemplating the first of several staged attacks on the base, which might serve as an excuse to invade Cuba. Withal, Nell Schwarzenbach maintains her equilibrium. Underlying the tension and her friends' worried letters is a more fundamental fact: "Whether we're here or not, and whether we're in danger, or uncomfortable, or tense, or whatever, isn't really the important thing. Castro will still be here, and that's what they ought to be worrying about. Communism in our backyard—that's the real menace."[47]

On February 2, 1964, the U.S. Coast Guard seized four Cuban fishing vessels, manned by thirty-eight crew members, which had strayed into U.S. territorial waters while trolling off the Florida Keys. The vessels, loaded with radio equipment, appear to have been ordered into U.S. waters by Cuban authorities as a deliberate provocation. The United States was only too happy to take the bait. After returning seven teenagers among the crew to Cuba, Florida officials detained the rest in Monroe County jail. In this, the age of rule by frat boys, Castro howled in protest, and the situation quickly escalated. On February 6, in a long-anticipated strike at the naval base, Castro shut off the water line connecting the base to the nearby Yateras River. By early evening the last drops of water trickled through the pipes at the base. At the time, the base held between fourteen and fifteen million gallons in reserve, enough, at the usual rate of consumption, to last approximately seven days. Meanwhile, two water barges headed to Guantánamo from Jamaica, while several water tankers prepared for duty along the eastern seaboard of the United States. Water on the base was instantly rationed. President Johnson announced that there was plenty of water to sustain naval operations at Guantánamo Bay. And he insisted that the United States would never be driven from Guantánamo. Meanwhile Castro, ever the generous defender of the meek and vulnerable, stated that he would permit water to flow for one hour a day to provide for women and children. By this time the Johnson administration had vowed to make the base independent of Cuba, which implied the installation of a desalination plant in the near future.

On February 8 a study group consisting of senior naval officers and representatives of the Joint Chiefs of Staff traveled to Guantánamo to assess the situation, examine the problem of Cuban labor on the base, and confront the challenges involved in making the base independent of Cuba. By February 10, pressure gauges at the naval base indicated that water was flowing to the base from the Yateras River, but naval officials declined to open the valves to accept it. Two days later, on February 12, 270 of the 2,400 or so Cuban commuters employed at the base were fired from their jobs. Naval officials had long had their eye on "security" risks among the Cuban labor force; these, along with a few recalcitrant workers and troublemakers, were the first to go. That same day, the navy announced that it would no longer permit dependents to accompany military personnel on tours to Guantánamo. Through a process of attrition, dependents would be gone within two years. "Suburban Living Is on Its Way Out as Gitmo Gears to Garrison Life," reported the *Navy Times*.[48]

On February 16, amid further dismissals of Cuban workers, the Cuban government accused base officials of stealing water above and beyond the one-hour, 114,000-gallon limit Castro had agreed to furnish for women and children. In fact, the base had not accepted any water since the initial shutoff, and the accusations and counteraccusations triggered a showdown between Castro and the base commander, famous in Guantánamo circles for providing the United States with its first "victory" over Cuban communism.

The base commander at the time of the water fight was a man named John D. Bulkeley, a decorated war veteran admired for evacuating General Douglas MacArthur and his family from Corregidor in March 1942 in the face of the Japanese advance, and promoted to vice admiral by John F. Kennedy. Kennedy himself was behind Bulkeley's assignment to Guantánamo Bay. Guantánamo, everybody in the navy knew, had the reputation of being the place where the navy sent senior officers before putting them on the shelf. Neither the president nor Bulkeley saw his new assignment that way. "That rascal Fidel Castro had been harassing our naval base at Guantánamo in every devious manner that he and his henchmen could think of," Bulkeley later recalled. "So Bobby Kennedy told me [privately] that the president wanted me to go down there and take charge of the base, stand up to Castro, and show 'that bastard with the beard who's boss in this part of the world,' as he put it."[49]

Bulkeley arrived at Guantánamo with all the confidence of a man who could never imagine why Castro could possibly resent an American colony on Cuban soil. "Gitmo is sure as hell not going to be another Pearl Harbor—for Castro . . . or anyone else," Bulkeley told a journalist shortly after his arrival. "Nothing fazes this man," the press reported dutifully. "Castro's going to find out he'll have his hands full—just like the Japs did."[50]

Nineteen sixty-four was an election year, and when news of the water fight broke out in the United States, President Johnson and presidential candidate Barry Goldwater competed to out-bluster each other. "If Castro thinks he can blackmail the Johnson administration out of Guantánamo," Johnson is said to have remarked, "he has totally misread his adversary." The United States must "be firm," Goldwater countered. "Castro's action has made the United States the laughing stock of the world. . . . Our flag has been spat upon and torn to the ground, and as an American I am sick and tired of it." The next day,

Goldwater boasted that he would be happy to lead the U.S. Marines in a charge on the Cuban pumping station, so long as "Castro [himself] promises to be" there.[51] Kennedy had personalized the conflict with Cuba. Johnson, Goldwater, and Bulkeley were only too happy to join the fray, notwithstanding Kennedy's lack of success in undermining the Cuban dictator. As the water fight escalated, one Guantánamo staff member recalled that "all of us around the admiral felt that, if it could be arranged, Bulkeley would like nothing better than to meet Castro in a one-on-one, no-holds-barred barroom brawl—winner take all."[52]

Meanwhile, the U.S. press service clamored for access to the naval base. Initially the Pentagon said no; such meddling was not in the "national interest."[53] Restricted access to press, civilians, and other prying eyes is partly what made the naval base so valuable. But the vacuum of U.S. news out of Guantánamo played right into Castro's hands. Beginning on February 16, U.S. Navy secretary Paul H. Nitze complained that news accounts out of Cuba accusing the base of stealing water were "gaining some currency in the US." Wasn't there something base officials could do to counter Castro's lies? Grant access to the U.S. press corps, came the obvious reply. Within days, more than a dozen reporters descended on the naval base. Bulkeley played the press like a fiddle. On the evening of February 17 he gathered a group of reporters and base officials at the northeast gate, where the water pipe from the Yateras River entered the naval base. There, amid flashing cameras and great fanfare, he excavated a large square of earth down to the Yateras pipeline, removing a thirty-eight-inch section. The U.S. pipeline was dry; accusations that the base was stealing water were a lie. Asked if superiors in Washington had ordered him to cut the pipe, Bulkeley replied no: he had simply informed the Pentagon that he planned to cut it unless otherwise directed; after all, Castro had called him "a liar."[54]

Bulkeley had ensured that the U.S. naval base would now have to provide its own water. Reading press and biographical accounts of the episode, one might conclude that Bulkeley had introduced liberal democracy to Cuba. Clearly the press relished the appearance of the United States coming out on top. "Almost overnight, John Bulkeley's hole in the ground near the main gate has become a sort of Guantánamo liberty bell," Bulkeley's biographer wrote years later (a telling metaphor for a U.S. triumph at this imperialist enclave). Cartoons of a brisk and businesslike Bulkeley cutting off Castro's pipeline (which, in the G-rated version, looks like nothing so much as a bullhorn) accompanied glowing descriptions of the Guantánamo commander finally forcing Castro to "Pipe Down."[55] This was a "tale of triumph," the London *Daily Telegraph* reporter Edwin Tetlow announced. "The U.S. has won a tactical victory in a tussle with Fidel Castro and in a more significant struggle with world communism. Such victories have been scarce enough."[56]

Bulkeley himself appears to have been on quite a high that night. Castro was rumored to be lurking in nearby Cuban hills during the pipe-cutting ceremony, his Colt .45 slung from a holster. Bulkeley favored the .357 Magnum, and it, too, was close at hand. Through much of the night after the pipe cutting, Bulkeley patrolled the base perimeter, "scrambling up one steep hill and down another" clad "in combat gear and carrying a loaded rifle." In this game of cops and robbers, the vice admiral was not going to be caught off guard. "In the darkness, the admiral threaded past mine fields, some real, some dummies, with their triangular red warning signs. His bodyguard, a Tommy gun–toting marine less than half Bulkeley's age, was hard put to keep pace."[57]

The water episode led to a public relations blitz, suggesting that the Johnson administration preferred to fight this cold-war battle with propaganda rather than outright espionage. That same year, Guantánamo officials set out to win the hearts and minds not only of Cubans on the base but also of nationals at other Caribbean ports. The plan was simply to outspend the enemy. For Cubans living and working on the base, there would be sumptuous Christmas dinners, Spanish-language movies, and rehabilitation of Cuban housing. Farther afield, there would be Girl Scout trips from the base to Jamaica, distribution of "materials" to other Caribbean ports, and disaster relief for Haiti following Hurricane Flora. Though the effect of such programs was hard to quantify, Guantánamo officials insisted that "the authorities and peoples of the countries within the GTMO Sector, CARIBSAFRON have been favorably influenced by the Cold War activities carried out by the command. The resources being devoted to Cold War activities are considered to be paying a worthwhile return." These initiatives did not completely take the place of muscle flexing. "There is ample evidence in this area that the readiness and capability of the United States to prevail in limited and general war is well-demonstrated, is credible, and has provided a deterrent to aggression," a report emphasized. With the Fleet Training Group keeping the bay full of warships, the base could be confident that Castro would behave himself. When "parades, static displays, demonstrations, air shows," and threat of war weren't enough, there was always a demonstration of America's material wealth: "The Navy and Marine Corps exchanges, commissary, certain clubs, beaches and other facilities are patronized by indigenous persons along with U.S. citizens," a report observed. "By this means indigenous personnel are afforded an opportunity to see, appreciate, and share in the bounty provided by our system of government."[58]

When Castro cut off the water in February 1964 the United States responded by firing roughly four-fifths of the Cuban commuters (consisting of "Cuban nationals," "Chinese, West Indians, etc") working on the base. Like cutting off the water pipe, cutting off the Cuban labor supply was designed to make the base independent of Cuban labor and thereby free of Cuban government interference. As early as 1961, Castro had forbidden Cubans to seek new jobs on the base, confronting the Americans with a labor deficit as Cubans retired or ceased working, and forcing U.S. officials to appeal to the Jamaican government for labor. In fact, a 1967 Guantánamo labor report suggests that, in releasing the Cuban workers, the Americans shot themselves in the foot. Among other advantages, "the Cuban commuters required practically no logistic support except for on-base transportation" and a few meals. By contrast, a replacement workforce from Jamaica or elsewhere required everything—from room and board to training and transportation. Moreover, the commuting population comprised men and women both. Again, by contrast, the Jamaican labor force consisted of men only. Less cut out for domestic maid service, they were unable to free up "dependent U.S. wives from household chores," thereby disqualifying American women from the base workforce.[59]

The firing of commuters had other unanticipated repercussions. Faced with the termination of their jobs, many commuters declared themselves exiles and appealed to naval officials for permanent residency on the base. This confronted the base with the prospect, unprecedented in U.S. military experience, of inheriting a permanent, aging occupational force that would one day be in need of geriatric care. (Indeed, to this day, there remain aging Cubans on the base whose medical requirements differ markedly from those of the conventional military population.) Curiously, many of this last category were Chinese, unwilling to return to Cuba or Communist China.[60] "Some of them are already old men incapable of work. Ultimately all of them will attain this status, imposing a potential geriatric problem upon the Naval Hospital." As if this weren't enough, the "same trend [of aging Chinese and Cuban residents alike] must be anticipated for requirements for caskets and burial plots in the Base cemetery."[61]

The balance of the 1967 Work Force Study addressed the difficulty caused by trying to replace mostly skilled so-called Cuban nationals, Chinese, and West Indians with mostly unskilled Jamaicans, which turns out to have been the only segment of its population that the Jamaican labor ministry was willing to part with. Many factors contributed to souring the relationship between the Jamaicans and their American hosts, from the fact that the Americans did not hide their preference for the old commuters, to substandard wages, poor housing, and the fact that U.S. officials did not allow families to accompany the Jamaican workers to the base.[62] But a wider chasm divided the Jamaicans from the American community: race. The 1967 report admitted as much. "The majority of the Jamaican workers are emotionally immature," the report suggests, and therefore cannot handle separation from their families. Separation "is a traumatic experience for them because of their fundamental and unsophisticated attitudes towards sex." Jamaican workers "lack a sense of responsibility for planning for the future and think in terms of day-to-day living." Inevitably among such a population there was a "high turn-over rate." No wonder, then, that "most American supervisors on the Base," both military and civilian, treated the Jamaicans in a "deprecatory and demeaning" manner. "The low productivity of the Jamaican, his lack of native industry, his color, his language, his body odor, are all subjects of disparagement and critical comment." As a result, training and assimilating the Jamaicans became extremely difficult, ultimately handicapping the base still more. For their part, the Jamaicans obviously recognized the "contempt" of their American hosts and resented the Americans' name-calling. (*Gooney* was a favorite term of opprobrium.)

Still, to identify a problem was not to fix it. Solutions to this problem remained elusive, thanks to the Jamaicans' innate character and to the peculiar race dynamics of Jamaican society itself. To begin with, "a black Jamaican finds it hard to have a natural, spontaneous relationship with a white person. . . . Taken from Africa as a chattel, then made a normal citizen of a society which sentenced him to remain an outcast, he accepted his inferior position and paid respect to the 'bossman.'" This, in turn, created suspicion, and led to "deceit," "cheating and stealing" among Jamaicans, who possessed "a dual morality." Combine this with Jamaicans' "national inferiority complex," and Guantánamo officials faced a tall order, indeed. The problem lay with Jamaica, where "racial equality exists," but where "it is an equality on the white man's terms, based on the presupposition that the white man has agreed to tolerate the black man, rather than on a belief in the black man's equal rights." U.S. liberty could do a lot, but whether it could rehabilitate the victims of such a society remained an open question.[63]

The change in the character of the Guantánamo labor force brought on by the water fight was palpable in the pamphlets that welcomed Guantánamo wives by the late 1960s. In 1958, Judy Spielman had been greeted by untroubled news of the racial composition of the Guantánamo Basin, along with enthusiastic reports about the ready availability of cheap but reliable maid service. There was an understanding, reports suggested, that only the fairest maids made it onto the U.S. base, living in close proximity to the officers and their families. In the late 1950s, Hal Sacks reports, the American Dream was alive and well. Suppose you wanted to host a private party of, say, ten couples? No problem. You could have the club send over a bar and bartender, along with food, all for around one dollar per guest. Getting cars washed and clothes made was equally convenient in these, the salad days. There may have been labor unrest on the base, never mind political upheaval in Cuba proper, but that didn't register in elite neighborhoods.[64]

What a difference a decade makes. The navy wives who arrived a decade after Judy Spielman received no blithe reassurances of Cuba's—much less the base's—racial composition, by now overrun with Jamaicans. To be sure, there is plenty of talk in their initiation pamphlet about the wholesomeness of small-town life, but gone are the promises of labor-free living. Indeed, the pamphlet's tone is comparatively subdued. "As indicated in this pamphlet," the 1968 edition reads, "Guantánamo Naval Base is comparable to a small city in the U.S. We have practically everything you would normally find in a small city," plus "a few extras, such as the lower cost of living here than stateside."[65] By 1968, prospective wives are greeted by long lists of what to bring, available recreation activities, opportunities for worship, along with a new warning about what not to say to the few remaining Cuban workers. In place of enthusiastic reports about what Cuban maids could do for Americans comes image after image of happy domesticity, along with incantations of the perfect life: "A suburban-like community has been carved out of a patch of scrub, thorn, palms, trumpet vines, and cacti," reads one banner. "Here and there a peanut butter sandwich, 'Gunsmoke,' a hamburger, baseball, and a merry-go-round," reads another. "More than a little Ohio, California, and West Virginia thrive in GTMO," reads a third.[66] If Jamaican labor had spoiled the demographic makeup of the base—so worrying to denizens of Oriente province going back centuries—one wouldn't have known it from that year's pamphlet. The pamphlet includes not a single photograph of any member of the Guantánamo community who is not white. Particularly notable in this edition is a centerfold of towheaded children, shirts off, on a jungle gym, accompanied by the caption "An Endless Summer of Family Activities." On the following page is an introduction to the base school, with yet another caption that reads, "The Battle for Truth." Make no mistake, the pamphlet informs prospective and arriving wives: "Happiness [means] being at home . . . with a purpose."[67]

The navy did all it could to ensure that nothing came between
Guantánamo and the myth of Mayberry. Just weeks before the
Bay of Pigs invasion, the public information officer at the naval
base informed his commander about a series of less-than-flattering
news stories due to be published by a reporter from Women's News
Service named Betty Reef. Based on the first piece out, the officer
concluded that Reef "tends to be selective in her quotes and paints a
slightly misleading picture" of the base. Beside pledging to promote
future journalists' contentment, the officer observed that the incident
"serves to point up the necessity for watchfulness to insure that the
journalist will write the truest picture of the situation at the Naval
Base."[68]

The problem recurred a few years later, in February 1965, when
base officials were discomfited when the Norfolk (Virginia) Ledger
published an article by journalist Elizabeth Chambers, who had
slipped onto the base camouflaged as a member of a singing troupe
from Old Dominion College. Among the titillating items in Chambers's story was a report of the group's contact with "sex starved marines." What in the world is going on down there? U.S. Navy officials
demanded. In reply, Admiral Bulkeley assured navy brass that he had
"personally seen to it that no suggestive or off color material is used by
the entertainers" who visit the base. In this case, Bulkeley doubted
that the entertainment slaked anybody's thirst for anything: "the entertainers used ankle length costumes of the gaslight era," though "they
did alter their costumes to above the ankle length which certainly was
welcome by some of the males in attendance."

More to the point, Bulkeley pledged to ensure that no similar
breaches of press censorship occurred on his watch. "I am now having
the Naval Station, who sponsors such groups, to ascertain well in advance of their arrival that only entertainers are coming and no newsmen are included unless authorized by [naval officials]. I will also see
that they are briefed that their visitation aboard is solely for entertainment and not for other activities."[69]

Controlling access to the base was important for two reasons. First,
in the propaganda war that broke out with Fidel Castro's rise in Cuba,

navy officials wanted to be sure that only the rosiest accounts of American values made their way across the Florida Straits. Second, by the mid-1960s, the naval base had begun to serve as a major transit station for Cuban refugees. In 1965, 72 Cubans crossed the fence onto the naval base. The next year the number of fence crossers nearly doubled. By 1967 it had risen to 515, before nearly doubling again the next year. The refugees created a dilemma for the base. According to the terms of the original treaty, the base and Cuba were obliged to return each other's fugitives. And yet the Cuban fence jumpers represented a huge propaganda victory for the United States, which wasn't about to return them to Castro. And so there was need for secrecy, as U.S. officials feared that violations of the terms of lease might put the base in jeopardy.[70]

Secrecy and lack of journalistic oversight allowed the navy to spin developments at the base to its advantage. It also enabled the navy to keep unfortunate, sometimes illegal, events under wraps. In mid-September 1966, for instance, two Cuban swimmers approached the USS *Willis A. Lee*, anchored in the outer harbor. According to that year's Command History, "at about 0130 the forward deck sentry observed a swimmer in the water some distance from the anchored ship, approaching. Ordered to move back and wait for the ship's boat, the swimmer continued to approach. Several shots were fired near, but not at, the swimmer and he was warned to move back." It turns out that there were not one but two swimmers in the water that night, a pair of brothers hoping to make it to the United States. One of the warning shots "had penetrated the forehead of the second swimmer, killing him instantly."[71] Now, killing hapless Cuban refugees in the water was supposed to be Castro's, not the navy's, stock-in-trade. The same Command History includes a mention of "the killings of numerous swimmers" by Cuban guards that very year. What was the mayor of Mayberry to do? Above all, base officials recognized, the need was "to avoid international repercussions and eliminate propaganda fodder." In the end, the surviving brother and five other swimmers "were secreted aboard the base for almost a week while intelligence personnel endeavored to persuade them not to disclose the circumstances surrounding the tragedy to anybody, including members of their families." What exact methods of enticement were used on the six Cubans, the Command History does not say. The victim "was encased and buried at sunrise in an unmarked grave in the base cemetery," with the commander and a few other officials on hand. In the end, all "agreed to secrecy, and the five were flown to Miami and paroled. All five kept the secret."[72]

Restricting access to journalists did not ensure favorable press. In December 1968 the *Pensacola* (Florida) *News Journal* carried a story by the journalist Tom Tiede about "the dreary life" at Guantánamo Bay. For once dispensing with the ballyhooed navy wife, Tiede focused on the sexual plight of the GIs since the coming of Castro. "Disgruntled GIs call Guantánamo 'celibate harbor,'" Tiede writes. "It hasn't got many women." Indeed, by Tiede's calculation there were roughly "2 women per square mile or one for every 400 males." Fewer than 100 of these were "unattached." This group included "a few Red Cross workers, some nurses at the hospital, a dozen or so dependents." The celibacy on the base made for recalcitrant marines. "Don't say I said this," a marine commander tells Tiede, "but I swear, if I could find some way to start a house of prostitution here, I think I'd do it." The base command did not trust the sailors and marines with the women available on the base. "Movie theaters are scrupulously segregated, and unmarried women are kept aisles away from unmarried men." Base authorities claimed to be aware of the problem, reminding Tiede of the myriad recreational activities available to the men. But the new base commander, James Hildreth, was courageous enough to look the problem squarely in the eye. He "established a liberalized Rest and Relaxation system which encourages the men to fly, whenever possible, to any one of several nearby, lively and girly islands," such as Haiti and Jamaica, both notorious for prostitution.[73]

"If you're going to smoke dope at a Navy base," a chief petty officer told the journalist Tom Miller in 1973, "one of the best places in the world is Guantánamo Bay, Cuba."[74] With Cuba closed off to U.S. liberty parties, marijuana and other drugs became the entertainment of choice, source after source reveals.[75] To my knowledge, Miller's essay, published in *Esquire*, was not banned from the base. But its tone and content call to mind "Guantánamo Blues" and could not have made base officials happy. By 1973 the reign of Fidel Castro was in its fourteenth year, which meant that it was also the fourteenth year of Americans' being denied travel privileges in Cuba. All the recreational facilities in the world (Miller described the U.S. naval base as "a 28,000-acre amusement park") could not make up for the sheer boredom.

Some things hadn't changed. For all the dope, amphetamines, and psychedelics that Miller encountered, booze remained the preferred avenue of escape. Sailors still sought sanctuary from this sanctuary in local Cuban bars, though by this time the only Cuban bars accessible to the base were Charlie's and another "Cuban-operated" bar located in "the Cuban Village" on a remote corner of the base. "Charlie's is a favorite spot for sailors trying to escape the American aura which covers the rest of the base. It has some degree of atmosphere, which is more than anyone claims for other drinking joints on the base. It gets its un-American atmosphere because it is un-American."

Like the base of Sacks's day, Miller's Guantánamo is a two-tiered place, satisfactory, perhaps, for officers and their wives; tedious for enlisted men. "The Guantánamo Good Life," Miller writes, "is a futile, busy attempt to fill up a year with recreational life devoid of human outlets. Masturbation, one hears, runs well ahead of fishing, sailing, horseback riding or football in leisure-time fulfillment." Indeed, "for the enlistees," Miller observes, clearly warming to the task, "Guantánamo is a good place to become an alcoholic. During the last twelve months gin has been the leading seller at the base Mini-Mart, with vodka a close second."[76]

Heavy drinking isn't all fun and games. Nor was the base as immune from the violence and crime afflicting U.S. communities as its defenders insisted. The year before Miller's visit saw the death of an eighteen-year-old civilian employee from an overdose of barbiturates and alcohol, the arrest of fifteen enlisted men for marijuana possession, and the conviction of a Jamaican contract laborer for assault with the attempt to commit rape.[77] That same year, navy officials established alcohol treatment centers at Guantánamo Bay and thirteen other overseas bases.[78]

Miller talks a lot about the segregation that divides Americans, Jamaicans, Cubans, and Filipinos on the base, but he doesn't mention racial segregation within the American ranks, which seems odd, given the events at Guantánamo and elsewhere in the several years before his visit. In 1968 it was hard to ignore the issue of racial segregation—even at the U.S. base.

Among the things Tom Tiede noticed on his visit a few years back was a sign at one of the outdoor movie theaters that read "Jamaicans and Cubans Sit Here."[79] Further investigation yielded many such signs. "There are more than 200 Jamaicans and Cubans at Guantánamo," Tiede observed, "but they are not allowed at any of the US clubs, US restaurants or US bathing beaches." The only places where they were allowed to mingle were at the Navy Exchange and on the sports field. Why the segregation? Tiede asked. Just naval policy dating back "God knows how many years," he was told. The policy continued because the navy found it "prudent." Indeed, Rear Admiral James Hildreth, the base commander, told Tiede, "There's a good reason for the segregation—trouble. We have to separate them in order to avoid trouble. Actually, we separate our married personnel from our unmarried personnel for about the same reason." Race had nothing to do with it. It was simply the fact that the customs of U.S. citizens and Cuban and Jamaican citizens did not "mix well." Jamaicans, especially, loved "to chatter," distracting American audiences. Jamaicans also had a propensity for violence. Besides, Hildreth remarked, apparently drawing on his own experience as well as venerable navy tradition, "I think they want to be by themselves. I think they prefer to be with their own people and so it's better that way."[80]

Tiede discovered base employees to be less than unanimous on that score. One Jamaican worker, though grateful for the opportunity the base provided to make a living, believed that it was not "a good idea to put up a sign which says black man 'Sit Here.' This is a U.S. base," he allowed, and obviously "the U.S. can do as it pleases, but that is a bad way to humiliate people. And I don't like it very much." Cubans shared this sense of resentment. The base occupied Cuban land, after all. Though there were too few African American sailors on the base for Tiede to canvass, one marine captain, a white man, told Tiede, "Why don't they just say: 'Jamaicans and Cubans Sit Downwind.'" Hildreth, on second thought, conceded that it might be time for a change. "That sign at the movie theater may not be really necessary."

On October 13, 1972, a fight erupted between white and black sailors aboard the aircraft carrier USS *Kitty Hawk*, stationed in the Gulf of Tonkin, off North Vietnam, leaving three crew members critically injured.[81] A few days later a second racial conflagration broke out aboard the oiler *Hassayampa* at Subic Bay in the Philippines. Four white sailors were injured, and eleven black sailors were detained at the correctional center at the base.[82] In the more serious episode aboard the *Kitty Hawk*, which involved more than one hundred sailors and forty-six injuries in the end, twenty-five enlisted men—all of them black—were brought before courts-martial.[83]

The incidents themselves and the disproportionate arrest of black sailors sparked an uproar in U.S. military and political circles. The navy's chief operations officer, Admiral Elmo R. Zumwalt, attributed the violence to racial reforms not keeping pace with expectations. In a draft memo, Admiral Zumwalt suggested that naval officers who did not make improved race relations a top priority should consider early retirement. Meanwhile, a panel of black officers protested that "the Navy has permitted the situation to exist where there is an incompatibility between being a member of a minority race and being a member of the Navy." The navy's recruiting slogan "You can be black and Navy, too" rang false. The intervention of NAACP executive secretary Roy Wilkins with navy secretary John Warner brought a temporary delay in the trials of the accused black sailors.[84]

All of which was on the mind of the *Washington Post* columnist Jack Anderson early the next year when he received word of race-based disgruntlement and unequal treatment emanating from Guantánamo Bay. In this case, the initial cause of complaint was the refusal by the navy to allow two black sailors accused of marijuana possession to retain a civilian lawyer. Civilian lawyers were no more welcome at Guantánamo than nosy journalists. When the accused tried to hire William Burleson, based in Washington, D.C., Burleson was denied access to the base. In fact, he managed to come on board after forging an official-sounding letter of invitation. But once at work on the case, he was informed by the navy that his clients had been convicted in a Guantánamo military trial—a premonition of things to come.[85]

Black friends of the accused told Anderson that the men had been "'tricked' into dropping civilian counsel by white Navy officers eager to avoid racial publicity. One black source told us he had been ordered not to talk with us about the case." But there seemed to have been more about the case than simply that. "Unpublished court filings . . . make clear why white officers want it hushed up," Anderson reported. "One paper charges that the daughter of commander Capt. Zeb Alford is herself guilty of the same possession charge." Moreover, other court papers noted that "the son of one of [the] senior officers was apprehended on the same charge as the accused." In that case, Captain Alford did not "enforce the law," but shipped the offending youth off the base. To make matters worse, Alford, having been photographed with his arm around the reigning black beauty queen, was quoted as remarking that he hoped the folks back home in Mississippi did not see him this way.[86]

Besides raising charges that compromising legal documents had been destroyed, court papers in the case, together with interviews of black servicemen, confirmed reports of racial division. When Anderson predicted that "the racial blowup on the aircraft carrier Kitty Hawk may be a mere firecracker compared with the pow[d]er keg now smoldering" at Guantánamo, Captain Alford's successor, Rear Admiral L. B. McCudden, disputed the portent as utter nonsense. Guantánamo had "no racial problem," he told Anderson. McCudden's denial was seconded by a *Post* reader and former neighbor of Alford's, who thought to change the subject. Alford was an upstanding man, the writer insisted; it was busybodies such as Jack Anderson who were the problem.[87]

In fact, there was a racial problem on the base, and like problems everywhere, this one had a history—or, rather, histories. In this case, the water fight of 1964 had changed the racial character of the base's labor force, just as civil rights advances in the United States threatened finally to penetrate navy ranks, making black servicemen more common and, at the same time, less willing to put up with second-class status.

By the time of Tom Miller's visit in 1973, the ratio of men to women at the naval base—though destined to evolve with the arrival the previous year of the first unaccompanied female officer in the base's history, along with its first female enlisted sailor—was still ten to one, "and Navy barracks are not quite the most comfortable place to openly share love with another man."[88] Haiti was the most convenient getaway. "Enlistees have a soft spot in their hearts for Haiti because it is one of the nearby R&R drop-off points, a chance to escape the contradictions of Guantánamo for the less cumbersome ones of Haiti," Miller continues, his story juxtaposed to a photograph of a bikini-clad woman dancing on a pool table at the Chiefs' Club. "Immediately upon landing in Haiti a serviceman gets into a cab and, with no words spoken, is taken to the door of a local whorehouse."[89]

Like many visitors to Guantánamo, where courtesy to guests is a stock-in-trade, Miller was invited to attend a dinner party at the home of Commander Alford. "Guests are beginning to arrive at the home of Margaret and Zeb Alford for a small dinner party," he reports. "Zeb is Captain of the Naval Station, a well-liked, outgoing man. He and Margaret socialize a lot." The Alfords' home is thoughtfully decorated in what Miller calls "modern style." Seashells are the leitmotif. "There is a fascinating ten-shelf display of a thousand shells Margaret has found on Cuban beaches, and a Picasso print rests on the bathroom wall, two feet above the toilet. Most of the evening's guests are young commissioned officers with a clean, liberal, white-collar attitude about things. The Alfords' eldest daughter acts as bartender while the Filipino houseboy Legaspi cooks a thirty-five pound red snapper caught two days previously."

The party starts off in the usual manner with small talk about recreational options on the base. It is interrupted when Alford's wife ("well into her third drink") sweeps away the veil of self-satisfaction. "'You know, you could go to parties for two years here and never hear a thought,'" she says. "Somewhat surprised at first, the others turn to her and agree." Still, several guests note that, if not *thoughts*, exactly, regular life at the base affords the population an occasional *idea*—in the banter of high school students, for instance, in callers to the base radio station, and in good "old-fashioned bigoted babble" down at the BOQ (bachelor officers' quarters). A late arrival finally turns the conversation to sex. The latecomer, a physician, wants to know how you can tell the difference between a sailor and a marine. Answer: it's how they respond to the problem of VD. "'It always happens right after they come back from R&R in Jamaica or Haiti. A Navy man will come in and whisper,' etc., embarrassed, circumspect; a Marine: 'Doc, I'VE GOT CLAP AGAIN.'" Guests dissolve into laughter "and more drinks are poured." Later, Commander Alford, cigar in hand, insists that "'Guantánamo doesn't lack anything any other Caribbean island resort has, except it has a fence around it. When the fence goes down it'll be the best assignment in the military.'"[90]

8

★

THE HAITIAN PROBLEM

Under the best conditions, sailing up the Windward Passage from the Caribbean Sea to the Atlantic Ocean can be difficult. When the wind is in your favor, the current is typically not. The Passage acts as a vortex, sucking water from the ocean into the Caribbean Basin and toward the Gulf of Mexico. At all seasons of the year, the Passage can be rough. It is frequently impassable for all but the largest ships. Still, an efficient, seaworthy vessel can make the journey in one piece, though the Passage almost always leaves a lasting impression.

Ask President Harry Truman. On February 25, 1948, Truman traveled to Guantánamo Bay from the southwestern tip of Haiti aboard the 243-foot presidential yacht *Williamsburg*, on a goodwill tour of the Caribbean Basin. With "groundswells whipped by a moderate gale," the *Williamsburg* "rolled and tossed about making it somewhat uncomfortable for all hands," in the understated words of the ship's log. "Nobody got seasick," the president told the press corps upon arriving at Guantánamo, his fingers crossed behind his back. Asked how he had stood up under the rough passage, the president quipped: "I stood up alright for the simple reason I didn't get up. I stayed in bed. Whenever I felt uneasy I just leaned my head back."[1]

The *St. Joseph*, a forty-foot, unpowered wooden sailboat, was neither seaworthy nor efficient. On August 5, 1977, it departed Port Salut, southwest Haiti, bound for the Bahamas with 101 passengers aboard. Five days later, on the night of August 10, the *St. Joseph* appeared off the mouth of Guantánamo Bay, having failed to clear the Windward Passage. The boat was taking on water, and many of its passengers were sick. Its captain headed for the naval base in the hopes of borrowing tools to patch a leak in the boat's rotting hull. Towed to a wharf on Windward Point, the *St. Joseph* was found to be too crowded to allow for immediate inspection and repair. The Haitians were brought ashore and provided shelter for the night, thus beginning a month-long stay at the naval base.[2]

These were hardly the first Haitian refugees to arrive at Guantánamo Bay. Since the Taíno cacique Hatuey first abandoned Hispaniola for Guantánamo in 1511, emigrants from today's Haiti have regarded southeast Cuba as a land of second chance. At the end of the eighteenth century, French colonists fleeing what would become known as the Haitian Revolution turned up at Guantánamo in droves, establishing a diversified agricultural economy while laying the foundation for Guantánamo City. The Guantánamo Basin continued to serve as an outlet for Haitian immigrants (until Fidel Castro restricted immigration after coming to power in 1959). In the eighteen months preceding *St. Joseph*'s call at Guantánamo Bay, two small boatloads of Haitian refugees had sailed to the U.S. base. The navy seized their boats and quietly returned the refugees to Haiti. Most of the Haitians who ended up at Guantánamo in the late twentieth century did so by accident, swept up in a whirlpool of natural and political currents that cut short their dreams of escape.

Haitians weren't the only refugees who arrived at the base in the second half of the twentieth century. After the Cuban Revolution, thousands of disgruntled Cubans also made their way to Guantánamo Bay. Beginning with a mere handful in 1960, their number rose from more than five hundred in 1967 to more than a thousand the following year. In a single episode in 1969, eighty-one Cubans shot their way past Cuban guards ringing the base perimeter, leaving sixty-nine compañeros behind. In the 1970s the flow of Cubans to the base diminished considerably before spiking again in 1980 and in the early 1990s. In contrast to the Haitians, most of whom were returned to Haiti, the vast majority of the Cubans who made it to the naval base ended up in the United States.[3]

At the time the *St. Joseph* departed Port Salut in the summer of 1977, U.S. policy toward Haitian refugees was fast evolving. After the dictator François Duvalier rose to power in Haiti in 1957, some forty-five hundred mostly wealthy Haitians fled to the United States. A second wave of thirty-five thousand Haitian professionals followed in the next decade. Hailing from the middle and upper tiers of Haitian society, these immigrants attracted little attention from U.S. officials. Settling largely in the Northeast, many in New York City, they quickly established themselves on a solid legal and economic basis.

In the late 1960s and '70s, a third group of migrants began to flee Duvalier-era Haiti. Poorer and less well connected than their predecessors, this group arrived in small boats off the Florida coast, unsettling local government officials and prompting the U.S. Immigration and Naturalization Service (INS) to warn of a potential flood of migrants from across the Caribbean Basin and Latin America. Thomas Jefferson's nightmare of over a century and a half earlier appeared in danger of becoming a reality.[4]

As evidence of trouble to come, the INS pointed to the roughly two thousand Haitians who applied for political asylum in the four years preceding *St. Joseph*'s visit to Guantánamo Bay. A mere 10 percent of those requests were granted, leaving eighteen hundred Haitians facing deportation hearings, their cases mired in immigration court. Meanwhile, thousands more Haitians continued to arrive in Florida. To forestall the flood and unclog the courts, the U.S. government launched a program to deport Haitian boaters on an expedited basis, denying them due process while summarily declaring them economic rather than political refugees, hence ineligible for political asylum. Which is more or less where things stood when the *St. Joseph* pulled into Guantánamo Bay.

Upon awakening at the naval base the morning after their arrival, the *St. Joseph*'s passengers discovered that the navy had seized their vessel and made arrangements to return them to Haiti. An examination of their boat "indicated that it would require about five working days to slow the leaks at a cost of about $650.00," the base commander reported, and "about 8 full working weeks to make the boat sea worthy at a cost of about $7200.00." Even then, much of the *St. Joseph*'s hull "was dry rotted and the feasibility of repair was doubtful." From the navy's perspective, the sooner the base was rid of the Haitians the better. They had "only become our responsibility because they landed on our property," a U.S. Defense Department official told journalists. "We hardly want to keep them there. We want them to go back where they came from."[5]

But the *St. Joseph*'s crew did not want to return to Haiti. When a bus pulled up to take them to the airfield, the refugees refused to climb aboard. Many had left home without proper documentation, they explained; they feared reprisals from the Haitian government. Reassurances on the part of naval officials that the Haitian government was preparing only the warmest welcome did nothing to persuade the refugees. They asked for their boat back and to be allowed to continue on their way. The navy refused, and when "all efforts, short of force," failed to get the Haitians aboard the buses, the navy arranged for the group to spend a second night.

The next day the *St. Joseph*'s crew awoke not to buses but to Haitian and U.S. government officials flown in from Port-au-Prince. Weber Guerrier, Haiti's director of immigration, and Andrew McKeon, vice consul at the U.S. embassy, personally greeted the migrants and urged them to return home. The officials were "successful in allaying the fears of the group as to possible retributions," the base commander observed, yet still the Haitians refused to depart for Haiti. As Guerrier and McKeon flew back to Port-au-Prince empty-handed, still "higher naval authorities" and U.S. State Department officials descended on the naval base. Over the next several weeks, American officials interviewed the Haitians to establish the validity of their asylum claims. In the end, four out of *St. Joseph*'s 101 passengers were granted political asylum. The rest were returned to Haiti.

Looking back on the Haitians' visit, the navy viewed the outcome with satisfaction. Though accustomed to dealing with scores of Cuban refugees at a time, the Haitians had tested base officials' "foresight, patience, and courtesy," according to the chief of naval operations. Still, the base had passed with flying colors. All praise for "the officers and men, Navy and Marine Corps, whose leadership and initiative were instrumental in resolving a potentially volatile situation."[6]

What could the Haitians expect upon returning home? A hint of what awaited the returnees was potentially discernible in the person of Weber Guerrier, the director of Haitian immigration, who, along with Andrew McKeon, had been so successful, in the words of the base commander, in easing the group's suspicions. The Haitians knew better. Retribution was Guerrier's middle name. Before assuming his current office, Guerrier had been commander of Fort Dimanche, the most notorious of Duvalier-era Haiti's prisons, "a place of execution" and "unrivaled cruelty," where individuals unlucky enough to end up were seldom heard from again.[7] A wolf in sheep's clothing, Guerrier was the point man of a Haitian security system that regarded asylum seekers as enemies of the state. In his new post, Guerrier enjoyed unimpeded access to new victims for the Haitian security system held in foreign detention centers such as Guantánamo Bay.[8]

In retrospect, navy and State Department personnel appear to have been credulous in accepting at face value Haitian officials' promises to treat the emigrants humanely. Surely, Guerrier and company did protest too much. Why would Haitian officials make such promises unless they were warranted? From the moment the *St. Joseph* arrived at the naval base, there was something grudging about the Americans' treatment of the Haitian refugees. If the United States granted the Haitians asylum, one State Department official remarked, it would "open a Pandora's box of attempted entries by refugees" into the United States. "They know the score," another observed, referring to the refugees; though a few might face punishment if returned to Haiti, "the great majority of considerations for leaving Haiti were economic." *The Washington Post* conceded that the United States was disinclined to admit the Haitians no matter what their motivation. To "have granted them political asylum could have strained relations with Haiti," the *Post* noted; "to have let them stay for economic reasons could have encouraged other Haitians to try the same thing."[9] Moreover, the Haitians were exacting a heavy toll on the naval base. "It is not clear how long the Navy will be able to continue providing for the 101," the *Post* reported. "Guantánamo is an isolated outpost, dependent for supplies on frequent Air Force planes and supply ships." The base faced "short-

ages of most goods," and yet "the laws of the seas demand that the
Navy feed, clothe, house, and provide medical care for the Haitians."
If reporters were skeptical about how 101 Haitians could discomfit a
naval facility capable of absorbing up to 1,000 Cuban fence jumpers
per year, they didn't say. And so a base that had stood up to Fidel Castro and the Russians became suddenly, disconcertingly, vulnerable in
the face of one hundred destitute refugees.[10]

The plight of St. Joseph's crew upon returning to Haiti from Guantánamo Bay would have been forgotten but for a lawsuit filed on behalf of five thousand Haitians denied political asylum in Florida in
the late 1970s. The lawsuit, Haitian Refugee Center v. Civiletti (1980),
accused the U.S. government of discriminating against Haitian asylum seekers on the basis of national origin, conduct outlawed by the
Immigration and Nationality Act of 1965.[11] In defending itself, the
government pointed to evidence about happy political conditions in
Haiti based partly on interviews of thirty out of the ninety-seven St.
Joseph passengers denied asylum at Guantánamo Bay. Besides extending the saga of the St. Joseph's crew, Civiletti illuminates U.S. government policy toward Haitian refugees, ultimately foreshadowing two
episodes from the 1990s when more than fifty thousand Haitian boaters (along with thirty-five thousand Cubans) were detained at Guantánamo Bay before being forcibly sent home.

Notably, it was during the crush of Haitian migrants that prompted
Civiletti that the U.S. government first considered exploiting Guantánamo's exceptional legal status—not Cuba and not the United States—
to deny Haitian asylum seekers the constitutional right to counsel, a
characteristic of both the 1990s migrant operations and the post-
9/11 prison camp. There are other parallels between U.S. government
conduct described in Civiletti and more recent developments at Guantánamo: the setting aside of established international protocols that
did not jibe with U.S. interests, the deliberate distorting of political
conditions abroad to promote U.S. government policy, the hyping of
the threat detainees in U.S. custody allegedly posed to the United
States, and, finally, the use of intimidation to compel outcomes desired by U.S. officials. In short, Civiletti reads like a primer for the
policies and behavior that has recently made Guantánamo notorious.

Haitian Refugee Center v. Civiletti originated in the INS response to the so-called Haitian Problem, when those thousands of Haitian boaters appeared off the Florida coast seeking political asylum. The rising volume of Haitian applicants coincided with pending changes to asylum procedures, which brought immigration hearings to a standstill. By June 1978 the number of unprocessed asylum claims exceeded six thousand, prompting INS officials to launch what became known as "the Haitian Program."[12]

Based on the conviction that the surest way to stanch the flood of refugees was to make their lives in the United States as miserable as possible, the Haitian Program authorized the immediate detention of refugees upon arrival in the United States. It terminated an existing policy that allowed detainees to apply for temporary work permits. And it introduced a set of administrative procedures designed to expedite the refugees' deportation. As if to comply with international and domestic laws that prohibited deporting refugees who might face political persecution upon returning home, the Haitian Program declared the Haitians *economic* refugees.

In the end, the Southern District Court of Florida found for the Haitians in *Civiletti*, confirming the charges of discrimination on the basis of national origin, and violations of due process.[13] District Court judge James Lawrence King was unsparing in his criticism of virtually every element of the Haitian Program. Whereas detaining the Haitians and forbidding them to seek temporary work was simply cruel, their expedited exportation was positively "callous." "Expulsion might well dissuade future migrants from leaving Haiti," Judge King conceded, "but it would do so by exposing Haitians to the persecution and death they feared."[14] Moreover, the Haitian Program described the refugees "as fitting into a broad class susceptible to uniform treatment," thereby violating the individual right to due process. There was nothing wrong with taking into account conditions in the country of origin with respect to *individual* asylum claims, King pointed out, but such conditions cannot serve as the basis for devising processing *procedures*. "The essence of procedural due process is that everyone re-

ceive the same fair hearing," the judge remarked, "regardless of the
merits of their individual claim. Economic refugees do not have fewer
procedural rights than political refugees, just as a criminal defendant's
procedural rights are not altered by his guilt or innocence."[15]

Judge King dismissed the government's claim that the Haitians
posed a threat to the local Florida community as "nothing short of
fantastic." The Haitians posed no considerable threat, nor did the local Miami community perceive one. "How can a group of poor, black
immigrants threaten a community?" King wanted to know. "What for
that matter, is a 'social threat,' if not the words of someone trying to
protect his own views of how society should exist? On such views the
Haitian program was founded."[16]

However shameful, the government's behavior in the case unsettled King less than what appeared to be its underlying motivation, for
more was involved here than discrimination alone. Racism itself was
the core of the issue, Judge King concluded, and the court simply
could not "close its eyes." The plaintiffs were "part of the first substantial flight of black refugees from a repressive political regime to this
country," Judge King remarked. "All of the plaintiffs are black. In contrast, for example, only a relatively small percent of the Cuban refugees who have fled to this country are black." Except in extraordinary
circumstances, "all of the Cubans who sought political asylum in individual hearings were granted asylum routinely." And yet "none of the
over 4,000 Haitians processed during the INS 'program' at issue in this
lawsuit were granted asylum. No greater disparity can be imagined."[17]

Judge King could not contain his astonishment at the government's
behavior. "Irony after irony plagues this case," he remarked. The Haitians embarked for the United States expecting to "reach a land of
freedom." They were met by "an Immigration Service which sought to
send them back to Haiti without any hearing, and a systematic program designed to deport them irrespective of the merits of their asylum claims." They had been "assured by good people in this country
that Miami was not Haiti, that they did not have to fear persecution
by the United States." And yet "their claims were denied without
any meaningful consideration." U.S. Haitian policy was "shocking
and brutal," Judge King wrote, "populated by the ghosts of individual
Haitians—including those who have been returned from the United

States—who have been beaten, tortured and left to die in Haitian prisons." It had to stop.[18]

King's ruling in *Civiletti* reflects a record of fact finding undertaken by the court about political conditions in Haiti. The conditions described in court documents transcend Duvalier-era rule itself (which came to an end in February 1986), and help explain why tens of thousands of Haitians ended up at the Guantánamo naval base in the early 1990s.[19]

In order to justify its characterization of the Haitian asylum seekers as economic refugees, the U.S. government had to demonstrate that Haiti was politically safe. If discrimination on the grounds of national origin was illegal according to U.S. law, forced repatriation of refugees to a country unable to guarantee their life and liberty violated both U.S. law and Article 33 of the United Nations Protocol Relating to the Status of Refugees (to which the United States became a signatory in 1968). To prove both the economic motive of the refugees and the existence of safe political conditions in Haiti, the defendants introduced a State Department study depicting glowing treatment by Haitian government officials of eighty-six recently returned asylum seekers, including thirty members of the *St. Joseph*'s crew. Too good to be true and conceptually flawed, the State Department report prompted the District Court to undertake an investigation of its own.[20]

Though not unprecedented, such fact finding in a case such as this is unusual. In general, federal judges wade cautiously into questions of foreign policy. "Immigration and naturalization matters implicate the conduct of foreign relations," Judge King conceded, thus they "pose the subtle risk that a decision on such questions might intrude on the political domain of the President and Congress." The court could not, for example, review an immigration case disputing discrimination specifically authorized by Congress. But it could indeed ensure that U.S. government agencies upheld congressional statutes and international protocols. Which is precisely what was at issue in *Civiletti*, and why Judge King concluded that the court could not weigh questions of discrimination and safe return without engaging in some research of its own. Conditions in Haiti, the Court discovered, were "stark, brutal, and bloody."[21]

To bend the will of a nation to the ambition of a single individual (or family) requires an immense security apparatus. It also often entails an impoverished and disenfranchised populace, a venal and obsequious elite, and an outside enabler. All three elements were present in midcentury Haiti as it emerged from twenty years of U.S. occupation (1915–1934) followed by twenty more years of indebtedness to and domination by outside economic interests, principally in the United States. When, in 1957, Haitian Army officials seized upon the slight and studious figure of Dr. François Duvalier to lend its rule legitimacy, it elevated a man infinitely more cunning than they, one able to channel widespread racial resentment against Haiti's light-skinned political, economic, and military elite into a populist crusade centered on himself. Recognizing its impending demise, Haiti's business community threw itself at Duvalier's feet.

The U.S. government facilitated Duvalier's rise to power. The simultaneous demise of Fulgencio Batista in Cuba stoked U.S. fears of Communist penetration along America's southern frontier. Duvalier shrewdly manipulated U.S. State Department officials, portraying himself as the defender of Western liberalism, all the while launching one of history's most authoritarian states. The U.S. government happily went along. The nation's "over-riding objective," a State Department official remarked, was "to deny Haiti to the communists." The secondary objective was to protect "private citizens and property interests in Haiti."[22] These goals were complementary. "To some extent," a CIA report later observed, "the incredibly low standard of living and the backwardness of the Haitian masses work against communist exploitation in that most Haitians are so completely downtrodden as to be politically inert."[23]

If combating communism was its principal aim in Haiti, the United States backed the right man. Nobody and nothing would be spared in the battle against communism, including liberalism itself. "Communist activities are declared to be crimes against the security of the state," Duvalier announced. "Any profession of Communist faith, verbal or written, public or private, any propagation of Communist or anarchist doctrines through lectures, speeches, conversations, readings, public or private meetings, by way of pamphlets, posters, newspapers, books, and pictures; any oral or written correspondence with local or foreign associations, or with persons dedicated to the diffusion of Communist or anarchic ideas; and furthermore, the act of receiving, collecting, or giving funds directly or indirectly destined for the propagation of said ideas"—all was strictly forbidden. Perpetrators of such crimes would be sentenced to death, their property "confiscated and sold for the benefit of the state."[24]

Besides recognizing the need for an outside sponsor, Duvalier understood that having turned to him to legitimate *its* rule, the army could not serve as his primary base of support. So he created an army of his own, the Volunteers for National Security (in French VSN for short), or Tonton Macoutes, named after the diabolical folk figure "Uncle Knapsack," who carted off naughty children on Christmas Day.[25] The Tonton Macoutes answered directly to Duvalier. Through the Macoutes, Duvalier's influence pervaded every element of Haitian society, from business to labor, from press to pulpit, from field to factory, from neighborhoods to schools, until finally infiltrating even the army itself.[26]

In denying political asylum to *Civiletti*'s petitioners, the U.S. government drew on a narrow interpretation of what constituted political resistance in Haiti based on the State Department report. According to the State Department, only intellectuals and political opposition leaders qualified as dissidents and hence potential victims of Duvalier oppression, a distinction that restricted asylum claims to a narrow class indeed. The court rejected the State Department classification. "The uncontroverted evidence at trial," Judge King observed, "demonstrates that the 'political opposition' is quite broadly defined" in Haiti. The State Department team failed "to consider the possibility that the claim of asylum itself may cause one to be classified among the political opposition."

Certainly, not every Haitian returnee endured such abuse. Still, the evidence revealed "a pattern one step removed from that." Asylum seekers were sure to be greeted with suspicion and regarded as opponents of the state. In Haiti this meant they faced a "substantial danger. Many will go to prison. . . . In prison, many will be beaten, perhaps even tortured, and some will die as a result." Meanwhile, others would live on in continuous fear "of a midnight visit from the Macoutes."[27]

Judge King conceded that individual accusations of abuse could be interpreted as isolated disputes between one Haitian citizen and the local prefect. This was "precisely the conclusion reached" by INS officials, who classified many such claims as "clearly lacking in substance." This made the court's fact finding indispensable. Based on its own evidence, the court concluded that "the Haitians in this class deserved something more than they received from the INS." Their so-called *economic* "claims were more political" than recognized; the government's "uniform rejection of their claims" betrayed "a profound ignorance, if not an intentional disregard, of the conditions in Haiti." The court's examination of political conditions in Haiti demonstrated that "some Haitians will be subjected to the brutal treatment and bloody prisons of Francois Duvalier upon their deportation. Until INS can definitely state which Haitians will be so treated and which will not, the brutality and bloodletting is its responsibility."[28]

During the events described in *Civiletti*, the U.S. government first broached the idea of exploiting Guantánamo Bay's ambiguous political and legal status to deny constitutional protections to individuals detained at the naval base. On August 20, 1978, the deputy commissioner of the INS, Mario T. Noto, sent a memo to his boss, Leonel J. Castillo, outlining a potential solution to the Haitian Problem. In the memo, Noto proposed detaining Haitians intercepted at sea at Guantánamo Bay rather than bringing them to Miami. At Guantánamo Bay, formally sovereign territory of Cuba, Haitians would have few if any constitutional protections and no access to lawyers, which INS officials had come to see "as part of the problem."[29]

In this instance, the U.S. government opted for the simpler recourse of summary asylum hearings followed by expedited deportation. But it learned the lesson of the Southern District Court's intervention. In the future, U.S. officials would take no chances, moving the detainment and processing of Haitian and Cuban refugees and enemy combatants offshore to Guantánamo, where they would remain beyond the purview of the American public and the reach of U.S. law. Or so, at least, they hoped.

As *Haitian Refugee Center v. Civiletti* unfolded in district court, two simultaneous migrant exoduses were under way in the waters south of Florida. One, the Mariel Boatlift, entailed some 125,000 Cubans embarking for Miami by boat from the port of Mariel, just west of Havana. The other remains largely unknown and unnamed: an exodus of tens of thousands of Haitians from diverse port towns and cities, most of them, too, hoping to make it to the Florida coast. The fate of the two groups could not have been more different. On the whole, the Cubans were welcomed to the United States, exiles from a Communist regime and sworn enemy of the United States; the Haitians were picked up at sea and returned to Haiti to face the autocratic tyranny of America's friend and the fierce foe of communism Jean-Claude Duvalier, François Duvalier's successor.

The Mariel Boatlift was a onetime deal. Conceived by Fidel Castro in 1980 to relieve a social and economic crisis, it was over in six months, halted by mutual agreement of Presidents Castro and Carter. By contrast, the Haitian exodus was spontaneous and open-ended. With political and economic conditions in Haiti in bad shape and unlikely to change, there was no anticipating an end to the exodus. Assuming office in January 1981, the Reagan administration felt compelled to act. The Haitian boaters jeopardized the nation's "welfare and safety," the president announced that autumn. To protect the nation, Reagan authorized the U.S. Coast Guard to halt, search, seize, and destroy any Haitian vessel suspected to be transporting refugees to the United States. Formally, the Alien Migrant Interdiction Operation (AMIO) acceded to the UN Protocol Relating to the Status of Refugees, which prohibited the return of refugees to a land in which they might be subjected to political or cultural persecution. According to the presidential order, passengers of seized vessels were to be transferred to U.S. Coast Guard ships and interviewed by INS officials to determine whether they had a "well-founded fear" of persecution if returned to Haiti. Those found to have such fear would be "screened in" to the United States, i.e., brought to Miami to file claims for political asylum. Those found to have no such fear would be delivered home. From the perspective of those who wanted to relieve the logjam of Haitian asylum seekers in Florida immigration courts, AMIO was a smashing success. In its first decade, twenty-eight of the approximately twenty-three thousand Haitians picked up by the U.S. Coast Guard made it to the United States. Of these, only eight were granted political asylum.[30]

Just as they had during the previous decade, U.S. officials succeeded in keeping the number of Haitian asylum seekers in the 1980s so low by once again distorting political conditions in Haiti. INS interviews aboard the Coast Guard cutters were public, compromising, and cursory. Having issued detailed guidelines intended to safeguard the refugees, the INS ignored those guidelines virtually to the letter.[31] Moreover, a remarkable presumption underlay AMIO: namely, that the United States had the right to sweep international waters between Haiti and the United States for Haitian migrants no matter where they might be headed. Formally, Reagan's order of autumn 1981 authorized the apprehension of only those Haitians bound expressly for the United States; in fact, any Haitian found at sea became a charge of the United States. The audacity of the program was matched only by its destructiveness, as one Duvalier enemy after another was delivered back into the hands of his or her persecutors.[32]

By the mid-1980s, with Haiti on the brink of famine, and 75 percent of Haitians living below the poverty line, a series of food riots erupted. As usual, Duvalier's security forces met the unrest with severe repression. Unusually this time, the Haitian people refused to back down. The murder of three young boys during an uprising in the city of Gonaïves in November 1985 sparked still wider protests that ultimately unseated Jean-Claude Duvalier. On February 7, 1986, amid persistent antigovernment demonstrations, the U.S. government airlifted Duvalier to France. It wasn't that the Reagan administration had wearied of Duvalier's repression; rather, it had become apparent that repression alone was no longer sufficient to keep a lid on popular unrest.[33]

Haitians greeted Duvalier's departure with jubilation. For the first time in a generation, ordinary Haitians were free to, of all things, simply *talk*. One journalist described the exhilarating sensation of "a million people talking all at once and all of a sudden." Instruments of civil society—newspapers, radio stations, political parties—sprang up as if overnight. Violence accompanied the celebration. After thirty years in power, the Duvalier state penetrated all aspects of Haitian society, and Haitians set about uprooting it with a vengeance. The most odious symbols of the state were the first to fall—the Duvalier flag and the

Tonton Macoutes. No few Macoutes were hurriedly and brutally dispatched.[34]

It is unfair to call a people who suffered as Haitians suffered under the Duvaliers naïve for reveling in their hard-won liberty. But with the U.S. government orchestrating the transfer of power, Haiti's liberation could not and would not last. Limited constitutional reform and a series of elections followed the change of government. But as in 1930s Cuba, the effect of these reforms was not to introduce liberal democratic governance to Haiti but to lend civilian veneer to ongoing military rule. From the U.S. perspective, liberal democracy was never the point. The point was a Haiti safe from "communism." Under the new Conseil National de Gouvernement (CNG) and its leader the Duvalierist general Henri Namphy, that is exactly what Haiti and the United States got. As the U.S. government and press praised General Namphy for his perspicacity and moderation, the Haitian people decried what appeared to be a return to old ways.

When, in April 1986, a crowd of unarmed demonstrators descended on the torture chambers of Fort Dimanche prison, the army beat back the crowd, guns blazing, leaving eight protestors dead and scores wounded. "By the end of its first year in office," according to one report, Namphy's regime "had openly gunned down more civilians than Jean-Claude Duvalier's government had done in fifteen years."[35] The next year was no better. In July 1987, wealthy landholders in the town of Jean-Rabel repressed a peasant uprising, killing hundreds of so-called communists. Random murders accompanied the orchestrated massacres, prompting one journalist to observe, as the year drew to a close, "something strange and terrible is taking shape in Haiti."[36]

The U.S. government response to renewed violence in Haiti was slow and tepid. Confronted by evidence of slaughter, U.S. ambassador Brunson McKinley claimed to have "no proof of such killings." Still another massacre in late November 1987 prompted the Reagan administration to formally suspend military aid to Namphy, though the CIA continued to funnel money his way to the tune of $1 million per year. By the end of the decade, U.S. intelligence officials appear to have been no more able to grasp the situation in Haiti than had the

State Department at its beginning. When, in November 1987, Haitian voters threatened to replace Namphy with the moderate human rights advocate Gérard Gourgue, Namphy suspended the new electoral council and declared a military dictatorship. The United States applauded. "The electoral council was being run by foreign leftists," Ambassador McKinley announced; "Gourgue was at least a Communist front man, if not a Communist himself."[37]

The following year began with a spectacularly fraudulent election that introduced a period of extreme instability in Haiti, culminating in September with the Saint-Jean Bosco Massacre—an attack on the congregation of a nettlesome liberal Catholic minister by the name of Jean-Bertrand Aristide. The desecrating of Aristide's church went too far for junior officers, who deposed Namphy while elevating yet another former Duvalier-era henchman, Brigadier General Prosper Avril. Avril followed his predecessor's script to the letter, governing by intimidation and extrajudicial killings. Inaugurated with the torture and public display of three dissidents in the autumn of 1989, Avril saw his reign come to a precipitous end the following March, after soldiers under his command killed a young schoolgirl while breaking up an antigovernment demonstration in the port of Petit Goâve. Avril resigned at U.S. insistence, his place taken by Ertha Pascal-Trouillot, a justice on Haiti's Supreme Court. The best that can be said of Pascal-Trouillot's brief but violent reign is that it served as the backdrop for Haiti's first free and fair democratic election. On December 16, 1990, by a margin far exceeding the estimation of U.S. intelligence officials, Haitians elected Jean-Bertrand Aristide president in a landslide, setting off a celebration to rival that which greeted the fall of the Duvaliers.

But just as in the aftermath of Jean-Claude Duvalier's demise, the popular celebration could not mask the resentment of Haitian elites. Even before Aristide was inaugurated early the next February, Roger Lafontant, a displaced Duvalier loyalist, launched a failed mutiny against Aristide's impending "communist dictatorship." This time, supporters of the president-elect struck back, rounding up and killing Tonton Macoutes while destroying property belonging to Lafontant's sponsors. While there is no denying the lawlessness that followed Lafontant's mutiny, it hardly reached the level described by the U.S.

press, which, like the U.S. government, seemed determined to undermine the Aristide government before it even came to power. "Burned bodies, cannibalism and torched homes give an aura of madness to the capital," wrote the Associated Press. "On Tuesday, two photographers took pictures of two men eating the flesh of a man who had been burned as hundreds of people looked on." Such sensationalism distracted American audiences from confronting the crimes perpetrated by Haiti's displaced leaders as when, several days before the new president took office, arsonists set fire to an orphanage founded by Aristide, killing four children.[38]

"Everyone who is anyone is against Aristide. Except the people"— the words of a Haitian businessman complaining to a reporter in the autumn of 1991, just weeks before Aristide was deposed in a military coup. Indeed, elite Haitians had good reason to lament Aristide's rise to power. For the first time in the nation's history, the Haitian government committed itself not to consolidate and expand the influence of the rich and powerful but to promote the interests of the poor. Critics in Haiti and the United States pointed to a few notorious examples of elite persecution to discredit the new government, but in fact, Haiti's transition to civilian leadership was distinguished by tranquility and moderation. The Aristide government confiscated no property, and its supposedly rabid followers killed not a single member of the old ruling class.[39]

Still, even moderate reform was too much for the opposition. On September 29, 1991, a group of Haitian Army officials launched a military coup, massacring a crowd mustered to protect the new president, while forcing Aristide's withdrawal from Haiti. This time, it was not the U.S. government that provided the means of exile but France, which sped the deposed president to Venezuela. At first the U.S. government publicly opposed the coup. Soon it changed its tune, blaming Aristide for his own downfall. Within days of coming to power, the military junta brandished papers allegedly documenting human rights abuses by the Aristide government. This was followed by "evidence" (fabricated with help from the CIA) that Aristide was mentally unstable, hence unfit for political office. Aristide was "a murderer and psychopath," one CIA officer testified before a hearing convened by U.S. senator Jesse Helms.[40]

The resurgence of Haiti's old guard pleased U.S. business interests, which wanted nothing so much as a return of low minimum wages and minimal labor protections to Haiti. But the violence attending the coup had an unforeseen consequence, as a new wave of emigrants departed Haiti's shores. In one of his first acts upon taking office, Aristide had dismissed the notorious *chefs de section*, local heads of the Tonton Macoutes, who had terrorized the Haitian people for over a generation. Upon assuming power, Raoul Cédras, leader of the military junta, promptly restored the section chiefs. With zeal that would have shamed the Duvaliers, the section chiefs hunted down Aristide supporters and prodemocracy activists throughout the country. In one case emblematic of the failure of U.S. Haitian policy, thugs in search of an alleged Aristide supporter torched the dental office of the man's brother, Frantz Guerrier, killing Guerrier's daughter and mother, who had taken refuge in his basement. Unsated, the killers returned a few weeks later and murdered the dentist's wife.[41] In another case, soldiers seized a woman named Yolande Jean, who had been working to promote adult literacy. Pregnant at the time, Jean was taken to the notorious Service des Recherches Criminelles police station, headquarters of the sadistic colonel Michel François, where she was beaten unmercifully and ultimately lost her baby.[42]

Within days of the coup, hospital morgues overflowed with victims; within weeks, the death toll exceeded fifteen hundred. Summary executions of entire families were not uncommon, as journalists described the worst violence they had seen in years. The scale of the violence was matched only by its audacity. Aristide supporters were cut down outside churches and in public squares. Brothers were taken out in front of siblings. Fathers were murdered before their children's eyes. In all, the coup displaced as many as two hundred thousand refugees, roughly half of whom fled to the Dominican Republic, while the other half, Frantz Guerrier and Yolande Jean among them, took to the sea.[43]

In the immediate aftermath of the coup, the George H. W. Bush administration suspended the forced repatriation of Haitian refugees. It

was no longer plausible to argue that Haiti was free of political persecution. In early October, as the number of Haitian boaters mounted,
the commander in chief of the U.S. Atlantic Command toured the
Guantánamo naval base in anticipation of using it to hold fleeing Haitians. The first refugees to arrive there in the aftermath of the coup
were not Haitians but rather a group of seventeen American missionaries who had escaped the violence in Haiti in four boats. Rescued by
the U.S. Coast Guard on October 10, the missionaries were unloaded
at the naval base before being flown home to the United States.[44]

Early the next month, the Coast Guard began picking up increasing numbers of Haitian boaters in the Windward Passage and Old
Bahama Channel. Official government narratives of this Coast Guard
sweep describe it as a "rescue" operation. There is no doubt that many
of the boats departing Haiti were unseaworthy and overloaded, and
that countless refugees perished in the exodus. But a *rescue* that ended
up returning the vast majority of refugees to face persecution, torture,
and sometimes death in Haiti did not feel beneficial to the Haitians.
At the very least, the experience of interdiction was profoundly alienating. "They burned our clothes, everything we had," Yolande Jean recalled, after having been picked up by a Coast Guard boat; "the
luggage, all the documents we were carrying." The Americans gave the
Haitians no explanation. "They just started towing our belongings, and
the next thing we know, the boat was in flames. Photos, documents. If
you didn't have pockets in which to put things, you lost them." Jean
managed to save a few precious papers by hiding them in a pocket.[45]
Moreover, the same presumption that inspired AMIO informed the
policy of President Bush: the United States had the right to seize any
Haitian boat bound no matter where, and detain, if not repatriate,
its crew.

On November 10, two Coast Guard cutters carrying nearly five
hundred refugees pulled into Guantánamo Bay and dropped anchor.
The base commander, Captain William C. McCamy, dispatched a medical team to care for the refugees aboard the cutters. Two days later,
alarmed by what his team found, McCamy informed Washington that
for the safety and health of all concerned he would off-load the refugees onto the base.[46] The Haitians were taken to a hastily erected
holding area known as Camp Bulkeley, out on the area known as

Radio Range (after the old radio antennas that once enjoyed unen-
cumbered access out into the Caribbean), along the Cuban coastline.
By mid-November, the number of boaters departing Haiti reached
new heights. To forestall the exodus, President Bush resumed forced
repatriations on November 18. A temporary restraining order out
of district court in Miami halted the president's order the following
day, prompting the president to establish a refugee camp at Guantánamo Bay. Four thousand Haitians came ashore at Guantánamo on
November 20.[47]

The majority of Haitians detained at Guantánamo were deposited
in Camp McCalla, which consisted of six separate facilities located on
the old airfield on Windward Point. Once Camp McCalla was completed, Bulkeley was reserved for special uses—to hold "screened-in"
Haitians awaiting transfer to the United States, for example, and, later,
for screened-in Haitians with HIV/AIDS. Still another facility, known
as Camp 7, was used as detention camp for uncooperative refugees. A
"Joint Task Force" (JTF) consisting of army, navy, air force, and marines personnel commanded the camps. The organization of the camp
followed standard military design, and included sections for families,
unaccompanied minors, and adult men and women. The camps could
accommodate up to 12,500 refugees at one time.

Determined to foster the refugees' cooperation, camp officials
charged the Haitians with electing representatives and maintaining
their living quarters (excepting sanitation). The JTF solicited volunteers to help with food preparation and, in some instances, with trans-
lation in the asylum screening process. To further encourage good
behavior, guards provided refugees with cigarettes, games, balls, tools,
construction material, and other "luxuries." U.S. officials also furnished the Haitians with a newspaper entitled *Sa K'pase* (*What's Happening*), prepared by the Military Information Support Team, known
by the acronym MIST, a branch of the Psychological Operations command. Published in both English and Haitian Creole, the paper informed refugees of the rules and recent development in the camps,
along with rosy accounts of life back in Haiti—apparently designed to
speed voluntary repatriations.[48]

The distinction between a refugee camp and a prison is razor thin,
and rests on the degree of trust and civility between the refugees and

their guards. Boredom and restlessness, the bane of many a detention operation, proved a challenge from the beginning. With little to do and even less space in which to do it, the social interactions between the mostly male U.S. military personnel and the screened-out Haitians especially deteriorated quickly. Guantánamo was "like hell," one witness recalled. Having fled Haiti after seeing his father and brother murdered by thugs who had been searching for him, this man couldn't bear to be "treated like animals." In the camps, he reported, "there are thousands of us. Children everywhere. There is so much confusion. Nobody knows what's happening." From the beginning, U.S. State Department officials pressured INS interviewers to screen *out* (i.e., return to Haiti) as many Haitians as possible, which made for tense relations between captives and captors. "If a cutter heading for Port-au-Prince still has space, more screened-in people will be questioned again," the same witness testified, or "if a person's story had even a small inconsistency, then he is told 'you are lying' and sent back" to Haiti.[49]

Confined for days on end in small camps, with limited social contact and little to keep them busy, it wasn't long before the Haitians began to feel like prisoners. As early as mid-December, after only three weeks in captivity, a demonstration broke out in Camp Bulkeley. Within several days, it spread to Camp McCalla, where Haitians confronted military guards with homemade weapons: tent poles, wooden rods ripped from cots, and chunks of asphalt. More than anything, the situation called for a mediator with knowledge of Haiti. When JTF commander George H. Walls tried to intervene, he was struck by a piece of asphalt; intervention by a representative of the Office of the High Commissioner for Refugees (UNHCR) accomplished little besides clarifying that the demonstrators wanted to speak to representatives in the United States. By December 15, when Walls called home for backup, the Haitians and their captors had come to regard one another as enemies.

The cultural chasm separating the two communities, already significant, yawned perilously that night, when U.S. soldiers dispatched to keep tabs on the demonstrators witnessed "what appeared to be a voodoo ritual." According to an official account, some of the Haitians "wrapped themselves in white sheets and walked to the four corners of the compound, which represented the four corners of the earth, to consult with the spirits." The Haitians "then drew strength from the earth by lying down on the ground near what appeared to be a make-shift voodoo shrine," which, the chronicler notes, "typically includes representations of Christian and voodoo religious figures and other objects shrouded with symbolic meaning, such as candles or glass jars." So menacing did this ritual seem that "the general and his staff worried that the next step might be a blood sacrifice of some sort." With no more knowledge of Haitian culture than the State Department team described in *Civiletti*, the U.S. officers were left to interpret the Haitians' actions on their own. "One officer thought some of the Haitians believed that a sacrifice would hasten the arrival of the 'magical bird' that would take them to Florida. Another officer remembered hearing about a threat by the malcontents to start throwing babies over the fence if their demands were not met within 48 hours."[50]

The Americans' interpretation of the Haitians' behavior could have been catastrophic. By the time the 302 marines dispatched from Camp Lejeune, North Carolina, descended on McCalla II at four o'clock on the morning of December 17 with fixed bayonets, the Haitians had been thoroughly dehumanized, their grievances dismissed. Wanting nothing so much as a taste of American freedom, they had become the dark, demonic *Other* that Americans feared in Haiti going back centuries. Only extraordinary discipline on the part of the refugees themselves prevented "Operation Take Charge" from becoming a blood-bath. "There is no question the Haitians were taken completely by surprise," read the government report, "and it was not a pleasant surprise. Grim-faced marines, some holding rifles, encircled the camp. Marine engineers wearing flack jackets and helmets and armed with breaching tools moved swiftly to make gaps in the wire through which the [marines], equipped with riot gear, entered the compound." When "the stunned migrants offered no resistance," the disturbance came to an end.[51]

In early December the district court in Miami replaced its temporary restraining order with a preliminary injunction, demanding that the Bush administration "implement and follow procedural safeguards adequate to ensure that Haitians with bona fide claims of political persecution are not forcefully returned to Haiti." Though overturned the following month, the injunction forced the INS to confront its dismal record in recognizing the real threat of political persecution confronting a broad class of Haitian refugees. For a time, the judicial intervention improved screening procedures at Guantánamo Bay. By mid-January 1992, the number of Haitians screened into the United States jumped precipitously to 85 percent, before falling back to 45 percent in February, then to a mere 2 percent in April. Overall, between October 1991 and June 1992, U.S. officials carried out some thirty-six thousand screening interviews at the naval base, "screening in" more than ten thousand Haitians, or roughly 28 percent.[52] Which is not to suggest that 28 percent was enough, or that Americans had finally overcome their anti-Haitian prejudice. Rather, it is simply to observe that the record could have been (indeed, had been) worse.

From the first, the State Department pressured INS interviewers to reduce the number of screened-in Haitians to an absolute minimum, which explains the rapid monthly decline in admittees in early 1992. In mid-December 1991, just as Frantz Guerrier's dental clinic was torched, the State Department informed the INS that "at this time we have no reason to believe the mere identification of an individual as an Aristide supporter put that individual at particular risk of mistreatment."[53] In early February, Commander Walls joined the everything-is-dandy-in-Haiti chorus, insisting that the repatriation of screened-out Haitians was going "smoothly," and that the returnees faced "no retribution," a claim he reiterated mid-month. In fact, neither the screening process nor the return of the exiles to Haiti was going smoothly, as more candid government reports allowed. Since mid-November 1991, when the Coast Guard first began picking up more and more refugees, the screening process had been slow, chaotic, and inefficient. In early February, INS agents lost the records of nearly two thousand screened-in refugees, a mistake that proved deadly for at least one of them. At the moment that Commander Walls was assuring the public about Haitian conditions, a young woman named Marie Zette was returned to Haiti despite protesting what she knew to be a death sentence. A few days later, at Guantánamo, Zette's name came up for transfer to Miami; there had been a mix-up. Zette's stay of execution came too late. Back in Haiti, she was murdered in her bed by

Tonton Macoutes. News of her fate arrived at Guantánamo later that month, borne by members of her fleeing family.[54]

Much of this migrant operation ("Operation GTMO" in military parlance) recapitulated the patterns of government behavior described in *Civiletti*. Some U.S. officials—Commander Walls comes to mind— seem simply to have accepted uncritically assurances by their colleagues that all was well in Haiti and that returnees would be greeted warmly upon arriving home. Others deliberately misrepresented the evidence before their very eyes. INS official Gunther Wagner, for example, having led three survey missions to Haiti, claimed that "95 to 97 percent of the [Haitian] people obviously have had no problems, and therefore would not be eligible for asylum." The majority of the asylum claims made by Guantánamo refugees, Wagner alleged, were simply "fraudulent."[55]

Having accepted the official line on conditions in Haiti, Guantánamo officials could easily mistake the desperation of Haitians slotted for return to Port-au-Prince as sheer defiance. In April 1992, ninety-six Haitians became "belligerent" after being loaded aboard the Coast Guard cutter *Tampa* for repatriation. Upon arriving in Haiti the following morning, the refugees refused to disembark, with some insisting that they would rather perish on the ship than confront what awaited them. "The negotiations eventually reached an impasse," according to the official line, leading U.S. military personnel to threaten to blast them off the ship with fire hoses. The threat sufficed to lure at least one Haitian ashore, and when he complained to witnesses that the Americans had used force, a Haitian policeman responded, "We have force here, too," raising a "ripple of laughter" on the dock. The laughter may have broken the tension, as the government chronicler suggests, but it could not alter the fate of the refugees, one of whom was Frantz Guerrier, the dentist, who was brutally beaten his second night back while asleep in his grandmother's bed.[56]

In fact, Guerrier need not have been aboard the *Tampa* that April day. With his dental office burned, and his mother, daughter, and wife murdered, Guerrier passed the "credible fear" test that qualified refugees for an asylum hearing in the United States. But his passage there was blocked after a blood test revealed that he was HIV-positive, which put him along with 230 other HIV-positive Haitians in social isolation and legal limbo on the base. On February 29, 1992, the INS announced that screened-in Haitians found to be HIV-positive would not be brought to the United States; they would remain at Guantánamo indefinitely while U.S. officials determined their fate.[57]

The testing of Haitians at Guantánamo Bay for HIV/AIDS began as a result of U.S. officials seeking assistance from allies in the region to relieve the crush of refugees. Belize and Honduras responded positively, but insisted that any Haitians brought to their countries be tested for HIV/AIDS. In the United States, the discovery that some Haitian refugees were HIV-positive triggered a 1986 law sponsored by Senator Jesse Helms prohibiting the admission of HIV-positive individuals. All the Haitian refugees on Guantánamo would have to be tested. Moreover, an INS official explained, initially screened-in Haitians found to carry the virus would be made to undergo a second screening interview more rigorous than the first. No longer would it suffice for HIV-positive refugees to demonstrate a "credible fear" of persecution upon return to Haiti. They would now have to prove to have a "well-founded fear"—precisely the bar required by judges at immigration hearings in the United States, only there, refugees facing such interviews were entitled to legal counsel. At Guantánamo, the INS denied refugees the right to legal counsel on the grounds that Guantánamo was part of Cuba, not part of the United States, hence outside U.S. constitutional jurisdiction. Besides, one INS official later testified, lawyers would only emphasize the strengths of their clients' claims.[58]

Even a finding of well-founded fear of persecution among HIV-positive Haitians did not result in transfer to the United States. The point of the double jeopardy was to clear Guantánamo of HIV-positive refugees, not speed their passage stateside. There remained the thorny problem of the 1986 law prohibiting the admission of HIV-positive individuals. Frantz Guerrier and company would simply have to wait.[59]

And wait they did, in conditions that one federal judge later likened to the sort of confinement typically reserved for hardened criminals. Yolande Jean described Camp Bulkeley, where screened-in HIV-positive Haitians lived in isolation, as "a space cordoned off with barbed wire. Wherever they put you," Jean explained, "you were meant to stay right there; there was no place to move. The latrines were brimming over. There was never any cool water to drink, to wet our lips. There was only water in a cistern, boiling in the hot sun. When you drank it, it gave you diarrhea. . . . Rats crawled over us at night. . . . When we saw all these things, we thought, it's not possible, it can't go on like this. We're humans, just like everybody else."[60] Frantz Guerrier was so repelled by life at Camp Bulkeley that he opted to return to Haiti, where at least he had a fighting chance.

By March 1992 the legal expedients hastily contrived by Florida attorneys to halt the forced repatriation were no longer in effect. In early February 1992, the Eleventh Circuit Court in Atlanta, having already lifted an injunction imposed by Miami District Court, vacated the injunction entirely, wiping it off the legal record. Haitians detained at Guantánamo Bay, the court declared, had "no substantive rights" under U.S. law. Toward the end of the month, the U.S. Supreme Court denied the Haitians' application for a stay of the Eleventh District Court's ruling along with a petition for certiorari (judicial review), leaving the Haitians at the mercy of the INS.

Enter another advocacy group, Haitian Centers Council, Inc., out of Brooklyn, New York, which filed a lawsuit on March 17 in New York District Court arguing that the new procedures announced by the INS at the end of February to rescreen HIV-positive refugees without the benefit of counsel violated both the First Amendment right to free speech and the Fifth Amendment right to due process. The government's plan to detain indefinitely those HIV-positive Haitians found to have a well-founded fear of persecution left them "in limbo." The Haitians were "people without a country. They can't get in. They can't get out. They can't get help, and now the government is saying no court can review what's going on." Surely such a state of affairs warranted "judicial intervention."[61]

Well, U.S. District Court judge Sterling Johnson demanded of INS officials, wasn't it true that the Guantánamo base was subject to the "complete jurisdiction and control" of the United States, and hence answerable to U.S. and international law? No, the government replied. The base was located on territory sovereign to Cuba. Neither the Immigration and Naturalization Act, the Administrative Procedures Act, nor Article 33 of the UN Convention and Protocol on the Status of Refugees created "judicially enforceable rights on the part of the individual Haitians on Guantánamo." The Haitians were "outside the United States and therefore they have no judicially cognizable rights in United States courts." Skeptical, Judge Johnson asked the government attorney if the government was really arguing that "Haitians, or anyone else at Guantánamo Bay, have no constitutional protection at all?" The government responded affirmatively, prompting Johnson to marvel, "You are saying, if I hear you correctly, that an agency like the INS, assuming they are arbitrary and capricious and even cruel, that the courts would have no jurisdiction because the conduct did not occur on US soil?" Precisely, the government counsel replied.[62]

In late March, alarmed by what he heard in court, Judge Johnson imposed a temporary restraining order halting the repatriations. On April 1 the parties were before him again, this time with the government arguing that admitting legal counsel to Guantánamo Bay for the refugees would be "meddlesome" and "adversarial" and would "slow things down."[63] On April 6, Judge Johnson replaced the temporary restraining order with a preliminary injunction upholding his previous ruling and granting plaintiffs' counsel the right to meet with their clients at Guantánamo Bay. The judge was unconvinced that the lawyers would prove any more meddlesome than the media, clergy, physicians, and numerous civilians already there. Moreover, he insisted, due process applied at Guantánamo, a facility under the full authority of the United States.[64]

Within hours, the government appealed Johnson's preliminary injunction to the Second Circuit Court in Manhattan. Before that court, the government argued that Judge Johnson's preliminary injunction would serve as a magnet, luring Haitians to the water at their peril, a noteworthy appeal from an administration that had not taken much interest in Haitians' well-being over the course of the previous twenty years.[65] The court denied the government's request, leaving the preliminary injunction in place. The government then appealed the Sec-

ond Circuit Court's ruling to the U.S. Supreme Court. On April 22 the
High Court stayed Judge Johnson's injunction, with Justice Clarence
Thomas casting the deciding vote.

The High Court's stay jump-started the "credible fear" hearings at
Guantánamo, where INS officials ordered their subordinates to clear
the place out.[66] Meanwhile, the surge in Haitian boaters that began in
early April continued unabated. More and more Haitians seemed determined simply to get to Guantánamo Bay, where, since the outbreak
of the coup, the odds of being screened into the United States had
risen from virtually nil the previous decade to roughly one in three. Up
to this time, in order to get to Guantánamo, boaters had only to make
it as far as the Coast Guard cutters ringing the Haitian coast, prompting many to take to the sea in virtually anything that would float. On
April 29, the Coast Guard ordered its ships to pull back beyond the
range of visibility from the shores of Haiti.[67]

Still, the flood of exiles continued. On May 19 more than 1,600 Haitians were plucked from the sea, the record for a single day since the
coup began. By May 20 the base commander announced the population
of the camp at 12,482, just 18 shy of capacity, prompting government
officials to suspend interdictions. Thereafter, only Haitian boaters in
mortal peril would be picked up at sea. By this time, 34,090 Haitians
had come ashore at Guantánamo Bay since the exodus began.

U.S. officials recognized that converting the decade-old Alien Migration Interdiction Operation to a search-and-rescue venture would
not stop desperate Haitians from taking to the sea. To that end, on
May 24, 1992, President Bush issued what became known as the "Kennebunkport Order," after the seaside town in Maine that was home to
the Bush vacation compound, from which the president announced a
new policy. From that day forward all Haitians picked up at sea would
be immediately returned to Haiti. No more transfer to Guantánamo,
no shipboard immigration screenings to establish either credible or
well-founded fear, no due process, no legal counsel, nothing. Haitians
who sought asylum in the United States could take their claims to the
U.S. consulate in Port-au-Prince, a notoriously unsympathetic place.

The Kennebunkport Order won immediate condemnation at home
and abroad. Critics said it violated Article 33 of the UN Convention
and Protocol on the Status of Refugees (prohibiting the return of refu-

gees to a place where they faced political persecution); the president had erected "a floating Berlin Wall."[68] Suddenly, Guantánamo, denounced for its brutal conditions and lack of constitutional protections, was defended as the least worst place to house refugees. Better to end up in Guantánamo—even with HIV—than to be returned to Port-au-Prince.[69]

When next the administration and its critics faced off in Brooklyn District Court, the plaintiffs sought a temporary restraining order, arguing that the Kennebunkport Order jeopardized the well-being of a vast class of Haitian returnees. Not so, argued U.S. solicitor general Kenneth Starr, whose very presence in district court signaled just how seriously the Bush administration viewed this case. "We have conducted over two thousand in-country interviews with repatriates. We have found no evidence of persecution or attacks on these individuals, none in our two thousand interviews."[70]

Just as in *Civiletti*, the government's glowing description of conditions in Haiti won the intense scrutiny of the Haitians' advocates. Between mid-November 1991 and May 1992, when the U.S. government was more or less abiding by the UN protocol and by U.S. statute law for the treatment of refugees, roughly 30 percent of Haitians screened at Guantánamo Bay passed the "credible fear" test, and were admitted to the United States for full asylum hearings. These numbers spoke for themselves: evidently *somebody* was facing persecution in Haiti. On May 31 six Haitians attempted suicide aboard a U.S. Coast Guard cutter heading for Port-au-Prince, with one leaping overboard in Port-au-Prince harbor.

On June 5, Judge Johnson issued his ruling. Unable to side with the Haitians due to a legal technicality, he nonetheless lambasted the government for making a mockery of Article 33. "It is unconscionable," the judge wrote,

> that the United States should accede to the Protocol and later claim that it is not bound by it. This court is astonished that the United States would return Haitian refugees to the jaws of political persecution, terror, death and uncertainty when it has contracted not to do so. The Government's conduct is particularly hypocritical given its condemnation of other countries who have refused to abide by the prin-

ciple of non-refoulement. As it stands now, Article 33 is a cruel hoax
and not worth the paper it is printed on.

Still, for all his indignation, the judge could do little to ease the
misery of the HIV-positive refugees. The question of their right to
counsel would remain moot pending a full trial, scheduled for late
October.[71]
Meanwhile, the U.S. military wasted no time in tearing down
Camp McCalla, just as it consolidated HIV-positive Haitians into
Camp Bulkeley. By mid-June the Haitian population at Guantánamo
was down to 2,500; by the first of July, only the 233 HIV-positive refugees remained.[72] As flawed as the screening process had been at
Guantánamo Bay, the closing of the camp was a catastrophe for many
refugees. When open to refugees, Guantánamo signified U.S. recognition of political repression in Haiti. The closing of the camps altogether bestowed political legitimacy on Haiti's military government.[73]
Life for the HIV-positive refugees detained at Camp Bulkeley was
difficult. In July 1992, as temperatures rose and as Camp McCalla
folded, the "residents" of Camp Bulkeley became increasingly exasperated by the continuing uncertainty over their fate and the constant,
coerced medical testing to which they were subjected. "We had been
asking them to remove the barbed wire" surrounding the camp, Yolande Jean recalled; "the children were playing near it, they were falling and injuring themselves. The food they were serving us, including
canned chicken, had maggots in it. And yet they insisted that we eat
it. Because you've got no choice. And it was for these reasons that we
started holding demonstrations."
On July 17, 1992, tension at the camp boiled over. When a shrug
became a push, a full-scale riot broke out between refugees brandishing sticks, stones, and anything else they could find and soldiers armed
with, among other things, a fire hose. The fire hose won the day, but
not before a few guards suffered minor injuries, auguring their return
in force.[74] The following day, an air force team swept the camp for
homemade weapons, rounding up the alleged instigators of the previous day's disturbance. Three Haitians were carted off to the brig,
thirty-nine others placed in isolation at Camp 7.[75] The JTF com-

mander praised the air force unit for conducting "themselves magnifi-
cently by incurring more injuries to themselves in their attempts not
to hurt the migrants."[76] The Haitians remembered the situation differently. "Since we left Haiti last December we've been treated like animals," one witness recalled. "When we protested about the camp back
then, the military beat us up. I was beaten, handcuffed and they spat
in my face. I was chained, made to sleep on the ground like animals,
like dogs, not like humans."[77]

Unfortunately for the U.S. government, the so-called Recapture of
Camp Bulkeley was recorded on videotape and later became a subject of review in Brooklyn District Court. Announced by the thunder of
a warplane flying low over the camp, the operation proceeded with a
bulldozer demolishing the gate as soldiers, clad in combat helmets and
vests, batons and shields in hand, rushed into the camp, driving the
refugees into small holding pens while ransacking their shelters. Soldiers bearing M-16 machine guns, some leading police dogs, accompanied the combat patrol into the camp. The JTF video depicted Haitians,
male and female, their hands bound behind their backs, being loaded
into vans. Children and pregnant women were among those arrested.[78]

The official military account speculated that "the riots were the
result of putting too much emphasis on improving the migrants' qual-
ity of life at the expense of relaxing camp control."[79] Give a Haitian an
inch and he'll take a mile. From mid-July 1992 forward, any semblance
of lax control vanished, and still the Haitians rebelled. When, by late
August, nearly six weeks after the riot, some of the Haitians remained
in Camp 7, their compatriots petitioned the military for their release.
The military denied the request, prompting the Haitians to storm the
compound and liberate the prisoners themselves. This time, when
base security arrived, the Haitians set fire to their camp, prompting a
still heavier military response, with more pushing, shoving, and ar-
rests. And so the cycle of violence continued, with protests, hunger
strikes, and, inevitably, more time in the brig.

Conditions at Camp Bulkeley deteriorated so precipitously that
even military officials joined in the criticism. On July 18 the head of
the Atlantic Command warned that the "creation of a 'penal' environment within the camp presents the opportunity for heavy criti-

cism from migrant support and humanitarian organizations. We have reached the point where such an environment stretches the margin of the interpretation of our humanitarian mission."[80] In September 1992, Admiral Paul D. Miller informed the Joint Chiefs of Staff that the health care at Guantánamo Bay did not meet the needs of HIV-positive detainees. Let's close this chapter of GTMO history, Miller urged his superiors. That December, a departing camp commander recommended moving the HIV-positive Haitians to the United States.

Still, the detainees languished. By January 1993, Yolande Jean and her colleagues had become so fed up with the uncertainty, forced medical treatment, and physical abuse that they began a hunger strike.[81] By March, Jean herself was so despondent that she contemplated committing suicide.[82]

Meanwhile, the advocates for the Haitians appealed their case to the Second Circuit Court in late June 1992. The Second Circuit had previously upheld Judge Johnson's preliminary injunction. Now it expressed bewilderment at the government's claim that it could do with the Haitians whatever it wanted so long as they were outside U.S. territory. Late the next month, the court issued a ruling prohibiting the refugees' direct return to Haiti. U.S. law applied at sea, the court announced. The Refugee Act of 1980 was unequivocal on the matter of forced return.[83]

The Supreme Court eventually stayed the lower court's ruling, but still the government wasn't satisfied. Later that summer the lead lawyer on the case announced that the Justice Department also wanted the court to vacate the Second Circuit's ruling that the U.S. Constitution applied at Guantánamo Bay, thereby preserving Guantánamo's place beyond the reach of law. But rather than taking the case directly to the Supreme Court, the government offered the Haitians' advocates a deal: if they agreed to the ruling being vacated, the government would grant them what they had sought all along, namely, access to their HIV-positive clients on the naval base. There would be no need for a formal trial. Advocates for Haitian Centers Council responded that they could not accept the deal without checking with their clients first. And so they gained access to Guantánamo Bay. What they found there so deeply offended their sense of justice that they rejected the government's offer to exchange permanent access for vacation. As a result, the legal case *Haitian Centers Council Inc. v. McNary* was "bifurcated" (split in two): the question of the Haitians' rights to a lawyer would go forward in Brooklyn District Court, though not before the result of the presidential election; the question of whether the U.S. Constitution applied at Guantánamo and at sea was headed for the Supreme Court the following spring.[84]

On January 14, 1993, less than a week before taking office, President-elect Bill Clinton abruptly dropped his opposition to the Bush administration policy of forcible return, thereby ensuring a trial in Brooklyn Federal Court. The next day, on January 15, the U.S. Coast Guard launched "Operation Able Manner," a blockade of the Haitian coast by twenty-two Coast Guard cutters. One week later, the Coast Guard reported that it had "saved and repatriated" 534 Haitians in the first week of the new operation, bringing the total number of Haitians "saved and repatriated" since the new year to nearly 3,500. The INS, generally unsympathetic to Haitian asylum claims, screened in roughly one fifth of the boaters picked up in the first two weeks of the new year, de facto acknowledgment that persecution persisted in Haiti.[85] In February, by a margin of 76 to 23, the U.S. Senate passed a resolution prohibiting all HIV-positive foreigners from entering the United States. If the Haitians on Guantánamo were going to get relief, it would come not from Congress but from the courts.[86]

On March 2, 1993, the U.S. Supreme Court heard oral arguments in the newly renamed case *Sale v. Haitian Centers Council*. According to the government attorney, neither the Immigration and Nationality Act of 1952 nor the 1967 UN Protocol on the Status of Refugees was intended to have extraterritorial effect, and so did not apply to Guantánamo. Much more than a technical question of law was at stake here, the government insisted. To apply the Constitution extraterritorially would only induce more Haitians to take to the seas, thereby putting more of them in jeopardy. It was both good law and sound policy to reverse the Second Circuit Court's ruling.[87]

Meanwhile, the plaintiffs, anticipating oral argument before a court that had twice sided with the government against the Haitians by a 5–4 majority, hoped to appeal to the so-called plain language predilection of conservative justice Antonin Scalia to win a majority, however slim. In 1968 the United States acceded to the UN protocol enjoining signatories not to "return a refugee in any manner whatsoever" to a setting where his life or liberty might be at risk. In 1980 the U.S. Congress amended a statute that authorized the attorney general to "withhold deportation of any alien" specifically "within the United States" to any country where he might be at risk, to read, "the Attorney General shall not deport or return any alien" to such a place. The old qualification "within the United States" was removed; a new one, "deport or return," was added. Plainly, the Haitians' counsel insisted, both the international protocol and the U.S. statute were meant to apply overseas. To deny the fact was to invite a world of chaos and lawlessness, in which nations could do whatever they wanted on the high seas or at ostensibly law-free places such as Guantánamo.[88]

Six days later, the plaintiffs were back in the more sympathetic surroundings of Brooklyn District Court, where Judge Sterling Johnson finally called to order the formal trial that would determine whether the U.S. Constitution protected the HIV-positive Haitians detained at Guantánamo Bay. Presented with eyewitness and video testimony describing abusive treatment of the HIV-positive detainees, as well as inadequate medical care, Judge Johnson grew incredulous at the government argument that U.S. law did not apply at Guantánamo Bay. "One of the problems I have," the judge told an INS attorney, was the government's contention that it had the unchecked authority "to take, kidnap, or abscond, whatever you want to call it, take a group and put them into a compound, whether you call it a humanitarian camp or a prison, keep them there indefinitely while there has been no charge leveled against them and there is no light at the end of the tunnel?"[89]

One week into the trial, yet another uprising broke out at Camp Bulkeley, with detainees setting fire to their lean-tos and pelting their captors with rocks. In reward for their recalcitrance, nearly forty refugees were hauled off to the brig, including Yolande Jean, who was so weak from her hunger strike that she was barely able to walk. The camp commander, Colonel Bud Paulson, set up an impromptu court-martial at the brig, inviting the alleged agitators to confess their crimes and express remorse. Those who refused to do so received sentences of up to three months in solitary confinement. Yolande Jean remembers approaching Colonel Paulson skeptically. "You are the judge," she murmured. "You are the lawyer. You are everything. What am I supposed to do?"[90]

Months later, Judge Johnson issued his ruling in *Haitian Centers Council v. Sale*. The judge sided with the plaintiffs on the essential issues before his court. The U.S. Constitution applied at Guantánamo, along with all due process protections and security against indefinite detention and unfair treatment. The judge ordered the government to let the detainees go. Judge Johnson's ruling echoes Judge King's ruling of thirteen years before. "The detained Haitians are neither criminals nor national security risks," Judge Johnson observed. "Some are pregnant mothers and others are children. Simply put, they are merely the unfortunate victims of a fatal disease. The Government has failed to demonstrate to this Court's satisfaction that the detainees' illness warrants the kind of indefinite detention usually reserved for spies and murderers."[91]

The government referred to Camp Bulkeley as a "humanitarian camp." The facts presented at trial suggested otherwise. "It is nothing more than an HIV prison camp presenting potential public health risks to Haitians held there."[92] Moreover, the First Amendment applied on Guantánamo, territory "under the complete control and jurisdiction of the United States government, and where the government exercises complete control over all means of delivering communications." Indeed, the judge observed, much of the information furnished to the refugees by the government was willfully inaccurate, and represented only the narrow "viewpoint of which the Government approves."[93] Ditto due process, Johnson ruled, quoting the Second Circuit Court. The plaintiffs "are not 'some undefined, limitless class of noncitizens who are beyond our territory,' they are instead an identifiable group of people who were interdicted by Americans in international waters pursuant to a binding Agreement Between the United States of America and Haiti, and who have been detained in territory that is subject to the exclusive control of the United States."[94]

The U.S. government aimed to put the Haitian refugees beyond the reach of any law. Judge Johnson refused to go along. "If the Due

Process Clause does not apply to the detainees at Guantánamo, Defendants would have discretion deliberately to starve or beat them, to
deprive them of medical attention, to return them without process to
their persecutors, or to discriminate among them based on the color of
their skin."[95] Nor was Johnson willing to endorse the Haitians' indefinite detention. "Testimony revealed that the Haitians were told that
they could be at Guantánamo for 10–20 years or possibly until a cure
for AIDS is found."[96]

Things did not go so well for the Haitians and their counsel at the
Supreme Court. On June 21 the High Court ruled 8–1, with Justice
John Paul Stevens writing for the majority, that international and federal prohibitions on returning refugees to Haiti applied only to refugees already in the United States. The United States could do whatever
it pleased with refugees at sea or at Guantánamo Bay. The U.S. statute
had no legal bearing outside the United States, according to the Court,
and both the text and the negotiating history of Article 33 precluded it
from applying extraterritorially. "Although gathering fleeing refugees
and returning them to the one country they had desperately sought to
escape may violate the spirit of Article 33," Stevens wrote, "general
humanitarian intent cannot impose uncontemplated obligations on
treaty signatories." There was no judicial remedy for the High Court to
draw on; Congress would have to pass new laws.[97]

In a scathing dissent, Justice Harry Blackmun chastised his colleagues for what he deemed to be a tortuous interpretation of the law.
In 1968, Blackmun noted, the United States acceded to Article 33 of
the 1967 UN Protocol on the Status of Refugees, which enjoined nations from returning "a refugee in any manner whatsoever" to a place
where he would face political persecution; in 1980, Congress "amended
our immigration law to reflect the Protocol's directives." Now, suddenly, a majority "decides that the forced repatriation of the Haitian
refugees is perfectly legal, because the word 'return' does not mean
return, because the opposite of 'within the United States' is not outside the United States, and because the official charged with controlling immigration has no role in enforcing an order to control immigration."
The majority opinion might have been at least comprehensible had

there been ambiguity in the law. But that was certainly not the case here. "The language is clear, and the command is straightforward." That should have been the end of the inquiry.[98]

In conclusion, Blackmun observed that the UN refugee convention of 1951 "was enacted largely in response to the experience of Jewish refugees in Europe during the period of World War II. The tragic consequences of the world's indifference at that time are well known. The resulting ban on refoulement, as broad as the humanitarian purpose that inspired it, is easily applicable here, the Court's protestations of impotence and regret notwithstanding." Moreover, the plaintiffs claimed no "right of admission to this country." Nor did they argue that the U.S. government had seized them illegally. They simply demanded "that the United States, land of refugees and guardian of freedom, cease forcibly driving them back to detention, abuse, and death. That is a modest plea, vindicated by the Treaty and the statute. We should not close our ears to it."[99]

Looking back on "Operation GTMO" in the autumn of 1994, Professor Harold Koh, who argued *Sale v. Haitian Centers Council* before the U.S. Supreme Court, noted several "troubling" things. First was President Clinton's continuation of the Bush administration's policy of forcibly returning Haitian refugees to Haiti without an asylum hearing. Second, Clinton adopted Bush's exploitation of the U.S. naval base at Guantánamo as a "rights-free" zone. Candidate Clinton had vehemently denounced both policies in the 1992 presidential campaign: "I am appalled by the decision of the Bush Administration to pick up fleeing Haitians on the high seas and forcibly return them to Haiti before considering their claim to political asylum," Clinton remarked in May 1992. "It was bad enough when there were failures to offer them due process in making such a claim. Now they are offered no process at all before being returned." These policies were "a blow" not only to long-recognized human rights conventions and U.S. statutory law, but also to "America's moral authority in the world."[100]

Still, politicians were politicians. More troubling to Koh was the judiciary's failure to act as a check on the executive branch. By denying the Haitians international and domestic legal protections, the Supreme Court simply followed the executive's lead: it read "unambiguous language as ambiguous," it ignored the express "object and purpose" of legal codes, it elevated "snippets of negotiating history into definitive interpretive guides," and it sanctioned the very injustices that international treaties on refugees had been "drafted to prevent." Cutting across political parties and branches of government, the logic of this development was nothing short of ominous. If, confronted by social and political crises, the U.S. government could deploy nonsensical semantic distinctions, tortuous misreadings of legal precedent, and claims about the existence of geographical spaces where no law whatsoever applies to set aside a universal prohibition like the refugee convention, what, Koh demanded, did this bode for other equally inviolable laws against torture or genocide?[101]

9

★

THE CHOSEN

On the morning of September 11, 2001, a dead finch lay on a sidewalk outside the entrance to Bulkeley Hall, administrative headquarters of the U.S. naval base at Guantánamo Bay. To Lieutenant Norman A. Rogers, public works officer on the base, this seemed an ill omen, indeed. Just minutes before, Rogers had been down on Fisherman's Point inspecting the desalination plant when the telephone rang. The base commander was on the line: the United States was under attack. Two passenger planes had struck the World Trade Center in New York City; a third had hit the Pentagon. A fourth was believed to have come down somewhere in the countryside outside Washington, D.C. Rogers was ordered to lock the gates to the plant and report immediately to headquarters. A native of New York State, he drove toward Bulkeley Hall with his aunt's image running through his mind. In recent days, her office was supposed to have relocated from the towers across the Hudson to New Jersey, but he couldn't be sure. For Rogers, as for so many New Yorkers and U.S. military personnel, the fallout from this day was bound to be intensely personal.[1]

Rogers arrived at Bulkeley Hall just after the first tower collapsed (an event that, as a structural engineer, he had thought to be "impossible"). Among the assembled staff, there was a palpable sense of giddiness, as if everyone was itching for a fight. To Rogers, giddiness seemed out of place in the face of what were sure to be grievous losses.

"Hey, guys," he remembers saying, "fifty thousand people work in those buildings; let's show a little respect." Like American bases the world over, Guantánamo immediately went into lockdown. There was talk of heightened security and of the commander issuing sidearms. In fact, seated in an isolated corner of a totalitarian state, the American community at Guantánamo Bay could not have wished itself a safer location. Still, the uniqueness of the moment was reinforced when the general in charge of Cuba's frontier guard called to pledge his nation's solidarity. "We weren't involved," he assured his American counterpart. "We've got you covered on this side. Nobody's coming over the fence."[2]

After a few tense days of curfews and impromptu security checks, life at the base returned to normal. For Rogers, "normal" in the days preceding 9/11 meant maintaining the base at minimal cost consistent with base security. The downsizing of Guantánamo began with the end of the migrant operations in the mid-1990s and the relocation in 1995 of the Fleet Training Group from Guantánamo Bay to Mayport, Florida. By the time Rogers arrived at Guantánamo in August 2001, most of the hard work associated with downsizing—eliminating programs and personnel—was complete. Rogers's mandate was to identify further savings. When the U.S. invasion of Afghanistan began on October 7, 2001, Rogers could no more imagine Guantánamo playing a central role in the war on terror than he could imagine himself being asked to lead it. This was not to be Guantánamo's moment.

"CENTCOM, PACOM, EUCOM—everybody was contributing in some way," navy commander Jeffrey Johnston recalled about the mobilization of U.S. forces in the immediate aftermath of 9/11. "Except us." By "us," Johnston meant SOUTHCOM, the U.S. Southern Command, based in Miami, Florida, whose job, among other things, is to oversee the Guantánamo naval base. In July 2004, Johnston, a civil engineer, would replace Norman Rogers as commander of public works on the naval base. In the autumn of 2001, Johnston was a junior officer working in antinarcotics construction along the Andean Ridge in South America. At that time SOUTHCOM was the smallest U.S. military command—"the card table at Thanksgiving dinner," in John-

ston's words. It had no troops to send into battle. "We felt disenfranchised," Johnston remembers; "the war was going on without us." To
make matters worse, there wasn't a senior officer on SOUTHCOM's
staff who didn't know somebody who had been killed or injured in the
terrorist attacks. Eager to do its part, SOUTHCOM could only watch
as everybody else was called to action. "For months it seemed like
there'd be nothing for us to do."[3]

But the kickoff of war in early October was followed by "a good
opening drive." Within a matter of weeks U.S. commanders found
themselves in possession of thousands of Taliban and al Qaeda prisoners, some of whom were believed to possess high-value intelligence.
The Bush administration wanted a place where interrogators could
talk to detainees "pretty thoroughly," Pentagon spokeswoman Victoria
Clarke told reporters later that winter, a place beyond the reach of
journalists and defense lawyers and the jurisdiction of federal courts.[4]
Starting in early November, rumors reached the naval base that the
Pentagon was considering Guantánamo, along with a few Pacific
Ocean atolls, as a possible site for a prison camp. Rogers found those
rumors hard to believe. "No one would be so dumb as to bring detainees here," he and his colleagues agreed. By contrast, the folks at
SOUTHCOM welcomed the thought of "being in the game." Soon
the chatter about using Guantánamo as a prison subsided, and Rogers
and Johnston and their colleagues went back to work.[5]

On December 11, 2001, in what appears to have been a case of conscious indirection, Secretary of State Donald Rumsfeld told journalists that the administration was still mulling the decision about where
to hold detainees. Afghanistan, U.S. shipboard, the detainees' countries of origin, and locations in the United States were all under consideration.[6] In fact, by early December, Guantánamo had emerged as
the administration's clear first choice. All other candidates were defi-
cient in one way or another—U.S. sites for not-in-my-backyard political reasons; foreign outposts because the Pentagon could not take for
granted even allied support for the kind of interrogations it envisioned;
U.S. protectorates such as Guam because they lacked immunity from
federal court oversight and were open to lawyers and journalists; fi-

nally, Afghanistan, because it was still far from stable. Guantánamo
met all these objections. Sovereign territory of a hostile state, it offered U.S. military personnel legal and diplomatic immunity. The U.S.
military strictly controlled access to the base, securing it from prying
eyes and enemies alike. Defense Secretary Rumsfeld later characterized Guantánamo as "the least worst place."[7] But allowing for the inconvenience entailed in transporting prisoners halfway around the
world, Guantánamo seemed an obvious choice to many U.S. military
officials.[8]

Many, but not all. Establishing a pattern that would hobble the war
on terror for the better part of a decade, civilian officials atop the Pentagon settled on Guantánamo as the site for a detention camp only
after studiously ignoring the expert counsel of career military officials
such as Norman Rogers. To Rogers, Guantánamo was absolutely not
the place for such a mission. To begin with, having worked in naval
intelligence, Rogers knew that secrecy was paramount in detainee operations, and that there could be no secrecy at Guantánamo Bay. As
more candid U.S. military personnel had long since acknowledged,
the naval base was surrounded by Cuban high ground. Perched on
nearby hills, "every camera-toting Cuban tourist and his sister enjoyed
comprehensive views of everything that went on at the base. Cuban
intelligence had photographs of every single person who stepped off a
US plane."

Furthermore, the logistics and the cost of building, manning, and
maintaining a prison on a base cut off from Cuba and nearly a thousand miles distant from the United States were prohibitive. Every piece
of building material, from the smallest tack to the largest bulldozer,
had to be shipped to Cuba by boat or plane. And this was as true of
human resources—soldiers, interpreters, interrogators, analysts, and
the associated service personnel—as of construction material. The
base had limited infrastructure and no hotels to accommodate the associated hordes. Construction at Guantánamo was "four times as expensive as at home, and ten times more difficult to complete." War
would only compound the logistical hurdles, as the buildup in Afghanistan monopolized cargo planes and transport ships alike. Finally, Rogers recognized, "there was the moral and legal risk of putting US
servicemen and women above the law." For years the *Army Field Man-*

ual had provided the military with an unequivocal code of moral and legal conduct. To choose a detention site where the manual might not apply was to expose military personnel to legal persecution. In short, from beginning to end, as Rogers saw it, the plan to use Guantánamo for detention and interrogation was ill-advised. "Better to simply declare the detainees enemies of the state and dump them in Leavenworth," he remembers thinking to himself. "Nobody would have even noticed."[9]

Rogers passed his arguments up the chain of command. How high those arguments proceeded is anybody's guess. As rumors that Guantánamo was in the running subsided, Rogers assumed that his opinion had been heard. He was wrong. In mid-December, SOUTHCOM received notice that Guantánamo was a finalist along with Guam as a detention site for the war on terror. Each command was to submit a proposal making the case for their place. "We really jumped on the opportunity," Jeff Johnston explained. Though not intimately involved with Caribbean operations, Johnston was a navy man. "I eagerly shoved myself into the process, offering advice about construction costs." By contrast, PACOM, the Pacific Command that oversaw the base at Guam, "didn't want the prison." Much closer to the theater of battle, they "had bigger fish to fry."

On December 23, 2001, six Learjets touched down on the runway at Leeward Point. If the Cubans were indeed watching, they saw exiting the planes a group of American politicians, dignitaries, and line officers that included Marine Corps general Michael R. Lehnert, veteran of 1990s migrant operations at Guantánamo, and the man slated to become the first commander of Joint Task Force 160, the unit in charge of detainee operations. Lehnert would not divulge whether or not JTF 160 was coming to Guantánamo. Rogers showed him around the base, taking him to sites that had been in use during the recent migrant operations. First they toured "Camp X-Ray," located at the end of Sherman Avenue, down the road toward the northeast gate. This site had been used as a short-term holding facility to isolate recalcitrant refugees and for Cubans who, having failed the screening process, were slated to return to Cuba. Forty primitive eight-foot-square chain-link cells remained at Camp X-Ray, catching Lehnert's attention. Years of neglect had left the cells in bad shape. Then the group proceeded to Radio Range, the largest continuous chunk of flat, developable property on the base, located over the hills and away from the heart of the naval community along the Cuban coastline. Formerly the site of some of the largest refugee camps, Radio Range retained plumbing and electrical infrastructure but little else.

In fact, Rogers and his colleagues tried to impress upon Lehnert that the place to situate a prison at Guantánamo, if at all, was Leeward Point, across the bay, away from the base population. There the JTF would enjoy freedom of movement and immediate access to the airfield in what was bound to be an "airfield mission." With no infrastructure in place on Leeward Point, Lenhert wasn't impressed. "You can't build a prison fast enough there," he told Rogers, providing a hint of what was to come. Besides, Lehnert didn't like the thought of his troops being isolated from the main naval community, including its many restaurants and recreational facilities. Leaving his chief of staff, the marine colonel William Meier, behind him, Lehnert departed Guantánamo late that day, his mind apparently made up. The next day, Christmas Eve, Rogers's phone rang yet again: "Start construction on the camp."

For Rogers and his staff, Christmas became a working holiday. All future holiday leaves, including Rogers's own, were immediately canceled. Folks already on vacation were summoned back. Even after they returned, Rogers and his crew were on "continuous mode," he remembers, "with each of us doing the work of two." As with every construction project at Guantánamo, the first task was to identify material and resources already at hand. Within minutes, Rogers embarked on the wholesale harvesting of chain-link fence from all over the base. They were soon in possession of hundreds of eight-by-eight-foot fence pallets that mirrored those used to construct the original Camp X-Ray. The size of the cells at X-Ray became the immediate object of criticism from inmates, activists, and even guards, who found them more suitable for animals than for human habitation. But the small size had nothing to do with exacting vengeance on the alleged perpetrators of 9/11. Rather, it reflected the way construction happened at Guantánamo, the new being built on top of the old with materials already at hand. "At no point," Jeff Johnston observed, "did engineers or architects grab a blank sheet of paper and say, 'Okay, where's the best place, what's the best way, to build a camp?' That's a luxury public works officials at GTMO never had."

Rogers and his crew worked away reconstituting fencing and welding "cages" amid immense pressure from the Pentagon, which called in every twelve hours to check on the status of the construction. On December 29, Rogers learned that the prisoners would arrive in two weeks. "We'll be ready," Colonel Meier assured his boss. "If necessary, we can bind detainees back-to-back, surround them in concertina wire, and guard them with M16s."

On Friday afternoon, January 11, 2002, after three weeks working at breakneck speed all the while enduring the Pentagon's constant badgering, Rogers and his crew were down on a dock of the bay celebrating the completion of 120 cells over some beers when a bus swept past escorted by military Humvees. The first detainees had arrived. Rogers was satisfied that he and his men had done the best they could with the materials at hand. Still, he knew that Camp X-Ray was inadequate to the task. For one thing, intelligence gathering would be exceedingly difficult in a setting where there was no isolating the detainees from one another, short of silencing them at gunpoint. For another, the ad hoc layout of the camp made moving detainees from cells to showers to interrogation rooms and back again inefficient, even dangerous. Moreover, the lack of basic infrastructure—of toilets in the cells, for instance, and the substitution of buckets—set the stage for future altercations between prisoners and guards. Finally, if bad for the prison population, conditions at X-Ray weren't much better for the guards. "It took nearly a month for us to get the showers running in the tent city" that housed the guard force, Rogers noted. "We knew that X-Ray sucked," Jeff Johnston allowed; "it simply didn't meet our needs." From a "mission standpoint," Rogers observed, "X-Ray was a dumb place."

So how, again, did the prison camp end up there? The answer, Rogers believes, has to do with a combination of factors. On the one hand, there was the general "arrogance" of Bush administration officials, who refused to entertain opinions different from their own. "We know what to do," said Rogers, mocking Pentagon chiefs; "now we're going to ram it down your throats."[10] On the other hand, and related to this, was a more specific desire to consolidate all aspects of national security policy in the hands of political appointees atop the Pentagon, including intelligence gathering and interrogation, formerly the province of the FBI and the CIA. To pursue intelligence as thoroughly as the Pentagon envisioned would require legal cover—finding a place where the law did not apply.[11] Sovereign territory of Cuba and hitherto ruled to be beyond the reach of federal courts, Guantánamo became the place.

But even here, as in the other ways that Guantánamo seemed like a good place to house a prison, the evidence was equivocal. Office of Legal Counsel deputy assistant attorney general John Yoo has been criticized for exemplifying the arrogant, go-it-alone style that characterized Bush administration foreign policy in the wake of 9/11, and for writing legal memos whose advocacy displaced dispassionate advice.[12] In the case of the December 28, 2001, Guantánamo memo, which Yoo describes as more like "a litigation strategy memo" than a close reading of existing law, his analysis was more cautious.[13] In this memo, while defending the constitutional immunity of Guantánamo Bay, Yoo anticipated the path by which due process and habeas corpus would make their way onto the naval base despite his own and his bosses' fervent objections.

In the Guantánamo memo, Yoo focused partly on court cases stemming from the migrant operations of the mid-1990s. The 1990s Guantánamo cases did not in fact address the question of habeas corpus (the Haitians and Cubans who passed through the base were not, formally speaking, *detainees*); rather, they were essentially debates about the applicability of due process—of the refugees' right to legal counsel. Administration officials believed that courts unwilling to grant refugees the right to counsel at Guantánamo were unlikely to extend habeas protection to al Qaeda or Taliban prisoners detained there. At stake was a cornerstone of Bush administration national security policy. "If a federal district court were to take jurisdiction over a habeas petition" emanating from Guantánamo Bay, Yoo warned Defense Department general counsel William J. Haynes, "it could review the constitutionality of the detention and the use of a military commission, the application of certain treaty provisions, and perhaps even the legal status of the al Qaeda and Taliban members."[14]

Yoo found the odds of a court assuming jurisdiction at Guantánamo unlikely. As evidence, he pointed to a Supreme Court ruling denying habeas to German agents seized and tried by American officials in China and imprisoned in Germany in the aftermath of World War II.[15] Aliens held in U.S. territory have indeed been granted habeas rights, the High Court acknowledged in *Johnson v. Eisentrager* (1950)—"presence in the country implied protection"—but such was not the issue in the case at hand, where the German prisoners remained outside U.S. "sovereign" territory, and where "the scenes of their offense, their capture, their trial and their punishment were all beyond the territorial jurisdiction of any court of the United States."[16]

Yoo assumed that the Court's logic in *Eisentrager* would apply at Guantánamo Bay, where the lease by which the United States occupied the base distinguished Cuban "sovereignty" from U.S. "jurisdiction and control."[17] Yoo conceded that the majority in *Eisentrager* appeared to conflate sovereignty and jurisdiction, possibly implying a "two-part test." But he insisted that this was not the Court's intention. The Court's meaning was unmistakable: where another country is sovereign, U.S. law does not apply. For confirmation, Yoo pointed to an earlier case affirming Cuban sovereignty at Guantánamo Bay (*Vermilya-Brown Co. v. Connell*, 1948), as well as to the more recent ruling in the Haitian and Cuban refugee cases (*Cuban American Bar Association, Inc. v. Christopher*, 1994), where the Eleventh Circuit Court of Appeals denied federal jurisdiction at Guantánamo Bay.

In making the case for Guantánamo, Yoo ignored some inconvenient facts. For example, invoking *Eisentrager* to bolster the argument against habeas jurisdiction at Guantánamo Bay, he slighted important differences between the two cases. In *Eisentrager*, for instance, the plaintiffs had been seized and tried in China and imprisoned in Germany, locations whose legal status was never in doubt and where the plaintiffs had an opportunity to defend themselves before a military commission. Compare that with a remote corner of Cuba over which the United States exercises de facto sovereignty and about which a supposedly sovereign Cuba has nothing to say, and the analogy to *Eisen-*

trager seems to wear thin. Combine this with the fact that no legal process recognized as valid anywhere on earth constrained U.S. treatment of detainees at Guantánamo Bay, and the analogy unravels.[18]

Nor was the precedent from the 1990s Guantánamo cases rock solid. Lower courts had repeatedly ruled against government assertions of a lawless Guantánamo. Though such rulings were ultimately vacated, at the very least they demonstrated an inclination among some federal magistrates to extend constitutional protections to executive actions undertaken in the absence of alternative legal recourse. According to Yoo, such meddling violated a key constitutional tenet that federal courts should steer clear of political questions unless authorized by congressional statute. The treatment of detainees was a case in point, and the president exercised authority "pursuant to the President's Commander-in-Chief and foreign affairs powers," Yoo wrote. "Without a clear statement from Congress extending jurisdiction to [Guantánamo Bay], a court should defer to the executive branch's activities and decisions prosecuting the war in Afghanistan."[19]

This is the gambit on which Yoo staked much of his legal advice in the aftermath of 9/11.[20] In the undeclared and open-ended war on terror, the president could do whatever he saw fit. "By definition, if it was authorized by the president," former national security advisor and secretary of state Condoleezza Rice told an audience in April 2009, in reference to Bush administration interrogation policy, "it did not violate our obligations under the Convention Against Torture. When the president does it, that means it is not illegal."[21] This argument makes many federal judges uneasy. Few contest the president's expanded powers in wartime, but those powers do not extend indefinitely. The president remains answerable to law.

Confident in his opinion, Yoo confessed doubt about the drift of the courts. Although "a district court cannot properly entertain an application for a writ of habeas corpus by an enemy alien detained at Guantánamo Bay Naval Base, Cuba," he argued, recent Guantánamo litigation suggested that "the issue has not been definitively resolved by the courts." Thus, Yoo cautioned Haynes, "there is some plausibility that a district court would entertain such an application."[22] Throwing caution to the wind, Haynes and his boss Defense Secretary Rumsfeld ordered prisoners brought to Guantánamo Bay early the next year.

On April 27, 2009, Condoleezza Rice defended Bush administration detention and interrogation policy in an interview at Stanford University. Asked how the United States could continue to perceive itself as a beacon of democracy in the face of evidence of torture and indefinite detention at Guantánamo Bay and elsewhere, Rice fell back on what has become a staple trope of ex–Bush administration officials. "Unless you were there in a position of authority after September 11th," Rice explained, "you cannot possibly imagine the dilemmas that you faced in trying to protect Americans." While there was lots of "second-guessing now," the only second-guessing that mattered to Rice was the hue and cry that would have ensued had thousands more Americans died "because we didn't do everything we could to protect them. If you were there in a position of authority," she continued, "and watched Americans jump out of 80-story buildings because these murderous tyrants went after innocent people, then you were determined to do anything you could that was legal to prevent that from happening again. And so I think people understand that."[23]

Rice may be right that the majority of Americans understand the dilemma of how best to defend the country against an unconventional enemy as she posed it.[24] Former top Bush administration officials continue to insist that their decision to rewrite legal codes prohibiting torture and inhumane treatment of enemy detainees was all that stood between Americans and a second terrorist attack. The historical record suggests otherwise. Criticism of Bush administration policy has not emerged only now, as Rice suggests; nor has it emanated largely from outsiders. Rather, internal opposition to the Bush administration policies was immediate and unequivocal.[25] The fact that high-ranking Bush administration officials, many of them, like Rice, new to the challenge of national security, chose to ignore the counsel of seasoned military and intelligence officials cannot make that advice go away.

If a unanimous call to protect Americans at any cost did not drive the U.S. detention and interrogation policies at Guantánamo Bay and elsewhere, what did? There are several explanations for this debacle, all of which coalesce around a politicization of national security policy at the expense of expertise. A leading authority on the history of torture maintains that torture occurs in democracies when "a national security bureaucracy overwhelms the democratic institutions that were designed to control it."[26] In this case, the reverse seems true: the torture and abuse of prisoners in U.S. custody in the wake of 9/11 is attributable to the transfer of national security policy out of the hands of seasoned military and national security experts and into the clutches of an intimate group of political ideologues.

Sometime in the first few months after 9/11, as the Bush administration cast about for novel interrogation techniques capable of softening up the most hardened terrorists, the telephone rang at the Joint Personnel Recovery Agency (JPRA) in Fort Belvoir, Virginia. On the line was William J. Haynes II, counsel to Secretary of Defense Donald Rumsfeld, who wanted to know what the agency tasked with training U.S. soldiers to resist enemy capture could teach Pentagon officials about inducing captives to talk. JPRA kept an archive of torture techniques used on American GIs by China, North Korea, and North Vietnam, among other autocratic states.[27] "Once we understood what [Haynes] was looking for," JPRA's Randy Moulton told the U.S. Senate Intelligence Committee, "we provided a . . . list of techniques."[28]

It would take these techniques the better part of a year to reach the prison at Guantánamo Bay. Meanwhile, no few senior military officials were becoming alarmed at the tenor and direction of this discussion. "We were absolutely marginalized," the retired rear admiral and navy judge advocate general Donald J. Guter lamented, in reference to his fellow judge advocates general. "I think it was intentional, because so many military JAGs spoke up about the rule of law." To Guter, there could be only one explanation for why the Bush administration sought a detention facility "outside the courts": "What they were looking for was the minimum due process that we could get away with. I felt like they knew the answer they wanted to hear."[29] Thomas Romig, Guter's army counterpart, remembered overhearing David Addington, legal counsel to Vice President Dick Cheney, warning fellow Bush administration officials not to involve Guter and Romig and their fellow JAGs in the decision-making process; they weren't "reliable." The outcome, Romig remarked, was "a disaster."[30]

The detainee-laden buses that whizzed by Norman Rogers and his construction team as it celebrated the feat of throwing up 120 prison cells in just over a fortnight was greeted at Camp X-Ray by JTF 160, a team of trained professionals from the U.S. Marine Corps base at Camp Lejeune, North Carolina, expert in the management and care of . . . *refugees*. Since the migrant operations of the 1990s, SOUTH-COM kept JTF 160 at its disposal, sending it down to Guantánamo once a year for refresher training. Though unfamiliar with Camp X-Ray, JTF 160 knew Radio Range like the back of its hand. "They were comfortable with Radio Range," Jeff Johnston explained. "They had maps and plans drawn up. They exercised annually down there, under strict review." Charged by the Pentagon to run the prison camp at Guantánamo, "SOUTHCOM defaulted to the same old pattern: they would take the plan they had in place, adapt it to the new demands, and say a prayer. Hopefully, it would work."[31]

Running a prison camp for the alleged perpetrators of 9/11 was different from running a refugee camp. It required different techniques. It also required more men than the JTF had at its disposal at Camp Lejeune. At Fort Hood, Texas, home to the Eighty-ninth Military Police Brigade, army specialist Brandon Neely discovered on the morning of January 6, 2002, that he would be deploying to a new prison facility at Guantánamo Bay. This was to be "a detainee facility, not an EPW (or Enemy Prisoner of War) camp," Neely remembered being told. Such a "detainee camp had never been run before"; "this would be the first time in history this had taken place since these people would not fall under the Geneva Convention." Due to depart for Guantánamo early the next day, Neely recalled having difficulty falling asleep that night. "I just kept thinking about what we were told that day—that we were going to come face to face with some of the worst people the world had to offer, and that these were the people who had attacked and killed so many people in our country."[32]

Though Camp X-Ray would be operational for only 110 days, it remains the iconic image from the Guantánamo detainee operation.[33] Neely first caught sight of it on the afternoon of January 7 as he and his fellow MPs made their way to that remote corner of the base. "We turned up . . . the dirt road to the tents. Off to the left you could see the sparks coming from this area where it looked like people were welding." Navy Seabees, the construction battalions under Rogers's command, were putting together the cells that would hold the detainees. Two days later Neely encountered the camp at close range. "It was like nothing I had ever seen before," he testified. "The cell—or cages as I call them—were small. 'Something like you would put a dog in,' I thought. And on top of that, it was all outdoors. Except for a small metal roof. The whole camp was rocks. No matter where you stepped you were stepping on rocks. But, 'Oh well,' I thought, 'I was not going to be staying here.'"

On January 9, 2002, forty-eight hours before the detainees were scheduled to arrive, Neely and his fellow MPs reviewed handcuffing and leg-shackling procedures. Neely had been assigned to an escort group that would be responsible for moving the detainees around the camp. The detainees "would be wearing a belt with cuffs," and the MPs would "grab the back of the belt with one hand and, with the other hand, grab their arm. Since escorting was a two-man job, one of the people escorting would force the detainee's head down while we walked so he could not see where he was going." Neely also underwent Immediate Response Force (IRF) training.[34] IRFs consisted of a group of five men, usually heavily armed, whose assignment was to overpower recalcitrant or uncooperative detainees.[35]

And that was all. Before departing Fort Hood, the MPs received no "special training for working at Guantánamo," Neely explained, and learned little or nothing about the Geneva Conventions. Indeed, at this point the relevance of the Geneva Conventions to the operation was far from clear. On the one hand, the MPs were told that the reason their own tents were rudimentary was due to Geneva's insistence that captors live no more than one step above their captives.[36] On the other hand, the MPs were told repeatedly that Geneva did not apply to this operation. The ambiguity on Geneva was compounded by a general lack of guidance about the safe and legal treatment of detainees. With the prisoners poised to arrive, no standard operating procedures (SOPs) constrained the guards' actions, Neely recalled; "we went out on a trial-and-error basis."[37]

The descriptions MPs got of their imminent charges made them indisposed to quibble over conventions of any kind. Like the U.S. public, Neely and his colleagues were told that the detainees had been "captured fighting the Americans in Afghanistan," which would prove true of less than 5 percent of the detainees.[38] The men due to arrive in a few days were "known terrorists" who had "helped in planning" the 9/11 attacks. "Our mission would be to guard these terrorists so the United States could get more info on attacks and possibly stop more terrorist attacks." If the aim of Neely's superiors was to gin up hostility among the guards, it worked. Even before the first detainee stepped off a bus at X-Ray, "a lot of us, including myself, were pissed off," Neely reported; "many people were out to get revenge for the havoc the United States had been through in recent months by these people."[39] In this the MPs only followed the example of their commander in chief, who in the immediate aftermath of 9/11 informed a group of advisors, "I don't care what the international lawyer says, we are going to kick some ass."[40]

Neely's confusion about the application of Geneva at Guantánamo emanated from on high. On the very day the first detainees arrived at the naval base, Defense Secretary Rumsfeld told reporters that the U.S. military intended "to, for the most part, treat [detainees] in a manner that is reasonably consistent with the Geneva Conventions." Journalists pressed the secretary to explain "which parts, which rights, privileges of the Geneva Convention" the detainees would be granted. "To the extent that it's reasonable, we will end up using roughly the Geneva standard," Rumsfeld replied. He hesitated to say exactly where the United States would "deviate from that or where we might exceed it." In the end, the U.S. military would "probably be on both sides of it modestly."[41]

Eight days later, Rumsfeld elevated a vague and inchoate standard of detainee treatment into official U.S. military policy. In a memo to General Richard Myers, chairman of the Joint Chiefs of Staff, Rumsfeld announced that "Combatant Commanders shall, in detaining Al Qaeda and Taliban individuals under the control of the Department of Defense, treat them humanely and, to the extent appropriate and consistent with military necessity, in a manner consistent with the principles of the Geneva Conventions of 1949."[42]

The ambiguity in Secretary Rumsfeld's orders would prove disastrous for detainees and guards alike, leaving the former defenseless and the latter vulnerable to war crimes prosecutions.[43] As Rumsfeld dodged the questions of a skeptical press, other Bush administration officials finalized the administration's policy on Geneva. Like other important legal opinions in the aftermath of 9/11, the groundbreaking document on the subject emanated from the Justice Department's Office of Legal Counsel and the person of John Yoo. On January 9, Yoo circulated a draft memorandum among national security agencies on the "Application of Treaties and Laws to al Qaeda and Taliban Detainees." The Pentagon had asked Yoo and his colleagues to answer "whether the laws of armed conflict apply to the conditions of detention and the procedures of trial of members of al Qaeda and the Taliban militia." Yoo concluded that the laws of armed conflict applied neither to al Qaeda ("a non-State actor") nor to the Taliban (rulers of a "failed state"). "Al Qaeda is merely a violent political movement or organization and not a nation-state," he wrote; hence "it is ineligible to be a signatory to any treaty." Further, "the novel nature of this conflict" made it doubtful "al Qaeda would be included in non-international forms of armed conflict to which some provisions of the Geneva Conventions might apply. Therefore, neither the Geneva Conventions nor the WCA [the War Crimes Act, the US law affecting Geneva] regulate the detention of al Qaeda prisoners captured during the Afghanistan conflict."

Nor could a "failed state" such as Afghanistan under Taliban rule trigger the Geneva Conventions, according to Yoo. The Taliban militia was no more "entitled to enemy POW status" under the Geneva Conventions "than al Qaeda itself." Furthermore, Yoo proceeded, even if Afghanistan were technically a functioning state, "the President has the constitutional authority to suspend our treaties with Afghanistan pending the restoration of a legitimate government capable of performing Afghanistan's treaty obligations." Besides, evidence suggested that the Taliban was so "intertwined with al Qaeda as to be functionally indistinguishable from it." This gave the Taliban more in common with an NGO "that used military force to pursue its religious and political ideology" than with a "functioning government."

Finally, Yoo addressed the question of whether the president was bound by so-called customary international law of armed conflict in his treatment of enemy detainees. Customary international law consists of broadly held, often unwritten norms and conventions—against torture, for instance. Yoo concluded that such law "does not bind or restrict the actions of the United States military, because it does not constitute federal law recognized under the Supremacy Clause of the Constitution." And yet, though customary international law did not bind the president, he retained the "constitutional authority as Commander-in-Chief to interpret and apply the customary or common laws of war in such a way that they would extend to the conduct of members of both al Qaeda and the Taliban, and also to the conduct of the U.S. Armed Forces towards members of those groups taken as prisoners in Afghanistan." Hitherto widely held to be binding on all parties (including U.S. presidents) at all times in all contexts, the customary international law of armed conflict became, according to Yoo, an instrument available to the U.S. president at his discretion.[44]

Yoo insisted that his Geneva memo was intended to clarify the conditions of detainee confinement rather than authorize abusive interrogation techniques, but that is not how many Bush administration officials interpreted it.[45] On January 11, just as the detainees arrived at Guantánamo, and as Rumsfeld parsed the fine points of detainee treatment before the press, William H. Taft IV, legal advisor to Secretary of State Colin Powell, wrote Yoo a note arguing that the memo was wrong on all scores.[46] Some of Yoo's mistakes were sophomoric. "The draft memorandum badly confuses the distinction between states and governments in the operation of treaties," Taft wrote. Failed states did not cease to be parties to treaties. Yoo's argument was "contrary to the official position of the United States, the United Nations and all other states that have considered the issue." Nor was Yoo correct that the president could simply suspend U.S. obligations under Geneva—a notion both "legally flawed and procedurally impossible at this stage." Finally, in claiming that nothing in the U.S. Constitution bound the president to abide by customary international law, Yoo ignored the very existence of international law itself.

This last mistake exposed Yoo's larger aim. "John," Taft wrote, "I understand you have long been convinced that treaties and customary international law have from time to time been cited inappropriately to circumscribe the President's constitutional authority or pre-empt the Congress's exercise of legislative power." Similarly, Taft understood Yoo's "desire to identify legal authority establishing the right of the United States to treat the members of the Taliban Militia in the way it thinks best." Taft himself shared Yoo's sentiment in both regards. Still, Taft could not endorse Yoo's conclusion to the president or secretary of state.

Two weeks later, David Addington, legal counsel to Vice President Cheney, would argue in a memo signed by White House counsel Alberto Gonzalez that the war on terror constituted a "new paradigm" in international relations, calling for new policies and procedures unanticipated by Geneva. In his response to Yoo, Taft anticipated this argument and flatly rejected it. "In previous conflicts," he noted, "the United States has dealt with tens of thousands of detainees without repudiating its obligations under the Conventions. I have no doubt we can do so here, where a relative handful of persons is involved." Cutting straight to the heart of the matter, Taft insisted that "only the utmost confidence in our legal arguments could . . . justify deviating from the United States' unbroken record of compliance with the Geneva Conventions in our conduct of military operations over the past fifty years." Yoo's legal analysis—"actually incorrect as well as incomplete"—scarcely amounted to that. "We should talk," Taft concluded, as if summoning an errant student to his office.[47]

Taft was hardly the first to push back against the Office of Legal Counsel rulings in the wake of 9/11. One colleague described Yoo's October 23, 2001, memo authorizing the domestic terrorist surveillance program as "weak" and "sloppy" and blind to relevant questions of law.[48] To Thomas Romig, Yoo's proposals on the subject of future military commissions would return the country to the days of "the Indian Wars. I looked at him and said, 'You know, that was 100-and-something years ago. You're out of your mind; we're talking about the law.'" Romig felt that high-level Bush administration officials regarded the concept of due process as so much "mumbo jumbo." For over a year, Romig struggled to haul national security policy in line with the law, before finally being told "the time for law has passed," that it was time "to take the gloves off."[49]

In defending his Geneva and subsequent memos, Yoo argues that it is wrong to confuse the legal rulings that issued from the Office of Legal Counsel with policy. The administration had asked the Justice Department for a reading of the law, and he and his colleagues had responded accordingly. The administration did not have to adopt those rulings as policy, Yoo insists. During the Korean and Vietnam wars, for example, the United States extended Geneva protections to combatants fighting for sides that had not signed the Geneva protocols. The Bush administration could have chosen to do so again. It had not. Yoo says that he made this point to Taft himself a few days after receiving Taft's dissent at a meeting in the White House Situation Room. "Oh," Yoo remembers Taft responding with relief, "good."[50]

Down at Guantánamo, Brandon Neely and his fellow prison guards viewed the ambiguity about whether Guantánamo applied as a license to "get some": to "inflict pain" and "get revenge."[51] Neely remembers the detainees' arrival that Friday afternoon in great detail. "Everyone," he reports, "including myself, was very nervous. We did not know when or how many detainees would be arriving that day to Camp X-Ray." After hours of anticipation, Neely learned that "the detainees were at the air strip" across the bay on Leeward Point, and that they were "being loaded up to bring to the camp." Neely started getting really nervous, almost scared. "Here it comes," he thought. "I am fixing to see what a terrorist looks like face-to-face." Neely's escort partner was as nervous as he. Indeed, "everybody in the camp that day was nervous and scared; you could literally hear a pin drop moments before that bus full of detainees arrived."

Led by "Marine humvees with .50 caliber guns mounted on them," the bus carrying the detainees pulled up to the gate. Upon contact, the MPs exorcised their anxiety on the detainees. "You could hear the Marines screaming at them 'Shut the fuck up! You're property of the United States of America now,'" Neely remembers. As an escort, Neely stood near the doors of the bus as one detainee after another was pushed down the stairs and into the grip of awaiting MPs. "The first person who got off the bus, I will never forget. It was a man with one leg. He was later called Stumpy by everyone." A short but heavy man, Stumpy hopped forward on one leg as MPs hollered at him to pick up the pace. The second thing off the bus was the detainee's prosthetic leg, which was casually tossed onto the ground. The detainees' attire is now the stuff of legend. "The prisoners arrived in orange suits. Some had orange ski caps. They had goggles on their eyes, earmuffs on their ears, surgical masks on their faces, and black gloves on their arms. They were hand-cuffed and leg-shackled. They had chains around their waists and a padlock on the back. The handcuffs were attached to the waist chain."

The manner of the detainees' transfer to Guantánamo Bay had been a cause of some concern among journalists and human rights officials. As early as January 3, Secretary Rumsfeld fielded questions on "the delicate, difficult, problem of transporting" the detainees from Afghanistan to Guantánamo Bay. "It's a long way," Rumsfeld conceded. "It's one of the disadvantages." The task would have to be carried out "very, very carefully," as "every time people have messed with these folks, they've gotten in trouble." These were, after all, "very well trained" and "hardened" men, "willing to give up their lives in many instances." US military officials would do their "best," using "the necessary amount of constraint so that those individuals do not kill Americans in trans-port or in Guantánamo Bay." Acknowledging the immensity of the task at hand, one reporter asked if the Defense Department had consid-ered using U.S. marshals, who had "tremendous experience" in escorting dangerous prisoners. "I have not addressed that," Rumsfeld confessed; he assumed that "military personnel" would handle the job.

A series of recent books argue that the torture and abuse that made Guantánamo and Abu Ghraib notorious was introduced at Guantánamo in autumn 2002 and then migrated to Iraq as part of a top-down, sys-tematic attempt on the part of high-level Bush administration officials to adjust interrogation techniques to meet the challenges of an unprec-edented enemy. If true, this cuts against the grain of the last century of modern torture history, which suggests that torture spreads horizontally rather than vertically as interrogators "pass on techniques . . . through low-level transmission between ordinary soldiers and policemen or by means of simple imitation on the job."[52] Such was the case during the Vietnam War, for instance, where the torture carried out by U.S. military interrogators proceeded without the authority (and perhaps even the knowledge) of top U.S. officials.[53] In fact, evidence from Brandon Neely and many others suggests that torture spread both ways at Guantánamo Bay. The abuse and torture of detainees in U.S. custody began long before General Geoffrey Miller showed up at Guantánamo Bay. It began with the first detentions of suspected al Qaeda and Taliban in places such as Kandahar and Bagram, Afghanistan, and migrated along with the detainees to the naval base at Guantánamo Bay.[54] Like Neely, soldiers in Afghanistan reported receiving "no specific training on the treatment of detainees"; rather, detainees "relied on their common knowledge in this area," employing "techniques they literally remembered from the movies." Expertise was a luxury circumstances didn't allow; there were simply "too many interrogations and not enough interrogators."[55]

Beginning in late January 2002, Secretary of State Rumsfeld became agitated at the lack of actionable intelligence emanating from Guantánamo Bay. With each passing day, the prospect of attaining useful information became attenuated. By mid-February it was obvious that Joint Task Force 160, which had been charged with overseeing the detention facility, was not up to the more critical task of obtaining information. On February 16 Rumsfeld commissioned JTF 170 to run the intelligence operation.[56] To lead JTF 170 the Pentagon selected Major General Michael Dunlavey, a man closely allied with Rumsfeld and other high-ranking Bush administration officials and whom one colleague described as "a tyrant and a strong Republican."[57]

Dunlavey's arrival in early March, together with Michael Lehnert's departure at the end of the month, signaled a change in emphasis at Guantánamo from detention to interrogation. From the first interrogations at Camp X-Ray, Lehnert had been concerned about the potential for detainee abuse. This concern mounted over the course of his over-lapping month with Dunlavey, when Dunlavey approached Lehnert with a list of proposed techniques designed to coerce detainees to talk.[58] Brandon Neely remembers becoming skeptical that many de-tainees were guilty of anything besides being in the wrong place at the wrong time.[59] By May even Dunlavey came to realize that many de-tainees weren't talking because they had nothing to say. When he took this message to Pentagon officials, he was informed that there would be no returning detainees to their home country; the interrogations should proceed.[60]

In June 2002 an alert FBI agent matched a fingerprint belonging to the supposed "twentieth hijacker," turned away by immigration offi-cials at the Orlando airport in August 2001, with that of a Saudi citizen named Mohammed al-Qahtani, picked up in Afghanistan in Decem-ber 2001 and held at Guantánamo Bay. To interrogate al-Qahtani, the FBI dispatched to Guantánamo a senior agent fluid in Arabic and knowledgeable about al Qaeda. Over the course of the next several months, using conventional rapport-building techniques, the agent got al-Qahtani to talk. Al-Qahtani confessed to attending an al Qaeda training session with several of the other hijackers, and to intending to join the 9/11 attacks. But that is about all he had to say, leaving some U.S. officials convinced that he must be hiding something. A conver-sation ensued: "There were lots of suggestions in August about what to do," Dunlavey remembered. "There were many 'brilliant ideas,' but the difficulty was that military interrogators were trained to interrogate militarily. . . . The opinion was that with more effective techniques we could make this work."[61]

Thus accelerated the hunt initially begun in the autumn of 2001 for what would become known as "enhanced interrogation" tech-niques, and the legal justification for implementing them. Bush ad-ministration officials continue to insist that these techniques bubbled up from the ranks. But evidence suggests they emanated directly downward from the White House and the Pentagon.[62] It was around this time that John Yoo sprang to action once more, authoring perhaps the most notorious of all his legal memorandums. Dated August 1, 2002, the so-called Torture Memo redefined torture to suit the policy of the Bush administration and to ensure that members of the administration who authorized or carried out torture would not be prosecutable under the War Crimes Act. "We conclude that torture as defined in and proscribed by Sections 2340-2340A, covers only extreme acts," Yoo wrote. "Severe pain is generally of the kind difficult for the victim to endure. Where the pain is physical, it must be of an intensity akin to that which accompanies serious physical injury such as death or organ failure." By this logic, detainees hung from meat hooks at Kandahar did not suffer torture. "Severe mental pain requires suffering not just at the moment of infliction but it also requires lasting psychological harm, such as seen in mental disorders like post-traumatic stress disorder. Additionally, such severe mental pain can arise only from the predicate acts listed in Section 2340. Because the acts inflicting torture are extreme, there is [a] significant range of acts that though they might constitute cruel, inhuman, or degrading treatment or punishment fail to rise to the level of torture." Yoo finished with a familiar refrain: if the president says an interrogation technique is necessary, it is not torture. He is the commander in chief.[63]

Exposed in the late spring of 2004, the Torture Memo was roundly repudiated. One legal scholar described it as "simply made of whole cloth. Well, not even. There's no cloth there at all. It is completely unsupported by, and contrary to, the plain words and structure of the [torture] statute." Another compared it to "discredited legal theories used by Latin American countries" to justify repression. Yoo's former teacher the Yale professor Harold Koh called the memo "perhaps the most clearly erroneous legal opinion I have ever read." Another critic simply dismissed it as a "disgrace." Yet another found that "it falls far below the minimum standards of professional competence." Conservatives chimed in as well as liberals. The conservative legal scholar Ruth Wedgwood observed that the memo called to mind "the 14th century, when an outlaw was treated like a wild beast."[64] With every additional memo, army judge advocate general Thomas Romig remarked, Yoo seemed to be moving the nation back in time.

Armed with the August 1 memo defining torture as something Americans would never do, David Addington, Alberto Gonzales, Jim Haynes, and the CIA lawyer John Rizzo flew down to Guantánamo in late

September 2002 to speak to personnel in charge of interrogating al-Qahtani. There they consulted with Dunlavey and JTF counsel Diane Beaver about how to induce al-Qahtani to talk.[65] Within a few months, and after an organizational review that unified the Guantánamo detention and interrogation commands under the command of General Geoffrey Miller, interrogators at the prison had a list of eighteen "enhanced interrogation" techniques approved by the Pentagon for use on al-Qahtani.[66] The interrogation log, publicly available, reveals that over the course of the next fifty-five days, al-Qahtani was systematically broken down. Among other things, he endured twenty-hour interrogations, forced shaving, forced nudity in the presence of a female, and various forms of sexual taunting and humiliation by a female, including straddling and rubbing. He was made to perform dog tricks, put in stress positions for prolonged periods of time, accused of homosexuality, made to wear women's underwear on his head, forced to pray before an "idol" shrine, told that his mother and sister were whores, shown pornographic pictures, made to dance with a male interrogator, told that other detainees would be told that he became aroused when searched by male guards, and threatened by military dogs.[67] "We tortured al-Qahtani," Susan Crawford, convening authority for the Office of Guantánamo Military Commissions, would later acknowledge. "His treatment met the legal definition of torture. And that's why I did not refer" al-Qahtani for prosecution.[68]

At Bagram air base in December 2002, two suspected terrorists were so violently kicked, punched, and slammed by U.S. soldiers that their muscle tissue disintegrated.[69] At Guantánamo Bay that same month, al-Qahtani's interrogation log suggests that his psyche underwent an analogous fate. What did this treatment accomplish? In June 2004, Gonzales, Haynes, and Haynes's deputy, Daniel Dell'Orto, told a press conference that the enhanced interrogation techniques used on al-Qahtani (and later others) had worked to elicit crucial intelligence and keep the nation safe. It is too generous to call this claim misleading. The only valuable information al-Qahtani divulged came from the FBI interrogation that preceded the deployment of the new techniques.[70]

———

By the time the detainees arrived at Guantánamo in January 2002, construction was already under way on a more permanent camp out on Radio Range, site of a large refugee camp from the mid-1990s, where sewer, water, and electrical lines were already in place. At this time in the Afghan war, the Bush administration did not intend to run a long-term prison operation at Guantánamo Bay. Norman Rogers was ordered to make the first three compounds of what became known as Camp Delta out of shipping containers, thereby ensuring their portability. Camps 1, 2, and 3, as the Delta units were called, were no less "half-assed" than X-Ray, Rogers remarked. SOUTHCOM intended to use Camp Delta "just long enough to build a real brick and mortar prison over on Leeward," Jeffrey Johnston explained, referring to the less-developed side of the naval base. By the time Johnston departed SOUTHCOM for a three-year stint in Barstow, California, "we had a master plan and pretty pictures that included not only prisons but a courthouse, housing, recreational facilities and all kinds of new development." Just as Rogers had originally predicted, the JTF did not like combining a detention mission with the everyday activities of the Guantánamo community. On the Windward Passage side of the base, "detainees in transport were treated like hothouse flowers." When detainees were on the move, all everyday activities came to an immediate halt.

But, like Guantánamo projects extending all the way back to those proposed by Spain's Mopox Commission over two centuries earlier, Leeward Prison "was a great plan not funded." Granted the money to construct a single "brick and mortar" prison at Leeward, General Geoffrey Miller declined. "On this the much-criticized Miller was spot-on," Jeff Johnston observes. "He didn't want to get stuck with half his operations at Windward and half at Leeward. So he built what became Camp 5 on Radio Range."[71] And there the prison has remained.

Brandon Neely left Guantánamo in midsummer 2002, several months before the enhanced interrogation techniques were deployed on al-Qahtani. Muslim chaplain James Yee, a native of Seattle, Washington, arrived at Guantánamo in November, just as the new techniques were being finalized. His precise role in the detention operation was less than clear, and right away Yee felt uneasy. Some of his uneasiness stemmed from the ambiguity about the Geneva Convention that

Neely himself noted. The president's announcement that Geneva would apply to detainees "to the extent allowed by military necessity" afforded the administration considerable "flexibility," Yee recognized. "One could argue that everything happening at the facility could be considered an act of military necessity."[72]

Geneva mandated that prisoners receive religious support, but if Geneva didn't apply at Guantánamo, what did this mean for Yee's mission? "It seemed I was here to do something that was not wholly supported," Yee remembers thinking. Was the point of assigning a Muslim chaplain to Guantánamo simply to give the world the impression that the United States was abiding by the dictates of Geneva? Yee's misgiving was exaggerated by the absence of clear marching orders. His predecessor at the prison cautioned that there was a notable absence of standard operating procedures "for the chaplain's operation inside the wire, nor is there a job description outlining the Muslim chaplain's duties and responsibilities." To compound matters, his predecessor warned Yee that Guantánamo was "not a friendly environment for Muslims, and I don't just mean prisoners." Sharing the detainees' religion and language automatically made the Muslim chaplains suspicious in the eyes of many GIs. In time, Yee would come to realize that the Muslim chaplains were as scrutinized as the detainees themselves. "We called the people watching us the 'secret squirrels,'" he noted. "We never knew who exactly they were."[73]

Yee's first encounter with Camp Delta left a strong impression. Like Neely, Yee thought initially of animals as he headed into his first block. "I had the distinct feeling of walking into an outdoor stall," he recalled. "The prisoners were held in two long rows facing each other across a narrow corridor. The cages were open-air and there was a tin roof overhead that trapped and baked the air." It smelled "like a locker room." There was no air-conditioning, no circulation. "At Camp Delta, the cages measured eight feet by six feet and the prisoners shared a mesh wall with two prisoners on each side and were in plain view of the detainee in the cage across the corridor." There was no privacy, and in an awkward moment, Yee met eyes with one of the detainees squatted in the corner of a cell and started to say a greeting before realizing "that he was using the toilet."[74]

When Yee arrived at the camp, detainees were allowed out of their "cages" for a quarter hour, every three days. Allowed "out" meant having access to a small pen less than two hundred square feet, into which the guards sometimes tossed a soccer ball. Bathing opportunities were limited to the detainees' day out. Religion was really all the prisoners had. And this is where Yee came in. The detainees were desperate to talk to him, and not just about religion, but about their innocence. Like Neely, it didn't take long before Yee began to question the accusations against some of the detainees in particular. Take the case of Omar Khadr, for instance, the fifteen-year-old Canadian citizen Yee first encountered with "a Disney book" in his hand, provided him by the detainee library. In the face of skepticism about the detainees' culpability, Guantánamo officials routinely point to an al Qaeda training manual known as the Manchester Document (found among the belongings of a terrorist cell in Manchester, England), which advises members, should they be detained by enemy governments, to make a claim of innocence. To Yee, the existence of the Manchester Document was inconclusive, to say the least. "Perhaps the act of steadfastly claiming innocence was a practiced al Qaeda strategy," he remarked, "but it would also be the response of an innocent person. How were these prisoners to prove their innocence if the act of seeming innocent was deemed a measure of their guilt?"[75]

Yee's testimony suggests that the systemic abuse Brandon Neely reported early on at Camp X-Ray overlapped with the initiation of the systematic torture of al-Qahtani and other Guantánamo detainees. With scarcely any degree of agency left to confirm their humanity, some of the detainees hurled insults at the guards (along with water, spit, urine, and feces). By the time Yee arrived, standard operating procedures enacted by the military dictated that guards not retaliate precipitously to detainee abuse. The SOPs were rarely followed. "General Miller had a saying that he'd often recite to guards when visiting Camp Delta," Yee recalled, "or whenever seeing troopers around the base. 'The fight is on!'" Miller would holler out—"a subtle way of saying that rules regarding the treatment of detainees were relaxed and infractions were easily overlooked." Just as he intended, Miller's remarks "pumped up" the guards, and many headed off to work "looking for trouble."

Cruelty took many forms at Guantánamo. As Immediate Response

Force beatings mounted over the course of the first six months, Yee made a point of visiting the detainee hospital. In one wing of the hospital not frequented by politicians and the press, Yee witnessed the force-feeding of a hunger striker reduced to eighty pounds. As one male nurse restrained the detainee, "another globbed petroleum jelly up his nose." The detainee's "screams could be heard throughout the hospital." On another visit to the hospital, the detainee engaged Yee. "Why am I here, Chaplain? This is no use. I've told them everything, and they keep asking the same questions. What more do they want?"[76]

Over the ensuing months, Yee's relationship to the MPs, never warm, deteriorated. He recognized that their job was very difficult and their preparation (like his own) inadequate.[77] But he also found it impossible to conceal his disapproval of the harassment to which the detainees were constantly subjected by the guards. His disapproval of the guards, in turn, was met by growing suspicion that he was on the wrong side. MPs began to follow him around the blocks, in violation of SOPs and despite his outranking them.[78]

Most of Yee's colleagues at Guantánamo were strikingly ignorant of Islam and disdainful of the elements they knew. MPs used this ignorance to their advantage, and seemed to delight in offending the detainees' beliefs. One thing both the guards and the intelligence staff knew well, however, was the strictures in Islam against inappropriate contact with women. These the U.S. military studiously exploited. "Female guards were often used to provoke the detainees," Yee noted. "Knowing that physical contact between unrelated men and women is not allowed under Islamic law, the female MPs would be exceptionally inappropriate in how they patted down the prisoners and how they touched them on the way to the showers or recreation."

Australian detainee David Hicks reported that he was offered prostitutes in exchange for intelligence. Yee couldn't confirm the presence of prostitutes at Camp Delta, but fellow interpreters described female interrogators disrobing during questioning of detainees. "One was particularly notorious and would pretend to masturbate in front of detainees. She was also known to touch them in a sexual way and make them rub her breasts and genitalia," while guards stood behind the prisoners, forcing them to watch. "Detainees who refused were kicked and beaten." U.S. officials' abuse of religion itself was no less pornographic.

One detainee described to Yee a ritual in which "prisoners were forced to sit in the center of a satanic circle drawn on the floor of an interrogation room. Lit candles outlined the circle and the prisoners were ordered to bow down and prostrate" themselves in the center. Then "interrogators shouted at the detainees, 'Satan is your God, not Allah! Repeat that after me!'"

In the several investigations the U.S. military has conducted of itself at Guantánamo Bay, it has conceded an incident or two in which a Qur'an was accidentally mistreated, after which rioting ensued. Yee testifies that the mistreatment of Qur'ans was a regular feature at Camp Delta. One particularly egregious incident set off a mass suicide attempt. Continued mistreatment of the Qur'an prompted the detainees themselves to propose a solution: we'll surrender our Qur'ans to you, so long as you cease abusing them. Not allowed; every cell must have a Qur'an. New SOPs authored by Yee specifically to end the abuse did little. Guards warned not to touch the Qur'ans themselves delighted in knocking the Qur'an stands to the ground.[79]

Yee's Sisyphean task to help the U.S. military distinguish between Muslim beliefs, on the one hand, and acts carried out by a few Muslim criminals, on the other, is perhaps best symbolized by an incident in which a staff member in the local chaplain's office approached him concerning an article about to come out in the next JTF newsletter. Produced by an outfit called the Servants of the Persecuted Church, the article told the story of an "Egyptian Muslim" named "Mohammed Farouk." Now, Farouk "hated Christmas," and "in an attempt to obey the Koran and please Allah," he and some friends "began to assault and harass Christians in their village." The group then "broke into Christian businesses, robbing, and vandalizing them," and so on. When Yee took this to the head chaplain, noting its violation of army regulations prohibiting religious intolerance, the chaplain agreed to withhold the newsletter's distribution, but only after checking first if indeed the Qur'an ordered the murder of all Christians.[80]

Yee's account of life at Guantánamo is corroborated by the linguist Erik Saar. An Arab-speaking sergeant in the U.S. Army, Saar was a graduate of the Defense Language Institute assigned to Guantánamo in December 2002 to assist the intelligence operation. Like Yee, Saar found himself underprepared for the assignment he'd been given, and surrounded by colleagues no more adequately prepared.[81] Like Yee, Saar found his first encounter with the MPs inauspicious, and his impression of MP treatment of detainees grew worse over time.[82] "The MPs just thought the detainees were treated too well," Saar remarked; "they were terrorists, responsible for 9/11, and their lives should be miserable."[83] In general, Saar found the MPs hostile to interrogators and linguists alike. Where the first were "screwing up the mission," ostensibly by constraining the punishments MPs could inflict on detainees, the linguists earned the MPs' undying enmity for talking to detainees. "What the fuck is wrong with you," Saar was asked; "are you one of them detainee lovers?"[84]

In many instances MPs were simply instituting the will of their commanders. "Always remember," Saar heard one lieutenant colonel tell his charges, "you guys should feel privileged to be here guarding this scum. These men are the worst of the worst. This place is reserved for those terrorists who either helped 9/11 or were planning future attacks against us when they were apprehended."[85] One didn't have to be a Muslim to worry about detainees who returned from interrogations with "a defeated look," their "head held low," their "eyes lifeless." After particularly "tough interrogations," some simply "huddled in a fetal position in the corner of their cells, staring off into space or even quietly crying."[86]

Saar, too, had a keen eye for the absurdity of detainee operations. After the suicide attempts, the camp assigned a "psych tech" to keep an eye on disconsolate detainees. "Do you feel hopeless?" one technician asked a detainee before moving on. "Seemed to me," Saar observed, "that asking these men if they were feeling hopeless was a little absurd, given their situation." Wasn't that exactly what interrogators "wanted them to feel? It was a little ridiculous that the psych team was trying to conduct damage control for everything the interrogators were trying to do, and I found that, in fact, there were certain detainees the psych techs didn't see because the interrogators wanted those guys depressed and dejected."[87]

No less absurd was the spectacle of forced inoculations. Unsurprisingly, detainees were hesitant to accept shots and medicine from U.S. personnel. "They think we're going to kill them," Saar explained to a psych tech sent to oversee one particular operation. After witnessing an IRF team brutalize an intransigent detainee, Saar remarked to himself, "There was something nonsensical about all this, of course. American soldiers on a tropical island brutally suppressing a man captured in the Global War on Terror—all for the sake of protecting him from the flu."[88]

As Saar became increasingly alarmed by the abuse he witnessed at Camp Delta, he found himself hoping that at least it was paying off. Running into a fellow linguist assigned to the interrogation group, Saar allowed that he hoped that this was all leading to a rich harvest of intelligence. "Maybe in the interrogations I'm not in," came the response.[89] Saar would get a chance to see the interrogation operation himself soon enough. Transferred from the Detainee Operations Group to the Detainee Intelligence Group, he immediately became aware of turf wars between military intelligence and the FBI. He overheard one military interrogator, grown tired of watching for weeks as an FBI agent deployed conventional rapport-building techniques with a detainee, remark, "Those goddamn agents sit in chairs across the table and talk to the guy all night like they were chatting with their best friend." One of the agents was actually growing a beard to demonstrate empathy with a detainee. "When are we going to get our hands on that bastard, sir?" the military intelligence official asked his boss.[90]

One of the first things Saar noticed upon transferring to the intelligence-gathering group was the marked discrepancy in training between the FBI officials, often with years of experience, and the military intelligence officials, often inexperienced and inadequately trained. Inscrutably, General Miller claimed the advantage in this contest went to the inexperienced. In "this testing lab in the global war on terror," Miller told journalists, "intelligence is a young person's game."[91]

The more Saar learned of the intelligence harvesting, the less the whole Guantánamo operation made sense to him. As commanders continued to insist that Guantánamo was yielding first-rate evidence that was saving people's lives, the whole detention operation came to seem like "a Potemkin village"—those "elaborate fake towns the eighteenth-century Russian field marshal rushed to build when Catherine the Great toured her empire." The military regularly carried out fake interrogations for visiting VIPs. "A façade would go up, like a set in an old movie. We'd put on quite a show—the camp's leadership had these events down to a science." In the days approaching an important visit, Saar recalled, the intelligence group would receive the itinerary and set to work. "My commanders staged the production carefully," Saar wrote. "A flurry of emails went back and forth among the JIG [Joint Intelligence Group] staff members about which detainee to schedule for these observations and what to ask him." Choosing a co-operative detainee, the interrogator "would simply go back over the material covered with him previously. A foolproof recipe for faux inter-rogations and the VIPs were none the wiser."[92] Politicians as well as investigative teams regularly returned from Guantánamo touting the treatment of detainees, especially the food and medical care, and downplaying the overwhelming evidence of torture and abuse.[93]

The deception of those outside Guantánamo Bay was matched by internal indirection. In February 2003 the intelligence community at Guantánamo Bay was summoned to a meeting presided over by a JAG lawyer whose job it was to update the staff on the detainees' status vis-à-vis the Geneva Conventions. The meeting had a peculiar feel, Saar remembered. The previous year, President Bush had vowed to abide by the Geneva protocols, where *appropriate and consistent with military necessity*, despite the fact that neither al Qaeda nor the Taliban qualified for Geneva protections. This, apparently, was changing. While offering nothing new, the visiting JAG officer took pains to re-view the administration's rationale. "This meeting was an explainer, and the military doesn't do explainers," Saar thought at the time. The administration "clearly felt" the issue "dicey enough that they had to stoop to providing us with some reasons, such as they were." Reasons for what? The closest the head of the Guantánamo intelligence opera-tion would come to saying it outright was this: "We still intend to treat the detainees humanely, but our purpose is to get any actionable intel-ligence we can, and quickly."[94]

In the ensuing weeks and months, the interrogations at Guan-tánamo grew rougher. Upon first transferring from the Operations to the intelligence group, Saar heard news of the techniques loosed on al-Qahtani. The problem with these new techniques, he recognized, was that "nobody had any experience with them. In the army you're trained for every event. No detail is too minor. Training, in fact, is all the army does when it isn't actually at war." Having long relied on the guidelines of the *Army Field Manual*, army interrogators were now being asked to disregard not only its rules but also its overarching philosophy: "Torture doesn't work, and in fact produces less reliable information because it has a tendency to induce victims to lie. Interrogators were taught that if they were skilled, they could get all the information they needed without going too far."[95]

The interrogations Saar participated in as a linguist confirmed the wisdom of the *Army Field Manual*. The premise behind the move to enhanced interrogation techniques was that conventional interrogation took time, and that the United States did not have the luxury of time in the war on terror. Violence does not speed up the harvest of intelligence, Saar suggests. On the contrary, it brings interrogation to a standstill. Saar contrasted an interrogation he witnessed by a CIA agent, who studiously "built a bridge" to a detainee, ending an interrogation session after two hours and promising to return and continue the session the next week, to that of a Defense Department interrogator, who relied on stress positions and uncomfortably cool room temperatures to soften up a detainee in advance of the interrogation. Where the CIA agent began her session by remarking, "I understand you speak some Spanish. Do you want me to talk to you in Spanish or would you rather we use Arabic?" her Defense Department colleague opened his interrogation with a curt "Are you going to cooperate with me tonight?" The outcome of the Defense Department interrogation seems preordained. As the detainee sat mutely, the interrogator became more and more frustrated and irate, before finally calling "the detainee a liar and every obscenity in the book."[96]

By April 2003, Saar was hearing more and more interrogators talking about "turning up the heat" on detainees. The expression had sexual as well as purely violent overtones, and Saar was present at a notable incident of sexual humiliation. One evening, a female army interrogator asked Saar to take the place of a Muslim colleague who she didn't think "would enjoy taking part in this one." The detainee they would be interrogating was "a piece of shit," Saar was told, and they "might have to turn things up a bit." The detainee in question was suspected of taking flight lessons, and had stopped cooperating with other intelligence agents. "I'm starting to take shit from above because he's not talking," the interrogator told Saar. "We need to try something new tonight."

The key to breaking this detainee, the agent concluded, was to alienate him from his Muslim religion, by which he seemed to be maintaining his strength. "We've gotta find a way to break that, and I'm thinking that humiliation may be the way to go. I just need to make him feel that he absolutely must cooperate with me and has no other options. I think we should make him feel so fucking dirty that he can't go back to his cell and spend the night praying. We have to put up a barrier between him and God."

When Saar arrived in the interrogation room, he found the detainee "short chained" by ankles and wrists to a metal ring on the floor, leaving him hunched over in an awkward position. Short-chaining may have been just the thing for a conventional roughing-up, but that is not what Saar's colleague had in mind on this night. She ordered the guards to seat the detainee in a chair, which would put his head about level with her waist. Then she began a striptease. "To my surprise," Saar wrote, "she started to unbutton her top slowly, teasingly, almost like a stripper, revealing a skin-tight brown army T-shirt stretching over her chest." Taunting him throughout, she circled behind him, "rubbing her breasts against his back." The taunting continued: "Do you like these big American tits, Fareek? I can see you are starting to get hard. How do you think Allah feels about this?" Sitting in front of him, the interrogator grabbed her breasts and asked him, "Don't you like big tits?" prompting him to look away. The script practically writes itself. "Are you gay?" she asked him when he averted his eyes.

Predictably, when this treatment did not induce the detainee to talk, the interrogator turned up the heat still more. The way to make a Muslim man feel too dirty to appeal to God, a Muslim colleague had informed her, was to touch him with what appeared to be menstrual blood. Braced by this suggestion, the interrogator returned to the room, repeated her banter with the detainee, then stood up, unbuttoned her pants, and informed him that she was having her period. She then circled behind him, touching him as if with menstrual blood. Returning to face him head-on, she removed her hands from her pants, revealing what looked like real blood on them, and wiped them on his cheek. "Who told you to learn to fly, Fareek? You fuck." At this point, the detainee screamed, spat, lunged, and struggled vainly to extricate himself from the chair. Summoned to the room, the MPs shackled the detainee to the floor, where he lay crying "like a baby, sobbing and mumbling in Arabic too distinct for me to understand," Saar remembered. "The only thing I picked out was, 'You American whore.'"[97]

The outside world was slow to comprehend the abuse and torture of detainees at Guantánamo Bay. "My gut tells me that the military is being very scrupulous," Human Rights Watch's Tom Malinowski remarked in June 2002. "Law enforcement professionals in this country understand that torture is a wonderful technique for getting confessions from innocent people and a lousy technique for getting truth out of guilty people."[98] Later that fall, *The New York Times* seemed to take at face value statements by Guantánamo officials that all was hunky-dory in the camps. "I don't want the U.S. Naval Base, Guantánamo Bay, to be viewed in a sense as anything unfair, brutal, human rights violations," Guantánamo commander Captain Robert A. Buehn remarked. "Certainly, that's not what's going on here." Similarly, General Rick Baccus, who replaced Michael Dulavey in April 2002, insisted that, "while the public debates the technicalities of how these people should be classified, we will continue to follow the traditions of humane treatment. In other countries, these detainees would not be heard from again."[99] The upbeat reports continued through the middle of the following year. While criticizing the legal limbo in which detainees found themselves in March 2003, the *Times* assured readers that there were "no credible reports of abuse or substantiated complaints about the physical conditions of detainees." The following May the paper announced that "all reports . . . indicate that prisoners have not been physically mistreated."[100]

Meanwhile, up in Washington, career intelligence officials became increasingly uncomfortable with the reports coming in from Guantánamo Bay. At the FBI, Marion "Spike" Bowman had, like many of the service JAGs, been left out of the discussion that led defense secretary Rumsfeld to sign off on the enhanced interrogation techniques in November 2002. Bowman, who had spent his career in navy intelligence and as judge advocate at the National Security Agency, among other appointments, was the person who fielded the calls from the concerned FBI agents at Guantánamo. Interrogation plans were advancing not only for al-Qhatani but also for Mohamedou Ould Slahi, another supposed high-value subject, the agents warned, both of which seemed misguided, amateurish, and illegal. Upon hearing from the agents, Bowman directed them to document what they were seeing so he could show the evidence to colleagues in the Defense Department. He then contacted Pentagon legal counsel William Haynes, among others. But Pentagon officials did not make for sympathetic interlocutors, and Bowman had a difficult time getting his reservations heard. Rumsfeld seems to have appointed Haynes general counsel at the Pentagon precisely because he knew Haynes would do his bidding. In this way Haynes was much like Gonzales, and indeed like many second-tier Bush-Cheney appointees. He performed dutifully, quashing independent thinking while leaving no tracks.[101]

At the Pentagon, Haynes "tried to control what everybody was doing there," Bowman reported. "I don't know whether he listened to anybody else on any of this or not." Moreover, Haynes himself wasn't "of a mind to say 'no' about anything." In short, Bowman's attempt to win an audience atop the Pentagon went nowhere. When the agents' report finally arrived on his desk in April 2003, Bowman passed it on to John Pistole, deputy assistant director, Counterterrorism Division, FBI, where it was delicately put aside.[102]

A democracy, according to a favorite cliché of the last several years, must fight its enemies with one hand tied behind its back, as if renouncing torture or enhanced interrogations amounts to a handicap. This is how the Bush administration saw it in the wake of 9/11, and continues to insist upon today. Evidence from Bowman and others suggests otherwise. By sidelining Bowman and countless other intelligence officials as it formulated national security policies in the wake of 9/11, the Bush administration needlessly handicapped the United States. First, the apparent illegality of U.S. policy exposed officials to criminal charges and alienated important allies. "Beyond any doubt," Bowman wrote John Pistole, what the United States was doing in Guantánamo "(and I don't know the extent of it) would be unlawful were these Enemy Prisoners of War (EPW). That they are not so designated cannot be license to do something that you cannot do to an EPW or a criminal prisoner." Should Bowman refer the evidence to the Defense Department inspector general? he asked Pistole. "Were I still on active duty, there is no question in my mind that it would be a duty to do so." Second, the new techniques impeded intelligence gathering and the prosecution of suspected war criminals. "These tactics have produced no intelligence of a threat neutralization nature to date and CITF [the Department of Defense's Criminal Investigation Task Force] believes that techniques have destroyed any chance of prosecuting the detainee."[103]

In an interview with the author Philippe Sands, Bowman articulated what exactly it was that troubled him so much about the enhanced interrogations. They elevate brute force over reason, taking us back to the Middle Ages. "I did not see any rational process—or any thought process—that went into the idea of how you were going to get information out of a person," Bowman told Sands. To tap the intelligence reservoir of an individual you have to treat detainees as individuals. The new paradigm betrayed no acknowledgment of that. In every single interrogation, Bowman observed, "You have to ask the question, what's it going to give me? If you can't answer that question, then the technique isn't harmless, it's dysfunctional."[104]

The FBI agent Ali Soufan confirmed Bowman's misgivings. In early 2002, Soufan, an experienced agent knowledgeable about al Qaeda and who worked on the USS *Cole* investigation and later interrogated Abu Zubaydah, traveled to Guantánamo Bay to emphasize the need for rapport-building techniques. Accompanying Soufan was Robert McFadden, another experienced interrogator who had worked with Soufan on the *Cole* investigation and who was now a member of the navy's Criminal Investigative Service (NCIS). Urged by Soufan to play by the book, Guantánamo military intelligence officials welcomed him with "blank stares," McFadden reported, as if "thinking, 'This is bullcrap.' Their attitude was, 'You guys are cops; we don't have time for this.'"[105]

In May 2009, Soufan testified before the Senate Judiciary Committee about enhanced interrogation techniques. "From my experience," he told the committee, "and I speak as someone who has personally interrogated many terrorists and elicited important actionable intelligence—I strongly believe that it is a mistake to use what has become known as the 'enhanced interrogation techniques,' a position shared by many professional operatives, including the CIA officers who were present at the initial phases of the Abu Zubaydah interrogation." Like Saar, Soufan insisted that, far from being faster—the principal defense of torture and enhanced interrogation—the new techniques, "from an operational perspective, are ineffective, slow and unreliable, and as a result harmful to our efforts to defeat al Qaeda."

Soufan defended the *Army Field Manual* from those who regarded it as outdated. "The Army Field Manual is not about being nice or soft," he observed. Rather, the proper distinction between the *Field Manual* and the new techniques is that the former is based on what Soufan called, echoing Bowman, "a knowledge-based approach." With the *Army Field Manual* as their guide, interrogators can outwit "the detainee by using a combination of interpersonal, cognitive, and emotional strategies to get the information needed." Such an approach, Soufan pointedly remarked, contrasts sharply "with the harsh interrogation approach introduced by outside contractors and forced upon CIA officials to use."[106]

In May 2010 the popular television drama *24* came to an end after an exhilarating eight-year run. Among other things, fans credited the show for its realism, and for fostering public debate about the relative merits of torture compared to, say, rapport building in eliciting intelligence. The two compliments are contradictory. Among seasoned intelligence officials, there is no debate. Torture doesn't work.[107] "Given the overwhelming negative evidence," journalist Anne Applebaum has written, "the really interesting question is not whether torture works but why so many people in our society want to believe it works."[108]

The depiction of intelligence collection in *24* informed Bush administration officials from top to bottom. Not only did Yoo and Homeland Security Chief Michael Chertoff cite *24* as inspiration, but popular depictions of torture influenced "young interrogators" on the ground in Iraq, retired army colonel Stuart Herrington found, where "the chain of command had this thirst for information and thought they could just tell the interrogators, you know, 'Take the gloves off. We need this information. We need it now.'"[109]

Like Soufan, Herrington, who has been conducting interrogations since the Vietnam War, senses "a watershed here with 9/11," whereby an old reliance on "guile and our wits, knowledge of human psychology, knowledge of the source itself, his language, his culture, the movement that he's a member of . . . together with a heavy dose of patience and stealth" was shunted aside by "a big myth" that information was "like a watertap that you can turn on by, you know, a brutal stroke, against the detainee." Just a few years ago, Herrington told the radio talk show host Terri Gross, it would have been "unthinkable" that "we would be having such a debate."

Haynes's stonewalling of Spike Bowman succeeded in delaying publication of FBI reports of abuse at Guantánamo Bay for two years, until December 2004.[110] But Haynes was less successful at brushing off the concern of navy general counsel Alberto Mora, when Mora caught wind of developments at Guantánamo in mid-December 2002. That month, Mora was approached by David Brant, chief of NCIS, one of whose staff members at Guantánamo Bay had come across the log of the al-Qahtani investigation. Unlike their army counterparts, naval investigators at Guantánamo Bay had experience in police work, hence knowledge about effective interrogation. What the navy staffers saw at Guantánamo alarmed them, and it wasn't long before Brant walked into Mora's office to deliver the solemn news. To Brant's relief, Mora was receptive, and within a few days, the two met again, this time with Brant brandishing the al-Qahtani log. "I was appalled by the whole thing," Mora recalled. "It was clearly abusive and assaultive. It was also clear it would get worse. It could lead to creep, where if the violence didn't work well, they would double it."[111]

Allegations of torture have become the principal sticking point in criticism of Bush administration detention and interrogation policy. Mora told journalist Jane Mayer that the distinction between torture and cruelty, the foundation of Yoo's memo, was not the point. "If cruelty is no longer declared unlawful, but instead is applied as a matter or policy, it alters the fundamental relationship of man to government. It destroys the whole notion of individual rights." Inherent rather than bestowed by government, such rights were universal, Mora explained. They applied "to all human beings, not just in America—even those designated as 'unlawful enemy combatants.' If you make this exception, the whole Constitution crumbles. It's a transformative issue."[112]

To Mora, then, this was a matter of principle, of ultimate ends, not mere procedures, and he determined to do everything in his power to bring the interrogation of al-Qahtani to a stop, even at a cost to his own career. After consulting with peers and receiving permission from his boss, navy secretary Gordon England, Mora went off to visit Haynes. On December 20, Mora dropped by Haynes's office, explained his opposition to the new techniques, and urged him to advise Secretary of Defense Rumsfeld to rescind his December 2 memo. Two and a half weeks later, on January 9, 2003, with no change to interrogation techniques, Mora returned to Haynes's office. There Mora conceded that, in theory at least, he could imagine an instance in which a detainee's knowledge of an impending terrorist attack might justify the use of torture, but surely this so-called burning fuse scenario did not apply at Guantánamo Bay. This was now more than a year after 9/11, and the intelligence value of the detainees had surely been attenuated. Again, Mora's objections met with no policy change, prompting him to approach Haynes yet again the following week, January 15, this time bearing an unsigned memo describing interrogations at Guantánamo as "at a minimum cruel and unusual treatment, and, at worst, torture," with which he vowed to go public if the Defense Department did not rescind the authorized techniques. That, finally, was language Haynes could understand. By day's end, Rumsfeld had revoked his December 2 memo authorizing the new techniques. Rumsfeld also promised to appoint a "working group" consisting of, among others, the military JAGs whose input Addington was determined to ignore. Mora had prevailed.

Or so it seemed. In fact, Rumsfeld had commissioned not one but two panels that January, a working group consisting of a range of opinion and that included Mora and his service peers, and an Office of Legal Counsel committee headed by Yoo and comprised of, among other figures, Alberto Gonzales; Michael Chertoff, head of the criminal division at the Department of Justice; and a coterie of other high-level Bush administration officials. Within a week, as the working group began its discussion, Yoo produced a lengthy draft memorandum more extreme than his so-called Torture Memo of the previous August. The new memo, signed in April 2003, ratified Guantánamo's status as a place beyond the reach of law and argued that the president, as commander in chief, had the authority to administer torture, including the gouging of eyes, dousing prisoners with "scalding water, corrosive acid, or caustic substance," "slitting an ear, nose, or lip, or disabling a tongue or limb." In what would become a familiar refrain, Yoo later told Mora that his new memo addressed questions of "law," not matters of "policy," a claim that appears not only naïve but incredible given the cross-fertilization of staff at the Pentagon and Justice Department.[113] If Yoo could not imagine the potential real-world effects of his opinion, he was indeed as unqualified for the job as William H. Taft IV originally suggested.[114] Meanwhile, the working group issued a draft report that ignored the reservations of Mora and the military JAGs about enhanced interrogation, while hewing to Yoo's latest opinion virtually to the letter. Upon seeing the draft report, Mora once again vigorously protested, warning Haynes not to let the secretary of defense sign off on the proposed techniques. The service JAGs who participated in the meeting also issued vehement written objections.[115] When no official working group report came out that spring, Mora assumed his protest had been heard and the report shelved. This was hardly the case. It took the revelations of torture and abuse at Abu Ghraib and the ensuing Senate hearings a year later to alert Mora to the fact that Rumsfeld had signed the final working group report that April, behind the backs of the military lawyers. In the intervening year, twenty-four new techniques (including one suggestively labeled "fear up harsh") had been operative at Guantánamo Bay—and had migrated to Iraq with the transfer of General Geoffrey Miller.[116]

In the end it was not a few good men but the U.S. Supreme Court that brought Bush administration policy at Guantánamo Bay to a precarious heel. The intervention of the High Court was set in motion as early as February 2002, when lawyers filed a habeas corpus petition, *Rasul v. Bush*, on behalf of two foreign nationals detained at the naval base. John Yoo's gamble of legal immunity at Guantánamo Bay would be tested. At first things seemed to be going Yoo's way. At the end of July, D.C. District Court judge Colleen Kollar-Kotelly dismissed the habeas petition due to lack of federal jurisdiction over foreign nationals detained at Guantánamo. The following March, the D.C. Circuit

Court affirmed the District Court's ruling, arguing that federal courts had no authority at Guantánamo Bay. Undeterred, the detainees' counsel filed a petition for writ of certiorari before the Supreme Court, which the Court granted the succeeding month, consolidating what were in fact three separate cases under the name *Rasul v. Bush*. Oral arguments occurred on April 20. On June 28, 2004, by a 6-to-3 majority, the High Court ruled in favor of the petitioners, affirming the right of Guantánamo detainees to challenge their detention in court.

The Court's ruling in *Rasul* was notable for several reasons. First, by appearances, anyway, John Yoo had lost. He had warned that a federal court *might* side with a challenge to Bush policy, but he certainly didn't expect that to happen. Second, Justice John Stevens, who wrote the majority opinion arguing that the United States was de facto sovereign at Guantánamo Bay, hence habeas applied there, was the same person who had earlier denied constitutional protections to Haitian migrants detained at Guantánamo in the 1990s.[117] What had changed over the intervening decade? Both the magnitude of the assertion of presidential power and its potential repercussions. "What is presently at stake," Stevens wrote in *Rasul*, "is only whether the federal courts have jurisdiction to determine the legality of the Executive's potentially indefinite detention of individuals who claim to be wholly innocent of wrongdoing." To this question, the majority offered a resounding yes.

Still, the Court was vague on exactly what form of relief should be granted the detainees. "Whether and what further proceedings may become necessary after respondents make their response to the merits of petitioners' claims are matters that we need not address now," the Court ruled, thereby passing the buck. The Bush administration was only too happy to seize back the initiative.[118]

Within days, the administration announced the establishment at Guantánamo of Combatant Status Review Tribunals (CSRTs), three-judge panels empowered to review the government's evidence against a detainee and make a recommendation to continue to detain or release him. In these tribunals, detainees had no right to counsel, but were provided with military "advisors." Nor were they allowed to review the evidence against them. More troubling, in constituting the

CSRTs, the government expanded its definition of what it meant to be an "enemy combatant." In *Rasul*, the government described an enemy combatant as someone who "was part of or supporting forces hostile to the United States or coalition partners in Afghanistan and who engaged in armed conflict with the United States there"; post-*Rasul*, the government significantly broadened that definition to include "an individual who was part of or supporting Taliban or al Qaeda forces," including "any person who has committed a belligerent act or has directly supported hostilities in aid of enemies."[119]

The potential for and evidence of abuse in this system is limitless. In 2009, D.C. District judge Kollar-Kotelly, who originally denied habeas corpus to Guantánamo detainees back in July 2002, reviewed the case of a Kuwaiti detainee named Fouad Mahmoud al-Rabiah and held at Guantánamo for seven years. The government's evidence against al-Rabiah was "surprisingly bare," Kollar-Kotelly remarked. The man had been held on the basis of a coerced confession that his interrogators acknowledged as dubious, and which the judge herself dismissed as "entirely incredible." Indeed, evidence in the detainee's record, which he was not allowed to see, "strongly supports" his claim of innocence. The judge saw "no evidence in the record that anyone directed any allegations toward al-Rabiah nor any indication that interrogators believed al-Rabiah had engaged in any conduct that made him lawfully detainable." Rather, "the evidence in the record during this period consists mainly of an assessment made by an intelligence analyst that al-Rabiah should not have been detained."[120]

Examples of such corruption abound. Lieutenant Colonel Stephen Abraham, who sat on the CSRTs for eight months, described the system as "geared towards rubber-stamping the detainees' prior designation as 'enemy combatants.'" As elsewhere throughout the Bush team's national security apparatus, the officials charged with compiling the evidence against detainees were "woefully inexperienced" in "the legal and intelligence fields." The same was true of the tribunals' recorders, true of the case writers, and so on. Detainees were held on the basis of charges that "lacked even the most fundamental earmarks of objectively credible evidence," Abraham observed. Detainees' files consisted of statements made in "indirect and passive forms without stating the source of the information or providing a basis for establishing the reliability or the credibility of the source." Judgments against detainees were often based on evidence that could not withstand "even the most cursory questions." Judgments in favor of detainees were typically reviewed and overturned, and greeted with the assumption that things had gone wrong. Among the evidence keeping numerous detainees confined at Guantánamo Bay was that provided by one Guantánamo captive, under duress, who claimed to have seen up to sixty of his fellows detainees in Afghanistan when they were in fact known to be elsewhere.[121]

Convinced by Bush administration propaganda that the CSRT system was humming merrily along—that Guantánamo held only the worst of the worst and that even these *worst* were being handsomely fed and cared for—the Republican-majority Congress passed the Detainee Treatment Act (DTA) in December 2005. The act banned the use of cruel, inhuman, and degrading treatment while stripping U.S. courts of habeas jurisdiction at Guantánamo Bay. Early the next year, the U.S. Supreme Court heard a challenge to the DTA's revocation of federal court authority at Guantánamo. For the second time in two years, the government lost, as the High Court rebuffed the other branches' assault on judicial authority. Moreover, the Court's decision in *Hamdan v. Rumsfeld* restored Geneva protections to Guantánamo Bay, upholding the plaintiff's challenge to the military commission system established there.[122]

Again Congress tried to limit federal judicial authority at Guantánamo by passing the Military Commissions Act in October 2006. Again, its attempt was rebuffed by the Supreme Court, this time in July 2008, just months before the presidential election, when, in *Boumediene v. Bush*, the Court upheld the habeas petitions of six supposed enemy combatants. As D.C. District Court judge Richard J. Leon remarked, when the case was remanded to him, the six petitioners whose detainee status was in question were no ordinary captives. Native Algerians, all were citizens or lawful residents of Bosnia at the time of their apprehension by American officials—"over a thousand miles away from the battlefield in Afghanistan"—for allegedly planning to travel to Afghanistan and take up arms against the United States. What was the evidence against them? Judge Leon couldn't exactly say. He did allow that "the Government relies exclusively on the information contained in a classified document from an unnamed source," a source, he pointedly remarked, that "is the only evidence in the record directly supporting each alleged detainee's knowledge of, or commitment to, this supposed plan." The government provided the Court no information by which to judge the source's credibility or reliability. Nor did it provide any corroborating evidence. Generously, Leon conceded that though the classified intelligence speaking to the credibility of the source may indeed have been "sufficient for intelligence purposes," it was insufficient "for the purposes for which a habeas court must now evaluate it. To allow enemy combatancy to rest on so thin a reed," he concluded, "would be inconsistent with this Court's obligation under the Supreme Court's decision in *Hamd[an]* to protect petitioners from the risk of erroneous detention"—the inspiration for habeas itself.[123]

In 2006, a lawyer familiar with the desolation and helplessness of death row had this to say about the Guantánamo prison camp: "I have been to death row in Texas, South Carolina, Missouri, Mississippi, Arkansas, and Indiana (the last being the site of the federal death row). I have been to more maximum-security prisons than I can recall. I have delivered the saddest news to men and women behind bars—parents have passed, children have been diagnosed, appeals have been denied. I have broken the news that a client's last chance for a reprieve has been turned down and his execution has been scheduled for a date in the near future. I have visited with clients late at night, in holding cells near execution chambers. Some paced nervously, others sat with a quiet dignity and peace. I have, only once, watched as a client of many years—a sixty-two-year-old great-grandmother—was put to death. But I have never been to a more disturbing place than the military prison at Guantánamo Bay. It is a place of indescribable sadness, where the abstract enormity of 'forever' becomes concrete: *this* windowless cell; *that* metal cot; *those* steel shackles."[124]

This description of the prison contrasts markedly with an account of the base from the early 1970s: "What is it about Guantánamo that makes it everybody's favorite, longed-for duty station? Perhaps it is one of those rare places in the world that seems to exist in everybody's dream vocabulary. Guantánamo evokes visions of a long-ago and far-away sort of place, a languid Caribbean paradise where the waves break on pristine beaches, and where the islanders shake down coconuts from trees when they want something to eat. Guantánamo today combines the nostalgia of the past with the adventure of a busy, growing naval base. There is just no place like it in the world."[125]

No place like it in the world. If not exactly true, this mythical Guantánamo, this "dream," remained authoritative really for centuries, until the Bush administration decided—against expert advice—to locate its prison camp there in the War on Terror. Since the Taíno cacique Hatuey first fled to Guantánamo from Hispaniola, Guantánamo had been a refuge for dispossessed individuals and groups. For the Taíno themselves, for the displaced New Englander John Drake (Admiral Vernon's prized guide), for French refugees from Haiti, for Cuba's founding fathers, for Fidel Castro (and Castro's enemies), and yes, even for Haitians with AIDS virtually imprisoned there in the 1990s, Guantánamo remained a land of second chance, a springboard that brought visitors to the bay a step closer to their dreams. Pirates once flocked there. American colonists turned U.S. imperialists called for its seizure. Once seized, Guantánamo became the supposed embodiment of the American Dream.

By the end of his term in office, George W. Bush, along with his second secretary of defense, Robert Gates, couldn't shed Guantánamo fast enough. Of course, the Guantánamo they wanted to shed was the prison, not the naval base. But whether the base itself can survive the sullying of its name is anybody's guess. More than a century after the Teller Amendment formally pledged the United States to leave Cuba to Cubans, the *Boumediene* decision virtually conceded title to Guantánamo Bay to the United States. Only now nobody seems to want it.

EPILOGUE

The history of the Guantánamo naval base exposes a fundamental paradox at the heart of American national identity between liberty and coercion. Domestically the paradox has been most visible in the interdependence of freedom and slavery, Manifest Destiny, and the dispossession of native peoples; internationally the paradox is starkest in the enduring vision of America as an empire of liberty, first described by Thomas Jefferson. Today this paradox plays out across the front pages of newspapers around the world, but there is nothing new about it at Guantánamo Bay. The United States intervened in the Cuban War of Independence in 1898 for the avowed purpose of ending Spanish tyranny. Its refusal to relinquish Guantánamo at the end of what Americans know as "the Spanish-American War" led Cubans to protest that they had exchanged one tyrant for another. Americans, meanwhile, bristled at Cuba's ingratitude, as if their selflessness demanded a reward.[1]

Despite its own beginnings as a cluster of colonies, the United States has been an expansionist, imperialist nation from its inception. The occupation of Guantánamo in 1898 fulfilled a yearning for an American foothold in Cuba dating back to the colonial era. Guantánamo was the first fruit of a harvest of territories, resources, and markets thought to be essential to U.S. prosperity and to the liberal democratic principles prosperity guaranteed. Guantánamo paved the way for the opening to U.S. business interests in Guatemala, Honduras, and Nicaragua, among other Latin American states, as well as the seizure and administration of the Panama Canal Zone. The taking of Guantánamo initiated the United States into an exclusive, if notorious, club of imperialist superpowers, and established a blueprint for American foreign policy lasting to this day. Conflating the expansion of national interest with the advance of freedom and democracy, the United States has intervened repeatedly in the affairs of sovereign nations, often against the express wishes of local popular majorities. Justifying these interventions politically and legally has not always been easy, and for over a century Guantánamo provided the laboratory and staging area where U.S. imperial ambition could be implemented beyond the scrutiny of the American public and the constraint of U.S. law.

Perched astride the Windward Passage, the strategic hub of the Western Hemisphere that cuts between Cuba and Haiti, Guantánamo has witnessed contests for local, regional, and global supremacy that date back centuries and have involved many of the world's great empires. Cuba figured centrally in European colonial competition, and Guantánamo Bay, with its deep and spacious harbor, could not help but become embroiled. Columbus left it to his successors to exploit the bay, though more as a harbor than as a home, as a lack of freshwater precluded intensive settlement for those without the means and manpower to tap neighboring resources. At once a vast anchorage and a warren of coves and inlets, Guantánamo became a favorite hideout of the legendary pirates of the Spanish Main who preyed (often with state sanction) on the merchant fleets of rival colonial powers. We may never know for sure who the first North American was to set eyes on the bay, but American colonists attended the successful British assault on Guantánamo of 1741. Thereafter Americans would keep Guantánamo closely in sight, constrained by exigency if not etiquette from intervening in Cuba's protracted battle for independence until the USS *Maine* blew up in Havana Harbor in early 1898. Logic, never mind the evidence, contradicted U.S. accusations that Spain had sunk the *Maine*. Spain had sought to avoid war with the United States at all costs. But logic was out of favor in an America bent on war and besotted with the propaganda of the Yellow Press. And so the war came, and with it, the happy coincidence of Guantánamo Bay.

The ensuing U.S. century at Guantánamo has consisted of periods of relative calm punctuated by fierce activity and hasty adaptation to unfolding global crises. The quiet and underused coaling station from which the United States strode triumphantly onto the global stage at the turn of the twentieth century scarcely resembled the boisterous depot to which the fleet repaired for fuel and refreshment during Prohibition. Prohibition-era Guantánamo, in turn, little resembled the base at which Batista's pilots refueled in their battle against the Cuban resistance. Nor did the Guantánamo that accommodated Batista in 1958 much resemble that dangled by Kennedy in an attempt to bait Castro into war just a few years later. Finally, Kennedy's Guantánamo differed markedly from the Guantánamo of presidents Carter and Reagan, which appeared so outdated by the 1970s and '80s that both men contemplated returning the base to Cuba. Only in the past decade or so has Guantánamo's role begun to stabilize. Guantánamo has become the place to hold refugees (more than eighty-five thousand Cubans and Haitians under the Bush and Clinton administrations in the 1990s) and prisoners of war—a never-never land within U.S. jurisdiction yet beyond the rule of law.

The American record at Guantánamo captures but half the story of the bay. Guantánamo Bay is part of Cuba, after all, and the U.S. century has a Cuban counterpart. A popular navy myth suggests that U.S.-Cuban relations—both in general and at Guantánamo in particular—remained healthy, cordial even, until Cuba's Communist revolution of 1959. The cordiality is said to have been palpable in the social interaction in the towns around the bay where Cuban and American navy bands sat shoulder to shoulder on holidays, and where American sailors unwound, innocently enough, when the fleet came in. Cubans know a different story. If there is one thing that unites diverse Cubans to this day, it is their shame at having consented to the U.S. occupation of Guantánamo in 1901. Nor are the many Cubans who labored at the base over the course of the U.S. century the free marketeers of American mythology. Hailing from an imperfect Cuba, they experienced American imperfections—exploitative labor conditions; gender, racial, and ethnic bias—firsthand. Long after New Deal legislation began to protect workers in the United States, Cuban labor on the base remained unorganized and unrepresented. Against this

exploitation Cuban workers fought relentlessly, sometimes successfully, grateful for the work no doubt, but mindful of the coercion symbolized by America's presence at the bay.

But so much for history; what does the future hold? In June 2006,
retired U.S. Army general Barry McCaffrey visited the Guantánamo
prison camp at the invitation of the United States Southern Command (SOUTHCOM). A former head of SOUTHCOM (1994–96),
now an adjunct professor of international affairs at the U.S. Military
Academy, McCaffrey knew the naval base intimately. The purpose of
the visit was to generate support for the camp just as Congress set to
work on what would become the 2006 Military Commissions Act. For
two days McCaffrey toured the camp, attended numerous briefings,
and observed a detainee interrogation—more or less the standard itinerary granted U.S. dignitaries and journalists.[2]

Much of McCaffrey's report recapitulated Joint Task Force (JTF)
talking points. "The JTF Guantánamo Detention Center is the most
professional, firm, humane and carefully supervised confinement operation that I have ever personally observed," McCaffrey remarked.
But not all of McCaffrey's report was boilerplate. The four-star general
could barely conceal his contempt for politicians who ("with no military experience and no kids in uniform"[3]) had jeopardized the physical
and emotional well-being and legal standing of U.S. troops. Years before Susan Crawford, convening authority for the Guantánamo military commissions, admitted that "we tortured Al Qahtani," McCaffrey
conceded that "during the first 18 months of the war on terror there
were widespread, systematic abuses of detainees under U.S. control
in Iraq, Afghanistan, and Guantánamo. Some were murdered and
hundreds tortured or abused."[4] The result was "enormous damage"
both to U.S. military operations and to the nation's international
reputation.[5]

Given the prison's continuing notoriety, McCaffrey concluded that
Guantánamo had suffered a mortal blow. "There is now no possible
political support" for the prison "going forward." Nor could the U.S.
military expect much from the base. "The great value of the platform

of Guantánamo was that it was a military space in which no Federal District Court had primary jurisdiction," McCaffrey explained.

> For that reason alone, Gitmo has over the past 45 years been the location of choice for U.S. migrant refugee operations (no appeal to the INS process) as well as other secret operations. No applicable foreign law, no foreign diplomatic intervention, no Federal Court civil orders, no nosy intervention by a U.S. Ambassador—only the exercise of unilateral U.S. military power and the tool of the Uniform Code of Military Justice. It was the perfect deal. No more.[6]

Yet five years after McCaffrey's visit, the Guantánamo prison camp is alive and well. The prison enjoys more public and political support today than at any time in its nearly ten-year history, notwithstanding President Obama's campaign pledge and inaugural promise to shut it down. In poll after poll taken over the course of the two years since Obama took office, the American public has overwhelmingly rejected the idea of closing the prison and transferring its population stateside, most recently in December 2010.[7] That same month, a Democratic Congress dealt a near-fatal blow to the administration's effort to close the prison by prohibiting the president from transferring detainees to the United States, from buying or constructing a prison on U.S. soil for the Guantánamo detainees, and from repatriating detainees without the signature of the secretary of defense—provisions enacted without parliamentary debate and virtually without public notice.[8]

Meanwhile, anticipating Congress's vote, the administration tried to make the best of a bad situation, assigning a legal team to address the most intractable issue confronting Justice Department officials, namely, what to do with the nearly fifty or so detainees considered too dangerous to release and yet thought to be unsuitable for trial by military tribunal, thanks to tainted evidence against them. To make indefinite detention more palatable, the administration will replace Bush administration "annual review boards" with "periodic review boards." Where the old boards consisted entirely of military personnel and provided the detainees no legal rights, the new ones will consist of an interagency panel of military and national security personnel, and will grant detainees both legal counsel and access to at least some incriminating evidence.[9]

Which raises the question of whether these changes are adequate for alleged enemy combatants detained in wartime. By all appearances, the torture and systematic abuse of detainees ended at Guantánamo long before Barack Obama took office. Indefinite detention continues there, but its legality has never been questioned by a single federal judge, liberal or conservative, and closing Guantánamo would only displace it to the United States. Moreover, the military commission system signed into law by the 2009 Military Commissions Act and now set to reopen at Guantánamo includes more protections— more judicial review, more limitations on coerced and hearsay evidence—than any prior military commissions, including Nuremburg.[10]

In short, one could argue that the Obama administration is only finishing the job begun at Guantánamo by JAG lawyers, human rights advocates, and the press, who have introduced a measure of law and transparency to what has long been an obscure place. Moreover, closing Guantánamo might inadvertently allow both the administration itself and the American public to sidestep the bigger question of how Guantánamo fits into the nation's larger detention archipelago. It is worth remembering that momentum began to build for closing Guantánamo just as escalating military engagement in Afghanistan and Pakistan swelled the ranks of detainees at Bagram air base and other detention centers beyond the purview of the American public and the reach of U.S. law. What is happening at Bagram? Where else is the United States detaining people? Under what conditions and for how long? The war against al Qaeda and the Taliban continues, but there have been no new arrivals at Guantánamo Bay.

And so a place that has come to symbolize America's fall from grace post-9/11 now demonstrates the power of symbols themselves to inhibit clear thinking. "The uproar over Guantánamo permits conflation of a whole congruence of ideas," observes David Barron, former head of the Office of Legal Council in the Obama administration. "It reveals how a set of practices, some of which may be more acceptable than others, became impossible to disentangle in our minds."[11]

Meanwhile, the more things change, the more things stay the same.

In February 2011, just as the new Guantánamo military commissions were set to restart, a detainee named Awal Gul died of a heart attack at the prison camp. Guantánamo officials described Gul as "an admitted Taliban recruiter and commander of a military base in Jalalabad." Gul's lawyer, Matthew Dodge, characterized that description as an "outrageous" slander. In three years of litigation, Dodge protested, the U.S. "government never claimed or pointed to any evidence that his client had run any Qaeda house or admitted providing support to Mr. bin Laden."[12] A few weeks later, President Obama defended what seemed to many observers to be the U.S. military's abusive treatment of Bradley Manning, the marine accused of leaking classified documents to WikiLeaks' founder, Julian Assange. Asked to explain why military officials thought it necessary to require Manning to sleep naked and appear nude before his guards, the president replied, "I have actually asked the Pentagon whether or not the procedures that have been taken in terms of [Manning's] confinement are appropriate and are meeting our basic standards. They assure me that they are."[13]

Still, even if wrong about the prison, is General McCaffrey right about the base? With its immunity from federal court oversight gone, has the base become at long last dispensable? McCaffrey is hardly the first to pronounce a premature requiem on the place. As the age of sail yielded to the age of coal, then coal to oil, and bases themselves to mobile carrier battle groups, there were always people around to make an argument for shutting down Guantánamo. From its earliest days, politicians and admirals alike criticized its geographical location, physical exposure, and expense. As early as 1934, the base commander, Admiral Charles Cooke, attempted to smother talk of removing the navy from Guantánamo. In his final report before stepping down, Cooke warned successors not to lose sight of the base's pivotal role in safeguarding hemispheric sea-lanes, thus anticipating its function in World War II. A generation later, when Adlai Stevenson suggested exchanging Guantánamo for a Soviet pledge to clear out of Cuba, President Kennedy and his senior staff wouldn't even consider it. And yet by the late 1970s and early 1980s, both the Carter and Reagan administrations gave at least passing thought to turning the base over to Cuba.[14]

Fifty years after Castro's rise to power, Guantánamo's strategic ir-
relevance is universally acknowledged. "Guantánamo serves no military
purpose, affords no strategic advantage," observes retired U.S. Marine
Corps general Jack Sheehan, former commander in chief of the U.S.
Atlantic Command (1994–97). "We're not going to attack Cuba. The
place exists now solely as a product of bureaucratic inertia."[15] Guantánamo was once important "as a political icon and covert platform,"
Barry McCaffrey has remarked. "As a strategic naval facility, it never
was important; it's always been a sump."[16] Today, adds Jeffrey Johnston, former commander of public works at the base, "Guantánamo
adds absolutely nothing to the navy. If Guantánamo disappeared, every ship would sail, every sailor would be trained. Moreover, the navy
would save fifty million dollars per year."[17]

Perhaps nobody knows the base like Jeff Johnston. For three years
(1999–2002), Johnston observed goings-on at Guantánamo from his
perch in SOUTHCOM. In 2004, he became the head of public works
at the base, a position he retained for five years, an unusually long
time in one place. Upon arriving at Guantánamo, Johnston discovered
that familiarizing oneself with Guantánamo meant getting to know the
Ghost of Guantánamo Past. To this day, the base remains littered with
land mines, unexploded ordnance, ancient, unused dry docks, the infrastructure of abandoned neighborhoods and migrant camps, not to
mention old wells and used shell casings dating back to the "Spanish-
American War." From the myriad minor things Johnston learned about
Guantánamo's history, one larger lesson stands out: "It is as wishful to
pronounce Guantánamo dead as it is futile to predict its future."

"Who knows what the future holds?" Johnson remarked. "If history
is any guide, the next Guantánamo will be nothing like past ones."
Migrant operations like those of the 1990s are unlikely to happen
again. Nor is there likely to be another prison. To Johnston, Guantánamo is as much about the valleys—the downtimes—as it is about
the peaks. "The valleys occur and everyone says, 'That's it! Gitmo's
done! We're out of here!' Then something comes along—racial fears,
fears of communism, Castro, the cold war, revolution in Haiti, terror-

ism, you name it—and someone says, 'Hey, use Gitmo!' after which comes, 'Okay, that's that. Close it down, Gitmo no longer matters.'"[18]

Cut through this noise and what do you find? "In quiet times," Johnston observes, "Gitmo is a silent bridge between history past and history future. There's a lull woven into Gitmo. Every day of doing nothing there is essential to tending the fields on which enormous world-changing events will transpire." As public works officer, Johnston felt "an obligation to the future charted by what happened in the past. Who in the world would ever have predicted GTMO's current and recent uses—that over the course of the last decade and a half, for example, Guantánamo would be the site of the only truly productive contact between the Cuban and U.S. governments" (during fence line meetings between the base commander and his Cuban counterpart)?[19] "We can't know what the future of GTMO will look like," Johnston insists. But of one thing we can be sure: "Guantánamo is now part of who we are."[20]

What do Cubans hope for the bay? "The U.S. Naval Base is the last vestige of the American intervention in Cuba over a century ago," the Cuban poet and writer Rafael Hernández observed a few years back. As fractious a people as anybody, "there is yet one thing that all Cubans, regardless of age or ideology, agree upon. We want the bay back. Not one single Cuban will say it's good for us." The base has brought the region's economic development to a standstill, Hernández explained. More than a political and military thorn in Cuba's side, it is an environmental disaster, with U.S. fighter planes buzzing the Cuban countryside, unexploded ordnance sprawled across the Guantánamo estuary, and nuclear submarines prowling about the harbor.[21]

Hernández is right about Cubans' fractiousness: many Cubans disagree with him about the U.S. base. Since the Taíno cacique Hatuey first fled Hispaniola for the Guantánamo Basin five centuries ago, Cubans have long looked on the region as a refuge from the repression, thuggery, corruption, and racial persecution besetting the rest of Cuba. Oriente province has long served as Cuba's frontier, Guantánamo as the nation's safety valve. For the past fifty years, Cubans fleeing the persecution of Castro's government have regarded the U.S. base as a vestige of imperialism, to be sure, but also as a haven. Cuban dissidents have climbed fences, tiptoed through minefields, and swum thirty miles against current, wind, and long odds to make it to the naval base.

Forward-looking Cubans can imagine a revolution finally ridding the nation of the Castros and their cronies. But they are not so naïve to think that such a revolution will be smooth or without its reverses. Keen readers of history, Cubans can foresee a liberal revolution giving way to a conservative reaction and so on in a cycle that could make a continued U.S. presence at Guantánamo as salutary as it is humiliating. Asked for their final word on the American presence in Guantánamo, a disparate group of Cuban exiles, all of whom risked their lives to get to Guantánamo and who spent months behind barbed wire there in 1994–95, replied simply: "Don't give it back."[22]

Which is not to say the United States shouldn't return the base to Cuba, only to suggest that Cubans themselves differ about its future—and that imperialism is rarely as straightforward as it seems.

NOTES

PREFACE

1. On a later trip to the naval base, I had a chance to interview a small planeload of Filipino workers heading home after six years. The several I spoke to signed successive two-year contracts (with two months' leave in between). They got their jobs through a Philippine government agency. For a monthly salary of five hundred dollars (which they sent directly home), they worked six eight-hour days per week at an hourly rate of roughly $2.60. Author interview, Filipino laborers, October 23, 2008, Guantánamo Bay (the Filipinos I interviewed requested to remain anonymous).

1 ★ REDISCOVERING GUANTÁNAMO

1. Francis Augustus MacNutt, ed., *De Orbe Novo: The Eight Decades of Peter Martyr D'Anghera*, vol. 1 (New York: G. P. Putnam's Sons, 1912), 94–95; J. M. Cohen, ed., *The Four Voyages of Columbus* (New York: Penguin Books, 1969), 170–71; and John Harmon McElroy, ed., *The Life and Voyages of Christopher Columbus, by Washington Irving* (Boston: Twayne Publishers, 1981), 239–42.
2. MacNutt, *Martyr*, 94–97, Carl Ortwin Sauer, *The Early Spanish Main* (Berkeley: University of California Press, 1966), 58; and Samuel M. Wilson, *The Indigenous People of the Caribbean* (Gainesville: University Press of Florida, 1997), 54.
3. Hortensia Pichardo Viñals, ed., *Documentos para la historia de Cuba*, tomo 1 (La Habana: Editorial Pueblo y Educación), 1984, 51.
4. MacNutt, *Martyr*, 95.
5. Peter Martyr reports that Columbus had taken this interpreter, whom he named "Diego Columbus," off "Guanahani (an island near by Cuba)"; ibid.

6. Cohen, *Four Voyages of Columbus*, 169–70.

7. The province of Guantánamo was among the densest areas of Taíno settlement in Cuba. (See www.hartford-hwp.com/archives/41/311.html.) Exactly how dense Taíno settlement was in the immediate vicinity of Guantánamo Bay is hard to say. Strained Cuban-U.S. relations at the bay over the past fifty years and U.S. development at likely archaeological sites at the U.S. naval base have hampered archaeological investigation. See Timothy R. Sara and William F. Keegan, *Archaeological Survey and Paleoenvironmental Investigations of Portions of U.S. Naval Station Guantánamo Bay, Cuba* (Newport News, Va.: Geo-Marine, 2004), chap. 3.

8. McElroy, *The Life and Voyage of Christopher Columbus*, 239–42; Cohen, *Four Voyages of Columbus*, 169–71; Sara and Keegan, *Archaeological Survey*, 15–41, 155–56, 170–71. Cf. Irving Rouse, *The Tainos: Rise and Decline of the People Who Greeted Columbus* (New Haven, Conn.: Yale University Press, 1992), chap. 3, 4, and 6; Samuel M. Wilson, ed., *The Indigenous People of the Caribbean* (Gainesville: University Press of Florida, 1997), chap. 12–14; and Samuel M. Wilson, "Cultural Pluralism and the Emergence of Complex Society in the Greater Antilles," paper delivered at XVIII International Congress for Caribbean Archaeology, St. George's, Grenada, July 1999 (available at uts.cc.utexas.edu/~swilson/wilson_iaca99.html).

9. Wilson, *Indigenous People of the Caribbean*, 17; and Rouse, *The Tainos*, 20.

10. Wilson, "Cultural Pluralism."

11. Franklin Knight, "Slavery and the Transformation of Society in Cuba, 1511–1760," Elsa Goveia Memorial Lecture, University of West Indies, Mona, Jamaica, March 22, 1988, 3; Anthony Pagden, *Peoples and Empires: A Short History of European Migration, Exploration, and Conquest, from Greece to the Present* (New York: Modern Library, 2001), 52.

12. Knight, "Slavery and the Transformation of Society in Cuba," 3; J. H. Elliott, *Empires of the Atlantic World: Britain and Spain in America, 1492–1830* (New Haven, Conn.: Yale University Press, 2006), 17–19; and C. H. Haring, *The Spanish Empire in America* (New York: Harcourt Brace Jovanovich, 1947), 23–27.

13. The term "long argument" is borrowed from Stephen Foster, *The Long Argument: English Puritanism and the Shaping of New England Culture* (Chapel Hill: University of North Carolina Press, 1991).

14. Carl Sauer has written that relations between Spaniards and Indians at Hispaniola began to fall apart in the spring of 1494, when one of Columbus's lieutenants removed the ear of a Taíno vassal in response to an alleged theft by Indians of Spanish clothing. If, indeed, this is the first case of formal violence perpetrated on the Indians of the New World, one must still reckon with the psychological upheaval and disorientation that the Spaniards' arrival exacted on Taíno communities; Sauer, *Early Spanish Main*, 84. Cf. Dave D. Davis, "The Strategy of Early Spanish Ecosystem Management in Cuba," *Journal of Anthropological Research* 30, no. 4 (Winter 1974): 294–314.

15. Juan Tomás Tavares K., *The Indians of Hispaniola* (Santo Domingo: Editores de

Santo Domingo, 1978), 48. See also Julia Tavares, *On the Trail of the Arawaks* (Ithaca, N.Y.: Cornell University Press, 1975).

16. Sauer, *Early Spanish Main*, 149.

17. Ibid. Dave Davis argues that Velázquez and the Crown learned from its annihilation of the Indians on Hispaniola, introducing a milder form of encomienda in Cuba; Davis, "Early Spanish Ecosystem Management in Cuba," 298–99.

18. Las Casas was one of several well-known critics of the Indian genocide. He came to his beliefs slowly, after first participating in the Spanish conquest of Cuba. To spare the Indians, Las Casas endorsed African slavery, though he came to regret this, too. At the time that he endorsed African slavery as an alternative to the forced labor of Indians, he was unaware of the cruelty of the African slave trade then under way at the hands of the Portuguese and Spanish slave traders, including Columbus himself. Once aware of it, he withdrew his endorsement, insisting that it was the only logical conclusion for a man of his religious and philosophical beliefs. Haring, *Spanish Empire in America*, 43–56; Pagden, *People and Empires*, 64–72; Robin Blackburn, *The Making of New World Slavery* (London: Verso, 1998),135–36; Lawrence Clayton, "Bartolomé de las Casas and the African Slave Trade," *History Compass* 7, no. 6 (July 2009): 1529–30.

19. Ladislao Guerra Valiente, *Las Huellas del Génesis: Guantánamo Hasta 1870* (Guantánamo: Editorial El Mar y Montaña, 2004), 11; Bartolomé de las Casas, "Hatuey," in Pichardo Viñals, ed., *Documentos para la Historia de Cuba*, 51–53.

20. Las Casas, "Hatuey," 51–53.

21. Manuel A. Iturralde-Vinent, "Meso-Cenozoic Caribbean Paleogeography: Implications for the Historical Biogeography of the Region," *International Geology Review* 48 (2006): 791–827; Walter Alvarez, "Eastbound Sublithosphere Mantle Flow Through the Caribbean Gap and Its Relevance to the Continental Undertow Hypothesis," *Terra Nova* 13, no. 5 (2001): 333–37; and J. Pindell, L. Kennan, K. P. Stanek, W. V. Maresch, and G. Draper, "Foundations of the Gulf of Mexico and Caribbean Evolution: Eight Controversies Resolved," in M. A. Iturralde-Vinent and E. G. Lidiak, eds., "Caribbean Plate Tectonics: Stratigraphic, Magmatic, Metamorphic, and Tectonic Events," *Geologica Acta* 4, nos. 1–2 (2006): 303–41. The geological composition of Cuba is immensely complicated, hence there is much division and debate about Cuba's paleogeological origin. See, for example, K. H. James, "Arguments for and Against the Pacific Origin of the Caribbean Plate: Discussion, Finding for an Inter-American Origin," in Iturralde-Vinent and Lidiak, eds., "Caribbean Plate Tectonics," 279–302. For schematic illustrations of the process described here, see www.scotese.com.

22. Levi Marrero, *Geografía de Cuba* (La Habana: Editorial Selecta, 1957), 610–18, Jacobo de la Pezuela, *Diccionario Geográfico, Estadístico, Histórico de la Isla de Cuba*, tomo 2 (Madrid: Imprenta del Establecimiento de Mellado, 1863), 496–512.

23. Ibid.

24. See José Barreiro, "Indians in Cuba," *Cultural Survival Quarterly* 13, no. 3

(1989): 56–60; and M. F. Pospisil, "Physical Anthropological Research on Indian Remnants in Eastern Cuba," *Current Anthropology* 12, no. 2 (April 1971): 229.

25. William E. Johns, "Dynamics of Boundary Currents and Marginal Seas: Windward Passage Experiment," Physical Oceanography: Annual Reports: FY06, Office of Naval Research; William E. Johns et al., "On the Atlantic Inflow to the Caribbean Sea," *Deep Sea Research* 1, no. 49 (2002): 211–43; and J. L. Sarmiento et al., "High-latitude Controls of Thermocline Nutrients and Low Latitude Biological Productivity," *Nature* 42, no. 7 (Jan. 2004): 56–60.

26. On the Coriolis effect, see www.uwsp.edu/geo/faculty/ritter/geog101/textbook/circulation/outline.html.

27. My explanation of this omits details available at earth.usc.edu/~stott/Catalina/Oceans.html.

28. Philip L. Richardson and Roger Goldsmith, "The Columbus Landfall: Voyage Track Corrected for Winds and Currents," *Oceanus* 30 (1987): 3–10.

29. See oceancurrents.rsmas.miami.edu/atlantic/canary.html.

30. On this boom-and-bust cycle in Cuba and Spain's other colonies, see Laird W. Bergad, *The Comparative Histories of Slavery in Brazil, Cuba, and the United States* (New York: Cambridge University Press, 2007), 12–14, as well as Louis A. Pérez Jr., *Cuba: Between Reform and Revolution* (New York: Oxford University Press, 1995), 27–31.

31. Pérez, *Cuba: Between Reform*, 38; Elliott, *Empires of the Atlantic World*, 224; Haring, *The Spanish Empire in America*, 223.

32. Pérez, *Cuba: Between Reform*, 38, and Elliott, *Empires of the Atlantic World*, 105.

33. Pérez, *Cuba: Between Reform*, 38–39; Elliott, *Empires of the Atlantic World*, 105–106.

34. Ibid.

35. Pérez, *Cuba: Between Reform*, 36–38; Guerra Valiente, *Las Huellas del Génesis*, 12–13.

36. Guerra Valiente, *Las Huellas del Génesis*, 127–29; Pérez, *Cuba: Between Reform*, 38–40.

37. Guerra Valiente, *Las Huellas del Génesis*, 127–29; Pérez, *Cuba: Between Reform*, 40–41, 46–7.

38. Ibid.

39. Elliott, *Empires of the Atlantic World*, 25; Haring, *The Spanish Empire in America*, 29.

40. Pérez, *Cuba: Between Reform*, 51–56.

41. Regino E. Boti, *Guantánamo: Breves apuntes acerca de los origenes y fundacíon de esta ciudad* (Guantánamo: Imprenta de el Resumen, 1912). Guerra Valiente, *Las Huellas del Génesis*, 18, represents a vast improvement.

42. Guerra Valiente, *Las Huellas del Génesis*, 12. On the nettlesome problem of contraband in Spanish colonies, see G. Earl Sanders, "Counter-Contraband in Spanish America: Handicaps of the Governors in the Indies," *The Americas* 34, no. 1 (July 1977): 59–80; George H. Nelson, "Contraband Trade Under the Asiento,

1730–1739," *American Historical Review* 51, no. 1 (Oct. 1945): 55–67; Alfonso W. Qiroz, "Implicit Costs of Empire: Bureaucratic Corruption in Nineteenth-Century Cuba," *Journal of Latin American Studies* 35, no. 3 (Aug. 2003): 473–511, esp. 476–79; and Virginia Lee Brown, "Contraband Trade: A Factor in the Decline of Spain's American Empire," *Hispanic American Historical Review* 8, no. 2 (May 1928): 178–89, esp. 182–83.

43. Guerra Valiente, *Las Huellas del Génesis*, 12.

44. For British troop levels, see Vernon to Newcastle, September 2, 1741, in *Original Papers, Relating to the Expedition to the Island of Cuba* (London: M. Cooper, 1744), Houghton Library, Harvard University, 91.

45. Edward Vernon to Thomas Pelham, Duke of York (and secretary of state for the Southern Department), July 29, 1741, in *Original Papers*, 29, 44.

46. Edward Vernon to General Thomas Wentworth, July 19, 1741, in *Original Papers*, 23; J.C.M. Ogelsby, "Spain's Havana Squadron and the Preservation of the Balance of Power in the Caribbean, 1740–1748," *Hispanic American Historical Review* 49, no. 3 (Aug. 1969): 477–79; Albert Harkness Jr., "Americanism and Jenkins' Ear," *Mississippi Valley Historical Review* 37 (1950): 75–76; and Richard Rolt, *An Impartial Representation of the Conduct of the Several Powers of Europe Engaged in the Late General War*, 4 vols. (London: S. Birt, 1749–50), 264.

47. Myron O. Stachiw, *Massachusetts Officers and Soldiers, 1723–1743: Dummer's War to the War of Jenkins' Ear* (Boston: New England Historical Genealogical Society, 1979), v–xxiv; Philip J. Greven, *Four Generations: Population, Land and Family in Colonial Andover, Massachusetts* (Ithaca, N.Y.: Cornell University Press, 1972), chap. 6–8; Douglas Lamar Jones, "The Strolling Poor: Transiency in Eighteenth-Century Massachusetts," *Journal of Social History* 8, no. 3 (Spring 1975): 28–54; Paul E. Johnson, "The Modernization of Mayo Greenleaf Patch: Land, Family, and Marginality in New England, 1766–1818," *New England Quarterly* 55, no. 4 (Dec. 1982): 488–516; and John J. Waters, "Family, Inheritance, and Migration in Colonial New England: The Evidence from Guilford, Connecticut," *William and Mary Quarterly*, 3rd ser., 39, no. 1 (Jan. 1982): 64–86.

48. *Boston Gazette*, April 14–21, 1740.

49. Stachiw, *Massachusetts Officers and Soldiers*, xiii, reports that nine hundred men from Massachusetts enlisted, but only five hundred headed south.

50. Reports of abuse ebb and flow but might still be described as constant. See, for example, *American Weekly Mercury* (Philadelphia), Nov. 17–24 and Dec. 20–27, 1726; *American Weekly Mercury*, Jan. 31–Feb. 7, and March 30–April 6, 1727; *Boston News-Letter*, March 19–26, 1730; *Weekly Rehearsal* (Boston), Sept. 10, 1733; *New England Journal*, Aug. 19, 1734; *Weekly Rehearsal*, April 4, 1735; *New York Weekly Journal*, March 13, 1737; and *Boston News-Letter*, April 14–21, 1737.

51. Stachiw, *Massachusetts Officers and Soldiers*, ix–xi; Elliott, *Empires of the Atlantic World*, chap. 8.

52. Though a licensed privateer, and therefore technically not a pirate, Fandino could evidently out-pirate them all. He is colorfully described in a letter from

Thomas Frankland, captain of the HMS *Rose*, to the secretaries of the Admiralty, June 16, 1742, quoted in J. K. Laughton, "Jenkins's Ear," *English Historical Review* 4, no. 16 (Oct. 1889): 748. On the distinction between pirates, privateers, buccaneers, and corsairs, see Peter Earle, *The Pirate Wars* (New York: St. Martin's Griffin, 2006).

53. Harold V. W. Temperley, "The Causes of the War of Jenkins' Ear, 1739," *Transactions of the Royal Historical Society*, 3rd ser., 3 (1909): 201–209, and passim. See also Stachiw, *Massachusetts Officers and Soldiers*, viii–xiii; Laughton, "Jenkins's Ear," 741–49; and Elliott, *Empires of the Atlantic World*, 232–34. Scholars have long debated whether Jenkins actually lost his ear aboard his ship rather than at some watering hole, never mind the question of whether the pickle paraded before Parliament lo those many years was actually *his* ear. Laughton, "Jenkins's Ear," 747, puts to rest at least the first question.

54. *Encyclopædia Britannica*, vol. 32 (New York: Encyclopædia Britannica, 1911), 1032–33; Elliott, *Empires of the Atlantic World*, 233.

55. *Boston Post Boy*, April 18, 1740. Vernon's medals are readily viewable online; see, for example, "Battle of Cartagena de Indias," Wikipedia.

56. On the idea that this campaign fostered a sense of "British transatlantic community," see Elliott, *Empires of the Atlantic World*, 232, which cites David Armitage, *The Ideological Origins of the British Empire* (Cambridge, UK: Cambridge University Press, 2000), 182–88. My reading of colonial newspapers is closer to that of Harkness, "Americanism and Jenkins' Ear," 75 and passim.

57. Harkness, "Americanism and Jenkins' Ear," 72–74; Vernon, *Original Papers*, 41. For an example of British hostility toward the Americans, see Sir Charles Knowles, *An Account of the Expedition to Carthagena with Explanatory Notes and Observations* (London: M. Cooper, 1743), 37–38, 55–56, which, after acknowledging the greenness of the British troops and officers, suggests that the Americans were much "worse."

58. Edward Vernon to Thomas Pelham, Duke of York, November 3, 1741, *Original Papers*, 152–53.

59. Ibid., 152. See also Vernon to Wentworth, Aug. 19, 1741, in *Original Papers*, 71.

60. From Port Royal, Lawrence Washington reports that the British suffered "about six-hundred" killed "and some wounded," and that "the climate killed us in greater numbers"; Lawrence Washington to Augustine Washington, May 30, 1741, Washington Family Papers, Manuscript Division, Library of Congress, Washington, D.C. The English writer Tobias Smollett served as surgeon's second mate on the Cartagena expedition and left two engrossing accounts of the illness he encountered. See his fictional *The Adventures of Roderick Random* (Oxford: Oxford University Press, 1979), 189–94, and his "Account of the Expedition Against Carthagena in the West Indies," in James P. Browne, ed., *The Works of Tobias Smollett*, vol. 8 (London, 1872), 442–55.

61. Vernon to the Duke of Newcastle, Nov. 3, 1741, in *Original Papers*, 152.

62. Lawrence Washington to Augustine Washington, May 30, 1741, Manuscript Division, Library of Congress, Washington, D.C.; Willard Sterne Randall, *George Washington: A Life* (New York: Henry Holt and Company, 1997), 20.

63. As a British parliamentarian, Vernon undoubtedly knew about the scarcity of land in the colonies; this is confirmed in Vernon to the Duke of Newcastle, July 29, 1741, in *Original Papers*, 44, where he writes that the establishment of a new British settlement somewhere in the Spanish West Indies "has long been in my Thoughts," if only "lately broke out into Execution."

64. Randall, *George Washington*, chap. 1.

65. Lawrence Washington to Augustine Washington, May 30, 1741.

66. E. Alfred Jones, ed., "The American Regiment in the Carthagena Expedition," *The Virginia Magazine of History and Biography* 30, no. 1 (Jan. 1922): 19.

67. The Virginians included Thomas Lee, Nathaniel Chapman, and John Mercer; the Englishmen, the Duke of Bedford, Virginia governor Robert Dinwiddie, and the merchant John Hanbury. Kenneth P. Bailey, *The Ohio Company of Virginia and the Westward Movement, 1748–1792: A Chapter in the History of the Colonial Frontier* (Glendale, Calif.: Arthur H. Clark Co., 1939), chap. 1. Cf. Eric Hinderaker, *Elusive Empires: Constructing Colonialism in the Ohio Valley, 1673–1800* (Cambridge, UK: Cambridge University Press, 1997), 135–39. For background on Lawrence Washington, see the long footnote 14 on pages 43–46 in J. M. Toner, ed., *The Daily Journal of Major George Washington, in 1751–2, Kept While on a Tour from Virginia to the Island of Barbadoes, with His Invalid Brother, Major Lawrence Washington* (Albany, N.Y.: J. Munsell's Sons, 1892).

68. Vernon to Duke of Newcastle, Nov. 3, 1741, in *Original Papers*, 152–53, which refers to a naval Council of War, Oct. 22, 1741, in *Original Papers*, 126; *Encyclopædia Britannica*, vol. 32, 1032–33.

69. Rolt, *Impartial Representation*, vol. 1, 267–68; Lawrence Washington to Augustine Washington, May 30, 1741.

70. Council of War quoted in Rolt, *Impartial Representation*, vol. 1, 266.

71. *The American Weekly Mercury*, out of Philadelphia, has two entries for a John Drake in its section on "shipping news," one "entered outward" for Boston aboard the sloop *Three Brothers*, on July 6, 1721, another "cleared outward" for Boston aboard the schooner *Philadelphia*, on July 27, 1721. In his July 19, 1741, letter to the Duke of Newcastle, Vernon allows that settlement of the Guantánamo Bay region had "long been in my Thoughts," thoughts that seem to date back to the previous December and his first encounter with Drake. See *Original Papers*, 44.

72. Declaration of John Drake, Mariner, July 10, 1741, *Original Papers*, 14–16.

73. "Testimony of Henry Cavelier, a carpenter of a British slave ship, imprisoned in Santiago and later released," *Original Papers*, 16–18.

74. Declaration of John Drake, *Original Papers*, 15–16.

75. Ibid., 15.

76. Francisco Cajigal de la Vega to Pedro Guarro, July 31, 1741, *Original Papers*,

200; Thomas Sturton, "An Account of Our March from the Camp at the Upper Barkadier on Augusta River, to the Village of Etteguava, and Back to the Camp," *Original Papers*, 195.

77. Sturton, "An Account of Our March," 196.

78. Vernon to Wentworth, July 19, 1741, *Original Papers*, 23.

79. Vernon to Lt. Thomas Sturton, July 24, 1741, *Original Papers*, 26. Vernon repeats the warning four days later; Vernon to Sturton, July 28, 1741, *Original Papers*, 30.

80. Vernon to Newcastle, July 29, 1741, *Original Papers*, 42. Travel literature, like classified advertising, is an inflationary medium. The sojourner's eye sees what it wants or needs to see, idealizing the ordinary, ignoring the unsightly, often failing to recognize the limits of its vision. "Give her the glass," Mark Twain once wrote; "it may from error free her, if she can see herself as others see her." There was no shortage of hyperbole and projection in Vernon's response to Guantánamo Bay. Vernon needed Guantánamo to compensate for Cartagena; the Americans needed Guantánamo to compensate for lack of land. But there was more to Vernon's and the Americans' responses than that. Guantánamo is indeed supremely situated at the heart of the Western Hemisphere—and superbly outfitted to make the most of its geographical fate. In ways that Vernon could scarcely have imagined, and despite great political and technological change, Guantánamo has retained its pivotal position in the modern Atlantic and American worlds, worlds it illuminates in compelling, often unexpected ways. See, among others, Mary Louise Pratt, *Imperial Eyes: Travel Writing and Transculturation* (New York: Routledge, 1992), chap. 1 and 3; James T. Campbell, *Middle Passages: African American Journeys to Africa, 1787–2005* (New York: Penguin, 2006), introduction; and Elliott, *Empires of the Atlantic World*, 88.

81. See, for example, *Original Papers*, 47, 50, 57, 95.

82. Vernon to Newcastle, Nov. 3, 1741, *Original Papers*, 153.

83. Harkness, "Americanism and Jenkins' Ear," 80.

84. See also *Boston Post-Boy*, Sept. 7, 1741, 3.

85. *Boston Evening-Post*, Sept. 21, 1741; *Boston Post-Boy*, Sept. 21, 1741.

86. Governor Shirley's Address to the Assembly reprinted in *Boston Post-Boy*, Sept. 28, 1741; see also the governor's proclamation of Oct. 16, 1741, Early American Imprints, Series 1: Evans Readex Digital Collections, no. 40244, Widener Library, Harvard University.

87. *Boston Post-Boy*, Sept. 28, 1741, 2.

88. Vernon to Newcastle, Nov. 3, 1741, *Original Papers*, 152.

89. Ibid.

90. Vernon to Newcastle, Nov. 26, 1741, *Original Papers*, 175.

91. Vernon to Newcastle, Dec. 1, 1741, *Original Papers*, 183.

92. Stachiw, *Massachusetts Officers and Soldiers*, xxii; Harkness, "Americanism and Jenkins' Ear," 87n131.

93. Olga Portuondo, *Guerra in el Caribe, 1741. Derrota británica frente a Santiago de*

Cuba (Santiago: Universidad de Oriente, 1987), 1–24, and Levi Marrero, *Cuba: Economía y sociedad*, S. A. Player, ed. (Madrid: S.A., 1993), 104.

94. Guerra Valiente, *Las Huellas del Génesis*, 17; Elliot, *Empires of the Atlantic World*, 233.

95. Guerra Valiente, *Las Huellas del Génesis*, 20–21.

96. Ibid., 22.

97. On these developments, see Robert S. Smith, "Spanish Mercantilism: A Hardy Perennial," *Southern Economic Journal* 38, no. 1 (July 1971): 8–10, John R. Fisher, "Commerce and Imperial Decline: Spanish Trade with Spanish America, 1797–1820," *Journal of Latin American Studies* 30, no. 3 (Oct. 1998): 461–70, 476.

98. Hugh Thomas, *Cuba, or the Pursuit of Freedom* (New York: De Capo, 1998), 73–74.

99. On the slow development of capitalism in Cuba, see Adelaida Zorina, "On the Genesis of Capitalism in Nineteenth-Century Cuba," *Latin American Perspectives* 2, no. 4 (March 1975): 11–13; and Bergad, *Comparative Histories of Slavery*, 15–18.

100. Laird W. Bergad, Fe Iglesias García, and María del Carmen Barcia, *The Cuban Slave Market, 1790–1880* (New York: Cambridge University Press, 1995), 23–26; Franklin W. Knight, "Origins of Wealth and the Sugar Revolution in Cuba, 1750–1850," *Hispanic American Historical Review* 57, no. 2 (1977).

101. Thomas, *Cuba*, 74–77.

102. Thomas, *Cuba*, 74–77; Guerra Valiente, *Las Huellas del Génesis*, 29–33; and Bergad, *Comparative Histories of Slavery*, 16–21.

103. José Guio y Sanchez y Maria Dolores Higueras, eds., *Cuba Ilustrada: Real Comisión de Guantánamo a la Isla de Cuba, 1796–1802* (Barcelona: Lunwerg Editores, 1991), 43, 53.

104. Ibid., 53–65.

105. Ibid., 66–67.

106. Guerra Valiente, *Las Huellas del Génesis*, 23–25; Guio y Dolores, eds., *Cuba Ilustrada*, 67.

107. Guio y Dolores, eds., *Cuba Ilustrada*, 72–73, 142–43.

108. Guerra Valiente, *Las Huellas del Génesis*, 27–29; Imilcy Balboa Navarro, "Guantánamo: de las Tierras del Rey a la Propiedad Contractual," in Josef Opatrný, ed., *Cambios y Revoluciones en el Caribe Hispano de los Siglos XIX y XX* (Praga: Editorial Karolinum, 2003), 133–35. Impatience with Spain's refusal to invest in Guantánamo Bay and other ports in Cuba was not limited to Spanish colonists and government officials. Nearly fifty years after Mopox, the editor of the U.S. periodical *De Bow's Review* lamented the empty and undeveloped state of Cuba's many promising harbors. "A great many of these fine harbors, where magnificent cities would long since have sprung up under a good government, are to this day places as deserted as when the isle was first discovered—360 years ago. There is now not even a fisherman's hut on their shores" (14, no. 2 [Feb. 1853]: 93).

2 ★ THE NEW FRONTIER

1. Thomas Jefferson to James Madison, Oct. 24, 1823, at www.memory.loc.gov/am mem/collections/jefferson_papers. On the United States's long dalliance with Cuba, see Louis A. Pérez, *Cuba and the United States: Ties of Singular Intimacy* (Athens: University of Georgia Press, 2003), 39–54 and passim.

2. On early British forays into the backcountry, see Eric Hinderaker and Peter C. Mancall, *At the Edge of Empire: The Backcountry in British North America* (Baltimore, Md.: Johns Hopkins University Press, 2003), 92–97 and chap. 5.

3. Born at Shadwell, Jefferson lived at the Randolph estate at Tuckahoe, along the banks of the James River, north of Richmond, for seven years starting in 1745. He returned to Shadwell at age nine. See Monticello website, www.monticello.org.

4. See query 2, A note on rivers, in Merrill D. Peterson, ed., *Thomas Jefferson, Notes on the State of Virginia* (New York: Library of America, 1984), 133–139, available at etext.virginia.edu/toc/modeng/public/JefVirg.html.

5. John Quincy Adams, *Writings of John Quincy Adams* (New York: The Macmillan Company, 1917), 373.

6. Note 2, query 4, on mountains, from Jefferson, *Notes on the State of Virginia* (Richmond: J. W. Randolph, 1853), 215. Jefferson was wrong about the origin of the Gulf of Mexico; see chap. 1.

7. Quoted in Paul Calore, *The Causes of the Civil War* (New York: McFarland, 2008), 200.

8. Peter S. Onuf, *Jefferson's Empire: The Language of American Nationhood* (Charlottesville: University Press of Virginia, 2000), 7, 60.

9. The great statement of this argument is Federalist 10; Onuf, *Jefferson's Empire*, 54; Drew R. McCoy, *The Elusive Republic: Political Economy in Jeffersonian America* (Chapel Hill: University of North Carolina Press, 1980); and William Appleman Williams, *Empire as a Way of Life* (New York: Oxford University Press, 1980), 39, 47.

10. Onuf, *Jefferson's Empire*, 80, 82.

11. First Inaugural Address; Onuf, *Jefferson's Empire*, 132.

12. Onuf, *Jefferson's Empire*, 58.

13. Franklin W. Knight, "The Haitian Revolution," *American Historical Review* 105, no. 1 (Feb. 2000): 103–108; Tim Matthewson, "Jefferson and Haiti," *Journal of Southern History* 61, no. 2 (May 1995): 211–13; and Susan Buck-Morss, "Hegel and Haiti," *Critical Inquiry* 26, no. 4 (Summer 2000): 821–37.

14. Knight, "The Haitian Revolution," 107–108; Matthewson, "Jefferson and Haiti," 211–13.

15. Matthewson, "Jefferson and Haiti," 232–33.

16. Hugh Thomas, *Cuba, or the Pursuit of Freedom* (New York: Da Capo, 1998), 77.

17. Thomas, *Cuba*, 75–80; Louis A. Pérez, Jr., *Cuba: Between Reform and Revolution* (New York: Oxford University Press, 1995), 70–75.

18. Ladislao Guerra Valiente, *Las Huellas del Génesis: Guantánamo Hasta 1870*

(Guantánamo: Editorial el Mar y Montaña, 2004), 41; Jacobo de la Pezuela, *Diccionario geográfico, estadístico, histórico de la isla de Cuba*, tomo 2 (Madrid: Imprenta del Establecimiento de Mellado, 1863), 497.

19. Oscar Zanetti and Alejandro García, *Sugar and Railroads: A Cuban History, 1837–1959* (Chapel Hill: University of North Carolina Press, 1998), 66–67.

20. "Annual Report on Foreign Commerce for the Year Ended September 1865," Guantánamo—Francis Badell, Consular Agent, 38 Congress, 2nd sess., serial set vol. 1227, sess. no. 11.

21. Guerra Valiente, *Las Huellas del Génesis*, 44–53.

22. Ibid., 64–65.

23. Thomas Jefferson, Second Inaugural Address, March 5, 1805, Avalon Project, Yale University, at avalon.law.yale.edu/19th_century/jefinau2.asp.

24. On the melting pot, see Jonathan M. Hansen, *The Lost Promise of Patriotism: Debating American Identity, 1890–1920* (Chicago: University of Chicago Press, 2003), 98–99.

25. Thomas Jefferson to the Miami, Potawatomi, Delaware, and Chipeway, Dec. 21, 1808, in Andrew Adgate Lipscomb, ed., *The Writings of Thomas Jefferson* (Charleston, S.C.: Nabu Press, 2010), 439; Onuf, *Jefferson's Empire*, 51.

26. Walter L. Williams, "United States Indian Policy and the Debate over Philippine Annexation: Implications for the Origins of American Imperialism," *Journal of American History* 66, no. 4 (March 1980): 811–27; Hansen, *The Lost Promise of Patriotism*, chap. 1.

27. Williams, *Empire as a Way of Life*, 69; Zoltan Vajda, "Thomas Jefferson on the Character of an Unfree People: The Case of Spanish America," *American Nineteenth Century History* 8, no. 3 (Sept. 2007): 273–92.

28. Williams, *Empire as a Way of Life*, 65.

29. Thomas Jefferson to James Monroe, Oct. 24, 1823, Thomas Jefferson Papers, Library of Congress.

30. James Monroe to Thomas Jefferson, June 30, 1823, Jefferson Papers.

31. John Quincy Adams's Account of the Cabinet Meeting of November 7, 1823, available at www.mtholyoke.edu/acad/intrel/jqacab.htm.

32. The Monroe Doctrine, Message of President Monroe to Congress, December 2, 1823, in Ruhl T. Bartlett, ed., *The Record of American Diplomacy: Documents and Readings in the History of American Foreign Relations* (New York: Alfred A. Knopf, 1964), 181–83.

33. Jefferson to William Carmichael, Aug. 2, 1790, at oll.libertyfund.org/?option=com_staticxt&staticfile=show.php%3Ftitle=803&chapter=86781&layout=html&Itemid=27); Thomas Jefferson to James Monroe, May 4, 1806, Jefferson Papers.

34. John Quincy Adams to Hugh Nelson, April 28, 1823, in Bartlett, ed., *Record of American Diplomacy*, 231–34.

35. Daniel Webster, Speech on the Panama Mission, U.S. House of Representatives, April 1826, in Robert F. Smith, ed., *What Happened in Cuba? A Documentary History* (New York: Twayne, 1963), 33–36.

36. Smith, *What Happened in Cuba?*, 36; Louis A. Pérez, Jr., *Cuba: Between Reform and Revolution* (New York: Oxford University Press, 1995), 104–10; Thomas, *Cuba*, 93–105.

37. Zanetti and García, *Sugar and Railroads*, 57; Ada Ferrer, *Insurgent Cuba: Race, Nation, and Revolution, 1868–1898* (Chapel Hill: University of North Carolina Press, 1999), 2.

38. See, for example, the intercepted letter presented to the British Parliament from a slave trader to fellow traders warning them to steer clear of Guantánamo. *Philadelphia Inquirer*, Aug. 13, 1825, 3.

39. Tom Chaffin, "'Sons of Washington': Narciso López, Filibustering, and U.S. Nationalism, 1848–1851," *Journal of the Early Republic* 15, no. 1 (Spring 1995): 93–94, 106–108.

40. Smith, *What Happened in Cuba?*, 38.

41. Ibid., 41.

42. James Buchanan to Romulus M. Saunders, June 17, 1848, in Bartlett, *Record of American Diplomacy*, 234–37; Smith, *What Happened in Cuba?*, 39–44.

43. William L. Marcy to Charles W. Davis, March 15, 1854, Smith, *What Happened in Cuba?*, 58–59, cf. 55. Cf. C. Stanley Urban, "Africanization of Cuba Scare," *Hispanic American Historical Review* 37, no. 1 (Feb. 1957): 29–45.

44. Robert E. May, *Manifest Destiny's Underworld: Filibustering in Antebellum America* (Chapel Hill: University of North Carolina Press, 2004), 270–72.

45. John Bach McMaster, *A History of the People of the United States, from the Revolution to the Civil War* (New York: D. Appleton and Company, 1921), 133–41; Tom Chaffin, *Fatal Glory: Narciso López and the First Clandestine U.S. War Against Cuba* (Charlottesville: University of Virginia Press, 1996), esp. chap. 2; Robert E. May, *The Southern Dream of a Caribbean Empire* (Gainesville: University Press of Florida, 2002), 24–30.

46. Ostend Manifesto, Oct. 18, 1854, in Smith, *What Happened in Cuba?*, 65.

47. Ibid., 64.

48. Ibid., 66.

49. Ibid.

50. George Fitzugh, "Destiny of the Slave States," *De Bow's Review* (Sep. 1854), in Smith, *What Happened in Cuba?*, 70; Maturin M. Ballou, *History of Cuba, or Notes of a Traveller in the Tropics* (Boston: Phillips, Sampson and Company, 1954), in Smith, *What Happened in Cuba?*, 72–73.

51. W. H. Holderness to Palmerston, Sept. 22, 1854, in Gavin B. Henderson, ed., "Southern Designs on Cuba, 1854–1857, and Some European Opinions," *Journal of Southern History*, 5, no. 3 (Aug. 1939): 375–76.

52. Robert Steven Levine, *Martin Delany, Frederick Douglass, and the Politics of Representative Identity* (Chapel Hill: University of North Carolina Press, 1997), 201–204.

53. Delany's planning did not advance far—in the nonfiction world, that is; see Martin Delany, "Annexation of Cuba," *North Star*, April 27, 1849. It advanced con-

siderably in his novel *Blake, or the Huts of Africa* (Boston: Beacon Press, 1970), part 2. See also James T. Campbell, *Middle Passages: African American Journeys to Africa, 1787–2005* (New York: Penguin Books, 2006), 72–76.

54. Sean Wilentz, "Who Lincoln Was," *The New Republic*, July 15, 2009, 24–47.

55. In the immediate antebellum era, annexationist sentiment on Cuba did not cut strictly along sectional lines; see McMaster, *A History of the People of the United States*, 139.

56. "Our Guantánamo Correspondence," *Weekly Herald* (New York), Dec. 12, 1857, 1.

57. "The Slave Trade," *Chicago Tribune*, July 9, 1860, 2.

58. Bradley Michael Reynolds, "Guantánamo Bay, Cuba: The History of an American Naval Base and Its Relationship to the Formulation of United States Foreign Policy and Military Strategy Toward the Caribbean, 1895–1910," Ph.D. dissertation, University of Southern California, 1982, 22.

59. Ferrer, *Insurgent Cuba*, 15–17.

60. Ibid., 47–56.

61. Ulysses S. Grant, Annual Message to Congress, Dec. 7, 1875, in Smith, *What Happened in Cuba?*, 82–84; Smith, *What Happened in Cuba?*, 85–87; Pérez, *Cuba*, 129–35; and Thomas, *Cuba*, 271–72.

62. Henry Cabot Lodge, "Our Blundering Foreign Policy," *Forum* (March 1895): 8.

63. Smith, *What Happened in Cuba?*, 85–87; Pérez, *Cuba*, 135–38; Thomas, *Cuba*, 272–80; and Ferrer, *Insurgent Cuba*, 93–99, 112–15.

64. Roosevelt quoted in Hansen, *The Lost Promise of Patriotism*, 22–23. Cf. Williams, "United States Indian Policy," 816–26.

65. Walter LaFeber, "A Note on the 'Mercantilist Imperialism' of Alfred Thayer Mahan," *Mississippi Valley Historical Review* 48, no. 4 (March 1962): 674–85.

66. Alfred Thayer Mahan, "The United States Looking Outward," *The Interest of America in Sea Power, Present and Future* (Boston: Little, Brown, and Company, 1897), 4–17; and Mahan, "Hawaii and Our Future Sea Power," in *The Interest of America*, 35–36.

67. Mahan, "Hawaii and Our Future Sea Power," 52; Mahan, "The Strategic Features of the Gulf of Mexico and the Caribbean Sea," in *The Interest of America*, 280–82; and Mahan, "A Twentieth-Century Outlook," in *The Interest of America*, 261.

68. Mahan, "The United States Looking Outward," 9–17.

69. Alfred Thayer Mahan, "A Twentieth-Century Outlook," in *The Interest of America*, 261, 226.

70. "Poor Spain in a Worry," *New York Times*, March 17, 1895, 17.

3 ☆ INDEPENDENCE DAY

1. "The Sunday at Camp McCalla," correspondence of the *New York Journal*, in *The Spanish-American War: The Events as Described by Eye Witnesses* (Chicago: Herbert S. Stone & Company, 1899), 94–95.

2. Stephen Crane, "Marines Signaling Under Fire at Guantanamo," *McClure's Magazine* (February 1899), 332.

3. Alex Szarazgat, *De la Conquista a la Revolución*, tomo 2 (Buenos Aires: Nuestra America, 2005), 12; Louis A. Pérez, Jr., *Cuba: Between Reform and Revolution* (New York: Oxford University Press, 1995), chap. 6; Hugh Thomas, *Cuba, or the Pursuit of Freedom* (New York: Da Capo, 1998), 264–309; and Philip S. Foner, *The Spanish-Cuban-American War and the Birth of American Imperialism*, vol. 1 (New York: Monthly Review Press, 1972), chap. 1.

4. *Philadelphia Inquirer*, Feb. 27, 1895, 1.

5. *Sioux City Journal*, Feb. 27, 1895, 1.

6. *New York Times*, Feb. 28, 1898, 5; *New York Times*, March 5, 1895, 5. Throughout the insurgency, *Times* articles continued to anticipate its demise long after evidence rendered such anticipations absurd, if not fraudulent.

7. *The Daily Picayune*, Feb. 27, 1895, 7. Similar reports occurred throughout U.S. newspapers; see, for example, *The Trenton Times*, Feb. 27, 1895, 4; *Boston Daily Journal*, Feb. 28, 1895, 1; *Idaho Daily Statesman*, Feb. 28, 1895, 3; and *The Kansas City Star*, Feb. 28, 1895, 6, the last of which, perhaps taking Spanish accounts of events in Cuba at face value, announced that "a very small revolution" in Cuba had been "dispersed easily."

8. Edwin T. Atkins, *Sixty Years in Cuba* (Cambridge, Mass.: The Riverside Press, 1926), 151–52.

9. Ibid., 138–40.

10. Ibid., 158; "Cuba's Rare Insurgents," *New York Times*, April 23, 1895, 5.

11. *New York Times*, May 3, 1895, 5.

12. Grover Cleveland, "American Interests in the Cuban Revolution," *Papers Relating to Foreign Affairs*, 1896, xxvii–lxii, available at www.mtholyoke.edu/acad/intrel/gc26.htm.

13. Gómez's two proclamations of July and November 1895 are available at www.historyofcuba.com/history/time/timetbl2b.htm#sca.

14. Weyler quoted in Pérez, *Cuba: Between Reform*, 165.

15. *Wheeling Register*, Jan. 19, 1896, 1.

16. Pérez, *Cuba: Between Reform*, 174.

17. Column from *The New York World*, reprinted in *The Kansas City Star*, June 29, 1896, 5.

18. See President Cleveland: "If Spain still holds Havana and the seaports and all the considerable towns, the insurgents still roam at will over at least two-thirds of the inland country. If the determination of Spain to put down the insurrection seems but to strengthen with the lapse of time and is evinced by her unhesitating devotion of largely increased military and naval forces to the task, there is much reason to believe that the insurgents have gained in point of numbers and character and resources, and are none the less inflexible in their resolve not to succumb without practically securing the great objects for which they took up arms."

President Grover Cleveland to Congress, Dec. 7, 1896. Papers Relating to Foreign Affairs, 1896, xxvii–lxii, U.S. Department of State, Washington, D.C.

19. Pérez, *Cuba: Between Reform*, 168–75.

20. Emory W. Fenn, "Ten Months with the Cuban Insurgents," *The Century Magazine* 56, no. 2 (June 1898): 307.

21. Ibid., 176.

22. President Cleveland to Congress, Dec. 7, 1896, Papers Relating to Foreign Affairs, 1896, U.S. Department of State, Washington, D.C., xxvii–lxii.

23. General Máximo Gómez to President Grover Cleveland, Feb. 9, 1897, available at www.historyofcuba.com/history/gomez4.htm.

24. *Herald* story published in the *Bismarck* (North Dakota) *Daily Tribune*, Dec. 31, 1897, 1.

25. Undersecretary of War Joseph C. Breckenridge to U.S. Army commander Lieutenant General Nelson A. Miles, Dec. 7, 1897, in Pichardo Viñals, *Documentos para la Historia de Cuba*, 513–14, available at www.historyofcuba.com/history/bmemo.htm.

26. Thomas, *Cuba*, 360–62.

27. Pérez, *Cuba: Between Reform*, 176–78; Thomas, *Cuba*, 372–81.

28. Thomas, *Cuba*, 376.

29. Lars Schoultz, *Beneath the United States: A History of U.S. Policy Toward Latin America* (Cambridge, Mass.: Harvard University Press, 1998), 139.

30. Estrada y Palma handed Janney a $2-million Cuban bond (6 percent interest), which, discounted in the United States, was worth half that. See Thomas, *Cuba*, 376; David F. Healy, *The United States in Cuba, 1898–1902: Generals, Politicians, and the Search for Policy* (Madison: University of Wisconsin Press, 1963), 26–27; and John Offner, *An Unwanted War: The Diplomacy of the United States and Spain over Cuba, 1895–1898* (Chapel Hill: University of North Carolina Press, 1992), 189.

31. Louis A. Peréz Jr., *The War of 1898: The United States and Cuba in History and Historiography* (Chapel Hill: University of North Carolina Press, 1998), 39–40; and Peréz, *Cuba: Between Reform*, 179.

32. Keeler's move to Boston seems to have been driven more by wanderlust than by lack of opportunity in Bangor, which, despite the long, cyclical economic depression at the end of the nineteenth century, was successfully diversifying from an economy based solely on lumber to one of pulp and paper manufacturing, communications, and transportation. See Sara K. Martin, "The Little City in Itself: Middle-Class Aspiration in Bangor, Maine, 1880–1920," M.A. thesis, University of Maine, 2001, chap. 1.

33. Frank Keeler, *The Journal of Frank Keeler*, ed. Carolyn A. Tyson (Quantico, Va.: Marine Corps Papers Series, 1968), 3.

34. *Boston Morning Journal*, March 25, 1898, 1.

35. Ibid.

36. Keeler, *Journal of Frank Keeler*, 3.
37. Robert Huntington Sr. to Robert Huntington Jr., May 4, 1898, Huntington Papers, U.S. Marine Corps Library, Quantico, Va.
38. Keeler, *Journal of Frank Keeler*, 4.
39. Huntington Sr. to Huntington Jr., May 4, 1898; Keeler, *Journal of Frank Keeler*, 4; Annual Reports of the Navy Department for the Year [hereafter ARND] 1898 (Washington: U.S. Government Printing Office, 1898), 441; and Charles L. McCawley, "The Guantánamo Campaign of 1898," *The Marine Corps Gazette* 1, 3 (Sept. 1916): 223.
40. A large-animal veterinarian assures me that "horses don't vomit," but one wonders if he has ever been off Cape Hatteras in heavy weather on a boat with a horse.
41. Huntington Sr. to Huntington Jr., May 4, 1898.
42. Keeler, *Journal of Frank Keeler*, 25.
43. Jack Cameron Dierks, *A Leap to Arms: The Cuban Campaign of 1898* (Philadelphia: Lippincott Company, 1970), 49.
44. Ibid., 49–50.
45. Robert Huntington, Sr., to Robert Huntington, Jr., May 27, 1898, Huntington Papers, U.S. Marine Corps Library, Quantico, Va.
46. Keeler, *Journal of Frank Keeler*, 5.
47. Herbert H. Sargent, *The Campaign of Santiago de Cuba* (Chicago: A. C. McClure & Co., 1907), 2:47 and 1:47, 83.
48. French Ensor Chadwick, *The Relations of the United States and Spain: The Spanish American War*, vol. 1 (New York: Charles Scribner's Sons, 1911), 318; ARND, 448.
49. Sargent, *The Campaign*, 1:83, 100, 2:102; Dierks, *A Leap to Arms*, 182.
50. ARND, 392.
51. C. F. Goodrich to William T. Sampson, May 19, 1898, ARND, 210–11.
52. Alfred Thayer Mahan, *The Interest of America in Sea Power, Present and Future* (Boston: Little, Brown, and Company, 1897), 26.
53. ARND, 210–11.
54. ARND, 397.
55. ARND, 399.
56. ARND, 489; Sargent, *The Campaign*, 1: 228–29; Chadwick, *Spanish-American War*, 1:356; Henry B. Russell, *History of Our War with Spain Including the Story of Cuba* (Hartford, Conn.: A.D. Worthington & Co., 1898), 63.
57. Keeler, *Journal of Frank Keeler*, 7.
58. Ibid., 37.
59. Ibid., 7.
60. Ibid., 9.
61. McCawley, "The Guantánamo Campaign," 229; Keeler, *Journal of Frank Keeler*, 11.
62. Robert Huntington, Sr., to Robert Huntington, Jr., June 19, 1898, Huntington Papers, 3.

63. Ibid.

64. Keeler, *Journal of Frank Keeler*, 13; McCawley, "The Guantánamo Campaign," 229–30.

65. J. F. Holden-Rhodes, "The Marines Would Stay," *Marine Corps Gazette*, November 1982, 69–70.

66. McCawley, "The Guantánamo Campaign," 232; Holden-Rhodes, "Marines Would Stay," 70.

67. Keeler, *Journal of Frank Keeler*, 13.

68. McCawley, "The Guantánamo Campaign," 232; Stephen Crane, "War Memories," in R. W. Stallman and E. R. Hagemann, eds., *The War Dispatches of Stephen Crane* (New York: New York University Press, 1964), 269. Crane seems to get the day of this activity wrong, implying here that this happened on June 13, where generally more credible sources such as McCawley and Keeler give the date for the arrival of journalists and new guns as the twelfth.

69. Arthur J. Burks, "Recall in Cuba," *Leatherneck* 30, no. 12 (Dec. 1947): 58.

70. Keeler, *Journal of Frank Keeler*, 13; Burks, "Recall in Cuba," 58–59.

71. Keeler, *Journal of Frank Keeler*, 14–17.

72. Felix Pareja to Arsenio Linares y Pombo, June 10, 1898, ARND, 450 (letter captured by the Cubans en route to Santiago).

73. Ibid.

74. ARND, 447, 453, 502.

75. See Captain McCalla's report of Feb. 11, 1902, in Chadwick, *Spanish American War*, 1:376–77.

76. Sargent, *The Campaign*, 99–100; Reynolds, "Guantánamo Bay," 125–27.

77. "Spanish Soldiers Starving," *New York Times*, July 9, 1898, 2.

78. Excerpt from the diary of José Muller y Tejeiro, ARND, 566.

79. Chadwick, *Spanish American War*, 1:312–13.

80. Sampson to Long, July 28, ARND, 614–15.

81. ARND, 449–50.

82. Robert Huntington Sr. to Robert Huntington Jr., July 29, 1898, Huntington Papers, 1.

83. Keeler, *Journal of Frank Keeler*, 38.

84. Ibid., 39; Robert Huntington Sr. to Robert Huntington Jr., June 19, 1898, Huntington Papers, 3.

85. Keeler, *Journal of Frank Keeler*, 13. See also the respectful firsthand description of Enrique Tomas y Tomas, the Cuban colonel in charge of the Cuban contingent, in Burks, "Recall in Cuba," 58–59.

86. *New York Times*, June 19, 1898, 1.

87. For evidence to the contrary, see Foner, *Spanish-Cuban-American War*, 1:359–68.

88. Sargent, *The Campaign*, 2:165–66.

89. Crane, *Dispatches*, 141–42.

90. Ibid., 146.

91. Ibid., 147.

92. Ibid.

93. *New York Times*, June 13, 1898.

94. Keeler, *Journal of Frank Keeler*, 20–21.

4 ★ A CRUEL AND AWFUL TRUTH

1. *New York Herald* interview with Máximo Gómez, Dec. 31, 1897, 1; García quoted in Philip S. Foner, *The Spanish-Cuban-American War and the Birth of American Imperialism*, vol. 2 (New York: Monthly Review Press, 1972), 355.

2. Carlos García Vélez, "Cuba Against Spain," in *The American-Spanish War: A History by the War Leaders* (Norwich, Conn.: Chas. C. Haskell and Son, 1899), 88–89.

3. Calixto García to William Shafter, July 17, 1898, quoted in Foner, *Spanish-Cuban-American War*, vol. 2, 369–70.

4. Elihu B. Root, "The Principles of Colonial Policy," in Robert Bacon and James Brown Scott, eds., *The Military and Colonial Policy of the United States* (Cambridge, Mass.: Harvard University Press, 1916), 161–62.

5. Walter L. Williams, "United States Indian Policy and the Debate over Philippine Annexation: Implications for the Origins of American Imperialism," *Journal of American History* 66, no. 4 (March 1980): 811–12.

6. Máximo Gómez, Diary, Jan. 8, 1899, at www.historyofcuba.com/history/gomez.htm.

7. Charles Emory Smith, "The War for Humanity," in Robert I. Fulton and Thomas C. Trueblood, eds., *Patriotic Eloquence Relating to the Spanish-American War and Its Issues* (New York: Charles Scribner's Sons, 1900), 290.

8. Ibid., 292.

9. Walter Hines Page, "The War with Spain, and After," *Atlantic Monthly* 81 (June 1898): 488.

10. John Henry Barrows, "The National Peace Jubilee," in Fulton and Trueblood, eds., *Patriotic Eloquence*, 14–17.

11. Franklin MacVeagh, "Not Mere Land Expansion," in Fulton and Trueblood, eds., *Patriotic Eloquence*, 240–42.

12. John Ireland, "America a World Power," in Fulton and Trueblood, eds., *Patriotic Eloquence*, 171–73.

13. Albert J. Beveridge, "March of the Flag," in Fulton and Trueblood, eds., *Patriotic Eloquence*, 27.

14. Ibid., 28–29.

15. William Jennings Bryan, "George Washington," in Fulton and Trueblood, eds., *Patriotic Eloquence*, 48–53.

16. Woodrow Wilson, "Education and Democracy," delivered at Columbia University, May 4, 1907, in Arthur S. Link, ed., *The Papers of Woodrow Wilson*, vol. 17, (Princeton, N.J.: Princeton University Press, 1966–1994), 135.

17. Herbert Pelham Williams, "The Outlook in Cuba," *Atlantic Monthly* 83, no. 500 (June 1899): 827.

18. Ibid., 829.

19. Alfred Russel Wallace, "America, Cuba, and the Philippines," *Daily Chronicle* (London), Jan. 19, 1899, 3.

20. Williams, "The Outlook in Cuba," 830.

21. Ibid., 832–36.

22. Ibid., 833.

23. Leonard Wood, "The Existing Conditions and Need in Cuba," *North American Review* 168, no. 510 (May 1899): 594.

24. Ibid., 594–95.

25. Ibid., 595.

26. Ibid., 597.

27. Ibid., 601.

28. Leonard Wood, "The Present Situation in Cuba," *Century Magazine* 58, no. 4 (August 1899): 639–40.

29. Horatio S. Rubens, "The Insurgent Government in Cuba," *North American Review* 166, no. 498 (May 1898): 562.

30. Ibid., 563.

31. Ibid.

32. Ibid., 564.

33. Ibid., 566–67.

34. Ibid., 569.

35. Máximo Gómez, Diary, Jan. 1899.

36. "Cubans Turn Bandits," *Evening News* (San Jose, Calif.), Oct. 5, 1898, 1.

37. "Cuba's General Resigns," *New York Journal*, Oct. 13, 1898, 3.

38. "General Wood Visits Guantánamo," *New York Times*, Nov. 11, 1898, 4.

39. "Guantánamo's Robinhood," *Idaho Daily Statesman* (Boise), Dec. 26, 1898, 1.

40. "Furnished Arms to Cubans," *Colorado Springs Gazette*, Dec. 26, 1898, 1; "Guantánamo Commission's Report," *New York Times*, Jan. 2, 1899, 2; "Investigation at Guantánamo," *New York Times*, Dec. 28, 1898, 3.

41. "Cubans Are Wrathy," *Morning Oregonian* (Portland), Jan. 25, 1899, 2.

42. Frances J. Higginson to Leonard Wood, Feb. 17, 1902, Leonard Wood Papers, Subject File: Cuba [1898–1902], Library of Congress, Washington, D.C. (hereafter cited as LWP).

43. Ibid.

44. Albert G. Robinson, "The Work of the Cuban Convention," *Forum* 31, no. 4 (June 1901): 401. Wood's over-optimistic reports of Cuban opinion were the subject of close scrutiny by American journalists, and seem to have caught Secretary of War Root and some members of Congress by surprise. See "Serious Situation in Cuba," *Springfield Daily Republican*, March 9, 1901, 6; Foner, *Spanish-Cuban-American War*, vol. 2.

45. Leonard Wood, *Civil Report on Cuba*, U.S. War Department, Washington, D.C., 1901, 21.

46. Order number 301, Military Governor of Cuba, July 25, 1900, Foreign Relations

of the United States, series available at digital.library.wisc.edu/1711.dl/FRUS, 1900, 358–59 (hereafter cited as FRUS).

47. Robinson, "Work of the Cuban Convention," 401.

48. Order number 455, Military Governor of Cuba, Nov. 9, 1900, in FRUS, 359–60.

49. The text of the Teller Amendment is available at www.etsu.edu/cas/history/docs/teller.htm.

50. Elihu Root to Albert Shaw, Feb. 23, 1901, in LWP.

51. "Cuban Problem Again Acute," *Pawtucket* (R.I.) *Times*, Jan. 29, 1901, 7.

52. Ibid.

53. Leonard Wood to Elihu Root, Jan. 4, 1901, in LWP.

54. "Cuban Problem Again Acute," 7.

55. Leonard Wood to Elihu Root, Feb. 27, 1901, in LWP.

56. Robinson, "The Work of the Cuban Convention," 401.

57. "Report on the Relations Which Should Exist Between Cuba and the United States," Feb. 26, 1901, in *Foreign Relations of the United States* (trans.), 1902, 361.

58. Ibid., 362.

59. Ibid., 362–63.

60. *The New York Times* cites a February 1 editorial from *La Nación* in support of liberal terms of U.S.-Cuban relations, which includes the lease of two coaling stations; *New York Times*, Feb. 15, 1901, 6; Root to Wood, Feb. 9, 1901, in LWP.

61. Wood to Root, March 4, 1901, in LWP. "Serious Situation in Cuba," *Springfield* (Mass.) *Daily Republican*, March 9, 1901, quotes the radical Cuban daily *La Patria* describing how Wood's misinformation on Cuban political sentiment swayed the administration and Congress into adopting Platt.

62. Wood to Root, Feb. 27, 1901, in LWP.

63. "Aspects of the Cuban Situation," *Springfield* (Mass.) *Daily Republican*, April 5, 1901.

64. "The Deed Is Done," *The State*, March 1, 1901, 4.

65. "The Sovereignty of Cuba," *New York Times*, Feb. 11, 1901, 6.

66. Ibid.

67. "A Stable Government in Cuba," *New York Times*, Feb. 18, 1901, 6.

68. Ibid.

69. "Meeting Not Harmonious," *Columbus Daily Inquirer*, March 29, 1901, 1.

70. Foner, *Spanish-Cuban-American War*, 2:603–11.

71. "Ponencia del Sr. Juan Gualberto Gómez, miembro de la comisión designada para proponer la respuesta a la comunicación del gobernador militar de Cuba," March 26, 1901, Apéndice H, in Emilio Roig de Leuchsenring, *Historia de la Enmienda Platt* (1961), 235–37.

72. Ibid., 240–41.

73. Ibid., 242–43.

74. Ibid.

75. Ibid.

76. Root's response quoted in Wood to Domingo Méndez Capote, April 3, 1901, in LWP.

77. Informe de la Comisión Designada para Avistarse con el Gobierno de los Estados Unidos, Dando Cuenta del Resultado de sus Gestiones, May 7, 1901, in Leuchsenring, *Historia de la Enmienda Platt*, 251–52.

78. Ibid., 254–55.

79. Adición al Informe Presentado por la Comisión Nombrada el Día de Abril Último, in Ibid., 263.

80. Comunicación del Gobernador Militar de Cuba, Trasladando el Informe del Secretario de la Guerra de los Estados Unidos, sobre Aceptación de la Enmienda Platt, June 8, 1901, in Leuchsenring, *Historia de la Enmienda Platt*, 271.

81. Wood to Roosevelt, Oct. 28, 1901, in LWP.

5 ☆ GUANTÁNAMO BLUES

1. Herbert Corey, "Across the Equator with the American Navy," *National Geographic*, 39, no. 6 (June 1921): 590.

2. Ibid., 591.

3. Ibid., 577.

4. Ibid., 580.

5. Ibid., 590.

6. Ibid., 591.

7. Ibid., 592–93.

8. The fullest account of this is Louis A. Pérez Jr., *On Becoming Cuban: Identity, Nationality, and Culture* (New York: Ecco Press, 1999), chap. 2. See also Robert B. Hoernel, "Sugar and Social Change in Oriente, Cuba, 1898–1946," *Journal of Latin American Studies* 8, no. 2 (Nov. 1976): 220; Carmen Diana Deere, "Here Come the Yankees! The Rise and Decline of the United States Colonies in Cuba," *Hispanic American Historical Review* 78, no. 4 (Nov. 1998), 733, 738–39; as well as Louis Pérez, Jr., "Politics, Peasants, and People of Color: The 1912 Race War in Cuba Reconsidered," *Hispanic American Historical Review* 66, no. 3 (Aug. 1986): 509–39.

9. Hoernel, "Sugar and Social Change," 221–22, 225–29; Deere, "Here Come the Yankees!" 735–38; Pérez, *On Becoming Cuban*, 221–24; Pérez, "Politics, Peasants, and People of Color," 509–12.

10. Hoernel, "Sugar and Social Change," 229–39.

11. Secretary Long cited in Bradley M. Reynolds, "Guantánamo Bay, Cuba: The History of an American Naval Base and Its Relationship to the Formulation of U.S. Foreign Policy and Military Strategy Toward the Caribbean," Ph.D. dissertation, University of Southern California, 1982, 155.

12. Henry Cabot Lodge, "Our Blundering Foreign Policy," *Forum* (March 1895): 8. See also Richard Olney, "International Isolation of the United States," *Atlantic Monthly* 81, no. 487 (May 1898): 577–88.

13. Naval War Board to John D. Long, Aug. 1898, in Robert Seager II and Doris D. Maguire, eds., *Letters and Papers of Alfred Thayer Mahan*, vol. 2, *1890–1901* (Annapolis, Md.: Naval Institute Press, 1975), 581–86.

14. Naval War Board to John D. Long, Aug. 15–20, 1898, in Seager and Maguire, *Letters and Papers*, 588.

15. Reynolds, "Guantánamo Bay," 229.

16. Ibid., 319, 355.

17. *New York Times*, "Revolt of Cuban Negroes Spreading," May 21, 1912, 5.

18. Wood quoted in Alejandro de la Fuente, "Myths of Racial Democracy: Cuba 1900–1912," *Latin American Research Review* 34, no. 3 (1999): 53; Pérez, "Politics, Peasants, and People of Color," 509–511.

19. De la Fuente, "Myths of Racial Democracy," 58–64; Aline Helg, "Race and Black Mobilization in Colonial and Early Independent Cuba: A Comparative Perspective," *Ethnohistory* 44, no. 1 (Winter 1997): 62–64; and Louis A. Pérez, *Cuba Under the Platt Amendment, 1902–1934* (Pittsburgh, Pa.: University of Pittsburgh Press, 2009), 148–51.

20. U.S. ambassador A. M. Beaupré to the secretary of state, Feb. 27, 1912, in FRUS, 243.

21. U.S. secretary of state Knox to U.S. ambassador to Cuba Beaupré, May 23, 1912, in FRUS, 245–46.

22. U.S. ambassador Beaupré to the U.S. secretary of state, May 24, 1912, in FRUS, 247.

23. The president of Cuba to the president of the United States, May 26, 1912, in FRUS, 247–48.

24. Taft to Gómez, May 27, 1912, in FRUS, 248; Gómez to Taft, May 27, 1912, in FRUS, 249.

25. Knox to Beaupré, May 29, 1912, in FRUS, 250.

26. Ibid., June 1, 1912, in FRUS, 252.

27. *New York Times*, "Warships to Cuba After Marines Land," June 6, 1912, 5.

28. Cuban foreign minister Manuel Sanguily to U.S. secretary of state, June 8, 1912, in FRUS, 259; Beaupré to Knox, June 9, 1912, in FRUS, 260; Beaupré to Knox, June 11, 1912, in FRUS, 262; and Helg, "Race and Black Mobilization," 63. For an eyewitness account of the U.S. Marines' expedition to Cuba, see John A. Gray (Maj., USMC), "Recollections of the 1912 Cuban Expedition," *The Marine Corps Gazette* 17, no. 1 (May, 1932): 45–48. On the analogy to post–U.S. Civil War, see Joel Williamson, *The Crucible of Race: Black-White Relations in the American South Since Reconstruction* (New York: Oxford University Press, 1984).

29. Beaupré to Knox, June 11, 1912, in FRUS, 262.

30. Michael R. Hall, *Sugar and Power in the Dominican Republic: Eisenhower, Kennedy, and the Trujillos* (Westport, Conn.: Greenwood Press, 2000), 39–43.

31. Jorge Domínguez, *Cuba: Order and Revolution* (Cambridge, Mass.: Harvard University Press, 1978), 17–18.

32. See Dudley W. Knox, Capt., U.S. Navy (Ret.), "An Adventure in Diplomacy,"

U.S. Naval Institute Proceedings 52, no. 2 (Feb. 1926): 273–87; FRUS, 1917, 367–431.

33. See conversation between the U.S. ambassador to Cuba, William Gonzalez, and Secretary of State Robert Lansing, in FRUS, Cuba, 1917, 368–410; "Fleet to Protect Americans in Cuba," *New York Times*, March 1, 1917, 12; and "Our Troops Guard 5 Points in Cuba," *New York Times*, March 13, 1917, 4.

34. Pérez, *Cuba Under the Platt Amendment*, 57–79.

35. Ibid., 59–61.

36. Ibid., 62.

37. Ibid., 70–73, 84.

38. Quoted in W. H. Brands, *T. R.: The Last Romantic* (New York: Basic Books, 1998), 569.

39. Pérez, *Cuba Under the Platt Amendment*, 139–43; Louis A. Pérez, Jr., *Cuba: Between Reform and Revolution* (New York: Oxford University Press, 1995), 215–20; Hugh Thomas, *Cuba, or the Pursuit of Freedom* (New York: Da Capo, 1998), 504–506.

40. Pérez, *Cuba Under the Platt Amendment*, 152–55, 227–29; Thomas, *Cuba*, 556–76.

41. Pérez, *Cuba Under the Platt Amendment*, 158–66; Pérez, *Cuba: Between Reform*, 241–44; Thomas, *Cuba*, 574–78.

42. K. C. McIntosh, "Guantánamo," *The American Mercury* 10, no. 37 (Jan. 1927): 106.

43. Evelyn Hu-DeHart, "Race Construction and Race Relations: Chinese and Blacks in 19th Century Cuba," in Wang Ling-chi and Lang Wungu, eds., *The Chinese Diaspora, Selected Essays* (Singapore: Times Academic Press, 1998), 78.

44. McIntosh, "Guantánamo," 110.

45. Ibid., 108.

46. Ibid., 111.

47. See Marion E. Murphy, *The History of Guantánamo Bay, 1494–1964* (U.S. Navy, 1953), chap. 5. Base officials never took kindly to criticism, particularly from women. See James F. Lloyd, lieutenant commander, U.S. Navy, to Rear Admiral E. J. O'Donnell, March 6, 1961, Command History Files, Navy Library, on the mildly critical article by Betty Reef in the *Overseas Press Bulletin*, Feb. 25, 1961; also, B. S. Solomon, captain, U.S. Navy, to Lieutenant Commander B. D. Barner, U.S. Navy, February 25, 1965, Command History Files, Navy Library, on journalist Elizabeth Chambers's infiltration of the naval base and her subsequent story, which appeared in the *Norfolk Ledger* that month.

48. See Fred S. Harrod, *Manning the New Navy: The Development of a Modern Naval Enlisted Force, 1899–1940* (Westport, Conn: Greenwood Press, 1979), introduction. The 1920s, the so-called Jazz Age, the age of flappers, was one of the most reactionary periods in U.S. history. The Red Scare, the epidemic of lynching and renewed commitment to segregation, immigration restrictions, and the Scopes trial are only a few of the era's hallmarks. See Lynn Dumenil, *The Mod-*

ern Temper: American Culture and Society in the 1920s (New York: Hill and Wang, 1995); Joshua Zeitz, *Flapper: A Madcap Story of Sex, Style, Celebrity, and the Women Who Made America Modern* (New York: Broadway, 2007); and Nathan Miller, *New World Coming: The 1920s and the Making of Modern America* (New York: Da Capo, 2004).

49. "Guantánamo Blues: A Taste of the Tropical Fruits of Prohibition, by a Navy Wife," *Liberty Magazine*, April 12, 1930, 19–20.

50. Ibid., 20.

51. Ibid.

52. Ibid.

53. Ibid., 21

54. Ibid.

55. Ibid.

56. Ibid., 22.

57. Ibid.

58. Ibid., 22–24.

59. Ibid., 24.

60. Ibid., 24.

61. Gerardo Castellanos, *Paseos Efímeros: Desfile histórico, Guantánamo Bijagual, Mantua, Remates de Guane* (La Habana: Editorial "Hermes," 1930).

62. In February 1930, Castellanos notes (page 180), Guantánamo City was once more opened to the Americans.

63. Castellanos, *Paseos Efímeros*, 183.

64. Ibid., 187–88.

65. Maynard Cooke Horiuchi to Jonathan Hansen, Sept. 20, 2005; Maynard Cooke Horiuchi to Jonathan Hansen, Oct. 1, 2005; Maynard Cooke Horiuchi to Hansen, Oct. 5, 2005; and Maynard Cooke Horiuchi, "US Naval Station, Guantánamo Bay, Cuba, Spring 1934 to April 1936," personal memoir of Maynard Cooke Horiuchi, in author's possession.

66. Horiuchi to Hansen, Oct. 1, 2005; Horiuchi to Hansen, Oct. 5, 2005.

67. Frank G. Carpenter, "American Mediterranean Must Be Guarded by Uncle Sam," *Boston Daily Globe*, October 15, 1905, SM3.

68. At different times, Cooke tried to do favors for Ernest Brooks, an Englishman and one of the area's largest growers. See J. G. Atkins, lieutenant commander, U.S. Navy, and aide to the commander in chief, U.S. Fleet, to Charles M. Cooke, Oct. 16, 1934, in Charles Cooke Collection, Box 7, Folder Osment, Hoover Institution Archives, Stanford University; Charles M. Cooke to William T. Osment, December 27, 1934, in Cook Collection, Hoover Institution Archives, Stanford University.

69. Horiuchi, "US Naval Station, Guantánamo Bay," 2–3.

70. Charles Cooke to William Osment, Jan. 14, 1935; William Osment to Charles Cooke, Jan. 15, 1935; Charles Cooke to William Osment, Jan. 16, 1935, all in Charles Cooke Papers, Hoover Institution, Stanford University. See also Hum-

berto Monteaguado, chief engineer, Secretaría de Obras Públicas, Jefatura del Distrito de Oriente, to Charles Cooke, April 20, 1936, with accompanying report; report about water supply, Commandant, U.S. Naval Station, Guantánamo Bay, Cuba, August 20, 1935, to chief of Bureau of Yards and Docks; and report on projects for supplying water to U.S. Naval Station Guantánamo Bay, Cuba, commandant, to chief of Bureau of Yards and Docks, all in Cooke Papers, Box 24, Folder U.S. Naval Station, Guantánamo, Hoover Institution Archives, Stanford University.

71. Cooke to Osment, Jan. 16, 1935; William Osment to Charles Cooke, Feb. 3, 1935, Cooke Papers.

72. Cooke-Osment correspondence, Feb. 19–21 and April 20, 1936, Cooke Papers.

73. "Guantánamo: Cloaca de Cuba," *Bohemia* (March 1938): 40, 46.

74. Jane Robinson Hartge, e-mail correspondence, Sept. 29, 2005.

75. "Relief Expedition to Haiti," Office of the Commandant, U.S. Naval Base, Guantánamo Bay, Cuba, Nov. 5, 1935. Charles M. Cooke Papers, Manuscript Division, Hoover Institution Archives, Stanford University.

76. Pérez, *Cuba: Between Reform,* 261–62.

77. Samuel Farber, *Revolution and Reaction in Cuba, 1933–1960: A Political Sociology from Machado to Castro* (Middletown, Conn.: Wesleyan University Press, 1976), 40–41; cf. Pérez, *Cuba Under the Platt Amendment,* 268–69; and Irwin F. Gellman, *Roosevelt and Batista: Good Neighbor Diplomacy in Cuba, 1933–1945* (Albuquerque: University of New Mexico Press, 1973), 42–60.

78. Farber, *Revolution and Reaction in Cuba,* 41–42.

79. Thomas, *Cuba,* 691–94.

80. Ibid., 43.

81. Ibid., 42.

82. Ibid., 43.

83. See, for example, Yuki Tanaka, *Japan's Comfort Women: Sexual Slavery and Prostitution During World War II and the U.S. Occupation* (New York: Routledge, 2001), esp. chaps. 1 and 5.

84. T. H. English, *Havana Nocturne: How the Mob Owned Cuba—and Then Lost It to the Revolution* (New York: William Morrow, 2007), 211.

85. Jana K. Lipman, *Guantánamo: A Working-Class History Between Empire and Revolution* (Berkeley: University of California Press, 2009), 109–117. Cf. Vern Bullough and Bonnie Bullough, *Women and Prostitution: A Social History* (New York: Prometheus, 1987); and Frederique Delacoste and Priscilla Alexander, eds., *Sex Work: Writings by Women in the Sex Industry* (San Francisco: Cleis, 1998).

86. Telephone interview, Doug White, Sept. 17, 2005.

87. Telephone interview, William Mills, Sept. 20, 2005.

88. Mills's account is confirmed by James C. Manning's unpublished novel *Swans of Cong,* based on his service in Guantánamo just after World War II, in author's possession.

89. "Reminiscences of Captain Roland W. Faulk, CHC, USN, Retired," U.S. Naval Institute, Annapolis, Md., 1975, 57.

90. Ibid., 58.

91. Ibid., 59–60.

92. "Your GTMO Home, Housing Information Manual," Public Works Center, U.S. Naval Base, Guantánamo Bay, Cuba, July 1958, 27.

93. Confidential Security Information, History of the U.S. Naval Base, Guantánamo Bay, Cuba, Command File, World War II, Operational Archives Branch, Naval Historical Center, Washington, D.C. The list of recreational activities dates from 1956. Pamphlet: "Living Conditions at the United States Naval Base, Guantánamo Bay, Cuba, 1956," Historical Collection, Guantánamo Naval Base.

94. Telephone interview, Peter C. Grenquist, Sept. 11, 2005. See also telephone interview, Peter Grenquist, July 9, 2009.

95. Telephone interview with Commander Harold H. Sacks, June 30, 2008.

96. Ibid.

97. Rex Lake, "Rex's Masterpiece," Sept. 9, 2009, in author's possession.

98. Ibid.

99. Compare Lipman, *Guantánamo*, 115.

100. Grenquist interview, July 9, 2009.

101. Ibid.

102. Ibid.

103. Gervasio G. Ruiz, "Guantánamo, Caimanera y La Base Naval Norte Americana," *Carteles* (May 7, 1950): 40–42.

104. Ibid., 41.

105. Ibid., 42.

6 ★ SEEING RED

1. Malcolm Byrne, ed., *The 1956 Hungarian Revolution: A History in Documents* (Washington, D.C.: National Security Archives Electronic Briefing Book, 2002); *New York Times*, Nov. 1, 1956, 38.

2. *New York Times*, Nov. 4, 1956, 1.

3. Byrne, *1956 Hungarian Revolution*, 3–4.

4. See www.time.com/time/personoftheyear/archive/covers/1956.html.

5. T. H. English, *Havana Nocturne: How the Mob Owned Cuba—and Then Lost It to the Revolution* (New York: William Morrow, 2007), xv–xvii.

6. Ryan's account of bullying by Cuban government troops is corroborated by Rex Lake, "Rex's Masterpiece." Lake lived in Caimanera from November 1956 to August 1958, and recounts numerous incidents of drunken Cuban soldiers randomly discharging their weapons in the direction of innocent civilians.

7. Samuel Farber, *Revolution and Reaction in Cuba, 1933–1960: A Political Sociology from Machado to Castro* (Middletown, Conn.: Wesleyan University Press,

1976), 138; Louis A. Pérez, Jr., *Cuba: Between Reform and Revolution* (New York: Oxford University Press, 1995), 284–87.

8. Pérez, *Cuba: Between Reform*, 284–88, Jorge Domínguez, *Cuba: Order and Revolution* (Cambridge, Mass.: Harvard University Press, 1978), 108.

9. Farber, *Revolution and Reaction in Cuba*, 160–62; Louis A. Pérez, "Cuba, c. 1930–1959," in Leslie Bethell, ed., *Cuba: A Short History* (Cambridge: Cambridge University Press, 1993), 83–84.

10. Farber, *Revolution and Reaction in Cuba*, 180–91; Pérez, "Cuba," 86–91.

11. The story of Cuban labor on the naval base is expertly described by Jana K. Lipman, *Guantánamo: A Working-Class History Between Empire and Revolution* (Berkeley: University of California Press, 2009), 39 and passim.

12. Lipman, *Guantánamo*, 16, 36–68.

13. Ibid., 48.

14. Ibid., 67–79.

15. Ibid., 29–31.

16. Ibid., 57–59.

17. Ibid., 75, 83.

18. Ibid., 91.

19. Ibid., 92–93.

20. Ibid., 94.

21. The following section is based on telephone interviews with Charles Ryan (Oct. 8 and 9, 2009) and Victor Buehlman (Oct. 14, 2009). Cf. Ramón L. Bonachea and Marta San Martín, *The Cuban Insurrection, 1952–1959* (New Brunswick, N.J.: Transaction Books, 1974); Thomas G. Paterson, *Contesting the Cuban Revolution: The U.S. and the Trampling of the Cuban Republic* (New York: Oxford University Press, 1995); Julia E. Sweig, *Inside the Cuban Revolution: Fidel Castro and the Urban Underground* (Cambridge, Mass.: Harvard University Press, 2002); and Van Gosse, *Where the Boys Are: Cuba, Cold War America and the Making of a New Left* (New York: Verso, 1993).

22. Author interview, Kevin N. Caffrey, Veteran, U.S. Marine Corps, Feb. 12, 2010, Cambridge, Mass.

23. Bonachea and San Martin, *The Cuban Insurrection,* 93.

24. "3 U.S. Youths Missing," *New York Times*, March 8, 1957, 5.

25. "U.S. Studying the Case of 3 Youths in Cuba," *New York Times*, March 31, 1957, 5.

26. "Batista Says Foes Have Quit Hideout," *New York Times*, March 31, 1957, 5; "Cuban Colonel: They're Not There," *New York Times*, April 13, 1957, 12.

27. *Time* magazine, March 18, 1957.

28. Louis A. Pérez, *Cuba and the United States: Ties of Singular Intimacy* (Athens: University of Georgia Press, 2003), 235; Bonachea and San Martín, *The Cuban Insurrection*, 244–45.

29. Telegram from Commander of the Naval Base at Guantánamo (Ellis) to the Chief of Naval Operations (Burke), June 30, 1958, FRUS, Cuba, 1958, 119.

30. Lake, "Rex's Masterpiece."

31. Ibid.

32. Ibid.

33. Bonachea and San Martín, *The Cuban Insurrection*, 245; Tad Szulc, *Fidel: A Critical Portrait* (New York: William Morrow, 1986), 438–39.

34. Szulc, *Fidel: A Critical Portrait*, 439.

35. Wollam quoted in telegram from the embassy in Cuba to the Department of State, July 3, 1958, FRUS, Cuba, 1958, 127.

36. See two telegrams from the embassy in Cuba to the Department of State, both dated July 3, 1958, FRUS, Cuba, 1958, vol. VI, 125–26.

37. Ibid.

38. Memorandum from the Chief of Naval Operations (Burke) to the Joint Chiefs of Staff, July 10, 1958, FRUS, 1958–60, Cuba, vol. VI, 140.

39. Nixon and Dulles quoted in Lars Schoultz, *Beneath the United States: A History of U.S. Policy Toward Latin America* (Cambridge, Mass.: Harvard University Press, 1998), 351–53. Cf. Greg Grandin, *Empire's Workshop: Latin America, the United States and the Rise of the New Imperialism* (New York: Metropolitan Books, 2006), 42–45.

40. See, for example, Memorandum from the Acting Secretary of State to the President, Dec. 23, 1958, FRUS, vol. VI, 1958–1960, 304–307.

41. Sweig, *Inside the Cuban Revolution*, 59.

42. Telegram from the embassy in Cuba to the Department of State, July 13, 1958, FRUS, Cuba, vol. VI, 152.

43. Telegram from the embassy in Cuba to the Department of State, July 13, 1958, FRUS, vol. VI, 153–54; telegram from the embassy in Cuba to the Department of State, July 12, 1958, FRUS, Cuba, vol. VI, 149.

44. Memorandum of Discussion at the 392nd Meeting of the National Security Council, Washington, D.C., December 23, 1958, FRUS, 1958–1960, vol. VI, 302–303.

45. Farber, *Revolution and Reaction in Cuba*, 198–201; Gary Prevost, "Cuba," in Harry E. Vanden and Gary Prevost, eds., *Politics of Latin America: The Power Game* (New York: Oxford University Press, 2002), 325–34; and Pérez, "Cuba," 92.

46. Memorandum of Conversation, Department of State, Washington, D.C., Jan. 9, 1959, FRUS, 109.

47. Stephen G. Rabe, *Eisenhower and Latin America: The Foreign Policy of Anticommunism* (Chapel Hill: University of North Carolina Press, 1988), 117–18.

48. Memorandum of Conversation, Department of State, Washington, D.C., Jan. 9, 1959, FRUS, 366.

49. Hugh Thomas, *Cuba, or the Pursuit of Freedom* (New York: Da Capo, 1998), 1198, 1256–57; Farber, *Revolution and Reaction in Cuba*, 216; Prevost, "Cuba," 334–35; Jorge Domínguez, "Cuba Since 1959," in Leslie Bethell, ed., *Cuba: A Short History* (Cambridge, UK: Cambridge University Press, 1993), 98–99.

50. Rabe, *Eisenhower and Latin America*, 128.

51. Memorandum of Discussion at the Department of State, Sept. 30, 1960, in

FRUS, Cuba, vol. VI, 1959–1960, 1079. See also editorial note on p. 1082, quoting Merchant as saying that "Castro would not be so stupid as to make an overt attack" on Guantánamo. Meanwhile, Admiral Dennison, commander in chief of the Atlantic Fleet, remarked that Guantánamo would be "useless to Castro."

52. Herter and Eisenhower quoted in Rabe, *Eisenhower and Latin America*, 172.

53. U.S. Policy Toward Cuba, Memorandum of Discussion at the 436th Meeting of the National Security Council, Washington, D.C., March 10, 1960, FRUS, Cuba, vol. VI, 1958–60, 834.

54. Fabian Escalante, *The Cuba Project: CIA Covert Operations, 1959–62* (New York: Ocean Press, 2004), 74.

55. Ibid., 86–93; Jesús Arboleya, *The Cuban Counterrevolution* (Athens: Ohio University Center for International Studies, 2000), 94–96.

56. Stevenson quoted in William N. Oatis, "Cuban's Guantánamo Attack Called Absurd by Stevenson," *Washington Post*, Aug. 25, 1961; Dennison quoted in "Reminiscences of Admiral Robert Lee Dennison, U.S. Navy (Ret.)," U.S. Naval Institute, Annapolis, Md., Aug. 1975.

57. Memorandum from CIA chief of operations Richard Helms to director of Central Intelligence McCone, Jan. 19, 1962, National Security Archive, Washington, D.C.

58. Program review by the chief of operations, Operation Mongoose (Lansdale), Jan. 18, 1962, FRUS, Cuba, vol. X, 1961–1963.

59. Memorandum for Brigadier General Edward G. Lansdale, USAF, assistant to the secretary of defense, from Brigadier General William H. Graig, DOD representative, Caribbean Survey Group, Feb. 2, 1962, Digital National Security Archive.

60. Memorandum from the chief of operations, Cuba Project, to Brigadier General William H. Craig, Feb. 19, 1962, Digital National Security Archive.

61. Memorandum for Secretary of State Robert McNamara from Chairman of the Joint Chiefs of Staff Lyman Lemnitzer, March 13, 1962, Digital National Security Archive.

62. Memorandum for U.S. National Security Advisor McGeorge Bundy from Acting Director Central Intelligence Marshall S. Carter, "CIA Action in Response to National Security Action Memorandum No. 181," Aug. 1962, Digital National Security Archive; Memorandum of Meetings of the Special Group, Augmented, to Discuss Mongoose, Aug. 16, 1962, FRUS, 1961–63, Cuba, Doc. 378; Memorandum of Meeting with President Kennedy, Aug. 23, 1962, FRUS, 1961–63, vol. XI, doc. 385.

63. Current Intelligence Memorandum, August 22, 1962, FRUS, Cuba, 1961–63, vol. XI, doc. 383.

64. See Laurence Chang and Peter Kornbluh, eds., *The Cuban Missile Crisis, 1962: A National Security Archive Documents Reader*, rev. ed. (New York: The New Press, 1999), introduction.

65. Telegram from Chief of Naval Operations (Anderson) to the Department of State, Aug. 24, 1962, FRUS, Cuba, 1961–63, vol. XI, doc. 389.

66. Memorandum from Director of the Bureau of Intelligence and Research (Hilsman) to Acting Secretary of State Ball, Aug. 25, 1962, FRUS, Cuba, 1961–63, vol. XI, doc. 390.

67. Carter to McCone, Cable, Sept. 7, 1962 (Excerpt), Digital National Security Archive.

68. See, for example, Report from the Chief of Naval Operations to the Secretary of State, Sept. 7, 1962, Digital National Security Archive; Summary of Items of Significant Interest, Sept. 7, 1962, Digital National Security Archive; as well as subsequent intelligence reports in idem.

69. Kennedy quote in Off the Record Meeting on Cuba, Oct. 16, 1962, The Cuban Missile Crisis, Avalon Project, Yale University, doc. 21.

70. Minutes of the 505th Meeting of the National Security Council, Oct. 20, 1962, The Cuban Missile Crisis, Avalon Project, Yale University, doc. 34.

71. Minutes of the 506th Meeting of the National Security Council, Oct. 21, 1962, The Cuban Missile Crisis, Avalon Project, Yale University, doc. 38.

72. Note to All Base Residents, October 22, 1962, Guantánamo Vertical File, U.S. Navy Library, Washington, D.C.; U.S. Naval Air Station, Guantánamo Bay, Cuba, Command Historical Report, 1962, Guantánamo Vertical File, U.S. Navy Library, Washington, D.C., 4.

73. Memo for Record, Cuba Fact Sheet, Oct. 27, 1962, Guantánamo Vertical File, U.S. Navy Library, Washington, D.C.

74. "Reminiscences of Admiral Robert Lee Dennison, USN (Ret.)," U.S. Naval Institute, Annapolis, Md., Aug. 1975.

75. Michael Dobbs, One Minute to Midnight: Kennedy, Khrushchev, and Castro on the Brink of Nuclear War (New York: Alfred A. Knopf, 2008), 124–25.

76. Memorandum for Director of Central Intelligence McCone from Deputy Director of Planning Richard Helms, Jan. 19, 1962, Digital National Security Archives.

7 ★ THE AMERICAN DREAM

1. Research Proposal NM 005 098, Preventive Medical Aspects of Field Vector Control, Bureau of Medicine and Surgery, Aug. 26, 1956, Spielman Papers, in author's possession.

2. Andrew Spielman to C. W. Sabrosky, Oct. 15, 1957, Spielman Papers. "The Guantánamo Bay Naval Base has acquired the reputation of a place in which eye-gnats are very annoying to man," Spielman wrote in an undated "Progress Report on an Eye Gnat Research Project at the US Naval Base at Guantánamo Bay, Cuba," probably around September 1957. Certain eye gnats, Spielman observed, "manifest this annoying and potentially dangerous 'eye-gnat' habit. They persistently attempt to crawl over and into various parts of the bodies of certain animals and of man. Some species are attracted to the eyes or other head orifices while others crawl over the feet or upon open sores and ulcers. In certain areas of the world, these flies vector trachoma or yaws, and they cause contaminative

conjunctivitis wherever they occur. Where eye-gnats are numerous, their nuisance value is sufficient justification of some sort of a control program. . . . Ordinary window screens are not a deterrent."

3. "Living Conditions at the United States Naval Base, Guantánamo Bay, Cuba, 1956," U.S. Navy, ii.

4. Ibid., 2.

5. Ibid., 12.

6. The federal minimum wage in the United States in 1956 was one dollar an hour in current dollars. Information Please Database, 2008 Pearson Education, Inc. At the low end, Cuban maids made just over one twentieth of that.

7. "Living Conditions," 12.

8. Ibid.

9. Author telephone interview, Commander Harold H. Sacks, U.S. Navy (Ret.), June 30, 2008.

10. Harold H. Sacks, Commander, U.S. Navy (Ret.), "Lt. Andrew Spielman Remembered," January 2007, in possession of the author.

11. This includes sailors living aboard ships. Confidential Security Information, History of the U.S. Naval Base, Guantánamo Bay, Cuba, Command File, World War II, Operational Archives Branch, Naval Historical Center, Washington, D.C., 9.

12. Nick Thimmesch, "'GITMO'—10 Years Later," *Newsday*, March 28, 1972.

13. Commander Leslie J. McCoy, quoted at www.defenselink.mil/news/newsarticle .aspx?id=31290.

14. Author interview with Commander Jeffrey M. Johnston, Oct. 14, 2005.

15. Author interview with Judy Spielman, June 19, 2008, Cambridge, Mass.: Daniel Spielman to F. R. DuChanois, May 22, 1957, Spielman Papers.

16. Andrew Spielman to K. L. Knight, April 22, 1957, Spielman Papers.

17. Andrew Spielman, "Progress Report on Eye Gnat Research Project NM 005 098.01 entitled 'Identification, Biology and Control of Eye Gnats (*Hippelates spp.*) at Guantánamo Bay, Cuba' for the period of October, 1–31, 1957," Spielman Papers.

18. Local planters, ranchers, and farmers also complained about eye gnats. Spielman speculated that sugar production and cattle ranching exacerbated the eye gnat problem in the region, as soil contamination from horse and cattle feces contributed to their abundance. Spielman, "Progress Report on Eye Gnat Research Project," 2, Spielman Papers.

19. Andrew Spielman to K. L. Knight, May 4, 1958, Spielman Papers.

20. Andrew Spielman to F. R. DuChanois, Sept. 6, 1957, Spielman Papers.

21. "Living Conditions," 15–16.

22. Ibid., 17–19.

23. Ibid., 17.

24. Author interview with Judy Spielman, June 19, 2008, Cambridge, Mass.

25. Andrew Spielman to F. R. DuChanois, April 24, 1958, Spielman Papers.

26. Andrew Spielman to K. L. Knight, June 25, 1958, Spielman Papers.

27. Fred S. Harrod, *Manning the New Navy: The Development of a Modern Naval Enlisted Force, 1899–1940* (Westport, Conn.: Greenwood Press, 1979); Morris J. MacGregor, Jr., *Defense Studies Series Integration of the Armed Forces, 1940–1965* (Washington, D.C.: Center for Military History, United States Army, 1985), available at www.history.army.mil/books/integration/IAF-fm.htm.

28. Peter C. Grenquist to Jonathan Hansen, Sept. 12, 2005; author interview, Peter C. Grenquist, July 9, 2009.

29. Telephone interview, Harold H. Sacks, June 30, 2008.

30. See   www.census.gov/population/www/documentation/twps0056/tabA-09.pdf; *1958 Coral Reef*, William T. Sampson School, Guantánamo Bay, Cuba. In 1950, South Carolina's black population was roughly 39 percent, Mississippi's roughly 45 percent, and Louisiana's roughly 33 percent. State and national figures changed little between 1950 and 1960. In these years, the U.S. census did not have a category for "Hispanics," and there were minuscule percentages of Native Americans and Asians.

31. Harrod, *Manning the New Navy*, introduction, chap. 1; Morris J. MacGregor, *Integration of the Armed Forces: Guide to Command of Negro Personnel* (NAVPERS—15092), Navy Department, Bureau of Personnel, Washington, D.C., Feb. 12, 1945.

32. Marine Corps commandant General Thomas Holcomb, quoted in MacGregor, *Integration of the Armed Forces*.

33. Tom Miller, "The Sun Sometimes Sets on the American Empire," *Esquire*, Vol. 80, September 1973, 100.

34. Jules B. Billard, "Guantánamo: Keystone in the Caribbean," *National Geographic*, 119, no. 3 (March 1961): 420–36.

35. Don Shoemaker, "Gitmo's OK Except for Landlord," *Minneapolis Star*, Nov. 16, 1968. Cf., for example, Tom Tiede, "The Dreary Life, One Woman for 400 Men," *Pensacola* (Fla.) *News-Journal*, Dec. 15, 1968.

36. Billard, "Guantánamo: Keystone in the Caribbean," 422–24.

37. "Teaching Overseas at the United States Naval Base in Cuba" (William T. Sampson School, 1968), 35.

38. Billard, "Guantánamo: Keystone in the Caribbean," 435.

39. Ibid., 432.

40. See Ed Kiester, "American Family in Guantánamo: An On-the-Spot Report," *Parade*, March 25, 1962, 6–10.

41. Billard, "Guantánamo: Keystone in the Caribbean," 432.

42. Ibid., 433.

43. Kiester, "American Family in Guantánamo," 6–10.

44. Ibid., 6–7.

45. Ibid., 7.

46. Ibid., 7, 10.

47. Ibid., 10–11.

48. Guantánamo Water Crisis, February 6–21, 1964, Guantánamo Vertical File,

U.S. Navy Library, Washington, D.C.; Water Crisis Facts and Occurrences, Public Information Office, U.S. Naval Base, Guantánamo Bay, Cuba, Feb. 1964, Guantánamo Vertical File, Navy Library, Washington, D.C., 1–3. "Suburban Living Is on Its Way Out as Gitmo Gears to Garrison Life," *Navy Times*, Feb. 26, 1964.

49. William B. Breuer, *Sea Wolf: The Daring Exploits of Navy Legend John D. Bulkeley* (Novato, Calif.: Presidio Press, 1989), 185.

50. Breuer, *Sea Wolf*, 188.

51. Ibid., 202–203.

52. Ibid., 208.

53. See, for example, Laurence Barret, "Guantánamo News Drought," *New York Herald*, Feb. 16, 1964; and Jack Raymond, "Cuba Base Ban for Newsmen," *Boston Globe*, Feb. 12, 1964, 1.

54. Water Crisis Facts and Occurrences, 3.

55. See, for example, the cartoon entitled "Cutting His Water Off," *San Francisco Examiner*, Feb. 19, 1964, 5C, as well as "Castro Can Pipe Down, U.S. Cuts Water Line," *Boston Globe*, Feb. 18, 1964, 1; "The Final Answer to Cuba on Water," *New York Herald*, Feb. 18, 1964, 1; and "Irate Admiral Cuts Guantánamo Mains," *New York Times*, Feb. 18, 1964, 1.

56. Breuer, *Sea Wolf*, 215, 244.

57. Ibid., 212.

58. Report from Commander, U.S. Naval Base, Guantánamo Bay, Cuba, to Commander, Antilles Defense Command, on Annual Cold War Activity Report, July 8, 1964, Guantánamo Command History, U.S. Naval Library, Washington, D.C.

59. Work Force Study, Aug. 15, 1967, appendix to 1967 Command History, U.S. Naval Library, Washington, D.C., vii–3, 8.

60. Ibid.

61. Ibid., vii–8.

62. Ibid., viii–12.

63. Ibid.

64. Telephone interview, Commander Harold Sacks, June 30, 2008.

65. "Your GTMO Home: U.S. Naval Base Guantánamo Bay, Cuba," Public Affairs Office, U.S. Naval Base, Guantánamo Bay, 1968, 1.

66. Ibid., 9.

67. Ibid., 16–17, 24–25.

68. Memorandum from Base Public Information Officer to Commander Naval Base, March 6, 1961, Guantánamo Vertical File, U.S. Naval Library, Washington, D.C.; "Gal Reporter Bucks Navy Red Tape," *Overseas Press Bulletin*, Feb. 25, 1961.

69. Admiral John D. Bulkeley to Admiral Needham, Feb. 1965, Guantánamo Vertical File, U.S. Naval Library, Washington, D.C. Cf. Captain B. S. Solomon to Lieutenant Commander B. D. Varner, Feb. 25, 1965, in Guantánamo Vertical File, U.S. Naval Library, Washington, D.C.

70. 1966 Command History, U.S. Naval Library, Washington, D.C., 17, and 1967 Command History, U.S. Naval Library, Washington, D.C., 3.

71. 1966 Command History, 18.

72. Ibid.

73. Tom Tiede, "The Dreary Life: One Woman for 400 Men," *Pensacola* (Fla.) *News-Journal*, December 15, 1968, 8E.

74. Tom Miller, "The Sun Sometimes Sets on the American Empire," *Esquire*, vol. 80, September 1973, 97.

75. Besides Miller, see Thimmesch, "'Gitmo'—10 Years Later," 1970 Command History, U.S. Naval Base Guantánamo Bay, Navy Department Library, Washington, D.C., 7, which reports seizure of more than thirty-two pounds of marijuana (estimated worth $25,760) at the base; 1972 Command History, U.S. Naval Base Guantánamo Bay, Navy Department Library, Washington, D.C., reporting a death from a drug overdose, along with the arrest of fifteen enlisted men on a drug-trafficking charge.

76. Miller, "The Sun Sometimes Sets," 186.

77. Command History 1972, 8, 26, 30.

78. Homer Bigarts, "Pioneer Navy Facility Leads Drive to Treat Alcoholism," *New York Times*, June 24, 1972, 33.

79. Tom Tiede, "Guantánamo Base Segregation of Facilities Being Done to Avoid Trouble," *Orlando Sentinel*, Dec. 17, 1968, 6A.

80. Tom Tiede, "Gitmo's Hired Hands Tied by Segregation," *Guam Daily News*, Dec. 14, 1968.

81. "Racial Clash Injures 33 on Carrier," *Washington Post*, Oct. 14, 1972, A3.

82. "Race Fight Injures 50 on U.S. Ships," *Washington Post*, Oct. 18, 1972, A48.

83. "Sailors Charged," *Washington Post*, Oct. 23, 1972, A9.

84. George C. Wilson, "Navy Mobilizing for Racial Reform," *Washington Post*, Nov. 5, 1972, A1.

85. Jack Anderson, "Guantánamo Base Is Powder Keg," *Washington Post*, Jan. 2, 1973, B11.

86. Ibid.

87. Robert A. Calavan, "A Neighbor Defends," *Washington Post*, Jan. 8, 1973, A21.

88. 1972 Command History, 18; Miller, "The Sun Sometimes Sets," 188.

89. Miller, "The Sun Sometimes Sets," 188.

90. Ibid.

8 ★ THE HAITIAN PROBLEM

1. Log of President Truman's Trip to Puerto Rico, The Virgin Islands, Guantánamo Bay, Cuba, and Key West, Florida, Feb. 20, 1948, to March 5, 1948, Truman Library, Independence, Mo.; "President Flies to Key West after Rough Voyage to Cuba," *New York Times*, Feb. 25, 1948, 1.

2. Enclosure (6), Command History, U.S. Naval Station, Guantánamo Bay, Cuba,

1977, U.S. Navy Library, Operation Archives, Navy History and Heritage Command, Washington Navy Yard; "Boat Leak Sends Haitian Refugees to Base at Guantánamo," *Washington Post*, Aug. 20, 1977, E5.

3. Command History, U.S. Naval Base, Guantánamo Bay, Cuba, 1968, U.S. Navy Library, Operation Archives, Navy History and Heritage Command, Washington Navy Yard; "81 of 150 Shoot Way Past Cuban Lines, Reach Guantánamo and Fly to Florida," *New York Times*, Jan. 9, 1969, 1; and Bryan O. Walsh, "Cuban Refugee Children," *Journal of Interamerican Studies and World Affairs* 13, no. 3/4 (July–October 1971): 413.

4. See *Haitian Refugee Center v. Civiletti*, No. 79-2086-Civ-JLK (S.D.Fla. July 2, 1980), discussed hereafter; and Gilburt Loescher and John Scanlan, "Human Rights, U.S. Foreign Policy, and Haitian Refugees," *Journal of Interamerican Studies and World Affairs* 26, no. 3 (August 1984): 337; Christopher Mitchell, "U.S. Policy Toward Haitian Boat People, 1972–93," in *Annals of the American Academy of Political and Social Science*, 534, Strategies for Immigration Control: An International Comparison (July 1994): 70–71.; Alex Stepick, "Unintended Consequences: Rejecting Haitian Boat People and Destabilizing Duvalier," in Christopher Mitchell, ed., *Western Hemisphere Immigration and U.S. Foreign Policy* (State College, Pa.: Penn State University Press, 1992), 133.

5. "Haitian Refugees at Guantánamo Base Pose Problems for US," *Washington Post*, Sept. 2, 1977, A17.

6. Enclosure (6), Command History 1977, 5.

7. *Haitian Refugee Center v. Civiletti*, No. 79-2086-Civ-JLK (S.D.Fla., July 2, 1980), 53–54.

8. Ibid., 43.

9. "97 Who Left Haiti Flown Back," *Washington Post*, Sept. 7, 1977, A20.

10. "Haitian Refugees at Guantánamo Base," *Washington Post*, A17.

11. See Case Summary, *Haitian Refugee Center v. Civiletti*.

12. Ibid., 73.

13. On the latter, see ibid., 76–80.

14. Ibid., 77–78.

15. Ibid., 76–77.

16. Ibid., 81.

17. Ibid., 8.

18. Ibid., 9.

19. Paul Farmer, *The Uses of Haiti* (Monroe, Me.: Common Courage Press, 2003), especially the chapter entitled "From Duvalierism to Duvalierism Without Duvalier," 90–120.

20. See *Haitian Refugee Center v. Civiletti*, 33–72.

21. Ibid., 28–31, 33. For more on so-called political question doctrine, see Nada Mourtada-Sabbah and Bruce E. Cain, eds., *The Political Question Doctrine and the Supreme Court of the United States* (New York: Rowan and Littlefield, 2007).

22. Farmer, *The Uses of Haiti*, 93.

394   NOTES TO PAGES 274–281

23. Quoted in ibid., 99.
24. Quoted in ibid., 94.
25. Ibid., 92.
26. Ibid.
27. *Haitian Refugee Center v. Civiletti*, 45–46.
28. Ibid., 73.
29. Ibid., 79.
30. William G. O'Neill, "The Roots of Human Rights Violations in Haiti," *Georgetown Immigration Law Journal* 7 (March 1993): 95–96, 117. Cf. Irwin P. Stotzky, "Haitian Refugees and the Rule of Law," *Guild Practitioner* 61, no. 3 (Sept. 2004): 167; Cheryl Little, "United States Haitian Policy: A History of Discrimination," *New York Law School Journal of Human Rights* 10, no. 2 (Spring 1993): 297; and Ruth Ellen Wasem, Specialist in Social Legislation, to the House Judiciary Committee, Subcommittee on International Law, Immigration, and Refugees, Nov. 15, 1991, cited in Little, "United States Haitian Policy."
31. Stotzky, "Haitian Refugees and the Rule of Law," 166–67; O'Neill, "The Roots of Human Rights Violations in Haiti," 95–96.
32. Little, "United States Haitian Policy," 296–99; *Haitian Centers Council v. Sale*, June 8, 1993, U.S. District Court for the Eastern District of New York, 823 F. Supp. 1028; 1993 U.S. Dist. Lexis 8215, 7.
33. Farmer, *The Uses of Haiti*, 100–107.
34. Ibid., 106–107.
35. Ibid., 109–10.
36. Michael Massing, "Haiti: The New Violence," *New York Review of Books* 34, no. 19 (Dec. 3, 1987): 45.
37. Quoted in Farmer, *The Uses of Haiti*, 121.
38. Ibid., 135–36.
39. Ibid., 144–48.
40. Ibid., 159–61. The evidence of U.S. deception and malfeasance here is overwhelming. See, among others, Tom Barry, "Interview with Haiti Expert Robert Maguire: Aristide's Fall: The Undemocratic U.S. Policy in Haiti," *Americas Program* (Silver City, N.M.: Interhemispheric Resource Center, Feb. 27, 2004); Irwin P. Stotsky, *Silencing the Guns in Haiti: The Promise of Deliberative Democracy* (Chicago: University of Chicago Press, 1997), chap. 1; Irwin P. Stotsky, "On the Promise and Peril of Democracy in Haiti," *University of Miami, Inter-American Law Review* 29, no. 1/2 (1997); Alex Dupuy, *The Prophet and Power: Jean-Bertrand Aristide, the International Community, and Haiti* (New York: Rowman and Littlefield, 2007), chap. 4; Robert Fatton Jr., *Haiti's Predatory Republic: The Unending Transition to Democracy* (Boulder, Colo.: Lynne Rienner Publishing, 2002), chap. 4; Anne-christine D'Adesky, "Père Lebrun in Context," in Deidre McFadyen, ed., *Haiti: Dangerous Crossroads* (Boston: South End Press, 1995), 175–80; John Canham-Clyne, "Human Rights à la USAID," *The Progressive* 58,

no. 9 (Sept. 1994): 25–26; James Ridgeway, ed., *The Haiti Files: Decoding the Crisis* (Washington, D.C.: Essential Books, 1994), esp. part 3; Allan Nairn, "Haiti Under the Gun: How U.S. Intelligence Has Been Exercising Crowd Control," *The Nation*, January 8, 1996, 11–15; Graham Hancock, *The Lords of Poverty: The Power, Prestige, and Corruption of the International Aid Business* (Boston: Atlantic Monthly Press, 1994); Peter Hallward, *Damming the Flood: Haiti, Aristide, and the Politics of Containment* (New York: Verso: 2008), introduction and chap. 1; and Andrew Reding, "Haiti: An Agenda for Democracy," World Policy Institute, Feb. 1996.

41. Brandt Goldstein, *Storming the Court: How a Band of Law Students Fought the President—and Won* (New York: Scribner, 2005), 98.
42. Farmer, *Uses of Haiti*, 223–24.
43. Ibid., 159, 221.
44. William R. McClintock, *Operation GTMO, 1 October 1991–1 July 1993* (USACOM, 1998), 9, 184.
45. Quoted in Farmer, *Uses of Haiti*, 223–24.
46. Ibid., 9, 185.
47. See *Haitian Refugee Center Inc. v. Baker*, Dec. 19, 1991, 950 F.2nd 685; Little, "United States Haitian Policy," 298–99; O'Neill, "The Roots of Human Rights Violations in Haiti," 114–15; McClintock, *Operation GTMO*, 13–14, 185–87.
48. McClintock, *Operation GTMO*, 24–25. Thanks to Gerald L. Neuman, several copies of the paper are in the author's possession.
49. Witness quoted in Goldstein, *Storming the Court*, 73–74.
50. Nicholas E. Reynolds, *A Skillful Show of Strength: United States Marines in the Caribbean, 1991–1996* (Washington, D.C.: History and Museums Division, Headquarters, U.S. Marine Corps, 1993), 14.
51. Ibid., 15.
52. Little, "United States Haitian Policy," 300–301.
53. Quoted in O'Neill, "The Roots of Human Rights Violations in Haiti," 105.
54. McClintock, *Operation GTMO*, 94. Zette's fate is described in Goldstein, *Storming the Court*, 99–101, 106–107.
55. Human Rights Watch, "Half the Story: The Skewed U.S. Monitoring of Repatriated Haitian Refugees," *Americas* 4, no. 4 (June 30, 1992): 3–4.
56. Reynolds, "A Skillful Show of Strength," 17; Goldstein, *Storming the Court*, 118, 126.
57. Cf. Farmer, *Uses of Haiti*, 226.
58. *Haitian Centers Council (HCC) v. Sale*, June 8, 1993, 823 F. Supp. 1028; 1993 U.S. Dist. Lexis 8215, 8.
59. Ibid., 8–9; Goldstein, *Storming the Court*, 98–99.
60. Goldstein, *Storming the Court*, 287; Jean quoted in Farmer, *Uses of Haiti*, 218.
61. Goldstein, *Storming the Court*, 77.
62. Johnson and Valentine quoted in ibid., 77–78.

63. Goldstein, *Storming the Court*, 107.

64. Ibid., 111.

65. Ibid., 114–45.

66. Quoted in ibid., 119.

67. McClintock, *Operation GTMO*, 195.

68. Goldstein, *Storming the Court*, 127–29.

69. Ibid.

70. Ibid., 138.

71. *Haitian Centers Council v. McNary*, June 5, 1992, U.S. Dist. Lexis 8452, 3–4; Goldstein, *Storming the Court*, 139, 148.

72. McClintock, *Operation GTMO*, 51, 202–203.

73. Human Rights Watch, "Half the Story," 4.

74. McClintock, *Operation GTMO*, 32, 203; Goldstein, *Storming the Court*, 140–41.

75. Farmer, *Uses of Haiti*, 229.

76. McClintock, *Operation GTMO*, 32.

77. Ingrid Arnesen, "HIV Prisoners," *The Nation*, January 4/11, 1993, 4–5.

78. Goldstein, *Storming the Court*, 273–75.

79. McClintock, *Operation GTMO*, 32.

80. Goldstein, *Storming the Court*, 269.

81. Ibid., 232–33.

82. Ibid., 234. Cf. Arnesen, "HIV Prisoners," 4–5.

83. Goldstein, *Storming the Court*, 143.

84. Ibid., 143, 148–49, 157–58.

85. McClintock, *Operation GTMO*, 208–209.

86. Ibid., 211–12.

87. *Sale v. Haitian Centers Council*, March 2, 1993, 509 U.S. 155; 113 S. Ct. 2549.

88. Goldstein, *Storming the Court*, 230–38; *Sale v. Haitian Centers Council*, 27.

89. Judge Sterling Johnson quoted in Goldstein, *Storming the Court*, 275–76.

90. Ibid., 268.

91. Johnson quoted in ibid., 287.

92. *Haitian Centers Council v. Sale*, 11.

93. Ibid., 13.

94. Ibid., 14.

95. Ibid., 14–15.

96. Ibid., 18.

97. *Sale v. Haitian Centers Council*, 10.

98. Ibid., 27–28.

99. Ibid., 37.

100. Clinton quoted in Harold Hongju Koh, "Reflections on Refoulement and Haitian Centers Council," *Harvard International Law Journal* 35, no. 1 (Winter 1994): 2n6.

101. Ibid., 5, 17–18.

9 ★ THE CHOSEN

1. Telephone interview with Norman A. Rogers, Nov. 8, 2010. Rogers asked that I not use his real name.
2. Ibid.
3. Author interview, Commander Jeffrey Johnston, U.S. Navy, Guantánamo Bay, Cuba, Oct. 28, 2008; follow-up telephone interview, Oct. 8, 2010.
4. Clarke quoted at abcnews.go.com/International/story?id=80277&page=1.
5. Author interviews of Rogers and Johnston, Nov. 8, 2010, and Oct. 8, 2010, respectively.
6. Department of Defensé News Briefing, Secretary Rumsfeld and General Myers, Dec. 11, 2001, available at avalon.law.yale.edu/sept11/dod_brief118.asp.
7. Department of Defense News Briefing, Secretary Rumsfeld, Dec. 27, 2001, available at avalon.law.yale.edu/sept11/dod_brief137.asp.
8. This was the opinion of Thomas J. Romig, judge advocate general, U.S. Army (2001–2005), for instance. In a conversation with Pentagon general counsel William J. Haynes II in early November 2001, Romig told Haynes that Guantánamo would be the perfect choice to conduct fair and efficient military tribunals in concert with short-term detention. "I was not in the least bit troubled by using Guantánamo for military commissions," Romig told me. "Once we got the rules straight, I expected that we could try these detainees and get them out of there within a year." Telephone interview with Thomas J. Romig, Oct. 11, 2010.
9. Rogers interview, Nov. 8, 2010.
10. Ibid. Here Rogers is in very good company, by no means limited to "liberals." Cf. among legions of other career military personnel, Thomas J. Romig; telephone interview, Oct. 11, 2010.
11. Rogers interview, Oct. 11, 2010.
12. Yoo has many critics, none more unremitting than Philippe Sands, *Torture Team: Rumsfeld's Memo and the Betrayal of American Values* (New York: Palgrave Macmillan, 2008), 230 and passim.
13. Author interview, John Yoo, Oct. 18, 2010, Berkeley, Calif.
14. Patrick Philbin, John Yoo Memorandum for William J. Haynes II, Dec. 28, 2001, 34–35, in Karen J. Greenberg and Joshua L. Dratel, eds., *The Torture Papers: The Road to Abu Ghraib* (Cambridge, UK: Cambridge University Press, 2005), 29–37.
15. Ibid., 29–30.
16. Ibid., 30.
17. Lease of Certain Areas for Naval Coaling Stations, July 2, 1903, U.S.-Cuba, T.S. No. 426, 6 Bevans 1120. Cf. Michael John Strauss, *The Leasing of Guantánamo Bay* (Santa Barbara, Calif.: Praeger, 2009), 78–103.
18. Joseph Margulies, *Guantánamo and the Abuse of Presidential Power* (New York: Simon & Schuster, 2006), 45–49. In making his case for the predominance of *Eisentrager*, Yoo understated the degree of U.S. sovereignty at Guantánamo Bay. "The fact that the United States can exercise some 'jurisdiction' and 'control' over

NOTES TO PAGES 312–314

the base is not the relevant factor for purposes of the analysis in Eisentrager," he wrote. But Yoo's "some" is disingenuous. U.S. control at Guantánamo is absolute, as Yoo himself undoubtedly knew at the time; see Yoo to Haynes, Dec. 28, 35.

19. Ibid., 36.

20. As if struggling to be heard, Yoo has written about presidential authority in wartime in three books published since 9/11: *War by Other Means: An Insider's Account of the War on Terror* (New York: Atlantic, 2006), see esp. chap. 6; *The Powers of War and Peace: The Constitution and Foreign Affairs After 9/11* (Chicago: University of Chicago Press, 2006), introduction and chap. 4; and *Crisis and Command: A History of Executive Power from George Washington to George W. Bush* (New York: Kaplan, 2010), esp. introduction and 401–427.

21. voices.washingtonpost.com/44/2009/04/30/rice_defends_enhanced_interrog .html.

22. Philbin, Yoo, Memorandum for Haynes, 37.

23. voices.washingtonpost.com/44/2009/04/30/rice_defends_enhanced_interrog .html.

24. Stephan Lewandowsky, Werner G. K. Stritzke, Klaus Oberauer, and Michael Morales, "Misinformation and the 'War on Terror': When Memory Turns Fiction into Fact," in Stritzke, Lewandowsky, David Denemark, Joseph Clare, and Frank Morgan, eds., *Terrorism and Torture: An Interdisciplinary Perspective* (New York: Cambridge University Press, 2009), 179–203.

25. Karen Greenberg, *The Least Worst Place: Guantánamo's First Hundred Days* (New York: Oxford University Press, 2009), 3.

26. Darius Rejali, *Democracy and Torture* (Princeton, N.J.: Princeton University Press, 2007), 22.

27. Scott Shane, "Soviet-style 'Torture' Becomes 'Interrogation' in the War on Terror," *New York Times*, June 3, 2007, Week in Review, 3; and Shane, "China-Inspired Interrogations at Guantánamo," *New York Times*, July 2, 2008, A1, 14.

28. U.S. Senate Armed Services Committee, "Inquiry into the Treatment of Detainees in U.S. Custody," Nov. 20, 2008, available at www.scribd.com/doc/14539734/ Inquiry-Into-the-Treatment-of-Detainees-in-US-Custody-Nov-20-2008, 179n179. Moulton's testimony jibes with that of Lieutenant Colonel Daniel J. Baumgartner, also of JPRA, who, prodded by evidence provided by the Senate committee, remembered communicating with Richard Schiffrin of the Pentagon's Office of the General Counsel in December about "the exploitation process and historical information on captivity and lessons learned." Testimony of Daniel J. Baumgartner Jr., USAF (Ret.), before the U.S. Senate Armed Services Committee, June 17, 2008, available at armed-services.senate.gov/statemnt/2008/ June/Baumgartner%2006-17-08.pdf.

29. Guter quoted in Tom Lasseter, "Day 4: Easing of Laws That Led to Detainee Abuse Hatched in Secret," June 18, 2008, Guantánamo: Beyond the Law project, McClatchy Washington Bureau, available at www.mcclatchydc.com/2008/ 06/18/38886/day-4-easing-of-laws-that-led.html#ixzz0nvz8fsuZ.

30. Addington quoted in Sands, *Torture Team*, 32; Comey quoted in Lasseter, "Day 4."

31. Johnston interview, Oct. 8, 2010.

32. Testimony of Specialist Brandon Neely, The Guantánamo Testimonials Project, Center for the Study of Human Rights in the Americas, University of California at Davis, available at humanrights.ucdavis.edu/projects/the-Guantánamo-testi monials-project/testimonies/testimonies-of-military-guards/testimony-of -brandon-neely.

33. The camp housed detainees from January 11 to April 29. See www.globalsecu rity.org/military/facility/guantánamo-bay_x-ray.htm.

34. In many accounts of the Guantánamo detention facility, the *I* in IRF is mistak- enly referred to as "Initial" or "Internal." Neely compounds this mistake by changing the "Response" to "Reaction." Neely, The Guantánamo Testimonials Project.

35. For a description and analysis of the IRFs, see Neely: "As far as IRFing is con- cerned, when I was there it went somewhat in this order: (1) The block guards would have a problem with a detainee (not listening, maybe saying something, or not following rules). The guards would then contact the duty officer for that shift. We were told 'If you were working a block and having a problem with one of the detainees and you couldn't handle it or get it under control, you should call the duty officer,' who was usually a E-7 (sergeant first class) or a 0-1 or 0-2 (first and second lieutenant). They would come to the block, assess the situation, and make the decision whether to take 'comfort items' away or call the IRF team into play. If the latter, then (2) the duty officer would come to the block with an interpreter and tell the detainee to do whatever he was told to and, if not, the IRF team would be called upon. (3) Once the IRF team was called upon and arrived on the block there was no 'I am sorry, I will do it' from the detainee; the IRF team was going to enter that cage and hog-tie that detainee." Cf. humanrights.ucdavis.edu/ projects/the-Guantánamo-testimonials-project/testimonies/testimonies-of-military -guards/an-analysis-of-the-immediate-reaction-force-reports.

36. See Convention III, Relative to the Treatment of Prisoners of War, 12 Aug. 1949, available at www.icrc.org/ihl.nsf/7c4d08d9b287a42141256739003e63bb/6fef8 54a3517b75ac125641e004a9e68.

37. Neely, The Guantánamo Testimonials Project. Neely's report of an absence of standard operating procedures at Guantánamo is confirmed by Specialist Luci- ana Spencer of the Sixty-sixth Military Intelligence Group. "When I began work- ing the night shift I discussed with the MPs what their SOP was for detainee treatment. They informed me that they had no SOP." R. Jeffrey Smith and Josh White, "General Granted Latitude at Prison," *Washington Post*, June 12, 2004.

38. See Mark Denbeaux and Joshua Denbeaux, "Report on Guantánamo Detainees: A Profile of 517 Detainees Through Analysis of Department of Defense Data," Seton Hall University Law School, 2006, available at law.shu.edu/publications/ GuantánamoReports/Guantánamo_report_final_2_08_06.pdf.

39. Neely, The Guantánamo Testimonials Project.

40. Quoted in Richard Clarke, *Against All Enemies* (New York: Free Press, 2004), 24.

41. Department of Defense News Briefing, Secretary Rumsfeld and General Myers, Jan. 11, 2002, available at www.defenselink.mil. Defense Secretary Rumsfeld himself seems to have remained vague on the extent to which the Geneva Protocols informed the Guantánamo operation through at least the end of January 2002. Asked by a skeptical press whether it wouldn't be wise to allow for some media access to the Guantánamo camp, a Rumsfeld suddenly solicitous of Geneva responded that "there is something in the Geneva Convention about press people around prisoners; that—and not taking pictures and not saying who they are and not exposing them to ridicule, which is the genesis, as I understand it, of the convention requirement." Department of Defense News Briefing, Secretary Rumsfeld, Jan. 22, 2002, available at avalon.law.yale.edu/sept11/dod_brief139.asp.

42. Memorandum for Chairman of the Joint Chiefs of Staff, Jan. 19, 2002, in Greenberg and Dratel, eds., *Torture Papers*, 80. See, for example, Rumsfeld's press conferences on January 16 and 20, at www.defenselink.com.

43. This is the source of the criticism of retired Marine Corps colonel Ann Wright. See www.codepink4peace.org/article.php?id=1335.

44. Memorandum for William J. Haynes II from John Yoo and Robert J. Delahunty (Yoo is known to be the principal author) on the Application of Treaties and Laws to al Qaeda and Taliban Detainees, Jan. 9, 2002, U.S. Department of Justice, in Greenberg and Dratel, eds., *Torture Papers*, 38–39.

45. Author interview, John Yoo, Oct. 18, 2010, Berkeley, Calif. As well as the following; see, for example, Colin L. Powell to Counsel to the President, undated, "Draft Decision Memorandum for the President on the Applicability of the Geneva Convention to the Conflict in Afghanistan," in Greenberg and Dratel, eds., *Torture Papers*, 122–25. Cf., John Barry, Michael Hirsh, and Michael Isikoff, "The Roots of Torture," *Newsweek*, May 24, 2004, available at www.globalpolicy .org/component/content/article/157/26905.html.

46. Your Draft Memorandum of Jan. 9, William H. Taft IV to John C. Yoo, Jan. 11, 2002, National Security Archives, available at www.torturingdemocracy.org/ documents/20020111.pdf. For a scholarly perspective on the Yoo memo, see Stephen P. Marks, "International Law and the 'War on Terrorism': Post-9/11 Responses by the United States and Asia Pacific Countries," *Asia Pacific Law Review* 14, no. 1 (2006): 42–74, esp. 61.

47. Taft to Yoo, Jan. 11, 2002. Addington is acknowledged to be the author of White House Counsel Alberto Gonzales's Jan. 25 memo to the president (actually written by David Addington) entitled "Decision re Application of the Geneva Convention on Prisoners of War to the Conflict with Al Qaeda and the Taliban," in Greenberg and Dratel, eds., *Torture Papers*, 118–21.

48. Jane Mayer, *The Dark Side: The Inside Story of How the War on Terror Turned into a War on American Ideals* (New York: Doubleday, 2008), 289.

49. Romig quoted in Lasseter, "Day 4"; author telephone interview, Thomas Romig, Oct. 10, 2010.

50. Yoo interview, Oct. 18, 2010. Despite continued objections from Secretary of State Colin Powell and his legal advisor William H. Taft, Yoo's Jan. 9 draft on Geneva was formalized by three subsequent memos. See Jay Bybee, Memorandum for Alberto R. Gonzales and William J. Haynes II, Jan. 22, 2002, in Greenberg and Dratel, eds., *Torture Papers*, 117; Gonzales, "Decision re Application of the Geneva Convention on Prisoners of War to the Conflict with Al Qaeda and the Taliban," in Greenberg and Dratel, eds., *Torture Papers*, 119–20; and President George W. Bush, Memorandum for the Vice President et al., on "Humane Treatment of al Qaeda and Taliban Detainees," February 7, 2002, in Greenberg and Dratel, eds., *Torture Papers*, 134–35.

51. In a recent book, Karen Greenberg argues that the first one hundred days or so represented salad days at Guantánamo compared to what it would become over the next several years, before administration of the camps was transferred out of the hands of General Michael Lehnert and into the hands of Generals Michael Dunlavey and Jeffrey Miller. That may be; I suppose it is a matter of perspective. But life is not experienced from Archimedean heights, and many individual detainees and guards remember things very differently. Compare the following discussion to Greenberg, *The Least Worst Place*, 213–14 and passim.

52. Darius Rejali, *Torture and Democracy* (Princeton, N.J.: Princeton University Press, 2009), 434. Rejali calls the informal pattern of torture proliferation as "the apprenticeship hypothesis."

53. Rejali, *Torture and Democracy*, 580–91. Just who ordered the "habitual" torture of Filipinos in the U.S.-Philippine War, 1899–1902, is not clear, though it is clear that high government officials knew about it; see Paul Kramer, "The Water Cure," *The New Yorker*, February 25, 2008, available at www.newyorker.com/reporting/2008/02/25/080225fa_fact_kramer. For more on the United States and torture, see Alfred W. McCoy, *CIA Interrogation: From the Cold War to the War on Terror* (New York: Metropolitan Books, 2006), 5–20 and passim.

54. Evidence of abuse at Bagram and Kandahar is overwhelming and undeniable. See Margulies, *Guantánamo and the Abuse of Presidential Power*, 135–37; Mayer, *The Dark Side*, 224–47. Cf. National Security Archive interviews of detainees Bisher Al-Rawi, Moazzam Begg, and Shafiq Rasul, available at www.torturingdemocracy.org, as well as Moazzam Begg, *Enemy Combatant: My Imprisonment in Guantánamo, Bagram, and Kandahar* (New York: New Press, 2007).

55. U.S. soldiers quoted in Rejali, *Torture and Democracy*, 433–34. As astounding as this may seem in the case of MPs, more astounding still are the statements of senior CIA officials that "case officers aren't actually trained in interrogation techniques"—that they never encountered "anyone who was a 'professional interrogator' in the agency." "We're not trained interrogators," one CIA official told Rejali; "to be honest, in those situations I really had no idea what I'm doing and I'm not the only one who has had this experience."

56. Greenberg, *The Least Worst Place*, 146–53.

57. On Dunlavey, see Sands, *Torture Team*, 37–39, 42–44; and Greenberg, *The Least Worst Place*, 164–68.

58. Greenberg, 172.

59. Neely testimony available at humanrights.ucdavis.edu/projects/the-Guantá namo-testimonials-project/testimonies/testimonies-of-military-guards/testimony -of-brandon-neely.

60. Sands, *Torture Team*, 43.

61. Dunlavey quoted in Sands, *Torture Team*, 44; see also 43–45.

62. Mayer, *The Dark Side*, esp. chaps. 8 and 9; Sands, *Torture Team*, 94–97, 227–29, and passim.

63. John Yoo, Memorandum for Alberto R. Gonzales, Aug. 1, 2002, on Standards of Conduct for Interrogations under 18 U.S.C. §§ 2340-2340A, in Greenberg and Dratel, eds., *Torture Papers*, 172–217.

64. Critics quoted in Mayer, *The Dark Side*, 152; Margulies, *Guantánamo and the Abuse of Presidential Power*, 90–91. For succinct critiques of the memo, see Margulies, *Guantánamo and the Abuse of Presidential Power*, 90–95; and David Cole, *The Torture Memos: Rationalizing the Unthinkable* (New York: New Press, 2009), introduction, esp. 20–25. Cf. Sands, *Torture Team*, 74–76, and Mayer, *The Dark Side*, 151–52.

65. Senate Armed Services Committee Hearing: The Origins of Aggressive Interrogation Techniques, available at www.levin.senate.gov/newsroom/release.cfm?id= 299242. On the Haynes JPRA discussions initiated in the immediate wake of 9/11, see note 28 about the first Haynes-JPRA discussion known to have taken place.

66. Again, high-level Bush administration officials insist that the idea for these techniques bubbled up from below; the evidence has come back to haunt them. Sands, *Torture Team*, 75–77, 224–32; Mayer, *The Dark Side*, 220–24.

67. Al-Qahtani's interrogation log available at ccrjustice.org/files/Al%20Qahtani%20 Interrogation%20Log.pdf.

68. Bob Woodward, "Detainee Tortured, Says U.S. Official," *Washington Post*, Jan. 14, 2009, available at www.washingtonpost.com/wp-dyn/content/article/2009/01/13/ AR2009011303372.html?hpid=topnews).

69. For a description of these lethal assaults, see Margulies, *Guantánamo*, 137.

70. Sands, *Torture Team*, 144–48.

71. Johnston interview, Oct. 8, 2010.

72. James Yee, *For God and Country: Faith and Patriotism Under Fire* (New York: Public Affairs Press, 2005), 47–48.

73. Ibid., 51.

74. Ibid., 52.

75. Ibid., 66.

76. Ibid., 73–74.

77. Ibid., 45, 85–88.

78. Army judge advocate Thomas Romig, celebrated in liberal circles for opposing Bush administration detention and interrogation policy, shared the MPs' suspicion of the Muslim chaplain. Telephone interview, Thomas Romig, Oct. 10, 2010.

79. James Yee, *For God and Country*, 115–22.

80. Ibid., 122–23.

81. Erik Saar, *Inside the Wire: A Military Intelligence Soldier's Eyewitness Account of Life at Guantánamo* (New York: Penguin, 2005), 46, 59, 71, 99.

82. Ibid., 55.

83. Ibid., 72.

84. Ibid., 73.

85. Ibid., 74–75.

86. Ibid., 65.

87. Ibid., 66–67.

88. Ibid., 90–95.

89. Ibid., 108.

90. Ibid., 151.

91. Ibid., 153.

92. I experienced this firsthand, on a tour of the prison in the autumn of 2008.

93. Romney quoted in Martha T. Moore, "Guantánamo Puzzles Candidates," *USA Today*, June 19, 2007, available at www.usatoday.com/news/politics/2007-06-18-gitmo-candidates_N.htm. Romney's pandering pales by comparison to that of Duncan Hunter, who came back praising the "honey-baked chicken" and "lemon-glazed fish"; Otto Kreisher and Toby Eckert, "Hunter Says Menu from Guantánamo a Proof of Good Care," *San Diego Union-Tribune*, June 14, 2005, available at www.signonsandiego.com/uniontrib/20050614/news_1n14gitmo.html. On a more serious note, see the Schmidt Report, a so-called investigation on allegations by the FBI of detainee abuse, available at www.cfr.org/publication/9804/schmidt_report.html. On the more general "pattern of deceit" at Guantánamo and elsewhere, see Margulies, *Guantánamo and the Abuse of Presidential Power*, chap. 8; and Stafford Smith, *Eight O'Clock Ferry to the Other Side*, chap. 5.

94. Saar, *Inside the Wire*, 159–63.

95. Ibid., 164–65.

96. Ibid., 166–73. Saar recounts other examples where intelligence and patience build trust, which generates information; e.g., 177–85.

97. Ibid., 220–28.

98. Eric Schmitt, "There Are Ways to Make Them Talk," *New York Times*, June 6, 2002, C1.

99. Katharine Q. Seelye, "Guantánamo Bay Faces Sentence of Life as Permanent U.S. Prison," *New York Times*, Sept. 16, 2002, A1.

100. Neil A. Lewis, "Detainees from the Afghan War Remain in a Legal Limbo in Cuba," *New York Times*, March 25, 2003, A21.

101. Sands, *Torture Team*, 118.

102. U.S. Department of Justice, Office of the Inspector General Report, May 2008, 126.
103. Sands, *Torture Team*, 121, 126–27.
104. Ibid., 118.
105. Michael Isikoff, "We Could Have Done This the Right Way," *Newsweek*, April 29, 2009, available at www.newsweek.com/id/195089.
106. Testimony of Ali Soufan before the U.S. Senate Judiciary Committee, May 13, 2009, available at judiciary.senate.gov/hearings/testimony.cfm?id=3842&wit _id=7906. The contractors Soufan refers to are Jim Mitchell and Bruce Jessen, the retired psychologists who imported SERE techniques into military interrogation and who shunted Soufan and McFadden aside in the questioning of Abu Zubaydah after he was picked up and taken to Thailand in March 2002. Among other treatment, Zubaydah was confined in a coffin-like box, slammed into walls, and waterboarded eighty-three times by Mitchell and Jessen, long after he had surrendered the information he had to Soufan and his associates. See Mayer, *The Dark Side*, 155–81; Shane, "Soviet-style 'Torture' Becomes 'Interrogation,'" 3; and Scott Shane, "2 U.S. Architects of Harsh Tactics in 9/11's Wake," *New York Times*, August 11, 2009, A1, 12.
107. See, for example, Steven Keslowitz, *The Tao of Jack Bauer*, iUniverse.com, 2009.
108. Anne Applebaum, "The Torture Myth," *Washington Post*, Jan. 12, 2005, A21.
109. Herrington interview, "TV Torture Changes Real Interrogation Techniques," *Fresh Air*, NPR, Oct. 10, 2007, available at www.npr.org/templates/story/story .php?storyId=15148243.
110. See Dan Eggen and R. Jeffrey Smith, "FBI Agents Allege Abuse of Detainees at Guantánamo Bay," *Washington Post*, Dec. 21, 2004, A1.
111. These events are described in Sands, *Torture Team*, 150–55; Mayer, *The Dark Side*, 224–37; and Margulies, *Guantánamo and the Abuse of Presidential Power*, 105–109.
112. Mora quoted in Mayer, *The Dark Side*, 219; cf. chap. 9.
113. Mayer, *The Dark Side*, 66–68, 229; Sands, *Torture Team*, 17–20, 212–213; Greenberg, *The Least Worst Place*, 46–47.
114. Mayer, *The Dark Side*, 228–33. In opposing Yoo's new memo and an accompanying new working group report, Mora was in good company.
115. See the written objections of Major General Jack L. Rives, USAF, Deputy Judge Advocate; Rear Admiral Micheal F. Lohr, USN, Judge Advocate General; Brigadier General Keven M. Sandkuhler, USMC, Judge Advocate General; and Major General Thomas Romig, USA, Judge Advocate General, available at www .torturingdemocracy.org/documents/20030205.pdf.
116. Mayer, *The Dark Side*, 228–32.
117. See previous chapter, and *Sale v. Haitian Centers Council*, June 21, 1993, available at www.law.cornell.edu/supct/html/92-344.ZO.html.
118. *Rasul v. Bush*, June 28, 2004, available at www.law.cornell.edu/supct/html/03 -334.ZO.html.

119. Margulies, *Guantánamo and the Abuse of Presidential Power*, 162–64.

120. Associated Press, "Kuwaiti Ordered Released from Guantánamo Bay," *New York Times*, Sept. 26, 2009, A15.

121. Andy Worthington, "The Guantánamo Whistleblowers," *Counterpunch*, July 2, 2007; see also Worthington's *The Guantánamo Files: The Stories of the 759 Detainees in America's Ille* (London: Pluto Press, 2007).

122. *Hamdan v. Rumsfeld*, Supreme Court of the United States, June 29, 2006, available at www.law.cornell.edu/supct/html/05-184.ZS.html.

123. *Boumediene v. Bush*, United States District Court, D.C. District, Nov. 29, 2008, available at ccrjustice.org/files/2008-11-20%20Boumediene%20ORDER%20-%20release%205%20of%206.pdf.

124. Margulies, *Guantánamo and the Abuse of Presidential Power*, 214.

125. From *Rules of the Road*, a Navy publication, quoted in Tom Miller, "The Sun Sometimes Sets," 97–100; 186–88.

EPILOGUE

1. On this paradox, see David Harvey, *Cosmopolitanism and the Geographies of Freedom* (New York: Columbia University Press, 2009), introduction and passim; William Appleman Williams, *Empire as a Way of Life: An Essay on the Causes and Character of America's Present Predicament, Along with a Few Thoughts About an Alternative* (New York: Oxford University Press, 1980); Andrew Bacevitch, *American Empire: Realities and Consequences of U.S. Diplomacy* (Cambridge, Mass.: Harvard University Press, 2002); Lars Schoultz, *Beneath the United States: A History of U.S. Policy Toward Latin America* (Cambridge, Mass.: Harvard University Press, 1998), chap. 19; and Jonathan M. Hansen, "American Empire as a Way of Life: The Search for Historical Alternatives," in Kenneth Christie, ed., *United States Foreign Policy and National Identity in the 21st Century* (New York: Routledge, 2009), chap. 8.

2. Memorandum for Colonel Mike Meese, Academic Report—Trip to Guantánamo, US Military Academy, June 28, 2006, 1–2.

3. Telephone interview, General Barry McCaffrey, USA (Ret.), April 19, 2010.

4. McCaffrey, Guantánamo Memorandum, 4; Crawford quoted by Bob Woodward, "Detainee Tortured, Says US Official," *Washington Post*, January 14, 2009, at www.washingtonpost.com/wp-dyn/content/article/2009/01/13/AR2009011303372.html.

5. McCaffrey, Guantánamo Memorandum, 4–5.

6. Ibid., 5; McCaffrey telephone interview, April 19, 2010.

7. See, for example, the Gallup poll of January 16, 2009 (www.gallup.com/poll/113893/americans-send-no-clear-mandate-Guantánamo-bay.aspx), the *USA Today*/Gallup poll of June 1, 2009 (www.usatoday.com/news/world/2009-06-01-gitmo_N.htm), the CNN poll of March 30, 2010 (www.miamiherald.com/2010/03/30/1554710/poll-americans-dont-want-obama.html), and the Rasmussen sur-

vey of December 15, 2010 (www.rasmussenreports.com/public_content/politics/
general_politics/december_2010/most_voters_worry_that_closing_Guantá
namo_will_set_dangerous_terrorists_free).

8. Charlie Savage, "Vote Hurts Obama Push to Empty Cuba Prison," *New York Times*, December 23, 2010, A18.

9. Executive Order: Periodic Review of Individuals Detained at Guantánamo Bay Naval Station Pursuant to the Authorization for U.S. Military Force, Office of the Press Secretary, The White House, March 7, 2011, available at www.white house.gov/sites/default/files/Executive_Order_on_Periodic_Review.pdf; Charlie Savage, "Detainee Review Proposal Is Prepared for Obama," *New York Times*, December 21, 2010, at www.nytimes.com/2010/12/22/us/22gitmo.html?_r=1.

10. Telephone interview with David Barron, former head of the Office of Legal Counsel in the Obama administration, October 13, 2010. In his May 2009 address on torture and indefinite detention at the National Archives, President Obama vowed that his administration would "no longer place the burden to prove that hearsay is unreliable on the opponent of the hearsay," though the journalist Robert Chesney has argued that this standard still falls well short of civil law protections. Barack Obama, "Remarks by the President on National Security," National Archives, Washington, D.C., May 21, 2009, at www.white house.gov/the_press_office/Remarks; Robert Chesney, "The Least Worst Venue," *Foreign Policy*, January 21, 2011, at www.foreignpolicy.com/articles/2011/01/21/ the_least_worst_venue?page=0,1. To Jonathan Hafetz, improvements in the commission system aren't good enough, given the Obama administration's adoption of its predecessor's broad interpretation of what can be characterized as war crimes. Jonathan Hafetz, "Reversal of Guantánamo Policy Will Harm US Reputation Abroad," DW-World.de, January 21, 2011, at www.dw-world.de/dw/ article/0,,14779114,00.html.

11. Barron interview, October 13, 2010.

12. "Lawyer Disputes Portrayal of Detainee," *New York Times*, February 5, 2011, A12.

13. Scott Shane, "Obama Defends Detention Conditions for Soldier Accused in WikiLeaks Case," *New York Times*, March 11, 2011, at www.nytimes.com/2011/ 03/12/us/12manning.html.

14. Commander Charles M. Cooke, Memorandum for Commander R. O. Davis, USN Office of Naval Operations, Sept. 26, 1937. Charles M. Cooke Papers, Manuscript Division, Hoover Institution, Stanford University. On Stevenson, see "Reminiscences of Admiral Robert Lee Dennison, USN (Ret.)" (Annapolis, Md.: U.S. Naval Institute, 1975), 405, and "Reminiscences of Vice Admiral Eli T. Reich, USN (Ret.)" (Annapolis, Md.: U.S. Naval Institute, 1983), 250–60; on Carter and Guantánamo, see National Security Council Memo, December 7, 1978, to Zbigniew Brzezinski, National Security Archive. On Reagan and Guantánamo, see *National Defense* 66, no. 370 (September 1981): 3.

15. Author interview, General John J. Sheehan, USMC (Ret.), January 25, 2007, Arlington, Va.
16. Telephone interview, General Barry McCaffrey, USA (Ret.), April 19, 2010.
17. Telephone interview, Commander Jeffrey H. Johnston, October 8, 2010.
18. Ibid.
19. Sheehan interview, January 25, 2007. Cf. Carol Rosenberg, "Disaster Drill Illustrates New Approach to Cuba," July 20, 2009, *Miami Herald*, available at www.palmbeachpost.com/news/content/state/epaper/2009/07/20/0720_cuban _troops.html?cxtype=rss&cxsvc=7&cxcat=0.
20. Ibid.
21. Author interview, Rafael Hernández, May 25, 2005, Cambridge, Mass.
22. Author interviews, Rolando Céspedez, Oscar Pila, Riquet Caballero Courguet, Francisco Suárez, Juan Raúl Llopis, and Manuel López, August 4, 2007, Miami, Fla., and Alberto Gonzales, June 3, 2008, Storrs, Conn.

ACKNOWLEDGMENTS

So many people contributed to the completion of this book that I hesitate to name them lest I leave anybody out. Thank you foremost to my wife, Anne, and to my children, Oliver, Julian, and Nathalie, whose love and joy and zest for life fuel my work and sustained this project from beginning to end. Thanks, too, to Richard Fox, David Hollinger, Jane Kamensky, Jim Kloppenberg, and Sayres Rudy, whose friendship, encouragement, and example provide continuous inspiration.

This book took shape in several institutional settings, some formal, some not. It sprang to life in the hospitable surroundings of the American Academy of Arts and Sciences, in Cambridge, Massachusetts, where I was visiting scholar (2003–2004) and where Leslie Berlowitz, Jim Carroll, and Jim Miller, among others, maintained a climate of dazzling intellectual stimulation. I am fortunate to be a member of a Boston-area writing group that has included Steve Biehl, Jane Kamensky, Steven Mihm, Mark Peterson, John Plotz, Jennifer Roberts, Seth Rockman, Dan Sharfstein, Conevery Valencius, and Michael Willrich. Their close reading of early chapters of this book set it on a firm foundation. I am likewise lucky to be based in Harvard University's Committee on Degrees in Social Studies, where Richard Tuck, Anya Bernstein, and a brilliant faculty and staff make coming to work each day exhilarating.

Jim Campbell, Roger Lane, and Scott Tromanhauser read a draft of the entire manuscript. Jim and Roger provided detailed and trenchant criticism, putting me permanently in debt. Bob Branfon, Kevin Caffrey, Jeff Kahn, Jim Kloppenberg, Sayres Rudy, and Alan Taylor read chapters and/or sections along the way, saving me from all manner of errors and infelicities.

Faculty and students at the following universities or think tanks commented generously on different iterations of this project: Brandeis University, Centro de Estudios de Información de la Defensa (Havana, Cuba), Columbia University, Harvard University, Oxford University, University of Georgia, University of Madrid, University of Sevilla, and University of Sydney.

Scholars and writers from many different fields provided direction and encouragement at critical stages. Sincerest thanks to Walter Alvarez, David Carlson, Mark Clague, John Coatsworth, Jay Cope, Jorge I. Domínquez, Don Doyle, Rafael Hernández, Manuel Iturralde-Vinent, William Johns, Carl Kaysen, Hal Klepak, Kris Lane, Dick Lehr, William Leith, Anthony Lewis, John Lewis, Jana Lipman, Tom Miller, Richard Millett, Louis Pérez, John Paul Rathbone, Theresa Roosevelt, Patrick Roth, Nancy San Martin, Robert Pendleton, Phil Richardson, Stephen Schwab, Paul Stillwell, Michael Straus, Stephen Webre, Samuel Wilson, and James Zackrison.

Research for this project took me on some memorable trips. On three visits to the Guantánamo Naval Base, I was greeted with astounding generosity and assistance by, among others, Admiral David Thomas, Captain Mark Leary, Commander Jeffrey Johnston, Pete Becola, Stacey Byington, Christopher Creighton, Clayton Helms, Earlene Helms, Harriet Johnston, Don King, JoAnn King, Robert Lamb, Paul Schoenfeld, Frank Simone, and Cy Winter. In Havana, Cuba, I benefited from the warmth and hospitality of Rolando Almirante, Boris Ivan Crespo, Luis M. Garcia Cuñarro, Jesús Bermúdez Cutiño, and Cynthia Newport. In Miami, Florida, I was welcomed and assisted by Alfredo Duran and Marcos Antonio Ramos, among others, as well as by Marlene Bastien, Steve Forester, Randy McGrorty, Myriam Mezadieu, Carol Rosenberg, Alex Stepick, and Irwin Stotzky. In Washington, D.C., Ingrid Ott, Doug Jones, General Jack Sheehan, and Wayne Smith all went way out of their way to help.

Thank you to the staffs of the following libraries: Widener Library (especially Lynn Shirey, librarian for Latin America); Houghton Library; the United States Marine Corps Research Library, Quantico, Virginia; the Navy Department Library, Washington, D.C. (especially Paul Tobin, Glenn Helm, and Ed Marolda); the British Library; Archivo General de Indias, Sevilla, Spain; the Cuban Historical Collection, University of Miami; the Library of Congress; the National Archives, Washington, D.C.; and the National Security Archive, George Washington University.

Various individuals defy categorization but provided much appreciated support somewhere along the line. Thanks to Tim Bartlett, Rob Chodat, Michael Coulson, Laura Fisher, Alex Gourevitch, Sarah Lovitt, Richard Pennington, Chuck Ryan, Glenda Sluga, John Straubel, Don Soldini, Liz Svezchenco, and Alfie Ulloa. I also want to salute my Spanish instructors: Lydia Jimenez, Monica Palacio, and especially Wega Firenze, the last of whom redefines what it means to be a teacher.

With tremendous savvy and just the right amount of force, Wendy Strothman, my friend and literary agent, nurtured this book to fruition. Many thanks, Wendy, for your unflagging faith. Anyone who has ever published with Hill and Wang/FSG knows the privilege it is to work with the teams assembled by Thomas LeBien and Jeff Seroy. At Hill and Wang, Dan Crissman proved wise beyond his years, setting the gold standard for what it means to be an editor. At FSG, publicist Steve Weil was accessible and focused throughout, bringing grace and equanimity to an often-maligned aspect of book publishing.

I know I am leaving people out. I burn a candle to the unnamed but not forgotten individuals who helped make this book possible. If, after all this help, mistakes remain, they are mine and mine alone.

Finally, this book is dedicated to my parents, Alix and Chris Hansen, whose unconditional love for me and support for this project are its ultimate sine qua non.

INDEX

Abraham, Stephen, 345
Abu Ghraib, 322, 343
Adams, John Quincy, 43, 52–54, 55–57
Addington, David, 314, 320, 325, 342
Administrative Procedures Act, 291
Afghanistan, 304–306, 322, 323, 352;
    war in, 304, 312, 317, 327, 346, 354
Africa, 6, 8, 14; slave trade, 34–35, 38,
    44, 49, 59, 361n18
agriculture, 18, 19, 32, 33, 34, 159, 160,
    266, 389n18; colonial, 32–34, 36–37,
    39, 47–50, 60, 67–68, 159, 160, 161;
    late-nineteenth-century, 79; of
    1900s–1930s, 150–51, 161–63,
    178–79, 180; of 1950s–1960s, 197,
    200, 221–22; planter community,
    32–37, 79–81; sugar, 36–37, 39,
    48–51, 58, 60, 69, 79–81, 83, 88,
    150–55, 159, 161–62, 174–75,
    178–79, 180, 181, 196, 197, 200, 222;
    see also specific crops
alcohol, 146, 149–50, 163–78, 384n6;
    naval base life and, 149–50, 163–78,
    188–90, 205, 239, 258, 259, 263–64;
    Prohibition, 146, 149, 164–78, 190,
    351; rum-running operations, 205
Alcudia, 38–39
Alford, Zeb, 262, 263, 264

Alien Migrant Interdiction Operation
    (AMIO), 277, 278, 283, 292
al Qaeda, 305, 329, 339, 340, 345, 354,
    355; prisoners, 305, 310–11, 318–19,
    323, 324, 334
al-Qahtani, Mohammed, 324;
    interrogation and torture of, 326, 327,
    329, 334, 338, 341, 342, 352
al-Rabiah, Fouad Mahmoud, 345
American Federation of Labor, 200, 201
American Revolution, 36–37, 45–47, 72,
    113, 160
Anderson, Jack, 261, 262
Andy Griffith Show, The, 235–36
annexation debate, 58–66, 145, 371n55
Aristide, Jean-Bertrand, 280–82
Army Field Manual, 306–307, 335, 340
Assange, Julian, 355
Atkins, Edwin, 79–81, 125
Atlantic Monthly, 116, 121
Auténtico Party, 201
Avril, Prosper, 280

Baccus, Rick, 337
banking, 161, 180
Baracoa, 224
Barron, David, 354
Barrows, John Henry, 117